TOBEY (TOBIE, TOBY)

GENEALOGY

THOMAS, OF SANDWICH

AND

JAMES, OF KITTERY

AND THEIR DESCENDANTS

By RUFUS BABCOCK TOBEY and CHARLES HENRY POPE

BOSTON, MASS.
PUBLISHED BY CHARLES H. POPE
221 COLUMBUS AVE.
1905

PREFACE.

THE preparation of this Genealogy was begun by the senior editor for his own gratification many years ago. A large correspondence grew up with persons of the name far and near and an accumulation of facts of general interest. The services of Mr. Harry E. Gifford were called into requisition to aid in the work of copying from private and public records, to arrange the matter thus found and carry on the correspondence. Personal matters compelled him to ask to be relieved from the work in 1901; and the help of Mr. Pope was obtained to continue the undertaking. At the end of a year the editors found themselves at the point of publication, as they felt, and asked for subscriptions for the issue of the work. The response was not sufficient to encourage the effort, and the editors, both heavily burdened with other cares and labors, laid the matter aside. The conviction at length forced itself upon them that the book ought to come out, and its publication was resolved upon.

While the work has been passing through the press much material has been obtained from careful search of public records and from correspondents. In but few cases have any of our applications for co-operation been refused or replies delayed beyond our necessary limits of time.

But we wish to thank most heartily the large number who have been exceedingly prompt and liberal in their assistance.

ILLUSTRATIONS

INTRODUCTION.

THE TOBEY (TOBIE, TOBY) family is an ancient and reputable one in England. Its origin would appear to the writer to be a familiar form of the Scripture name Tobias, often given as a Christian name, derived after the analogy of Davy from David, Willey from William, etc.

The earliest record of the name, in any of its forms, in New England is found in the annals of the General Court of Massachusetts Bay Colony. They relate to a man who seems to have been in the country only a few years, and who does not appear to have been related to the Sandwich or Kittery pioneers.

"6th Octobr, 1634, FRANCIS TOBY being fined 10£, hee is discharged of the same."

The man was again before the Court in less than a year.

" 7th July, 1635, ordered that Francis Toby (for misdemeanor by him committed) shalbe bound to his good behaviour and shall putt in suretyes for the same, or else to remaine in holde."

Whatever his offence the Court softened towards him, for we read

" 8th July, 1635, There is viii £ of Tobeyes fine of x £ remitted him."

"June 7, 1636, John Jobson, shipmaster, undertooke and bound himselfe in a sum set of 10£ to answear [answer] for Frauncis Tobey any damage not exceeding 10£."

The same date Jobson was discharged from his surety, and the fact was again recorded under date of Sept. 6, 1636.

What was the offence? The record does not intimate; very likely some mere informality, the breaking
of some petty rule or "red tape." The laws of the
Colony were so angular that even such orderly persons as Sir Richard Saltonstall, Ensign Jennison, Mr.
John Humphrey, with many others, had fines imposed
on them in those days. The man was a person of
some standing, we judge, for the notary Thomas
Lechford has a record of a suit about an apprentice
who had been placed by "Francis Toby, of Rotherhith,
county Surrey, shipwright" in the year 1635, and we
judge the two sets of records refer to the same person.
But he does not show himself here after Jobson ex-
tricates him from the mazes of Puritan law. Possibly
we might find by search that he was connected with
one or more of the Tobies who came here and cast in
their lot permanently with the people of New England;
but there is nothing now known in this direction.

The next man of this name to appear in our New
England records was THOMAS TOBEY (also called
Tobe, Toby, Tobie and Tobye in the public docu-
ments of the day), who was a very early settler in the
town of Sandwich, at the head of Cape Cod Bay, in
Plymouth Colony.

Freeman in his History of Cape Cod quotes the
following entry concerning this man:

"Thomas Tobie, Sr. subscribed 7 shillings for the meeting
house the 6 mo. 7, 1644."

Perhaps Thomas had been in the plantation still
earlier; some one has invented the tale that he had
been living on Long Island before this time and came
thence to the Plymouth Colony settlement. But all
probabilities are against this theory, and not a line of
evidence has been produced to prove the statement.

We may well believe that he had come from some

English home not long before the date of his helping
in the erection of Sandwich meeting-house in 1644.
His biography will be given as fully as our knowledge
will allow in later pages.

HENRY TOBYE was a resident of Exeter, New
Hampshire, "5th day, 4th month, 1639," when he signed
the "Combination" of planters, and was still living
there in 1640 when the instrument was re-affirmed.
He had died or removed before "12th, 8th month,
1649," we infer from a deed of John Bursley to Edward Gilman bearing this date, conveying among
other tracts of land "one house lot that was Henrye
Tobies," with all the meadows and privileges which
went with the lot. All search for other items about
this Henry has failed to disclose any trace of him.

But not far away from Exeter, at the mouth of the
Piscataqua river, in Kittery, Maine, dwelt JAMES
TOBEY, in the latter part of that seventeenth century.
The incomplete records of town, church and colony
at that period give us no note of the man earlier than
June 24, 1687, when a lot of land was granted to him
by the town in its orderly apportionment of lands; and
the hand of an Indian warrior took his life 21 May,
1705, cutting off his son and namesake James Tobey,
Junior, the same day. But we shall see that he left
several sons and daughters, through whom a large
progeny has descended. Of him and his descendants
as full accounts as possible will be given in succeeding
pages.

We thus see that there were four Tobies in New
England in colonial times: *Francis*, a transient resident of Boston; *Henry*, for a few years a landholder
in Exeter, then vanishing from our sight as the former
had done; *Thomas*, of Sandwich, and *James*, of Kittery, who gave their strength and lives to the founding

of our nation and whose blood has flowed on in the lives of thousands of worthy descendants in this and other names.

Two important questions arise at this point: First, Were the Sandwich and Kittery pioneers related? Second, Whence came they?

To the first it may be said that there is no similarity of Christian names in the two groups which suggests connection, and no correspondence or community of interest which indicates it. To the second our only reply is that neither of the colonists left on record a line that points to his birthplace or relations.

The writer believes that search in the Probate and parish records of England — the country from which every token indicates that they came — would result in discovering the origin of both men, with many items concerning their circumstances and the condition and history of their ancestors. May it not be hoped that the interest developed by this book will lead a number of the family throughout the United States to combine with the writer soon and secure such a search? Correspondence is solicited.

In making up this book we place the Sandwich branch first, for the reason that it appears in colonial records many years the earlier, and the dates of marriage of the sons lead to the belief that Thomas was somewhat the older man. So in constructing the title we arrange the different spellings of the name in the order of the number of persons following them, as shewn in our correspondence, in directories, and in public records and books, conceding equal honor to each of the three forms presented.

The most *prevalent* spelling of the name by persons of the Sandwich and Kittery families has been *Tobey*. Yet it is but fair to observe that of the sons of Thomas Tobey of Sandwich, Nathan signed his name "Tobie," and Gershom his "Toby," while the oldest grandson, Thomas, spelled his "Tobye."

PART FIRST

THOMAS OF SANDWICH AND HIS DESCENDANTS

THOMAS TOBEY OF SANDWICH AND HIS DESCENDANTS.

1

THOMAS[1] TOBEY (recorded also as Toby, Tobye, Tobe and Tobie in the town and colonial records), came at an early date to Sandwich in Plymouth colony, Massachusetts. The town was settled by ten men of Saugus (afterward Lynn), in the spring of 1637; but we have few items of town proceedings for a long time, the earliest pages of the old book being lost. The earliest mention of this man is the statement quoted by Freeman in his History of Cape Cod:

"Thomas Tobie Sr. subscribed 7s. for the meeting house on the 6 mo., 7. 1644."

The town records of Sandwich are much mutilated at the beginning, and this entry does not now appear; but it was undoubtedly read by Mr. Freeman before the book had lost so many of its early pages.

The statement has been made by a number of persons that "Thomas Tobey came from England to Long Island early in the seventeenth century and remained there till about 1640, when he came to Plymouth Colony and settled at Sandwich." But I find no evidence whatever that this is correct. Indeed there were removals of settlers *from* Sandwich and other Massachusetts towns *to* Long Island. Rev. William Leverich, minister of Sandwich at an early day, removed to Oyster Bay, L. I., in 1658. But all

probabilities are against the legend that Thomas Tobey
or any other man of his period, having resided on
Long Island, migrated eastward to Sandwich!

In the town annals Thomas Tobey appears as a man
of good sense and energy, called by his neighbors to
act in various public capacities which required more
than usual ability and judgment. Nov. 7, 1652, he
was one of a committee appointed to take care of all
the fish that were taken by the Indians within the
borders of the town, and have them sold for the benefit
of the town treasury; he was also one of those desig-
nated to oversee the cutting up of the whales which
not infrequently drifted or were driven ashore on the
flats, and sometimes became the occasion of serious
strife between the inhabitants.   He brought suit
against a neighbor in 1653 " for retaineing a yearling
calfe," but lost his case. His tax for the year 1654
was 2 shillings, 6 pence. He subscribed 5 shillings
toward the building of " a place for publick meetings "
in 1655, and a pound a year toward the support
of a minister in 1657. In the latter year we find
his name among those who took the oath of fidelity
to the colony. In 1658 he was chosen constable, an
office requiring accuracy in accounts and energy in
collecting taxes as well as handling prisoners, etc.;
was sworn at the court in Plymouth, June 1, 1658.
In the same year he was chosen one of the " Ratars,"
i. e. assessors of rates or taxes. The town paid him
4 shillings on a certain occasion for " haveing the
strangers to Plymouth," which perhaps refers to his
being sent, as constable, with wayfarers, believed
to be Quakers, to place them in the jail at the seat of
government. He was one of the highway surveyors
and " pundor " or pound-keeper in 1660; on a committee to lay out a new pound in 1662; on a committee of reference in 1664–5; appointed to meet
with Barnstable men about boundary in 1659; a jury-

THOMAS: FIRST GENERATION.   17

man in 1663 and 1668; excise officer from 1662 to
1668; member of a grand inquest in 1670; in charge
of the letting out of town lands in 1668. 23(2)1675
his name appears in the first list of townsmen extant.
A council of men was selected in 1676 to " hire men to
goe out upon the scout for the town," and to assign
soldiers to duty, furnish amunition, etc., in the time
of King Philip's war; and he was one of the three
citizens to whom this important duty was assigned.

Lands for Rev. John Smith, the minister of the
township, were laid out in 1673 by a committee of
which Thomas Tobey was a member. He contributed
to the repairs of the meeting house in 1676; acted as
an auditor on the accounts of the constable with Mr.
Bourne in 1678.

Liberty was granted him to have additional land
in July, 1681, and he was anthorized to look for it,
having the assistance of Mr. Bourne and Mr. Edmond
Freeman in the search; "if any can be found he is to
have fifty or threescore acres thereof upon report to
the court," runs the record. [Plym. Col. Rec.]   A
tract of ten acres "formerly granted to Samuel Knott,"
was also laid out to him in 1699. His name is one of
the twenty who were members of the Sandwich church
" when Mr. Cotton was ordained Nov. 28, 1694."
[Oldest page of the church record extant.]

The first marriage of Thomas Tobey of which we
know is thus recorded in the town book of Sandwich:

" Thomas Tobie and Martha Knott were married the 18th of
November, Anno 1650."

Martha was a daughter of George Knott, one of the
ten founders of Sandwich, and his wife Martha. Mr.
Knott had died about a year before this marriage,
leaving a will in which he anticipated that Martha
would marry Thomas Dunham, who had " pretended "
to be " contracted " to the girl; but the family disap-

proved of the match, and Dunham married another
maiden while Martha yielded to the wooing of "Thomas
Tobie," and became the mother of seven sons who
lived to maturity and whose descendants have done
credit to her.

Mrs. Knott, Martha's mother, lived in Sandwich
some years, as the records show; her life was not free
from trials, for she was one of those persons who, having attended religious services away from the regular
place of worship (Quakers or Baptists), were brought
before the court for "non-attendance," a fiction which
persecutors in Europe had long practised and from
which Puritans did not at first cut loose. Samuel
Knott, a brother of Mrs. Tobey, survived his brother-
in-law, and was remembered in his will.

Mrs. Martha Tobey died at some time not on record,
and her husband married, second, after 1689, certainly,
Hannah, widow of Ambrose Fish. As "Mrs. Tobey"
she took care of William Cleare and Elkanah Smith
in their sickness, and the town voted March 20, 1705,
to pay her 24 shillings. She survived Mr. Tobey
and died in March, 1720–1, leaving a will which con-
veys much interesting information about family connections; we give it below.

The records of Sandwich, as we have seen, gratify
our desire for details of Thomas Tobey's life to a limited
extent. In the Probate records of Barnstable county
we further discover that he was one of the appraisers
of the estate of Sergt. Benjamin Foster, Oct. 16, 1690.
At the date of his will in 1710 he was evidently in
full possession of his faculties, as is definitely shown
by the particular bequests and arrangements he made.
Notice that he remarks upon his age; that he mentions each of his surviving sons and gives legacies to
the representatives of those who had passed away;
that he tells the number of his surviving daughters
if he does not gratify our curiosity by calling them

by name; that he makes the fact apparent that his second wife was a widow when he married her by bequeathing to her the property she brought at their marriage; separate wifely property not being recognized then to any extent save when a widow married whose children's rights had to be guarded; and the testimony given to his former marriage by the provision for life—care and decent burial of the surviving brother of his former wife.

THE WILL OF THOMAS¹ TOBEY.

I, Thomas Toby of Sandwich in the County of Barnstable in New England being Aged and weak of body yet thro' the mercy & goodness of God of Disposing mind and memory and calling to mind the uncertainty of this Transitory Life I am Desirous according to my Duty to sett things in order before God shall call me hence and therefore Do make this my Last Will & Testament hereby Revoking and Disannulling all former Will & Wills by Word or writing heretofore by me made; and do hereby Constitute and Declare this to be my Last Will & Testament in manner and form following viz : my Will is To Comitt my Soul to God in Jesus Christ who gave it and my Body to Decent buryal when God shall pleas to call me hence and as Touching my worldly estate which God hath beyond my Deserts bestowed on me my will is to Dispose of it as followeth.

Impr. my Will is that all my Debts in Right or Conscience to any persons due, Together with my funerall Charges shall be first paid and Discharged by my Executors hereafter Named in convenient Time out of my estate.

Item. I do hereby Give bequeath and further Ratify and confirm unto my Loving son John Toby his heirs and assigns forever that Lott of upland which I formerly Gave to him Lying near ye now Dwelling house of Joseph Foster in Sandwich aforesd being now in ye Tenure and occupation of sd Joseph Foster according to the known bounds yr'of.

Item. I will and bequeath unto my Loving son Samuel Toby his heirs & assigns forever the stone end of my Dwelling house in which ye sd Samuel now dwelleth and the one half of my Barn now in his possession and his Improvement and the moyety

or one half part of my old field so called part of which the
sd Barn standeth on according as it is now divided and fenced
in by itself and he to have that side on which sd barn now
standeth; and I also give and bequeath unto him the sd Samuel
Toby his heirs and assigns forever my Lott of Land Lying near
ye now Dwelling house of Edward Dillingham and Adjoineth
to That called ye twenty acres; sd Lott being by estimation
six acres be it more or less and is bounded as ye fence now
stands; and ye orchard & piece of upland fenced in with it and
the piece of fresh meadow Adjoining to it together with my
piece or parcell of meadow ground or salt marsh Lying below
ye now Dwelling House of Eliakim Tupper; only Reserving
to my son Garshom convenient ways to his Lands within these
Lands.

Item. I will and bequeath unto my Loving son Garshom Toby
the other half of my sd old field by the barn which is now in
his occupation & improvement with a convenient way to it
where it is now used at ye head of ye other half and also the
Little pasture called the hors pasture att ye foot of ye other
piece before mentioned; and also all ye Right of my Lands on
ye westerly side of ye way that Leads Down to the House in
which sd Samuel now Dwells and the neck of Land behind
and att ye Southwest end of sd Dwelling house and so extending all Round between the Mill pond and sd fresh meadow and
so home to the farm of my son Jonathan Toby Togather with
all my meadow and marsh Lying below the now Dwelling
House of Widow Ruth Chipman between sd house and ye
Town Harbour near Skaffold point so called and also ye Least
piece of my meadow in ye on pasture neck so called Lying
between ye meadow of Shubal Smith and Jashub Wing with
all my meadow & upland Lying between the fords so called
having the meadow of William Bassett on the one side and ye
meadow of Mr. John Smith & Stephen Skeffe Esq on ye other
side Together with all my meadow and marsh Lying over ye
creek on Sawpit neck side as also all my upland adjoyning to
that meadow excepting two acres att ye uper end; Together with
the other part of my Dwelling House being the southwest end
of it; and also the other half of my sd barn with free Egress
and Regress To and from the same; All which sd Parcels of
upland and meadow ground to be to the only proper use &
behoof of him the sd Garshom Toby his heirs and assigns for
ever.

And I Do also will and bequeath unto them the sd Samuel
Toby & Garshom Toby my sons their heirs and assigns forever
my Lott of land in ye Towneck so called and my twenty acres
of Land formerly Given to me by Quachatasett Indian Sachem
Lying near Snake pond as also my twenty acre Lott and my
forty acre lot that is yet to be Taken up and Divided; as also
all my Right in the Comon or undivided Land in sd Town of
Sandwich all which is to be equally Divided between them;
But the Condition on which I give all the sd Lands & meadows
unto the sd Sam'l & Garshom is that they or their heirs exec'rs
or admin'rs Do Keepe maintain yr uncle Samuel Knott During
ye Time of his Naturall Life both with food Drink Lodging
and apparill and to allow him a decent Buryal after his death.

Item. I do give and bequeath unto my son Jonathan Toby
his heirs and assigns forever ye Lands on which he now Dwells
and in his possession and my biggest piece of meadow in sd
ox pasture.

Item I give and bequeath unto my grandson Thomas Toby
of Yarmouth besides what I have already given him one heifer
of two years old and one shilling in money.

Item. I give and bequeath unto my son Nathan Toby his
heirs & assigns forever all those my Lands att & near his Dwelling house now in his possession and the two acres of Land
before Reserved in Sawpit Neck.

Itm. I Give and bequeath unto my Grand daughter Sarah
Toby the daughter of my son Ephraim Toby Deceased that
Lott of Land on which her mother Hannah Toby now dwells
and to her heirs and assigns forever; provided that she Live
to ye age of one and twenty years or marry but if not then to
be Equally Divided amongst all my sons Then surviving.

Itm. I Give and bequeath unto Hannah my Loving Wife all
the Estate which she had when I married her and what she now
hath which she gott by her own Labour or that was Given to
her; and one Cow and all ye money which she shall have of
mine in her hands at Time of my Death.

Item. I Give and bequeath unto each of my three daughters
five shillings apiece; and what other Estate shall be left of myne
when Debts Legasys & Funerall charges are paid out my will
is that it be Equally Divided to and between them the sd Sam'l
and Garshom Toby whom I Do ordain & constitute to be Joynt

Executors to this my will.   In testimony whereof I have hereunto sett my hand & seal this 29th of March 1709–10.

THOMAS TT TOBY   [Seal]
his mark & seal

Signed, sealed & Declared To be his Last Will & Testament
In the presence of
Wm. Bassett Sen'r.
Wm. Bassett Jun'r.
Thankfull Bassett.

Proved April 9, 1714.
[Barnstable Prob. Bk. 3, p. 352, *et seq.*]

WILL OF THE WIDOW OF THOMAS' TOBEY.

Hannah Tobie of Sandwich being Weak of Body yet of Per-
fict minde and memory Do make This my Last Will and Testament   . . .   I give unto Seth Fish my Loving son the sum
of Twenty Shillings to be paid to him out of my estate as a
Token of my love.   I do Give and bequeath unto my six children hereafter mentioned : all and singular w'soever shall be
found within Doors or without which Doth of Right belong to
me in manner and form as followeth : viz :   To my son Samuell
Tobye and my daughter Abiah Tobye his wife one full third
part of my estate.   And to my son Garshom Tobye and my
daughter Mehitable Tobye his wife another third part of my
estate.   And to my son Eliakim Tupper and my daughter
Joannah Tupper his wife the other third part   . . .   This
third day of March, Annoque Domini one thousand seven hundred and twenty 1720 twenty one.

HANNAH   TOBYE.   (Seal.)
her marke

In Presence of these
Witnesses.
Eldad Tupper
Temperance Bourne
her marke
Elizabeth Tupper

The will was probated the last part of the month.   The
estate was appraised at £ 95 : 15 : 3.

Children, order unknown:

2. i.   Thomas,* b. in Sandwich, Dec. 8, 1651.

3. ii.   John, birth-date unknown; townsman in 1681; father in 1684.

4. iii.   Nathan, birth-date unknown; townsman in 1681; father in 1686.

5. iv.   Ephraim, birth-date unknown; townsman in 1681; father in 1691.

6. v.   Jonathan, birth-date unknown; townsman in 1694; father in 1694.

7. vi.   Samuel, birth-date unknown; townsman in 1699; father in 1697.

8. vii.   Gershom, birth-date unknown; townsman before 1702; father in 1697.

Besides these sons there were "three daughters," as we learn from the father's will. If they were his own children it seems strange that he did not specify their names or those of their husbands. Documents of the vicinity and period have been searched for clues but no trace of these "daughters" has been found. It is not impossible they may be the three daughters of his second wife Hannah (by her former husband Ambrose Fish), who are named in her will at a later date; two of them had married sons of Mr. Tobey and the third was a neighbor.

Notice that the widow speaks of her "six children" but specifies her three daughters and their husbands.

2

THOMAS² (*Thomas¹*), born in Sandwich, Dec. 8, 1651; died in Yarmouth, Feb. 2, 1676–7; married Mehitabel, daughter of John Crow (name since called Crowell) of Yarmouth ("Nobscusset"). She survived him, and died a widow in 1723. He removed to Yarmouth (the eastern part now Dennis), and in the same place his descendants continued.

Att the prerogative Court held at Barnstable march the 6th 1688 : 9 The settlement of the estate of Mr. John Crow Sen Late of Yarmouth deceased was ordered as followeth (that is to say) that John Crow the eldest son of the sd deceased to have and Injoy the house and all the Lands of his sd deceased Father after the death of his mother mehittable Crow and the sd mehitable Crow to have and Injoy the third part thereof dur-

ing her natural Life and three pounds In Apparel to Samuel
Crow the son of the sd deceased and Just debts being paid the
sd Mehitable the relict of the sd deceased to have the third
part of the rest of the estate; mehittable crow and Lidya Crow
the Daughters of sd deceased having had already considerable of theirs) the other two thirds of his personal estate to be
equally devided between his children Samuel Crow Jeremiah
Crow Elizabeth Crow Susanna Crow and Hannah Crow and
the sd John Crow the son of sd deceased to pay out of his own
estate the sum of twenty shillings to Thomas Toby grandson
of sd deceased within a twelve month after the date above
written and to his sd brother Samuel Crow the sum of forty
shillings presantly after the marriage or death of the sd mehittable Crow his mother.

[Barnstable Prob. Bk. 1, p. 26.]

The fact that the son Thomas was the only representative of this family to receive a legacy from his
grandfather Tobey in 1710, seems to show that he
was the only one then living; such evidence is simply
negative, but the fact that we find no trace of any
other child of this Thomas[2] in the colony is further
evidence that Thomas[3] was the only survivor of this
family.

Child:

9. i.   Thomas,[3] b. Feb. 2, 1678.

3

JOHN[2] (*Thomas[1]*) born and resident in Sandwich,
was enrolled as one of "the townsmen to vote for
officers" 27 June, 1681. Chosen to see to the due
observance of the law relating to horses March 22,
1693–4. Married Jane ———. He died Dec. 26,
1738.

THE WILL OF JOHN TOBEY, Sen.

In the Name of God Amen I John Tobey Sen'r of Sandwich
in the County of Barnstable in the Province of ye Massachusetts Bay in New England do make and Ordain this my last

will and Testament and in the first place I Give my Soul to God Humbly Intreating Pardon and Acceptance Through the merits of Jesus Christ and as to my worldly Estate wherewith it hath pleased God to favour me that Remains undisposed of my Just debts and funeral charges being first Satisfied and Paid I Dispose of in manner following

Imprimis I Give to my Beloved wife Jane if she survive me the use of all my Personal Estate or movables that shall not be Disposed of hereafter in this my will During her widowhood or Natural life

Item, I Give to my son Thomas all my Cloaths or wearing Apparell

Item I Give to my son John five shillings.

Item I Give to my son Eleazer five shillings

Item, I Give to my son Eben'r five shillings

Item, I Give to my Son in Law Richard Garret five shillings

Item, My will is that as to the Residue of my estate that shall Remain after my wives Decease that it be Equally Divided between my two daughters Mary Clark and Reliance Ewer or their heirs that they share & Share allike in all the said moveable or Personal Estate.

Finally I Hereby nominate and appoint my son John and my Son in law Thomas Ewer the Exec'rs of this my last will and Testament in witness whereof I have hereunto set my hand and seal this ninth Day of July 1733 in the seventh year of his Majesties Reign.

Signed Sealed and Published as
    the Last will and Testament   his
of the said John Tobey in Presence of us   JOHN ✕ TOBEY [Seal]
    Benjamin Fessenden   mark
    Ebenezer Perry
    Rebecca Fessenden
                Proved Feb 1738.

Children:
    i.   Mary,[2] b. March, 1684-5; m. ——— Clark.
10. ii.   John, b. February, 1686-7.
    iii. Martha, b. June, 1688; m. Richard Garrett.
11. iv. Thomas, b. August, 1690.
12. v.   Ebenezer, b. September, 1692.
    vi. Reliance, b. March, 1695; m. Thomas Ewer.
13. vii. Eleazer or Eliezer, b. Jan. 2, 1699-1700.
    2

4

NATHAN² (*Thomas¹*), born in Sandwich at a date
not now known, was enrolled as a townsman of the
plantation June 27, 1681, and was referred to in honorable ways in after years in the same place.

He married (according to the Sargent Genealogy)
Mary Sargent* who was probably the mother of Seth
and Deborah. The long interval between the recorded
births of children from 1689 to 1697 may indicate
that he married his second wife about the latter date.
She was Sarah Fallowell, of whose connections we
have the following very interesting particulars in a
deed of land.

"Nathan Tobey of Sandwich, Samuel Barrow, of Middleborough and Susanna, his wife, and Sarah Tobey, being heirs
to the three fourth parts of the estate which our grandmother
Sarah Fallowell and our uncle William Fallowell, both late of
Plymouth, died seized of; and whereas the court, 13 June,
1729, settled the whole upon our brother William Tobey, of
Plymouth," they deeded their shares to John Cooper and
Nathaniel Thomas June 26, 1729, in confirmation of a deed
which William had made to the same parties.

The date of Nathan Tobey's death is not recorded
but may be inferred from the date of his will and the
time of its probating.

THE WILL OF NATHAN TOBEY, SEN.

November the 26th 1721.
In the Name of God Amen. Nathan Tobie of the Town of
Sandwich In the County of Barnstable In the Massachusetts
Bay In New England Sen'r being in his right mind, this being
his last will and Testament hath ordered thus:
I give to my wife Sarah Tobie my whole estate and the
improvement of it my house and all my land both at home &
abroad as Long as she Lives to order and Dispose of it as

* She was a granddaughter of William Sargent, "haberdasher of hats" in
Northampton, Eng.; a pioneer in our Charlestown and Malden where he was
an active citizen, a deacon and lay-preacher, whence he removed to Barnstable
with his sons John and Samuel and daughters. He died Dec. 16, 1682.

she thinks fit and her four children after her Nathan Susanah William and Sarah Tobie, Excepting one forty acre Lot lying up at a place called Peters Pond which I Reserved for my son Seth, and as for my daughter Deborah I give unto her five shillings and one shilling to each of her children. My beloved wife Sarah Tobie being my Executor as witness my hand

NATHAN TOBIE.

the mark of ✔
Jashub Wing
the mark of / Henry Landers

Proved April 5th 1722.

[Barns. Prob. Bk. 4, p. 52.]

The widow returned an inventory, the property being appraised at £ 586: 18: 06. After her death the son Nathan was appointed administrator of both estates and guardian of his brother William, July 24, 1724. Division was made to the children: Nathan, William and Sarah Tobie and Susannah Barrow, Aug. 28, 1725.

Children:

14. i. Seth,[3] b. Monday, March 24, 1686.
ii. Deborah,[*] b. Jan. 26, 1689.
iii. Jemimah, b. March 31, 1697.
iv. Susannah, b. March 11, 1698–9 ; m. Samuel Barrow.
15. v. Nathan, b. Sept. 28, 1701.
16. vi. William, b. May 3, 1706.
vii. Sarah, b. Aug. 30, 1708 ; m. Barnabas Tobey, No. 69.

5

EPHRAIM[2] (*Thomas*[1]), born in Sandwich; married Hannah ———; who survived him. He was enrolled as a townsman, 27 June, 1681. The mark of his cattle was recorded in 1689,—

" a halfe pennie on ye Right eare the hind side and a piece .cut out of the toppe of the same ear like a mackerill taile."

* Is she the Deborah Tobey who married in Boston, Jan. 20, 1707, Benjamin Ivory?

He lived but a short life, dying before Sept. 29, 1693, when the inventory of his estate was taken, which his widow presented in court Oct. 4 following. It showed household goods, tools, cattle, a Bible, etc.; total, £45:13:00. " Widow Hannah Tobey " was admitted to the church April 14, 1700. She died before May 20, 1714, when Nathaniel Otis was appointed administrator of her estate.

Children:

    i.   Benjamin,[2] b. in Sandwich, " son of Ephraim Tobie,"
           March 24, 1691. Probably died before 1709.

   ii.   Sarah, remembered in the will of her grandfather in
           1709.

6

JONATHAN[2] (*Thomas[1]*), born in Sandwich and resided there; was " accepted as a townsman " 22 Jan. 1694, a grand juror Feb. 27, 1696–7. A fence viewer in 1700–1. Married " Remembrance " or Remember ———. She joined him in a deed of the homestead; recorded 30 March, 1748–9. She died Nov. 3, 1732. He died in 1741.

THE WILL OF JONATHAN TOBEY, SEN.

I, Jonathan Tobey of the Town of Sandwich in the County of Barnstable in the Province of the Massachusetts Bay in New England husbandman being at present in tolerable health of Body and of Disposing Mind and Memory Through the Mercy and Goodness of God but considering the uncertainty of this Present Life and the certainty of approaching Death Either sooner or Later I do make this my Last will and Testament hereby Revoking and Disannulling all other and former will or wills Testament or Testaments by me heretofore made Ratifying and Confirming this and no other To be my Last Will and Testament. And Principally and first of all I Recommend my Soul to God In Jesus Christ and my body to a Decent Christian Burial at the Discretion of my Executor hereafter Named and as for the Temporal Estate wherewith God hath Blessed me in this Life I Give Demise and Dispose thereof in manner and form following That is to say.

Impr. My Will is that all my Just Debts and funeral charges and the Legacies hereafter given in this my will shall be first paid by my Executor out of my Moneys and the Debts due to me as far as they will Extend and the Rest out of my stock of creatures.

Item. I will and Bequeath to my Daughters Deborah Mariah Remember and Abigail five pounds apeace.

Item. I will and bequeath to my Grandson John Clark Twenty shillings.

Item. I will and bequeath to my Grandson Jonathan Clark the sum of four pounds money.

Item. I will and bequeath to my Daughter Mercy the Use and Improvement of my new house chamber During Life and a feather bed and furniture and one cow.

Item, I Will and Bequeath to my Daughter Mary the sum of Fourty pounds in money and a feather bed & Furniture and one cow.

Item. I will and Bequeath to my sons Samuell Jonathan and Nathaniel their respective Heirs and assigns forever all my Estate in Housing Lands and Meddows whatsoever I also give them my said three sons all my Tools and Utensils that are used about Husbandry and my Arms and Ammunition and one feather bed and furniture Equally among them.

Item. I will and Bequeath the Rest of my household Goods To my Daughters Mercy and Mary Equally.

Item My will is that after the before mentioned Legacies Funeral Expenses and Just Debts are paid what Remains of my Stock of Creatures shall be Equally Divided betwixt my said three sons and my Daughters Mercy & Mary and I do constitute and appoint my Eldest son Samuell to be Executor of this my Last Will & Testament.

In witness whereof I have hereunto set my hand seal the sixth day of September Anno Domini one thousand seven hundred & thirty-eight.

JONATHAN TOBEY [L.S.]
. his J mark

Signed Sealed and Declared to be his Last
Will and Testament in Presence of:

Sam'll Jennings.

her
Abigail / Perry
mark

Ruhama Jennings.

Proved Aug. 4, 1741.
[Barns. Prob. Bk. 6, p. 86.]

Children:

1. Deborah,[2] b. Dec. 30, 1694.
ii. Elizabeth, b. Sept. 15, 1697.
iii. Maria, b. Jan. 12, 1700–1.
iv. Remember, b. Aug. 16, 1703. Remember Tobey m.
Cyrano Tilson of Chilmark at Sandwich, Jan. 12,
1730–1.
18. v. Samuel, b. Sept. 11, 1707.
vi. Mercy, b. Oct. 6, 1710.
vii. Abigail, b. May 28, 1713.
viii. Mary, b. Feb. 2, 1715.
19. ix. Jonathan, b. Aug. 6, 1718.
20. x. Nathaniel, b. June 30, 1721.

7

SAMUEL,[2] (*Thomas*[1]), born in Sandwich and dwelt
there; died "9. 22, 1737" (Nov. 22, 1737). Married
Abiah, daughter of Ambrose and Hannah Fish, born
in Sandwich, Sept. 2, 1678; her mother was her husband's step-mother as we have seen.

He resided in Sandwich; was chosen one of the
grand jurors "March 8, 1699 also 1700"; a surveyor
of highways in 1700; a tithing man in 1709. He
educated his children as well as was practicable, and
gave Samuel the course at Harvard in preparation for
the ministry.

THE WILL OF SAMUEL TOBEY, SEN.

In the name of God, Amen. I, Samuel Tobey of Sandwich
in ye County of Barnstable In ye province of the Massachusetts
bay in New England not knowing but yt my Departure out of
the world by Death is at hand do make and ordain this to be
my last will and testament hereby revoking cancelling and an-
nulling all others and in the first place I commend my Soul to
God thro the merits of Jesus Christ to be sanctified and saved
and my body I commit to the earth by a decent burial at ye
Decression of my executor hereafter named and as to that
worldly estate wherewith it has pleased God to favour me my
Just Debts and funeral charges being first satisfied and paid I
Dispose of in manner following:

٦٠Imprimis I give to Abiah my beloved wife ye one third of my estate both real and personal to be used and improved by her for her benefit and comfort During her being my widdow and if any part of my personal estate be remaining at her Death which I now give her my will is that she have Liberty to dispose of it to whom of her children she pleases.

. Item I give to my beloved son Corenelios Tobey my sword he having rec'd considerable from me in my life

Item I give to my beloved son Zacheus twenty shillings to be paid him by my sons Jonathan and Eliakim each ten shillings within twelve months after my Decease he having had also what I Designed him in my lifetime

Item I give unto my beloved son Jonathan the one half of all my lands meadows marsh and swampy ground Together with my house and barn in equal partnership and proportion with his brother Eliakim (Excepting and Saving to Eliakim as hereafter saved and excepted) he paying the several legacics wch in this my will I appoint him to pay

Item I give to my beloved son Eliakim Tobey the other half of all my lands meadows marsh and swampy ground Togeather with my house and barn in equal partnership with his brother Jonathan also I give him free of any Division or partnership to him his heirs and assigns forever my piece of land and orchard below the way over against my dwelling house also my piece of land and low ground near to the town neck gate in Sandwich he paing the several Legacies which in this my will I appoint him to pay. These lands and meadows in partnership with and between my son Jonathan and Eliakim I give to them their heirs and assigns forever.

Item. I give to my beloved son Samuel a good preaching bible To be bought by my sons Jonathan and Eliakim.

Item I give to my beloved son Thomas Twenty pounds to be paid by my sons Jonathan and Eliakim, Ten pounds each within half a year after he comes to be one and twenty years of age

Item. I give to my daughter Joanna Spooner five shillings to be paid by my son Jonathan

Item I give unto my Daughter Tabath Freeman five shillings to be paid by my son Eliakim these daughters having received at their marriage wt I Designed for them

Item I give to my Daughter Ruth two Beds with furniture To them that is to say feather Bedds with the remainder of ye

two thirds of the household stuff after her mother has taken her
third also I give her Liberty To live in the home during her
being a single woman

Item I give unto my grandson Jabez* five pounds on his
coming To be twenty one years old To be paid by my sons
Jonathan and Eliakim fifty shillings each of ym and my will is
that he be put out to some good trade by my Execut'rs hereafter named when he comes to be about fourteen years of age

Item I give to my sons Jonathan and Eliakim the remainder
of my personal and moveable estate not otherwise Disposed of
in this my last will and testament The better to enable them to
pay my just debts Finally I hereby nominate and appoint my
beloved wife Abiah Tobey Exec'x and my sons Jonathan Tobey
and Eliakim Tobey Executors of this my last will and testament In witness whereof I have hereunto set my hand and
seal ye forth day of September Domini one thousand seaven
hundred and thirty seaven Signed Sealed and Declared to be the
last will and testament of ye sd Samuel Tobey In presence of
John Bates Nathaniel Bassett Benjamin Fessenden.

his
SAMUEL x TOBEY [Seal]
mark and seale

Proved October 17 1737.

[Barns. Prob. Bk. 5, p. 302.]

Children:

    i.   Joanna,² b. May 22, 1697; m. Nov. 29, 1716,
         Benjamin Spooner of Dartmouth.

21. ii. Cornelius, b. Sept. 12, 1699.

    iii. Tabitha, b. Nov. 9, 1701; m. May 9, 1726, Joseph
         Freeman.

22. iv. Zaccheus, b. Jan. 13, 1703–4.

    v.   Ruth, b. Sept. 8, 1706.

23. vi. Jonathan, b. May 13, 1709.

24. vii. Eliakim, b. Oct. 19, 1711.

25. viii. Samuel, b. May 8, 1715.

26. ix. Thomas, b. Aug. 14, 1720.

27. x.   Elisha, b. July 14, 1723.

* "My grandson Jabez Tobey," who thus received a bequest from his grandfather, was not 14 years old at that time (1737). His parentage has not yet
been ascertained by the writer. He married at Dartmouth, March 2, 1748,
Anna Spooner; and had children: Philip, b. Sept. 10, 1750, and Tabitha, b.
May 11, 1752. Jabez Tobey of Dartmouth, cordwainer, bought land there Feb.
23, 1753.

8

GERSHOM[2] (*Thomas*[1]), born in Sandwich; married
first, April 29, 1697, Mehitabel, daughter of Ambrose
and Hannah Fish, mentioned in her mother's will on
a previous page; she was born May 19, 1680, and died
after 1720. He married second, Hannah Nye; she
died Oct. 27, 1748.

Gershom Tobey, with Richard and John Landers, all of
Sandwich, bought land in Bridgewater 25 May, 1730, and
sold the same 15 July, 1731.

He resided in Sandwich; appears in the list of
townsmen, "transcribed from the old Booke of Records," June 25, 1702; was one of the men chosen to
see to the "due observance of the law about swine"
in 1718, and held other town offices.

He made his will Jan. 31, 1757, and died probably
only a short time previous to March 6, 1759, when it
was probated.   .

THE WILL OF GERSHOM TOBEY, SEN.

I, Gershom Tobey Sen'r of Sandwich in the County of Barnstable In the Province of the Massachusetts Bay in New England yeoman being under Bodily Indisposition but of Disposing
mind and memory through the mercy & Goodness of God &
considering the uncertainty of the Present Life and the certainty
of approaching death I do make this my last will and testament
and principally and first of all I Recommend my soul to God
in Jesus Christ and my body to a decent Christian Burial at
the Discression of my Executor hereafter named and as Touching such worldly estate wherewith it hath Pleased God to Bless
me in This Life I give demise and Dispose of the same in the
following manner and form
    Imprimis My will is and I do Give and Bequeath unto my
son Silas Toby & to his heirs and Assigns forever all my upland
& swampy ground near his now Dwelling house on each side
the way that comes from Jashub Wing's to his house and also
half my Salt & fresh meadow betwixt Sawpit Neck & the
Great ford creek also the woodlot Lying near Nathaniel fishes

houses also my Part of a Twenty acre Lot in Partnership with
Eliakim Tobey & my Land in sheep Pasture lots at a place
called the Opening also my Lot of Land lying Landersas
Swamp Being all in the Town of Sandwich

Item I Give & Bequeath unto my son Barnabas Toby his
heirs and assigns forever one half of my salt & fresh meadow
Betwixt sd Sawpit Neck & the Great ford Creek also my Land
which is Inclosed with fence that Lieth near Southward from
his now Dwelling House Joyning to the Lane that leads up to
Grassey Pond

Item I Give & Bequeath to my son Ephraim Toby one hundred Pounds old Tennor or the Value thereof in Lawfull money
to be Paid him by my three sons Silas Barnabas and Gershom
Equally betwixt them within one year after my Decease

Item I Give to my son Gershom Toby his heirs & Assigns
forever my now Dwelling house & all the land adjoyning
thereto Including that land called the Park also my orchard
also my barn and the Land adjoyning thereto to extend to the
Lands of John and Thomas Smith called the Twenty acres
together with my Land & meado at the Island sd meadow
adjoyning to the mill creek and also my Land & meadow Lying
to the westward of the Great ford Creek & also all my Land
in Sawpit neck so called & my half wood lot runing up to the
westward of the Great hollow & also my wood lot adjoyning
to the head of the Inclosed Land given to my son Barnabas
By this my will & Lying to the southward thereof I also Give
my son Gershom all my Husbandry Tools and utensils

Item I Give and Bequeath to my daughter Temperance a
fether Bed a coverlid & a Pair of sheets

Item I Give & Bequeath to my Daughter Mehitable my
Brass kittle and a pair of Curtains & Vallents one coverlid &
a Looking Glass and all my Puter

Item I Give & Bequeath to my Daughter Jerusha all the
Best of my household Goods that are not disposed of Before in
this my will

Item my will is that my Just debts & funeral expenses shall
be paid out of my Quick stock But if it should not hold out to
be enough then my will that my three sons Silas Barnabas &
Gershom shall Pay Equally betwixt them what shall fall short
and if my Quick stock shall overpay my Debts and funeral
expenses the Remainder with my apparel shall be equally divided betwixt my sd three sons

Item I Give & Bequeath to my sons Barnabas & Gershom and to their heirs and assigns forever my Lot of Land in the Last division in Sandwich lying near the Round Swamp & Southward from it I also Give to my son Gershom all the hay corn and meat that I shall die seized off

Lastly I do ordain and appoint my son Silas Toby to be the Sole Executor of this my Last will & testament & I do hereby utterly Disalow and Revoke all & every other will or wills heretofore By me made Ratifying & Confirming This & no other to be my Last will & Testament In witness whereof I have hereunto set my hand and seal the thirtyfirst day of January Adom'i 1757 Signed Sealed Published Pronounced and Declared by the said Gershom Toby to be his last will and Testament In Presents of us ye subscribing witnesses.

Joseph Foster   GERSHOM TOBY [L. S.]
Cornelius Toby Junr
Silas Bourn
        Proved March 6, 1759.
[Barns. Prob. Bk. 9, p. 435.]

Children :

    i.   Jerusha,[2] born March 23, 1697–8 ; married June 22, 1719, Seth, son of John and Elizabeth (Bourne) Pope, born Jan. 3, 1701, died in 1769. [Pope Family (Plymouth line), page 290.]

   ii.   Temperance, b. April 21, 1701.

28. iii.   Silas, b. Nov. 4, 1704.

29. iv.   Barnabas, b. July 22, 1708.

30. v.   Ephraim, b. July 22, 1711.

   vi.   Mehitable, b. Dec. 23, 1714.

31. vii.   Gershom, b. Sept. 24, 1720.

9

THOMAS[3] (*Thomas,*[2] *Thomas*[1]), born in Yarmouth, Feb. 2, 1676; is said to have married first, a daughter of George Crow (Crowell).

He married at some time, as we learn from his will, Rebecca ——, who seems to have been a widow when he married her, from the circumstance that he refers to property she owned before her marriage to him; yet he may have been her first husband, and the reference may be to the dower given to her by her father.

He resided in that part of Yarmouth which later became the town of Dennis. He died in 1757, leaving the following will.

Children, order not positively known :

33. i.   Thomas,[4] b. about 1704.
34. ii. Seth, b. about 1716.
     iii. Mehitabel, m. —— Taylor.
     iv. Rebecca, m. —— Parker.
     v.   Desire, b. 1707; m. at Yarmouth, May 28, 1730, James Sears; she d. July 28, 1781. He d. at Ridgefield, Conn., March 17, 1781. [Sears Gen.]

THE WILL OF THOMAS TOBEY, THE THIRD.

In the Name of God Amen I Thomas Toby of Yarmouth in the County of Barnstable In the Province of the Massachusetts Bay in New england Yeoman, being week & sick of Body but of sound mind and memory Blessed be God for it & calling to mind the mortality of my body and knowing that it is appointed for all men once to Dye do make & ordain this my last will & Testament In form and manner as followeth first I bequeath my Soul Into the hands of Almighty God my Maker, hoping through the meritorious Death & Passion of Jesus Christ my only Saviour and Redeemer to receive free Pardon of all my Sins and as for my Body to be buried in a decent Christian Burial at the discretion of my Executors hereafter nominated nothing doubting but at the General Resurrection I shall receive the same again by the Almighty Power of God and as Touching such worldly estate wherewith it hath pleased to God to Bless me in this life I Give demise and Dispose of the same in the following form and manner.

Imprimis I give and bequeath unto Rebecca Tobey my dearly beloved wife the Liberty to Live in the East room of my dwelling house and sufficient firewood for her to burn cut fit for the fire at the door during her widowhood and I give her likewise sixty pounds of meat pork and beef in proportion yearly and eight bushels of Indian corn and four bushels of Rye yearly and

I Give her one cow and to be kept for her summer and winter on my estate during her widowhood and I Give her one Iron pot and skillet to use and a Linnen Spining wheel & one third part of the beading that hath been made by her since we married togeather To her own disposal and my will is my wife shall have liberty to pass and repass to fetch water out of my well and to use the cellar to put in beer & soap &c during her widowhood. I Give the abovesaid articles to my said wife as her Dowry and my will is my said wife shall have all the moveable Estate that she brought with her when we came togeather to be at her own disposal forever.

Item I give unto my Daughter Mehetable Taylor Twenty shillings lawful money. Item I give unto my second Daughter Rebecca Parker Twenty shillings lawful money. Item I give unto my Daughter Desire Sears Twenty shillings lawfull money as Legacies. Item I give unto my Son Thomases Three sons each of them a small Bible all these abovesd Legacies to be paid out of my moveable Estate. Item I give unto my son Thomas Tobey the West end of my Dwelling house and the one half part of all the rest of my buildings and also five acres of Land that lyeth adjoining unto his own land that he bought of Elisha Hall and the onethird part of all my meadow both fresh and salt meadow and I likewise Give unto my son Thomas Tobey the one half part of all my upland and woodland & the one half of my moveable estate both in doers and out doers after my wives Decease and the abovesaid legacies and my will is that my two sons shall have the half Lott of woodland called the Oak Lott equall between them as they have begun to divide it. Item. I Give unto my son Seth Tobey the Eastward end of my Dwelling house and one half part of all the Rest of my other buildings and the one half part of all my upland & woodland that I have not yet Disposed of and also two thirds of all my meadow both fresh and salt and one good feather bed and bolster and coverlid and blanket with the one half part of all my moveable estate both Indoors and without I give all the abovesaid estate both Real and personal unto my said two sons Thomas Toby & Seth Toby to them their heirs executrs and assigns forever and I ordain constitute and appoint my said two sons Thomas and Seth Tobey to be my Executors to this my last Will and Testament revoking and disallowing all other wills and Testaments In witness whereof I have hereunto set

my hand and seal this twenty.second Day of October one thou-
sand seven hundred & fifty one.
Signed sealed & published   THOMAS TOBYE [L. S.]
 in presence of
John Vincent.
Samll. Vincent.
Joseph Staple.
       Proved March 15, 1757.
[Barns. Prob. Bk. 9, p. 274.]

10

JOHN³ (*John,*² *Thomas*¹), born in Sandwich, February, 1686; resided there; "John Toby, Jr." was
chosen for "the petit jury for the superior court," 5
March, 1727–8.

He was married in Bridgewater, Aug. 30, 1710
(by Elisha Brett, Justice of the Peace) to Mary Jennings (probably the daughter of Ephraim and Deliverance Jennings, and born Jan. 1, 1719–1720).

Children :
 i. Thankful, b. Dec. 29, 1712.
 ii. Reliance, b. Nov. 23, 1713; m. Aug. 30, 1733,
   Ebenezer Goodspeed of Barnstable.
 iii. Mary, b. July 23, 1715.

11

THOMAS³ (*John,*² *Thomas*¹), born in Sandwich in
August, 1690; I think he must be the following:

"Thomas Tobie married July 12, 1711, Mary Damen."
[Scituate records.]
 "Thomas Toby of Scituate, husbandman, with wife Mary,"
sold "one fifth of all the estate which our honoured father
Zechariah Damon late of Scituate died seized of" to John Da-
mon, Feb. 17, 1730.

He probably resided afterward near the boundary
of his native town in the district which had been incorporated as Hanover, and then attended church at
his old home; for we read "Thomas Tobey was dis-

missed from the church of Scituate to that of Sandwich, Jan. 18, 1741." Thomas Tobey of Hanover, having died, administration of his estate was granted March 7, 1753, to Luke Tobey of Rochester. The property, very small, was given to the widow, Mary.

Children :

   i. Deborah ;'* m. June 4, 1731, Isaac Borden, also of Hanover.

   ii. Jane, bapt. Oct. 2, 1720, at the 2d church of Scituate.

35. iii. Elisha, "   "   "

   iv. Mary, "   "   " ; admitted to the church, æ. 17, Dec. 14, 1735; m. June 19, 1738, James Torrey, Jr.

   v. Martha, bapt. Aug. 13, 1721.

   vi. Thomas, bapt. "in private, being sicke," March 23, 1723-4.

   vii. Ann,* admitted to the church June 20, 1742.

36. viii. Luke.*

12

EBENEZER³ (*John,*² *Thomas*¹), born in Sandwich in Sept. 1692, and resided there some time; removed to Falmouth; married in the latter place June 30, 1715, "Mercy Hatch of Falmouth." Was chosen to a subordinate town office at Sandwich in 1720, and filled about every office in the gift of the citizens of Falmouth in later years.

Children :†

   i. Abigail,⁴ b. March 26, 1716; m. Nov. 29, 1739, Elisha Tobey of Hanover (No. 35).

   ii. Jean, b. March 22, 1718-9; m. Feb. 15, 1740, John "Your" [Ewer].

   iii. Mercy, b. July 26, 1722; m. March 19, 1749-50, David Hatch.

42. iv. John, b. May 24, 1724.

43. v. Silas, b. in Falmouth in 1732-3 (month and date not given).

---

* Placed in this list by inference.
† Perhaps "Nancy" was his daughter, who, "of Falmouth," m. in 1747, Silas Bush. [Freeman's Cape Cod.]

13

ELEAZER³ or ELIEZER³ (*John,² Thomas¹*), born in Sandwich Jan. 2, 1699, and resided there. Was chosen one of the fence-viewers in 1728. He married first, Martha ———, who died Dec. 6, 1732. He married second, June 14, 1733, Margaret Fish.

He died intestate. The inventory of his property, taken Feb. 22, 1745, was presented in court five days later by the widow Margaret. She was appointed guardian to the younger children March 14, 1745; James chose Peleg Laurence of Sandwich as his guardian, June 3, 1746. Land was set off Dec. 11, 1753, "to the eldest children, James, Mary, Rebeckah and Martha," and "to the five younger children, Eleazer, Bethiah, Mehitable, Jane and John."

Children :

    i.   Mary.⁴
    ii. Rebeckah.
    iii. Martha; m. Jan. 1, 1740–1, Shubael Ewer, of Sandwich.
44. iv. James.
45. v. Eleazer.
    vi. Bethiah; m. at S. Aug. 26, 1764, Isaac Keen, of Marshfield.
    vii. Mehitable.
    viii. Jane; m. July 12, 1762, Micah Jones, of Barnstable.
46. ix. John.

14

SETH³ (*Nathan,² Thomas¹*), born at Sandwich, March 24, 1686; married Feb. 5, 1719, Hannah Weeks; she died at Sandwich, Dec. 26, 1740; he died Jan. 15, 1740–1. He left no will; his death following so soon after his wife's may intimate a time of prevalent sickness and much depression.

Children:

    i. Mary,⁴ b. May 7, 1720.

47. ii. Seth, b. July 29, 1721.
    iii. Benjamin, b. June 11, 1723.
48. iv. Nathan, b. Feb. 13, 1725–6.

15

NATHAN[3] (*Nathan,*[2] *Thomas*[1]), born in Sandwich,
Sept. 28, 1701; married Sept. 25, 1726, Thankful
Foster; was chosen to a minor town office in 1731.

He made his will, " advanced in age," Jan. 17, 1787;
it was probated April 23 following; bequeathed to
Susanna, widow of his deceased son Joseph, and their
children Timothy, William, Barnabas, Silvanus and
Benjamin ; to grand daughters Ann Bowles and
Sarah Hatch; to his two daughters Maria, wife of
Joshua Tobey, and Thankful, wife of James Faunce.
Daughter in law Susanna, executrix.

Children:

   i.   Stephen,[4] b. April 30, 1727; no evidence that he
       was living at the time of his father's death.
49. ii. Joseph, b. Sept. 22, 1728.
  iii. Maria, b. Nov. 24, 1731; m. Joshua Tobey (No.
      60).
  iv. Thankful, b. Jan. 11, 1738–9 ; m. Nov. 4, 1773,
      James Faunce.

16

WILLIAM[3] (*Nathan,*[2] *Thomas*[1]), born in Sandwich,
May 3, 1706; married Ann ———. He was elected
to the humble office of hog rieve in 1734. He died
Nov. 16, 1737.

His will dated Nov. 15, 1737, probated Nov. 20
following, bequeathed all his property to his wife Ann;
after her decease it should go to Joseph and Maria,
children of his brother Nathan Tobey.

18

SAMUEL[3](*Jonathan,*[2] *Thomas*[1]), born Sept. 11, 1707;
married April 3, 1735, Experience Ellis.   Resided in
3

his native town of Sandwich and lived a long and worthy life. He died in 1791, leaving the following will:

In the name of God amen I, Samuel Tobey of Sandwich in the County of Barnstable in the Commonwealth of Massachusetts, yeoman, being advanced in years, but thro divine goodness of sound and disposing mind & memory, do make this my last will and testament and first I commend my soul to God hoping for mercy through Jesus Christ and my body to a decent burial at the discretion of my Executor hereafter named and as to my worldly estate I give demise and dispose as follows.

Imprimis I give devise and bequeath to my beloved wife Experience and to her heirs and assigns forever a piece of upland adjoining my salt meadow lying near John Perry's mill also I give and bequeath to my beloved wife Experience all my notes of hand, and all my household goods and book debts forever to her own disposal and all my quick stocks, also I give and bequeath unto her the improvement of all my real estate so long as she shall remain my widow during life.

Item. I give and bequeath to my daughter Remember Swift besides what I have already given her one Spanish milled Dollar.

Item I give and bequeath to my daughter Mary Tobey besides what I have already given her one Spanish milled Dollar.

I give and bequeath to my Daughter Cynthia Bassett besides what I have already given her one Spanish milled dollar.

Item I give and bequeath to my Daughter Cochie Nye besides what I have already given her one Spanish milled Dollar.

Item. I give and bequeath to my two Grandsons Nathaniel Tobey and John Tobey the sons of my son Samuel Tobey deceased two Spanish milled Dollars. viz one dollar to be paid to each of them, the reason I give them no more is because I have already given their father deceased his proportion of my estate.

Item I give and bequeath to my son Nathaniel Tobey, besides what I have already given him one Spanish milled Dollar and all my wearing apparel the reason I give him no more is because I have already given him his proportion of my estate.

Item I give and bequeath to Matthias Tobey and Stephen

Tobey my sons besides what I have already given them, one Dollar to each of them the reason I give them no more is because I have already given them their proportion of my Estate.

Item I give, devise and bequeath to my son William Tobey and his heirs and assigns forever all my land that lieth on the Westward side of the Country road to the little Bay lying between the land of Thomas Burgess and Jonathan Wing also the upland that is called Tobeys upland that I own and the meadow that lieth on the southwesterly side of the Great upland and Cohematant Island, that I have heretofore not disposed of also a piece of salt meadow and a piece of upland about one third of an acre lying at the foot of my homested land and meadow by the eastward side of the Little Bay beginning at a creek by the said Little Bay, runing by said creek up to a spring in the Old orchard piece thence to the westward to a cedar bush on the bank so as to include all the salt meadow that lieth to the southward of the abovesaid Creek and about one third of an acre of upland, reserving a cartway without gates or bars for them that shall own or improve the upland that joins said meadow for them to go to the Little Bay, also I give, devise and bequeath unto my son William Tobey and his heirs and assigns forever one half of the salt meadow that lies near Elnathan Ellis house the south side of said meadow. Also one half of my woodland that is not within fence and is to the eastward of the Country road the northeast side of said Land, also the improvement of one half of my orchard but not the land nor liberty to set out no more trees the north side of said orchard forever provided and the conditions here is that if my son William Tobey shall pay one half of my just debts and funeral charges and the expense and cost of settling my estate after my decease and one half of the Legacies given to my four daughters and one half of the Legacies given to my two grandsons—Nathaniel and John Tobey and one half of the Legacies given to my three sons Nathaniel Tobey, Matthias Tobey and Stephen Tobey the one half of the Legacies amounting to four Spanish milled Dollars and one half, my will and meaning is for my son William Tobey to pay all just debts the whole of them where I have signed the security with him, reserving the improvement of his mother.

Item I give devise and bequeath unto Samuel Tobey Jr. my Grandson, son of my son Ellis Tobey his heirs and assigns forever all the remainder of my lands and meadows and buildings of every kind of real estate, wherever and whatever after the decease of my beloved wife Experience and the decease of my son Ellis Tobey and his wife Lydia and if she the said Lydia should survive my son Ellis and marry then in that case for her not to have any improvement of any part of my estate, provided and the conditions hereof is that if my Grandson Samuel Tobey Jr. pays one half of my just debts, funeral charges and expense and cost of settling my estate after my decease and pays all just debts of his father Ellis Tobey where I have become bound and signed with him, I mean for the said Samuel to pay the whole of them and pay unto his Grandmother or her heirs or assigns twelve Spanish milled Dollars and pay one half of the Legacies given to my four Daughters and one half of the Legacies given to my two grandsons Nathaniel Tobey and John Tobey and one half of the Legacies given to my three sons Nathaniel Tobey, Matthias Tobey and Stephen Tobey the whole of that I mean for my Grandson Samuel Tobey Jr. to pay as Legacies with what he has to pay to his Grandmother Amounting to sixteen Spanish mill Dollars and one half, my will and meaning is for all the Legacies to be paid in twelve months after my decease.

Item, I give and bequeath to my son Ellis Tobey the improvement of all the lands and meadow and buildings that I have given to my grandson Samuel Tobey Jr. as long as he shall live and not to come into improvement till after the decease of my wife Experience. And I give & bequeath to Lydia wife of my son Ellis Tobey if she should survive my son Ellis the same improvement as I have given her husband Ellis Tobey so long as she shall remain his widow and no longer, also I give to my son Ellis my Gun and Sword, the reason I give him no more is because I have already given him his proportion of my estate.

Finally I constitute and appoint Stephen Rennet of Sandwich in the County of Barnstable and Commonwealth of Massachusetts yeoman sole executor of this my last will and Testament hereby revoking all other or former will or wills by me at any time made ratifying this to be my only last will & testament. In witness whereof I have hereunto set my hand and seal this nineteenth Day of April A.D. one thousand seven hundred and ninety-one.

SAMUEL TOBEY [L. S.]

Signed, sealed, published and pronounced by the said Samuel Tobey as and for his last will and testament in presence of us
Thomas Burges.
Covell Burges.
Ebenezer Raymond.

Proved Dec. 20, 1791.

[Barns. Rec. Bk. 27, p. 202.]

Children:

i. Remember,[4] b. Oct. 31, 1735; m. Capt. Ward Swift, Jan. 9, 1755-6.
ii. Matthias, b. Dec. 23, 1736; d. 17 Dec., 1737.
51. iii. Ellis, b. Oct. 21, 1737.
52. iv. Samuel, b. May 26, 1739.
53. v. William, b. March 5, 1740-1.
54. vi. Nathaniel, b. March 1, 1742-3.
55. vii. Matthias, b. Jan. 29, 1744-5.
56. viii. Stephen, b. Feb. 7, 1746-7.
ix. Mary, b. Nov. 6, 1749.
x. Cynthia, b. May 21, 175[3]; m. Oct. 10, 1773, Joseph Bassett.
xi. Celia, b. May 21, 1757; m. Oct. 10, 1773, Jonathan Ellis.
xii. "Cochie"; m. —— "Nye" (known only from the will of her father).

19

JONATHAN[3] (*Jonathan,*[2] *Thomas*[1]), born in Sandwich, Aug. 6, 1718; married at Plymouth, Feb. 19, 1740, Deborah Swift, of Plymouth. [Plymouth co. rec.] She survived him, and was appointed guardian of the children mentioned below, July 25, 1755. He was chosen to a town office in Sandwich in 1746.

He died before Jan. 15, 1755, when Thomas Swift and Samuel Tobey were appointed administrators of his estate. In the inventory of his estate " gun and sword and all war stores," valued at 17 shillings and 6 pence, are mentioned among other items.

Children:

57. i. Jonathan,[4] b. Dec. 24, 1740.
  ii. Deborah; she and Silas Swift were published Dec. 17, 1765.
58. iii. Lemuel.
  iv. Bathsheba; married Seth Fish of Sandwich, Dec. 5, 1765.
  v. Lydia; is she the "Lydia Tobey b. at Sandwich, June 16, 1748, who married Micah Blackwell, Nov. 23, 1766"?
  vi. Elizabeth.
  vii. Mercy.
59. viii. Thomas, born March 26, 1753.

20

NATHANIEL[3] (*Jonathan,*[2] *Thomas*[1]), born in Sandwich, June 30, 1721; was living when his father made his will in 1738.

Nathaniel Tobey of Sandwich and Elizabeth Godfrey of Chatham were married at Chatham, Oct. 17, 1756.

21

CORNELIUS[3] (*Samuel,*[2] *Thomas*[1]), born Sept. 12, 1699; married Deborah, daughter of John and Elizabeth (Bourne) Pope, born Jan. 6, 1702–3; he died in 1792.

He resided in Sandwich; was chosen to a subordinate town office in 1728; was a deacon of the church.

"Cornelius Tobey of Sandwich, co. Bristol, blacksmith," bought for £110 of Timothy Ide of Rehoboth 7 June, 1748, lands lying part "in a Narragansett township of land of Number four lying part in Quabbin a Place so called and part at the West of and adjoining to Hatfield, in the co. of Hampshire," etc. Part of this he sold 15 May, 1771, to Nathan Alden of Middleboro, Plymouth co., for £40; land specified as in Greenwich, Hampshire co. Another tract in the same region he purchased 27 June, 1748, for £150, and a third the same day for £200.

THOMAS: THIRD GENERATION. 47

"Cornelius Tobey of Sandwich, gentleman," made a deed of gift of a portion of this Connecticut valley land to his daughter Patience Feb. 4, 1755, which she and her husband Thomas Bassett of Sandwich conveyed back to him 15 April, 1763, that he might sell it to James Foster of Rochester a few days later: the region now specified as Chesterfield, co. Hampshire. He also gave a part of the land to his son, "Elisha Tobey of Sandwich, physician," 3 Dec. 1754; and sold another tract for £200 to Isaac Rogers of Greenwich, 7 July, 1779.

He made his will Dec. 3, 1791; bequeathed to daughter Deborah Nye and her daughter Mary; to granddaughter Deborah Smith, daughter of his deceased daughter Patience; to her sons William and Cornelius Bassett and her grandson Samuel Bassett; to daughter Joanna Pope; to granddaughter Bathsheba Paddleford, daughter of deceased son Elisha; to grandsons Heman, Meletiah and Joshua Tobey, sons of deceased son Cornelius, and to his son Elisha; mentioning Cornelius' wife Lois and daughters Hannah Bourne and Betsey Tobey; to son Joshua.

Children (order not known):
- i. Deborah, married July 12, 1763, Barnabas Nye.
- ii. Patience, married Feb. 13, 1746, Thomas Bassett.
- 60. iii. Joshua.
- 61. iv. Cornelius.
- v. Lemuel, died Feb. 17, 1749.
- vi. Joanna, married Feb. 15, 1761, Elisha, son of John and Mercy (Swift) Pope.
- vii. Betsey, died Oct. 14, 1813.
- 62. viii. Elisha.

22

ZACCHEUS[3] (Samuel,[2] Thomas)[1], born in Sandwich, Jan. 13, 1703–4; married Jan. 1, 1726–7, Sarah, daughter of John and Elizabeth (Bourne) Pope, born March 25, 1705–6; he died Feb. 1, 1798, aged 96 years."

He bought of Benjamin Spooner, Sept. 19, 1726, land in Dartmouth, which he made his "homestead farm"; afterwards bought many other tracts. His wife Sarah joined with him in a deed of gift to their son Elnathan, Dec. 17, 1778. They united in a quit-claim deed of Pope heirs Jan. 24, 1754. He made a division with Content Dexter of land they owned in common 22 July, 1755; he gave lands to his sons Prince and Noah in 1778.

He was first ensign, then captain,* and later major of the 2d regt. of Bristol co. militia.

Children:

63. i.   Elnathan,⁴ b. Jan. 11, 1727–8.
64. ii.   Samuel, b. Feb. 9, 1729–30.
65. iii. John, b. July 29, 1732.
66. iv.   Zaccheus, b. Dec. 2, 1734.
67. v.   Zoeth, b. July 14, 1737.
68. vi.   Lot, b. Sept. 26, 1739.
69. vii. Prince, b. June 7, 1741.
    viii. Elizabeth, b. April 24, 1743.
70. ix.   Noah, b. March 8, 1745.
    x.   Mary, b. Sept. 9, 1747. [See No. 52.]

23

JONATHAN³ (*Samuel,*² *Thomas*¹), born in Sandwich, May 13, 1709; married first, Dec. 17, 1732, Abigail Lewis. He bought the homestead farm of William Parker in Rochester, June 6, 1738, and there married second, Sept. 26, 1738, Elizabeth Cannon. She joined him in a deed of this place,—*recorded* 30 March, 1748. They removed to Dartmouth; sold other Rochester lands to Zaccheus Tobey 28 Jan., 1743, and lands in

* "Dartmᵒ 2ᵈ May, 1758—These may Certify that Elnathan Spooner has given to Jonathan Delano the sum of five pounds, thirteen shillings & four pence, as an Inducement to him to Inlist into his Majesties Service in the present Expedition against Canada, which I esteem as so much done Towards a Turn. as witness my hand. Zaccheus Tobey, Capt." [An old paper in possession of the Spooner family, William Spooner, p. 131.]

"that part of Dartmouth called New Bedford" 9 Dec.,
1776. He gave his homestead in New Bedford to his
son William 19 March, 1785.

Jonathan Tobey, of New Bedford, gentleman, made
will May 19, 1788, bequeathing to his wife; children
William, Jonathan, Seth, Cornelius, Sarah Snell and
Abigail Taber; grandchildren Cynthy, Seth and James
Warren; son William residuary legatee and executor;
probated Oct. 1, 1793.

Children (order of birth unknown):

	i.	Sarah,⁴ born Aug 28, 1733 ; married ——— Snell.
	ii.	Abigail, born Nov. 7, 1736; married Nov. 21, 1756, Jabez Taber.
71.	iii.	Jonathan.
72.	iv.	Seth.
73.	v.	Cornelius. Cornelius Toby, Jr., was a private in Capt. Simson Fish's co., as per muster and pay roll Sept., 1778; service on alarm at Dartmouth and Falmouth.
	vi.	Mary; m. (published in Dartmouth Aug. 27, 1768) James Warren.
74.	vii.	William.

24

ELIAKIM,³ (*Samuel,*² *Thomas*¹), born Oct. 19, 1711;
married April 17, 1740, "Abigail Bassett, Jr." Resided in Sandwich, was one of those chosen "to order
the fireing of the woods in this Town"—for the making of tar—11 March, 1745-6.

Eliakim Tobey was a member of a committee of the
people of Plymouth county in 1774, who asked officers
of the colonial militia to resign rather than aid in the
enforcement of acts injurious to the people. [See
No. 61.] He died in 1780.

WILL OF ELIAKIM TOBEY.

In the Name of God Amen. I Eliakim Tobey of Sandwich
in the County of Barnstable in the State of Mass'tts Bay, Hus-

bandman, being weak in Body, but thro' Divine Goodness of Sound & Disposing mind & memory, do make this my last Will & Testament And first, I Humbly recommend my soul to the mercy of God : thro' Jesus Christ, & my Body to a Decent Burial, at the Discretion of my Executor hereafter named ; & my worldly Estate I Give, Demise and Dispose as followeth.

Imprimis. I Give and bequeath to my beloved wife, Abigal, in Lieu of her Dower, or power of thirds in my Estate, one cow & six sheep, and during her Continuing my Widow, the Improvement of all my Real Estate & of all my Household goods, not herein otherwise Disposed of, and if she marry again, I give her Seventy Spanish milled Dollars, to be paid either in Silver or so much other current money as shall be sufficient to purchase so many Spanish milled Dollars and then her Improvement of my real Estate and Household goods to cease.

Item I Give and bequeath to my two Grandsons Alvin Nye & Anselm Nye, sons of my daughter Lucy deceased to each two Spanish milled Dollars to be paid either in Silver or current money sufficient to purchase sd Spanish milled Dollars each to be paid at twenty one years of age ; & if either Dye before that time the Survivor to have ye whole. I also give them equally between them to have all the Household Goods, that was their mothers which I may be in possession of at my decease.

Item I Give and bequeath to my daughter Elizabeth Nye my two best feather beds & all the bedding, furniture & appurtenances belongiug to them ; I also give her so much more of my household Goods, to take after my wifes term expires, as being added to ye beds & furniture above given her, and to what I have otherwise given her & kept a written account of, shall in the whole be of the value of one hundred & seventy eight Spanish milled Dollars, but if sd household goods shoald prove insufficient to make the whole of that value the Deficiency to be made up in Spanish milled Dollars or other money, sufficient to purchase them so that Elizabeth have in the whole the real Value of one hundred & seventy eight Spanish milled Dollars.

Item I Give Devise & bequeath to my son Samuel Tobey his heirs & assigns forever all my Land, old orchard & swampy Ground, lying on the westerly side of the Country Road where his Dwelling House & shop now stands ; and also two acres of my Land lying on the easterly side of the country Road, at the Northerly end adjoining to Gershom Tobeys Land and the road.

Item I Give Devise and bequeath to my son William Tobey his heirs and assigns forever four acres of my field or Pasture that adjoyns to Edward Dillinghams Land to be taken of at the end next to Country Road.

Item I Give Devise & bequeath to my son Lemuel Tobey & to his heirs and assigns forever my field whereon my Dwelling House Stands (excepting the two acres above given to Samuel) and my dwelling House and also all the remainder of my field adjoyning to Edward Dillinghams Land; & also my Chest with Drawers in it, & my Desk & my watch, that was my son Anselms & all my Cash, Notes of Hand & Bonds now in my possession provided that Lemuel pay the Just Debts of my son Anselm that yet remain unpaid.

Item. I Give Devise & bequeath to my three sons, Samuel, William & Lemuel and to their Heirs & assigns forever to be equally Divided between them, all my salt & fresh meadow, all my Woodland, and all other my Lands and real estate, not herein otherwise Disposed of particularly my barn and corn houses Standing on the land given to Lemuel and for the same to continue on sd Land with full Liberty of a way to the same doing as Little Damage as may be to Lemuels Land. In like manner I give them my pew in the Meeting House and all my Husbandry tools, Quick Stock and what is due to me upon Books and all other my Personal estate not herein otherwise Disposed of; Provided they each pay one third part of my Just Debts (excepting Anselms) funeral charges, and the Legacies to my wife, Daughter and grandsons when due, according to the true meaning of this my will.

Item my will is that my sons Samuel, William & Lemuel come into possession of the real estate herein Devised them, when my wifes term expires and not before.

Finally I Constitute & appoint my son Samuel Tobey sole Executor of this my last will and Testament hereby revoking all other or former Will or Wills by me made and ratifying and confirming as my only last Will & Testament: In confirmation and Witness whereof I have hereunto set my hand & seal this twenty third Day of February in the year of our Lord one thousand seven hundred and eighty.

ELIAKIM TOBEY [L.S.]

Signed sealed Published and
Pronounced by the sd Eliakim Tobey
as his Last will and Testament
in presence of
    Joshua Tobey
    Abra Williams
    Hannah Smith
            [Proved May 9, 1780]
[Barns. Prob. Bk. 2, p. 5.]

Children :

75. i. Samuel,⁴ b. Feb. 20, 1740–1.
   ii. William, b. Jan. 8, 1744–5; died May 4, 1746.
  iii. Lucy, b. Aug. 26, 1747; m. April 2, 1767, Elisha
       Nye.
76. iv. William, b. March 2, 1750–1.
77. v. Anselm, b. Dec. 8, 1752.
78. vi. Lemuel, b. Oct. 30, 1755.
  vii. Elizabeth, b. May 20, 1757; m. —— Nye.

25

Rev. SAMUEL³ (*Samuel,*² *Thomas*¹), born in Sandwich, May 8, 1715; married Sept. 6, 1738, Bathsheba, daughter of Timothy Crocker, of Barnstable, born April 2, 1717; she survived her husband.

He was graduated at Harvard College in 1733. Was invited to preach at Berkley, Jan. 1, 1736; "called" Aug. 3, 1736, and ordained pastor of the church Nov. 23, 1737, and remained in office forty-four years, until his death. His salary was £100 per annum and the Sabbath day contributions; he stipulated that payments should be on a basis of "silver at 26 shillings per ounce." He did very excellent work in his parish and pulpit, and was highly honored and beloved.

He had a deed of land from Joseph Dean and others 17 Sept., 1737. He bought 50 acres of land in Berkley of Ebenezer French, May 3, 1738. He purchased

a tract in Middleborough in 1759, which his son Nathaniel and son-in-law Paull divided, etc., in 1791.
He died suddenly, Feb. 13, 1781, leaving no will; his eldest son, Samuel Tobey, Esq., administered on his estate. The inventory was taken June 20, 1781; it shows a small but finely selected library of classical and theological works, 75 books enumerated by title, and "242 pamphlets"; abundant household supplies and farm stock, and a hundred acres of land with buildings; total, £660-15. This was divided to the widow Bathsheba and children: Samuel, Nathaniel, Enoch, Paul, Silas, Timothy, Bathsheba, Isaac, "Sela Dean" and "Alatha Paull."

Children:

i. Celia,' "Sela,"b. Wed., Aug. 29, 1739; m. Dec. 6, 1759, Abial Dean, of Assonet Neck.

ii. Samuel, b. Tues., Aug. 11, 1741; d. May 28, 1743.

79. iii. Samuel, b. "the first day of the week," June 5, 1743.

80. iv. Timothy, b. Wed., Sept. 25, 1745.

81. v. Nathaniel, b. Monday, Aug. 17, 1747.

82. vi. Isaac, b. Thurs., July 20, 1749.

83. vii. Enoch, b. Mon., Sept. 2, 1751.

viii. Aletheia, "Alatha," b. "on ye Sabbath," March 3, 1754; m. (pub. Sept. 4, 1773) Edward Paull, of Taunton.

ix. Bathsheba, b. Thurs., Sept. 9, 1756; m. Dec. 5, 1782, Gideon Babbitt, of Dighton.

x. Abigail, b. Sabbath day, Feb. 4, 1759; d. Nov. 28, 1778.

84. xi. Paul, b. about 9 o'clock, Sabbath Day night, Sept. 6, 1761.

85. xii. Silas, b. about 10 o'clock, Sabbath Day night, Sept. 6, 1761; twin with the above; d. unmarried at Port au Prince, W. I.

26

THOMAS[3] (*Samuel,[2] Thomas[1]*), born Aug. 14, 1720; married Feb. 27, 1740-1, Elizabeth, Swift.

She died March 30, 1748-9. He resided in Sandwich. Was a tithing man in 1745; precinct clerk in 1747. He died before Oct. 14, 1761, when Zaccheus Tobey of Dartmouth was appointed guardian of Thomas Tobey, a minor above 14 years old, son of Thomas Tobey, late of Sandwich.

Children:

86. i. Sylvanus,[4] b. June 19, 1741.
87. ii. Thomas, b. Jan. 5, 1745-6.
88. iii. Seth, b. Nov. 29, 1748.

28

SILAS[3] (*Gershom,*[2] *Thomas*[1]), born Nov. 4, 1704; died Dec. 14, 1790; married Nov. 21, 1734, Mary Dillingham.

Residence, Sandwich; chosen for petit jury in 1733. In his will, dated April 1, 1774, proved March 15, 1791, he left his estate to his wife Mary and sons Prince, Silas and Stephen.

Children:

93. i. Prince,[4] b. March 9, 1736-7.
94. ii. Silas, b. March 20, 1739-40.
95. iii. Simeon, b. April 9, 1744.
96. iv. Stephen, b. May 2, 1747.

29

BARNABAS[3] (*Gershom,*[2] *Thomas*[1]), born July 22, 1708; married Oct. 23, 1743, "Sarah, daughter of Nathan Tobey, of Sandwich." She died Nov. 21, 1747. He married second, Anne Tobey, perhaps widow of William, No. 16. Resided in Sandwich; was chosen to a town office in 1741. He died between Jan. 14 and March 16, 1763. Query: Was this his widow?

"Ann Tobey and Francis Phinney, both of Sandwich, were married at S. May 30, 1764."

WILL OF BARNABAS TOBEY.

In the Name of God Amen this fourteenth day of January A.D. 1763 I Barnabas Tobey of Sandwich in the County of Barnstable yeoman being of perfect mind and memory Do make and Ordain this to be my Last Will and Testament first I Recommend my soul Into the Hands of God that Gave it and my Body to the Earth to be Buried in Decent Christian Burial at the Discretion of my Executrix hoping for a Blessed Resurrection and as Touching my Worldly Estate I give Demise & Dispose of it in the following manner and form.

Imprimis. My Will is that my Piece of upland that lies adjoyning to Daniel Wings Land and my Piece of Salt Meadow that fell to me by my first wife that Lyeth adjoyning to Gershom Tobeys and Nathan Tobeys meadow all in Sandwich aforesd be first sold by my Executrix to [pay] all my Just Debts & funeral charges.

Item I Give and Bequeath to my Beloved Wife Ann Tobey to her and to her Heirs forever all my Personal Estate as household furniture Quick stock farming Tools notes Bonds Book Debts Servants and Also the over plus of the aforementioned Land & meadow if Any Remain after my Just Debts and funeral charges are paid I also Give to my Wife the Improvement of all my Real Estate (except the aforesd Lands and meadow) during her Natural Life and then After my said Wives Decease Item I give & Bequeath to Barnabas the son of Joseph Tobey of said Sandwich to him and his heirs and assigns forever my piece of Land in sd Sandwich Lying Between Zacheus Wings and Nathan Tobeys Land reserving the Improvement to my said wife during her natural Life Item I give and Bequeath to Prince Tobey of sd Sandwich to him his heirs and assigns forever my Dwelling house and all my Piece of Land adjoyning in said Sandwich and all the Buildings Thereon reserving the Improvement to my said wife as abovesd. Item I give and Bequeath to Elisha of Sharon the son of my brother Ephraim Tobey deceased and to the aforesd Prince Tobey to them and their heirs and assigns forever all the Remaining part of my Real Estate not before herein Disposed off only Reserving the Improvement thereof to my wife during her Natural Life as above mentioned that is all my upland salt and fresh meadow & woodlotts in sd Sandwich to the sd Elisha

Tobey & prince Tobey to be equally divided Between them and their heirs and assigns Exclusive of the Land & meadow to be sold as aforesd and what I herein before Bequeathed sd Barnabas Tobey & sd Prince Tobey and their heirs and assigns forever Finally I do hereby constitute & appoint my Beloved wife Ann Tobey to be my sole Executrix of this my Last Will and Testament and I do hereby Revoke & annul all other Wills Testaments & Executors by me in any way before willed or Named Ratifying this and only this to be my Last will and Testament In witness whereof I have hereunto set my Hand and Seal the Day and Year first above written   Sign'd Seal'd Deliv'd and Declared by sd Barnabas Tobey as his Last Will & Testament in presence of us

Gershom Tobey.
Ignatius Dillingham.
Silas Turner.

his
BARNABAS + TOBEY [L. S.].
mark and seal

(Proved March 16, 1763.)

[Barns. Prob. Bk. 12, p. 340.]

Child:

Barnabas,[4] b. Nov. 14, died 27, 1747.

30

EPHRAIM[3] (*Gershom*,[2] *Thomas*[1]), born at Sandwich, July 22, 1711; married Reliance ———. He removed to Sharon, Connecticut.

Children:

97. i.   Elisha,[4] b. Jan. 2, 1738.
98. ii. Jesse, b. Jan. 26, 1740–1.
     iii. Mehitable, b. June 10, 1743; married in 1746, at Sharon, Conn., Daniel Ticknor.
99. iv. George, b. Sept. 2, 1745.
100. v. Benjamin, b. Jan. 11, 1747–8.
     vi. Martha, b. Jan. 29, 1753.
101. vii. Ephraim, b. Aug. 16, 1755.

31

GERSHOM[3] (*Gershom,*[2] *Thomas*[1]), born Sept. 24, 1720; married Oct. 30, 1746, Mary Foster.
Children:
  i.   Sarah,[4] b. Dec. 29, 1747;* married March 10, 1774, Barzillai Ellis; both of Sandwich.
102. ii. Gershom, b. about 1749.

FOURTH GENERATION.

33

THOMAS[4] (*Thomas,*[3] *Thomas,*[2] *Thomas*[1]), born about 1704; married Mary ———. Resided at East Yarmouth, since called Dennis. Was admitted to the church Aug. 17, 1760.

His will, dated March 8, 1787, presented for probate Aug. 9, 1791, spoke of himself as being "infirm in body," etc.; bequeathed his house, buildings, cattle, furnishings, and all his property, to his three sons.
Children:
120. i.   Stephen,[5] b. June 28, 1741.
121. ii. Knowles, b. May 22, 1744.
122. iii. Samuel, b. April 1, 1746.

34

SETH[4] (*Thomas,*[3] *Thomas,*[2] *Thomas*[1]), born in Yarmouth (Dennis) in 1716; married first, Zipporah ———. He married second, Betsey, daughter of Dr. John and Deborah (Crowell) Sears, born at Yarmouth Dec. 3, 1750, who had married first, Benjamin Howes and was then his widow. She was mentioned as "Betsey Tobey" in the will of her father.

Lieut. Seth Tobey was admitted to the church of

* Believed to be this " Sarah."

4

East Yarmouth Aug. 13, 1775. He died Aug. 31, 1801, aged 85. [Freeman.]
Child:
123.   Seth,[5] b. Nov. 18, 1769.

35

ELISHA[4] (*Thomas,[3] John,[3] Thomas[1]*), born about 1716, baptized Oct. 20, 1720, in the part of Scituate which was afterward incorporated as Hanover.

"Elisha Tobey of Hand Over and Abigail Tobey of Falmouth" were published at the latter place Feb. 18, 1738. She was a daughter of Ebenezer (No. 12) and Mercy (Hatch) Tobey.

Elisha was dismissed from the church of Scituate to that of Falmouth Jan. 18, 1746.

36

LUKE[4] (*Thomas,[3] John,[2] Thomas[1]*), whose administering on the estate of Thomas of Scituate and Hanover seems to indicate this relationship, resided in Rochester in 1753. He married there, Aug. 30, 1750, Hannah Swift. He died in 1776, and Samuel Jenney administered on his estate March 4, 1776.

43

SILAS[4] (*Ebenezer,[3] John,[2] Thomas[1]*), born at Falmouth 1732–3; married at Falmouth, July 31, 1761, Bethiah Rowley; he died Jan. 1, 1783, "æ. 50." He was a town officer at various times. He did valiant service in the Revolutionary war. [Compare with No. 94.]

Silas Tobey, private, on Lexington alarm roll of Capt. Joseph Palmer's co. which marched on the alarm of April 19, 1775, from Falmouth; served 3 days; residence, Falmouth, Barnstable co.; *also*, served at Falmouth and Dartmouth on alarms, Sept. 1778, 8 days, same co., Freeman's regt.; *also*, Feb. 4, April 2, and May 16, 1779; *also*, appears among a list of men

THE OLD FREEMAN HOUSE IN DENNIS.   BUILT ABOUT 1700.
A TYPICAL HOUSE OF THE PERIOD.

belonging to a company stationed at Naushon who signed a petition for increase of wages or their discharge in case request was not complied with, dated Naushon, Aug. 10, 1777; *also*, private on muster and pay roll, Capt. Elisha Nye's co., Feb. 12, to April 20, 1777; served 2 months and 8 days; stationed at Elizabeth Islands; *also*, in a list of 6 months men raised by the town of Falmouth for service in the Continental Army during 1780, July 19, to Dec. 31; roll dated at "Hutts," near West Point, N. Y.; *also*, private, Capt. Ebenezer Smith's co. late Col. Calvin Smith's (6th) regt. in service Jan. to Dec. 1782; for wages, etc.; reported died Jan. 1, 1783; *also*, appears in a list of men belonging to the 6th regt. on clothing account, Jan. 1, 1778, to Dec. 31, 1782.

His widow presented claim for wages due him as a soldier, March 30, 1784; order paid April 5, 1784.
Children:

    i.   Silva,* b. June 20, 1763. Sylvia Tobey was published at Dartmouth May 18, 1786, to Isaiah Tower.
    ii.   Ebenezer, b. Sept. 10, 1765.
130. iii.   Zimri ("Zimry"), b. June 10, 1767.
    iv.   Mary, b. March 30, 1769.
    v.   Zuriel, b. March 29, 1771.
    vi.   Fanny, "Fanney," b. June 14, 1773.
131. vii.   Silas, b. April 21, 1776.

44

JAMES[4] (*Eleazer,*[3] *John,*[2] *Thomas*[1]), born in Sandwich about 1732.

James Tobey was a private, on muster and pay roll of Capt. Jacob Lovell's company, Col. Freeman's regiment; served 6 days on an alarm at New Bedford and Dartmouth in Sept., 1778.

46

JOHN[4] (*Eleazer,*[3] *John,*[2] *Thomas*[1]). born in Sandwich, (called "John Tobey, Jr."; married Mercy, "daughter of Thomas and Deborah (Sears") Howes of Yarmouth, born May 25, 1732. He died Jan. 23, 1803. His widow died before Dec. 17, 1807, when her estate was settled. Resided in Sandwich.

John (Tobey) appears among a list of officers of the Mass. Militia as first lieutenant in Capt. Baruch Bassett's co. of the Barnstable co. regt., commissioned Feb. 21, 1776; *also*, on certificate of election, dated Watertown, April 10, 1776, given by Col. Nathaniel Freeman, certifying that the above was chosen first lieutenant of a co. raised in Barnstable co. to reinforce the Continental army Nov. 1775; joined the army Dec. 10, 1775; *also*, lieut. in Capt. Berechiah Bassett's co. of Barnstable co. regt.; service as a reinforcement to the Continental army Dec. 10, 1775; dated Watertown, April 10, 1776; *also*, on roll for travel to and from camp at Cambridge, dated Jan. 13, 1776; residence Sandwich.

WILL OF JOHN TOBEY.

In the Name Of God, Amen. I John Tobey of Sandwich in the County of Barnstable, Gentleman, being advanced in life, but through the goodness of God of sound and disposing mind and memory, sensible of my own mortality and minded to set my house in order before I go hence to be here no more forever, and in order thereto do make this my last will and testament in manner as follows, viz.

In the first place I commend my soul into the hand of that merciful God that gave it, and my body I commit to the dust in humble hope of a glorious resurrection to immortal life & as to such worldly estate as God hath been pleased to bless me with I give and dispose of the same as followeth.

Imprimis. I give and bequeath unto my beloved wife Mercy Tobey the use and improvement of one half of my real estate, during the time she shall continue my widow, and also during the said term the use of all my indoor household furniture.

Item. I give and bequeath unto my son, Josiah Tobey, and unto his heirs and assigns forever, a note of hand I hold against him, and any other demand I may have against him the said Josiah.

Item. I give unto my son John Tobey and unto his heirs and assigns a piece of salt marsh, lying at Fullers Point, which I bought of Abraham Crocker, containing about three loads; also all the land which I own lying between Nye's road so called & the old road leading from my dwelling house to Sandwich town the Falmouth road and the road leading to Cotuit; meaning all my land, contained in the Gore formed by said roads—allowing him a way to the Pond for water through my land where it will be least prejudicial to my other heirs, to be through gates & bars.

Item. I give and bequeath unto my son, Reuben Tobey and unto his heirs and assigns forever a note which I hold against my said son Reuben for one hundred dollars and interest, or any other demand I may have upon him.

Item. I give and bequeath unto my son Eleazer Tobey and unto his heirs and assigns forever all the demands which I may have upon the said Eleazer Tobey at the time of my decease

Item. I give and bequeath unto my Daughters, Mehitable Bourne Sarah Crocker, & Matilda Weeks the sum of ten Dollars each to be paid them by my two sons, Thomas & James in twelve months after my decease, to them and to their heirs & assigns.

Item. I give and bequeath unto my daughter, Rebekah Tobey the use of the new bedroom in the westerly part of my house and a privilege in my dwelling house and fire wood found for her and provisions for her comfortable support, during the time she shall remain single. I also give her my best bed to her and her heirs; and in case my said daughter should marry I give her one hundred dollars to be paid her by my two sons Thomas and James; I also give her the sum of ten dollars to be paid by my two sons aforesd at the time of the legacies above mentioned become due to my daughters before mentioned.

Item. I also give unto my four daughters Mehitable Bourne, Sarah Crocker, Matilda Weeks and Rebekah Tobey, all my household furniture, after their mother's term of improvement has expired to be equally divided between them, excepting my meat barrels, cranes, &c. to them their heirs and assigns forever.

Item. I give unto my sons, Josiah, Reuben and Eleazer and unto their heirs and assigns forever my wearing apparel equally to be divided between them.

Item. I give unto my two sons, Thomas and James, and unto their heirs and assigns forever all the residue and remainder of all my Estate both real and personal of every name or nature and wherever the same may be consisting of lands, buildings, livestock, farming utensils, Notes of hand, book debts, &c. or of any other name; they allowing their mother the improvement of one half of my real estate and paying out the legacies in this my will and finding for my daughter Rebekah fire wood and provisions, during the time she shall remain single, and also paying my just debts, funeral charges and the charges of settling my estate and performing every condition in this my will mentioned.

Finally. I constitute and appoint my two . sons, Thomas Tobey and James Tobey Executors to this my last will and testament, and I do hereby ratify and confirm this and this only to be my last will and testament. In testimony whereof I have hereunto set my hand and seal this fourteenth day of May, in the year of our Lord, one thousand eight hundred.

JOHN TOBEY [L. S.].

Signed, sealed, published, pronounced & declared by the sd John Tobey to be his last will & testament, in presence of us

Jona. O. Freeman.   Barnabas Ewer.   Alice Ewer.

Proved Feb. 11, 1803.

[Barnstable Prob. Bk. 33, p. 66.]

Children:

    i.   Mehitable,[3] b. Aug. 21, 1760.
132. ii. Josiah, b. Dec. 1, 1761.
    iii. Sarah, b. Aug. 2, 1763; m. Feb. 21, 1788, Josiah
          Crocker; rem. to Pawlet, Vt.; d. May 26, 1847,
          [J. J. C.]
    iv.   Rebecca, b. Jan. 24, 1765.
133. v.   John, } b. Dec. 31, 1766.
    vi.   Mercy, }
134. vii. Reuben, b. Feb. 3, 1769.
135. viii. Thomas Howes, b. Oct. 1, 1770.
    ix.   Matilda, b. June 6, 1772.
136. x.   Eleazer, b. Jan. 7, 1775.
137. xi. James, b. Jan. 4, 1778.

47

SETH[4] (Seth,[3] Nathan,[2] Thomas[1]), born in Sandwich July 29, 1721; married first, Abigail ——; married second, Mary Moxom of Sandwich.

We know very little about his life. It seems probable that he was a seafaring man; the administrator of his estate was a captain. The property was not large. The times were distressingly hard in those days of many wars and little manufactures and commerce.

He left, as the records show, a child by each of his two wives.

His estate was administered upon Aug. 7, 1773, by Enoch Tupper, mariner; one item in the inventory was seven-fifteenths of a wood lot. "Thirds" were set off to the widow Mary March 24, 1774.

Children:

138. i.   Benjamin,⁵ "of Seth and Abigail Tobey," b. Feb. 27, 1750.

ii.   Abigail, "of Seth and Mary Tobey," b. June 14, 1762; m. ―――― Hoxie; [family tradition.]

48

NATHAN⁴ (*Seth,³ Nathan,² Thomas¹*), born in Sandwich Feb. 13, 1725–6; appears to be the man who married in Boston, May 10, 1747, Anne Thwing.

49

JOSEPH⁴ (*Nathan,³ Nathan,² Thomas¹*), born in Sandwich Sept. 22, 1728; married at Falmouth, Feb. 19, 1754, Susanna Parker, who survived him, and was a legatee of his father in 1787, with her children Timothy, William, Sylvanus, Barnabas and Benjamin. Resided in Sandwich. He died Nov. 1, 1786, according to a memorandum of his son William.

Children:

i.   Anna,⁵ b. Nov. 15, 1755.

ii.   Sarah, b. Oct. 28, 1757.

140. iii.   William, b. Sept. 9, 1759.

141. iv.   Barnabas, b. March 20, 1761.

142. v.   Lewis, b. June 17, 1763.

143. vi.   Timothy, b. Sept. 19, 1765.

144. vii.   Sylvanus, b. June 4, 1769.

145. viii.   Benjamin.

51

ELLIS[4] (*Samuel,[3] Jonathan,[2] Thomas[1]*), born Oct. 21, 1737; married Jan. 11, 1759, Lydia Perry.

Ellis Tobey was a private on muster and pay roll of Capt. Ward Swift's co., Col. Freeman's regt.; enlisted Sept. 6, 1778.

Children:

    i.   Emma,[5] b. Oct. 11, 1760.
    ii.   Mehitable, b. April 12, 1763.
146. iii. Samuel, b. July 19, 1765.

52

SAMUEL[4] (*Samuel,[3] Jonathan,[2] Thomas[1]*), born in Sandwich, May 26, 1739; married there Jan. 26, 1769, Mary Tobey. Was she his cousin Mary, daughter of Zaccheus and Sarah (Pope) Tobey? He died before his father, who bequeathed in his will (1791) to "my two grandsons Nathaniel Tobey and John Tobey, sons of my son Samuel Tobey, deceased."

Children:

147. i.   Nathaniel.[5]
148. ii. John.

53

WILLIAM[4] (*Samuel,[3] Jonathan,[2] Thomas[1]*), was born in Sandwich, March 5, 1740–1. He married a wife named Maria who outlived him. We find no record of his life-work. He died about the beginning of the year 1798. Elisha Perry was appointed to administer on his estate Jan. 22, 1798, and his widow Maria was made guardian of his minor children, Archelaus and Franklin, Dec. 11, 1800.

[Consult the Revolutionary Rolls in the Appendix.]

Children:

149. i.   William.[5]
150. ii.   Tristram.
151. iii. Archelaus.
152. iv. Franklin.

54

NATHANIEL⁴ (*Samuel,³ Jonathan,² Thomas¹*), born March 1, 1743–4. Nathaniel Tobey married at Falmouth, Nov. 28, 1773, Mary Tobey.
He removed to Lee. There he married March 19, 1782, Deborah Finney, who was received to the church with him May 5, 1793.

Nathaniel Tobey was ensign on muster and pay roll of Capt. Micah Hamlin's co., Col. Simeon Cary's regt., enlisted Feb. 2, 1776; served 6 days; roll dated March 30, 1776; *also*, (Nathaniel Tobie) corporal on muster and pay roll of Capt. William Ford's co., Col. John Brown's regt. from July 21 to Oct. 27, 1780; *also*, private on muster and pay roll of Capt. Abel Babbitt's co., Col. John Hathaway's regt. for service at Rhode Island on alarm from Aug. 1 to 7, 1780; *also*, appears on a list of men who paid money to John Ellis, as a bounty for 3 years' enlistment, dated Lee, March 25, 1781; *also*, private on muster and pay roll of Capt. Josiah Yale's co. from Oct. 12 to 20, 1781; marched on alarm from Lee and Lenox to Stillwater by order of Brig. Gen. Rossiter.

Children:

	i.	Experience,⁵ b. Dec. 28, 1782.
154.	ii.	Samuel, b. Oct. 22, 1784.
	iii.	Marah, b. Sept. 18, 1786.
	iv.	Cynthia, b. May 17, 1792.
	v.	Barnabas, b. and d. in 1795.

55

MATTHIAS⁴ (*Samuel,³ Jonathan,² Thomas¹*), born Jan. 29, 1744–5; married in Sandwich [about 1769], Hannah, daughter of Stephen and Maria (Bourne) Nye, born May 10, 1751, [Freeman], died at Machias, Me., Sept. 27, 1835.

Matthias Tobey was reported as lieutenant on muster and pay roll of Capt. Joshua Tobey's co. enlisted July 1, 1775; as lieutenant appears in an account dated Boston June 22, 1776, of provisions delivered Micah Hamblin's co. of Col.

Marshall's regt.; residence, Sandwich; *also*, " Matthew Toby,"
first lieutenant, on a return of officers of Michael Hamblin's
[company] Col. Thomas Marshall's regiment; dated Council,
July 5, 1776; *also*, on a return of Captain Matthias Tobey's
company, Col. Allen Willard's regt., for mileage from Fort
Edward to Sandwich, dated Boston, Jan. 1777; *also*, return of Capt. Matthias Tobey's co., Col. (late col.) Hallett's
regt., for service at Rhode Island on alarm, July 14 to Nov. 2,
1780.

He removed to Machias, Me.; resided at the Port;
died Nov. 7, 1818.

Children:

159.　i.　　Zenas,* b. about 1771.
160.　ii.　　Elisha, b. 1773.
161.　iii.　Matthias, b. 1775.
　　　　iv.　Rebecca, b. 1777; m. Jireh Phinney (his second
　　　　　　wife).
　　　Children:
　　　　　　1. Edmund Phinney.
　　　　　　2. Matthias Phinney.
　　　　　　3. John Phinney.
　　　　　　4. Rebecca Phinney; m. Nathaniel Marston.
　　　　　　5. Samuel Phinney.
　　　　　　6. Albert S. Phinney.
　　　　　　7. Zenas Phinney.
　　　　　　8. Temperance Phinney.
　　　　v.　Temperance; m. Alvin Phinney.
　　　　　　Child: Alvin Phinney. Jr.

56

STEPHEN[4] (*Samuel,*[3] *Jonathan,*[2] *Thomas*[1]), born in
Sandwich Feb. 7, 1746–7; married Nov. 5, 1772, Lydia
Ellis.

He removed to Lee; his wife Lydia was received
to the church and baptized Sept. 21, 1783. He was
elected a surveyor of lumber in 1790 and at other
times.

See in the Appendix the entries of Revolutionary
services of Stephen Tobeys, not easy to separate.

Children recorded at Lee :

  i. Nathaniel,' b. and d. in 1775.
  ii. Remember, b. April 11, 1777.
  iii. Celia, b. April 10, 1780; m. June 26, 1800, John Rathbun.
163. iv. Stephen, b. Dec. 20, 1782.
 — v. Lydia, b. July 7, 1785.
164. vi. Nathaniel, b. Feb. 17, 1788.
165. vii. Asael, b. Nov. 21, 1790.
  viii. Sarah, b. June 17, 1793.
  ix. Mary, b. and d. March 12, 1799.

57

JONATHAN[4] (*Jonathan*,[3] *Jonathan*,[2] *Thomas*[1]), born in Sandwich, Dec. 24, 1740; married Dec. 27, 1764, Sarah Lewis of Sandwich. He died before the summer of 1781, as we learn from an interesting document still extant, the indentures of his son's apprenticeship.

  Child:

169. Jonathan,' b. Jan. 10, 1771; apprenticed to his father's brother Thomas of Rochester, cordwainer, to learn the trade, June 6, 1781. His mother Sarah consented and signed the articles, in which the relationship was declared.

58

LEMUEL,[4] (*Jonathan*,[3] *Jonathan*,[2] *Thomas*[1]), was born in Sandwich about 1744, was one of the children placed under the mother's guardianship after the father's death in 1755. Compare with Nos. 78 and 89.

Lemuel Tobey, private, on muster and pay roll of Capt. John Grannis' company, July 4 to Dec. 31, 1775; served 6 months 13 days; stationed at the Elizabeth Islands; *also* sergeant, on a return of Capt. Ward Swift's company for bounty allowed for service on secret expedition to Rhode Island,

Oct., 1777; residence Sandwich; *also*, sergeant, on a pay
abstract of Capt. Simeon Fish's company, Col. Freeman's regiment, for service 4 days; marched on alarm at Falmouth,
Sept., 1779, by order of Brig. Otis.

59

Dea. THOMAS[4] (*Jonathan*,[3] *Jonathan*,[2] *Thomas*[1]),
born in Sandwich March 6, 1753; died May 2 (or June
1), 1831; married first, at Rochester, Oct. 17, 1772,
Elizabeth (Betty) Norton; married second, March 2,
1780, Abigail Smith, born July 9, 1757, died April
18, 1794; married third, Oct. 5, 1794, Keziah Lincoln,
born April 1, 1756, died May 3, 1801; married fourth,
in New Bedford ("Dea. Thomas Tobey of Rochester"), Nov. 4, 1801, Mercy, daughter of Isaac Pope,
of N. B.; she sold her share in her father's estate
April 8, 1807, Dea. Tobey signing with her; married
fifth, in N. B., Sept. 8, 1814, Mehitable (Hitty or
Hetty), daughter of Jireh Willis, of N. B. [Deed of
heirs Aug. 3, 1825.] She outlived him, and died before Oct. 6, 1838. [Nantucket Inquirer.]

He was apprenticed July 27, 1767, to Josiah Burges
to learn the trade of cordwainer (shoemaker), his
brother Jonathan overseeing the arrangement; Ellis
Tobey was one of the witnesses. He took his nephew
Jonathan into the business many years afterward, as
we have just seen. He bought land in Rochester
April 9, 1776, in 1779, 1781 and 1791; and sold land
at various times. Was an active man in town and
church affairs, highly respected. Chosen deacon of the
Mattapoisett Church June 21, 1791; delegate to the
ordination of Oliver Cobb at Sippican in 1799, etc.
He signed his will March 12, 1829; it was proved
Aug. 7, 1832. He bequeathed his estate to his wife
Hetty, his sons Lemuel and Isaac S. Tobey, his
daughters Elizabeth, wife of Ebenezer Nye, and Abi-

gail, wife of Francis Nye, and to his grandson, Job T. Tobey, son of Isaac S.

Thomas Tobey of Rochester was a private in Capt. Clap's company of Col. Cotton's regiment, May 2 to Aug. 1, 1775, dated Oct. 7, 1775; also, private in a list of men mustered in Plymouth co. to serve in Capt. Sparrow's company, Col. Nye's regiment, by a return made between Sept. 10 and 15, 1777, by James Hatch Muster Master; also, to serve until Jan. 1, 1779; residence Rochester; also, private on muster and pay roll of Capt. Nathaniel Hammon's company, Col. or late Col. White's (4ᵗʰ Plymouth County) regt., for service at Rhode Island at on an alarm from July 30, to Aug. 8, 1780.

Children:

175. i. Lemuel,' b. July 20, 1781.
     ii. Thomas, b. Feb. 27, 1782; bapt. in March, 1783; d. May 20, 1788.
176. iii. Isaac Smith, b. Jan. 19, 1785; bapt. March 20, 1785.
     iv. Matthew, b. May 8, 1787; bapt. Sept., 1787; d. in New Orleans, La., July 23, 1812.
     v. Elizabeth, b. Sept. 16, 1789; m. Ebenezer Nye.
        Children :
        1. Reuben Nye, b. Oct. 26, 1806.
        2. Abigail T. Nye, b. Sept. 11, 1808.
        3. Matthew T. Nye, b. June 1, 1815.
        4. Harriet N. Nye, b. July 5, 1818.
        5. Ebenezer Nye, b. Sept. 22, 1823.
     vi. Thomas, b. Dec. 27, 1792; d. June 22, 1793.
     vii. Abigail, b. July 16, 1795; bapt. ("child of Thomas and Kezia Tobey") in 1795 [Church record.]; m. Francis Nye.
        Children :
        1. Elizabeth Tobey Nye, b. Sept. 26, 1817; d. Aug. 15, 1847.
        2. Charles Henry Nye, b. Dec. 8. 1821.
        3. Francis Augustus Nye, b. Dec. 1. 1823.
        4. Benjamin Lincoln Nye, b. July 1, 1828; d. Sept. 6, 1858.

60

Joshua[4] (*Cornelius,*[3] *Samuel,*[2] *Thomas*[1]), born about 1729; married Nov. 12, 1752, Maria, daughter of Nathan Tobey (No. 15), born Nov. 24, 1731. He died in 1794. Residence, Sandwich. He commanded a company at the opening of the Revolution. See under Nos. 55 and 187.

In his will, dated March 18, proved May 18, 1794, he bequeathed to his wife Maria; sons Stephen, Nathan, Lemuel and Cornelius; daughters Fear and Deborah, and grandchildren Hannah, Joannah, Silvanus and Benjamin, children of his deceased daughter Catharine Gibbs.

Children:

	i.	Catharine,[5] b. March 21, 1753; m. Aug. 25, 1774, Silvanus Gibbs.
187.	ii.	Stephen, b. May 6, 1755.
188.	iii.	Nathan, b. Feb. 1, 1757.
189.	iv.	Lemuel, b. May 12, 1760.
190.	v.	Cornelius.
	vi.	Fear.
	vii.	Deborah.

61

Cornelius[4] (*Cornelius,*[3] *Samuel,*[2] *Thomas*[1]), born about 1734; died Oct. 8, 1778; resided in Sandwich; married Feb. 1, 1756, Lois, daughter of John and Mercy (Swift) Pope, born May 25, 1738. He held a commission in the local militia company, but resigned it when the British government had become so oppressive that the people began to rebel.

"Whereas application has this day been made to us, military officers of the companies of militia in Sandwich, by certain gentlemen said to be appointed by the Body of the People, to apply to us to resign our military commissions: We hereby transmit our resignation of our respective commissions to the chief colonel of the regiment, to be by him transmitted to the Captain general; and that we will not by any ways or means assist in carrying into execution the late acts of Parliament; and that we will not accept of any commission in consequence of or in conformity to said acts, or under any unconstitutional regulations. As witness our hands.

John Smith   Cornelius Tobey
Elisha Bourne
Silas Bourne   Micah Blackwell"
" Sandwich, Oct. 3, 1774 "

Children:

i.   Patience,* b. July 17, 1756. Samuel Fessenden
     and Patience Tobey were married at Sandwich
     April 21, 1774.
ii. Elisha, b. Feb. 14, 1758; bapt. July 5, 1761; d.
     young.
iii. Deborah, b. Dec. 26, 1759. Deborah Tobey of
     Sandwich and Ebenezer Bourne of Wareham were
     published at W. Sept. 2, 1782.
iv. Alithea, b. March 29, 1762.
191. v.   Heman, b. Dec. 11, 1763.
192. vi. Melitiah, b. Feb. 8, 1766.
vii. Hannah, b. April 20, 1768; m. ——— Bourne.
viii. Joanna, b. Feb. 21, 1770.
193. ix. Joshua, b. Aug. 5, 1772.
x.   Betty (Betsey), b. Nov. 27, 1774; d. Oct. 14,
     1813.
194. xi. Elisha, b. Feb. 2, 1777. " Elisha Tobey died May
     26, 1817." [Record, family of Melitiah.]

62

Dr. ELISHA[4] (*Cornelius,*[3] *Samuel,*[2] *Thomas*[1]), born July 14, 1723; died accidentally May 10, 1781; married Jan. 12, 1745–6, Desire Newcomb, born May 21, 1725, died Jan. 25, 1778. He graduated at Harvard College in 1743. Was a physician, resided in Dartmouth (afterwards New Bedford), and bought land there June 12, 1753. Had an extensive practice in the county. He was elected representative to the General Court in 1770. His residence is still standing (1902), an antique, gambrel-roofed house, in the
5

north part of Acushnet village. [Hist. N. B.] He
made his will April 25, 1781; it was probated Oct. 2
following; he bequeathed to daughter Deborah Swift,
son Lemuel, son William, daughters Bathsheba Pad-
dlefoot, Desire, Patience and Abigail Tobey, sons
Elisha and Cornelius. Refers to lands in Greenwich
in Hampshire County, which we find he received of
his father 3 Dec. 1754; mentions Bathsheba's two
children.

Elisha Tobey, private, on muster and pay roll of Capt. Isaac
Pope's company, Col. Wm. Shepard's regiment (the 3[d] Mass.
regiment), enlisted for 9 months, July, August, October, 1778;
Jan. 5, 1779, on a certificate of service given by Capt. Isaac
Pope, who certifies that the above-named Elisha Tobey, who
was drafted into Capt. Nathaniel Hammond's co. in 1778, has
now joined his company; also on rolls for March and April,
1779.

Children:

195. i.   Lemuel,[4] b. Feb. 27, 1748-9.
     ii. Bathsheba (Bathshua), b. Sept. 1, 1751; m. John
          Paddelford of Taunton; (published April 28,
          1769).
     iii. William, b. Aug. 7, 1753.
196. iv. William, b. March 20, 1755-6.
     v.   Desire, b. Aug. 24, 1758; m. Aug. 15, 1784,
          Christopher Hammond.
     vi. Patience, b. Feb. 13, 1760-1; married April 13,
          1785, Capt. John Langworthy; he died Dec. 17,
          1800.
197. vii. Elisha, b. Jan. 18, 1764.
     viii. Abigail, b. Aug. 2, 1766; died Aug. 20, 1837;
          married at New Bedford, Sept. 23, 1792, Laban
          Coffin, of Sherburne.
          Children:
              1. John Starbuck Coffin, b. Aug. 6, 1793.
              2. Andrew Swain Coffin, b. July 19, 1795.
              3. Mary Coffin, b. Feb. 15, 1797.
              4. Phebe Coffin, b. Jan. 18, 1799.

5. Lydia Coffin, b. Jan. 29, 1801.
6. Sarah Coffin, b. March 6, 1804.
7. Eliza Coffin, b. March 5, 1806.
  ix. Deborah, b. July 16, 1767; m. —— Swift;
    died Dec. 12, 1802.
198. x. Cornelius, b. July 10, 1768.

63

ELNATHAN[4] (*Zaccheus,*[3] *Samuel,*[2] *Thomas*[1]), born
Jan. 11, 1727–8. He married in Dartmouth, Sept. 3,
1749, Deborah, daughter of John and Phebe (Spooner)
Taber, b. May 25, 1731. He bought a tract of land
in Dartmouth, Nov. 28, 1761. They sold this homestead farm and other lands, Dec. 23, 1777.

He removed to Conway, Hampshire co.; bought for
£88, 14 shillings, 3 Oct. 1778, part of Lot No. 21.
He sold for £80, Aug. 11, 1787, to Amaziah Tobey,*
a tract of land adjoining one he had previously sold
to Zaccheus Tobey; sold another tract to Amaziah
Oct. 17, 1793.
  Child:
    Sarah,[5] b. Jan. 11, 1754.

64

SAMUEL[4] (*Zaccheus,*[3] *Samuel,*[2] *Thomas*[1]), born in
Dartmouth, 9 Feb. 1729–30; married first (published
13 Aug. 1752), Esther Rider; married second, Abigail ——.

Became a "mariner," *i. e.* a sea captain. Bought
land in Dartmouth, 20 Sept., 1762. Resided in New

---

* Amaziah Tobey, born 1764: married Nov. 14, 1787, Molly, daughter of
Lieut. Micajah and Anna (Crowell) Sears, born Sept. 24, 1773. [Sears Genealogy.] She died in Conway Dec. 10, 1851, "aged 88 years."[!] He removed to
Conway; bought land of Elnathan Tobey, Aug. 11, 1787. He sold land adjoining his home Jan. 7, 1797, and part of the tract on which he lived Feb. 15, 1837.
His land and property was assigned, and was sold by the assignee May 29, 1846,
his wife Molly conveying her right of dower. He died Aug. 24, 1853, "aged 91
years."

Bedford, where he bought land 17 Feb. 1797. Made
his will Nov. 8, 1797, proved Feb. 2, 1819, bequeathing all to his wife Abigail.

65

JOHN' (*Zaccheus,*[3] *Samuel,*[2] *Thomas*[1]), born July
29, 1732; married in Dartmouth (pub. Dec. 3, 1754)
Jan. 9, 1754–5, Mary Bennett; she died in 1820,
" aged 85 years "; he died Sept. 24, 1811.

They sold land to Daniel Bennett 25 Oct. 1786.
They joined March 10, 1796, with John Taber, attorney to his children; Abraham Shearman, guardian to
John Bennett; and Seth Spooner, guardian to Sherman, all heirs of Desire Bennett, in a sale of their
rights in certain lands.

John Tobey of New Bedford, yeoman, " advanced in years,"
made will March 28, 1811, probated Nov. 5, 1811; bequeathed
to wife Mary; daughter Salvina Bennett, widow of Daniel Bennett; Ruth Whelden; Parnell, widow of Consider Smith;
Mary Mason; Reuben son of Reuben Mason; Betsey M.,
daughter of Timothy Tallman; William Bliss, son of Richard
Mason; to Job and Hannah, children of Thomas Cook; Joseph
Whelden and Salvina Bennett, executors.

Children :
i.   Salvina,[5] m. (pub. Sept. 30, 1780) Daniel Bennett.
ii. Thankful, b. about 1756; m. (pub. in Dartmouth,
     Sept. 12, 1778) Capt. Reuben Mason; he died
     Nov. 2, 1806, in his 50th year; she d. Aug. 19,
     1802, in her 46th year.
     Children :
       1. Richard Mason.
       2. Reuben Mason.
       3. Charles Mason.
       4. Ruth Mason, m. Capt. Joseph Whelden.
       5. Parnel Mason, m. (1) Consider Smith; m.
          (2) in Nov. 1812, Joshua Morse.

Child :
Edward Morse, m. Caroline Terry, and
had a daughter, Lydia A. Morse, who
m. Benjamin White, whose son Alden
White, a prominent citizen of Acushnet,
has contributed information regarding
this line.
6. Mary Mason.

66

ZACCHEUS[4] (*Zaccheus,*[2] *Samuel,*[2] *Thomas*[1]), born at
Dartmouth, Dec. 2, 1734 ; married first, (pub. Dec. 1,
1756) Anne Sampson : married second, Ruhama ——.
They sold land in Dartmouth May 1, 1778, and March
15, 1798, sold other land.

Zaccheus Tobey, of Butternuts, Otsego co., N. Y.,
yeoman, released a mortgage on land in New Bedford,
14 Aug. 1784; " Ruhamy Tobey " was one of the witnesses.

Zaccheus Tobey, private on muster and pay roll of Capt.
Manassah Kempton's co., Col. Freeman's regt. for service at
Rhode Island on alarm from Sept. 27, to Oct. 29, 1777, on a
secret expedition.

Child :
199.   Zaccheus,[5] b. 1757.

67

ZOETH[4] (*Zaccheus,*[3] *Samuel,*[2] *Thomas*[1]), born in
Dartmouth July 14, 1737; married first ——; mar-
ried second, in Middleborough, Jan. 10, 1782, Abigail
Keen of that place.

Zoeth (Zoath) Tobey, private on muster and pay roll of
Capt. George Claghorn's co., Col. Abiel Mitchell's regt. from
July 31 to Oct. 31, 1780 ; Bristol Co. regt. raised to re-inforce

the Continental army, by resolve of July 22, 1780; *also*, on a
warrant to pay officers and men of Capt. Claghorn's co., dated
March 27, 1781; *also*, private on muster and pay roll of Capt.
Henry Jenne's co., Col. John Hathaway's regt., Aug. 2 to 8;
1780; 2ᵈ Bristol Co. regt.; service at Rhode Island on an
alarm; roll certified at Dartmouth.

Children :

201. "Zoeth, Jr."[5] b. Sept. 15, 1764.

68

Lot[4] (*Zaccheus*,[3] *Samuel*,[2] *Thomas*[1]), born in Dart-
mouth, Sept. 26, 1739; married first (published Jan.
30, 1761), Keziah Jenne. Lot Tobey and Elmener
Dexter of Dartmouth intended marriage Dec. 30, 1775.
Lot Tobey married in New Bedford, Jan. 7, 1790,
Abigail Tompkins.

He bought tracts of land in Dartmouth in 1771,
1779, etc.

With wife Abigail he sold land in New Bedford,
May 11, 1792. He sold land alone 9 May, 1798.

Lot Tobey was a private on the muster and pay roll of Capt.
Henry Jenne's co., Col. John Hathaway's regt., Aug. 2 to 8,
1780, at Rhode Island on an alarm.

Keziah Tobey, of New Bedford, singlewoman,
and Sasson Worth of the Little Nine Partners in the
state of New York, blacksmith, with Ruth his wife,
sold their rights in marsh land in New Bedford, formerly belonging to their grandfather Job Jenne 23
March, 1793.

Having removed to Greenfield, Greene co., New
York, his daughter Sarah joined him June 14, 1804,
in a deed of land in New Bedford.

Children :

   i. Sarah.[5]
  ii. Keziah.
 iii. Ruth; m. Sasson Worth.

69

PRINCE[4] (*Zaccheus,[3] Samuel,[2] Thomas[1]*), born in Dartmouth, June 7, 1741; died in Conway, July 7, 1810, married Jan. 5, 1765 (published Aug. 2, 1764) Jane Delano ("Jean Delano, Jr."), born Dec. 30, 1743; died Nov. 4, 1837.

He became a sea-captain; resided some years at Dartmouth, then removed to Conway, where he spent the remainder of his days.

"Prince Tobey, mariner, of Dartmouth," bought land in Rochester, June 18, 1771; "Prince Tobey, gentleman, of Dartmouth," sold land in Rochester to Zaccheus Tobey, Jr., March 2, 1778.

He bought of Stephen Rawson, in 1778, for £700, Lot No. 66 (except 4 acres previously sold).

Prince Tobey appears as private on a pay abstract of Capt. Benjamin Dillingham's co. for service on sea coast at Dartmouth for 3 months; enlisted April 15, 1776; *also*, as first lieutenant among a list of officers of the Massachusetts militia in the 12th company of the 2[d] Bristol co. regt.; commissioned April 27, 1776; *also*, private on muster and pay roll of Capt. Simeon Fish's co., Col. Freeman's regt., Sept. 1778; service on alarm at Dartmouth and Falmouth. Compare with No. 93.

Prince Tobey of Conway, in the county of Hampshire, made his will May 1, 1809; it was probated Sept. 11, 1810. He bequeathed to his wife Jane the improvement of one-third part of his homestead farm and buildings, all his household furniture, one horse, side-saddle, cutter, harness and a third part of his neat stock, to be used and improved by her during her life; the furniture to be then divided between his daughters. He bequeathed to his son Elijah and his daughters Deborah, Elizabeth and Sarah, one dollar each; and the same sum to each of his grandchildren, Pollisa, Richard, Jane and Cordelia Bond. To his sons Elisha and Prince $400 and all the land in Lot 67 in Conway which was owned by the late Ezra Tobey, deceased, to be divided between them. To daughters Christiana and Pamelia $200 apiece when they arrive at the age of 21. The remainder of the estate to his son Benjamin whom he appointed executor.

Children :

i. Silas,[1] b. Oct. 10, 1765; d. Aug. 21, 1769.
ii. Elijah, b. Jan. 31, 1767.
203. iii. Deborah, b. May 22, d. Sept. 1, 1768.
iv. Deborah, b. March 9, 1770; m. ———— Faxon; d. 1842.
v. Elizabeth, b. May 22, 1772; m. Rev. Josiah Godard.
vi. A son, b. May 28, d. "35 days after," 1774.
vii. Jane, b. Aug. 26, 1775; m. March 5, 1796, Consider Bond; d. Jan. 7, 1804.
viii. Ezra, b. April 8, 1777; d. March 17, 1807.
204. ix. Elisha, b. Feb. 22, 1779, at Conway.
x. Joseph, } b. Jan. 23, 1781; { d. Sept. 22, 1800.
205. xi. Benjamin, }
xii. Sarah, b. May 27, 1783; m. June 10, 1806, William Holloway.
xiii. Prince, b. Jan. 22, 1785.
xiv. Christiana, b. May 4, 1787; d. Sept. 9, 1809.
xv. Pamelia, b. March 23, 1789; m. March 15, 1812, Cyrus Holloway of Sherburne.

70

NOAH[4] (*Zaccheus,*[3] *Samuel,*[2] *Thomas*[1]), born in Dartmouth, March 8, 1745. Served in the Revolutionary War; was enrolled in a company of men who marched from Dartmouth to camp under command of Capt. Benjamin Dillingham and arrived there Feb. 15, 1776. Received a deed of part of his father's homestead.

Noah Tobey of Dartmouth bought land in Conway by the west end of Lot 61, 29 March, 1777. He sold the land and buildings in Conway, "whereon he is now living," Nov. 28, 1789, his wife Sally joining in the deed.

The family removed at some time to Ballston, Saratoga county, N. Y.

Children:

206. i. Herman.
ii. Samuel.
iii. Abigail; m. ———— Stewart.

71

JONATHAN[4] (*Jonathan,*[3] *Samuel,*[2] *Thomas*[1]), born in Dartmouth Dec. 4, 1740; married there Dec. 28, 1777, Love White, born at Nantucket, Aug. 12, 1758, died April 29, 1839; he died Aug. 18, 1816.

Jonathan Tobey, Jr., husbandman, of Dartmouth, bought land there 10 July, 1793.

Jonathan Tobey, yeoman of New Bedford, made will Nov. 2, 1811; probated Oct. 29, 1816; bequeathed to wife; children John, Silas, Jonathan, Marchant, William, Cornelius, Leonard, Abishai, Sarah and Love. The three youngest boys to " be learned to read, write and cypher so much as is suitable for children to be put out to a trade," and then to "be put out to some useful trade." Jonathan was made residuary legatee and June 1, 1819, made guardian of Leonard, Abishai H. and Love M.

Children, recorded in Dartmouth:

211. i. John,[5] b. Aug. 31, 1779.
212. ii. Silas, b. Aug. 23, 1781.
    iii. Molly, b. Aug. 12, 1783; d. July 11, 1785.
    iv. Sarah (Sally), b. June 26, 1785; m. Salisbury Sherman.
213. v. Jonathan, b. July 12, 1787.
214. vi. Marchant, b. April 3, 1791.
215. vii. William Isaac, b. July 6, 1793.
216. viii. Cornelius, b. May 26, 1796.
217. ix. Leonard, b. Jan. 6, 1799.
    x. Love Marchant, b. April 28, 1801; m. April, 1820, Jesse Sears. She d. in Acushnet June 23, 1879.
218. xi. Abisha Huxford, b. Sept. 5, 1804.

72

SETH[4] (*Jonathan,*[3] *Samuel,*[2] *Thomas*[1]), born in Dartmouth; married (published in D. June 1, 1770) Mary Williamson of Middleborough. She died Oct. 17, 1799.

Seth Tobey, corporal, is entered on company returns of Capt. Egery, Col. Danielson's regiment, May 4, to Aug. 1, 1775; another return of the same is dated at Roxbury Oct. 6, 1775, residence Dartmouth; *also*, private on pay roll of Capt. Manasseh Kempton's co. in Col. Carpenter's regt. for service at Rhode Island on alarm, July 26, to Aug. 29, 1777.

Seth Tobey of New Bedford, mariner, sold to Peleg Huttleston, 15 Sept., 1789, land in N. B., in the village called Oxford, on the East side of Acushnet Harbour.

He died in 1793; his widow was appointed administratrix Oct. 1, 1793, and appraisal was made April 30, 1794. Joseph Bates was appointed guardian of " Seth Tobey, son of Seth Tobey, late of N. B., being a minor above the age of 14 years," May 7, 1799.

Seth and Ebenezer Williamson Tobey sold in February and May, 1802, lands which had belonged to their father Seth and on which he had formerly lived.

Children :

      i.   Ansel.[5]
219. ii. Seth.
220. iii. Ebenezer Williamson.
     iv. Mary.
     v.   Sarah, b. Dec. 21, 1784; m. Sept. 19, 1802, Thomas Terry.

74

WILLIAM[4] (*Jonathan,*[3] *Samuel,*[2] *Thomas*[1]), born in Dartmouth about 1755; married Ruhama [Taber]. They lived in the homestead which had formerly belonged to Thomas Taber in 1803. [Bristol Deeds 113, 484.] He received a deed of gift of his father, Jonathan Tobey's homestead farm in New Bedford, 19 March, 1785. " William Tobey 2ᵈ "* of New Bedford,

---

* William Tobey, Jr., married in New Bedford, June 25, 1795, Almy Shearman. In the division of the real estate of Jacob Shearman, late of New Bedford, 1 Oct., 1804, one of the portions was set off to his daughter "Amity Tobey," adjoining the dower of the widow Abiah Shearman.

with wife Ruhama, sold 19 March, 1795, lands inherited from his father, Jonathan Tobey; other tracts Sept. 4, 1823. [See Revolutionary Rolls in Appendix.] "Mr. William Tobey died at New Bedford, Jan. 14, 1835, æ. 80."

William Tobey 2ᵈ of New Bedford was appointed guardian, June 5, 1819, of the children of Seth Tobey late of Hudson, N. Y., to wit: William Tobey, Jr. and Elizabeth Tobey, above the age of 14 years, and Amy, Melora, Seth I. and Isaac S., under 14 years. [Bristol Co. Prob. Rec.]

75

SAMUEL⁴ (*Eliakim,³ Samuel,² Thomas¹*), born in Sandwich, Feb. 20, 1740-1; remained in his native place long enough to perform a good part in the struggle for independence and then removed to Maine. Was in Waterville about 1784; soon after removed to Fairfield, near by; built the first framed house there; was a farmer; town clerk for twenty years; a justice of the local court. Though he had lost a leg he made his way well on a wooden one and accomplished a great deal. He died suddenly,—dropped down in the road.

He married Mary ———, who was born in 1749.

Samuel Tobey of Sandwich was chosen 2d Lieutenant of the 1st Sandwich company (Capt. Simeon Fish) in the 1st Barnstable regiment, March 19, 1776; commissioned 1st Lieut. June 5, 1778; was one of the officers in Capt. Elisha Hedges' co. detached from his brigade by Brig. Joseph Otis and put under Maj. Winslow of Col. Doane's regiment, Barnstable, Jan. 7, 1777; was on the roll of Capt. Fish's co., Sept. 1778; service on alarm at Dartmouth and Falmouth.

Children:
  i.   Abigail,⁵ b. 1769.
  ii. Lucy, b. 1771.

222. iii. Samuel, b. 1773.
223. iv. Eliakim, b. Jan. 25, 1776.
224. v. Nymphas, b. 1778.
225. vi. Nathaniel, b. 1780.
226. vii. Stephen, b. 1783.
227. viii. Ansel.
228. ix. William.
  x. Mary, b. 1790.
  xi. Celia, b. 1792; m. (pub. at Falmouth Dec. 4, 1814) Stephen Nye.

76

WILLIAM[4] (*Eliakim*,[3] *Samuel*,[2] *Thomas*[1]), born March 2, 1750-1; married March 17, 1778, Hannah Crocker.

[See Revolutionary Rolls in Appendix.]

In the name of God Amen. I, Hannah Tobey of Sandwich in the County of Barnstable, widow, being advanced in years but through divine goodness, of sound and disposing mind and memory do make ordain and declare this instrument to be my last will and testament revoking all others.

Imprimis. All my debts are to be paid and the legacies herein after bequeathed are to be discharged as hereafter directed.

Item. I give and bequeath to Hannah Tobey and to William Tobey children of my son Jonathan Burr Tobey the sum of fifty dollars each to be paid them by my executors when they arrive at the age of twenty-one years.

Item. I give and bequeath to my son Jonathan Burr Tobey the sum of five dollars to be paid to him by my Executors in one year after my decease.

Item. I give to my daughter Grace Bursley wife of Heman Bursley and to my daughter Abigail Nye wife of Obed B. Nye and to their heirs all my real and personal estate of every name and nature.

I constitute and appoint Heman Bursley and Obed B. Nye Executors of this my last will. In witness of all and each of the things herein contained, I have hereunto set my hand and seal this sixth day of February in the year of our Lord one thousand eight hundred and twenty-eight. Signed sealed and declared by the above named Hannah Tobey to be her last will and testament in presence of the testator and of each of us have hereunto subscribed our names as witnesses.

Heman Tobey.   HANNAH TOBEY [L.S.]
Seth F. Nye.
Abram Nye.

Proved June 10, 1828.

Bk. 47, p. 181.

Children b. at Sandwich :

   i.   Grace,⁴ b. Oct. 5, 1778; married Heman Bursley.
   ii.   Abigail, b. Dec. 15, 1783; married Col. Obed B. Nye.
  iii. Lydia Barker, b. April 5, 1790; died early.
229. iv.   Jonathan Burr, b. May 30, 1794.

77

ANSELM⁴ (*Eliakim,³ Samuel,² Thomas¹*), born Dec. 2, 1752. Referred to in his father's will in 1780, as having passed away before that time.

Ansel Tobey, private on muster and pay roll of Capt. Elisha Nye from Jan. 4 to Feb. 2, 1776, and from April 5 to Sept. 1, 1776; *also*, sergt. on a return of Capt. Ward Swift's co. for bounty allowed for service on secret expedition, Oct. 1777; *also* sergt. on roll of Capt. Simeon Fish's co., Col. Freeman's regt. in Sept. 1778, 11 days.

78

LEMUEL⁴ (*Eliakim,³ Samuel,² Thomas¹*), born Oct. 30, 1755.

Lemuel Tobey, private, on muster and pay roll of Capt. Joseph Palmer's company, Col. Josiah Whitney's regiment, for service at Rhode Island; served 2 months, 3 days; dated South Kingston, July, 1777; *also*, private, on muster and pay roll of Capt. Simeon Fish's company, Col. Freeman's regiment, Sept., 1778; service on alarm at Dartmouth and Falmouth; *also*, private, on muster and pay roll of Capt. Crandon's company, Col. John Hathaway's regiment, Aug. 2–8, 1780; served 6 days.

Inherited land in Sandwich from his father in 1780.

'79

SAMUEL[4] (*Samuel,*[3] *Samuel,*[2] *Thomas*[1]), born in Berkley, June 5, 1743; married Sept. 6, 1768, Experience Paull, of Berkley; he died Dec. 18, 1823.

He learned the trade of cordwainer, but pushed out into general mercantile business. May 11, 1769, he bought land of Stephen Webster; later he purchased other lands.

He and his son Apollos were in partnership as " traders " Oct. 28, 1800, as shown in records of deeds. He was a citizen of prominence, an Esquire or Justice of the Peace, a man of efficiency and usefulness.

Samuel Tobey of Berkley was a private on the muster roll of Capt. Joseph Batt's co. (Burt's co.) Col. Edward Pope's regiment, for service at Rhode Island on the alarm of Dec. 8, 1776.

Children:

 i. Achsa,[5] b. Jan. 29, 1769; m. Dec. 2, 1788, Roger French of Berkley, and was living in 1853 at Barnard, Vt.

230. ii. Apollos, b. Sept. 15, 1770.

 iii. Ruth, b. June 18, 1772; living at S. in 1853.

 iv. Betsey, b. March 11, 1774; m. Jan. 12, 1794, Tisdale Porter of Berkley; she d. June 15, 1795.

 v. Samuel, b. May 12, 1776; d. Feb. 3, 1787.

231. vi. Enoch, b. Nov. 5, 1778.

 vii. Peddie, b. Nov. 17, 1780; m. Thomas Richmond; living at Medfield, in 1853.

 viii. Bathsheba, b. Oct. 17, 1782; m. Oct. 10, 1804, Rev. Abraham Gersher, of Dighton.

 ix. Rowena, b. March 16, 1785.

232. x. Silas, b. March 21, 1787.

80

TIMOTHY[4] (*Samuel,*[3] *Samuel,*[2] *Thomas*[1]), born in Berkley, Sept. 25, 1745; married (intention) Oct. 9, 1773, Mary Holloway. He removed to Shelburne, Hampshire co., Mass.; sold, Oct. 28, 1783, to his brother Nathaniel, land in Middleborough, inherited from his father. Removed to Conway; died there, "Capt. Timothy Tobey," Jan. 18, 1812. "Widow Tobey," who died there March, 1835, may have been his wife.

Timothy Tobey, second lieutenant, in a return of officers on board the armed sloop Freedom, John Clouston, commander; ordered in council Sept. 4, 1776, that officers be commissioned; *also,* on a pay abstract for wages of two men and ration allowance, admitted from previous roll of Brig Freedom, as returned by Capt. John Clouston, dated Boston, Jan. 16, 1777; 6 months and 9 days rations allowed; omitted from previous roll.

Timothy Tobey, private on a pay abstract of Capt. Elijah Walker's (7th) company for service at Rhode Island, 1780; in Col. John Hathaway's regt., Brig. Gen. George Godfrey's (Bristol Co.) brigade; co. marched to Tiverton, R. I., on the alarm of Aug. 2, 1780.

Children:

233. i. Silas.[5] 234. ii. Samuel.

81

NATHANIEL[4] (*Samuel,*[3] *Samuel,*[2] *Thomas*[1]), born in Berkley, Aug. 17, 1747, and there resided. He married Abigail, daughter of Stephen Burt.

Nathaniel Tobey was private on muster and pay roll of Capt. James Nichol's co., Col. Edward Pope's regt.; served 13 days on alarm at Rhode Island of Dec. 8, 1776; residence Berkley.

He bought land in Middleborough in 1783, which was sold Oct. 20, 1837, by his son Nathaniel, who had removed to Tompkins county, N. Y. Owned land in Freetown, which he and his wife sold July 3, 1793.

Nathaniel Tobey, yeoman, of Berkley, made will Dec. 31, 1801; probated March 2, 1802; bequeathed to his wife Abigail; daughter Cynthia Pierce and grand children Alvin and Lucinda Pierce; daughters Nabby and Philena Tobey; sons Nathaniel and Samuel Tobey.

Children:

i. Cynthia,* b. Oct. 23, 1773; pub. in Berkeley to Silas Pierce of Middleborough, April 2, 1796.

ii. Abigail (Nabby), b. Dec. 2, 1775; m. Feb. 24, 1803, David "Taulbut" (Talbot).

235. iii. Alvin, b. May 20, 1778; not mentioned in father's will.

iv. Philena (Filena), b. April 9, 1781; m. Dec. 20, 1801, Eli Hathaway.

v. Nathaniel, b. Nov. 4, 1784.

236. vi. Samuel, under 14 at his father's death, 1802.

82

ISAAC[4] (*Samuel*,[3] *Samuel*,[2] *Thomas*[1]), born in Berkeley, July 20, 1749; married first (intention July 11, 1772), Lydia, daughter of Col. George Williams; he married second, Deborah, daughter of Benjamin Williams, Esq.

Isaac Tobey was lieutenant on muster and pay roll of Capt. Jotham Houghton's co., Col. Samuel Denny's (2d) regt., Oct. 24 to Dec. 1, 1779. He received a pension from Jan. 22, 1833, "aged 84 years"; resided in Franklin County, Mass.; annual allowance, $83.44; sum received $250.32. Service in Mass. State troops.

He was a carpenter and shipwright; bought land in Dartmouth in 1773 and 1774; removed to Barre, and July 9, 1785, sold to Ephraim Caswell land in Berkley which he had inherited from his father.

He removed to New Salem, where he acquired land which he sold Sept. 9, 1796; his wife sold her share in the estate of Joseph Foster, late of New Salem. He removed again to Hawley, where he passed the remainder of his long and honorable career. Was a deacon of the church, an active, useful man.

He died June 5, 1845. His will, dated 11 July, 1837, proved 21 July, 1845, gave his wearing apparel to his son William; his real estate to his son John; his household furniture to his daughters Ann Carter, Deborah, wife of Theodore Field, Mary W., wife of Ephraim Williams, and Bathsheba Wing, widow; all his pension money to be divided between them also; William and John executors. A voucher attached affirms that he was a pensioner, having served the country in the Revolutionary war; that he left but the six children mentioned in the will.

Children, the eldest, born in Dartmouth, the rest recorded in Barre, except the youngest:

237. i.   William,⁵ or Williams, b. Feb. 23, 1773.
     ii.   Isaac, b. July 19, 1779 ; d. before his father.
     iii. Anne, b. Dec. 8, 1781 ; m. Thomas Carter.
     iv.   A son, b. and d. Oct. 21, 1783.
238. v.   John, b. Jan. 17, 1785.
     vi.   Deborah, b. April 11, 1787 ; m. Theodore Field.
     vii. Joshua, b. Feb. 21, 1789 ; d. in 1821. His brothers and sisters joined in a quitclaim deed of his estate to their father, 19 April, 1821.
     viii. Samuel, b. March 7, 1791 ; went West; was in business at Fort Meiggs, Ohio ; d. before March 1, 1821, when his father requested administration of his estate by Capt. John Tobey of Buckland, which was granted.
     ix.   Mary Williams, b. March 29, 1793 ; m. Ephraim Williams.
     x.   Bathsheba, b. ———— ; m. ———— Wing, and was a widow in 1837.

83

ENOCH⁴ (*Samuel,³ Samuel,² Thomas¹*), born in Berkeley, Sept. 21, 1751; mar. Rebecca Littlefield, of Newport, R. I. Was a "mariner," *i. e.*, sea-captain. Sold, Sept. 4, 1784, land which had been "set off" to him from his father's estate.

6

Enoch Tobey, private on muster and pay roll of Capt.
Joseph Batt's (Burt's) company, Col. Edward Pope's regt.,
for service at Rhode Island on the alarm of Dec. 8, 1776;
residence, Berkeley; Bristol County regt. in camp at Warren,
R. I.

The inventory of his estate, taken Sept. 26, 1789,
was presented in court Nov. 3, following, by his
brother Samuel.

84

PAUL[4] (*Samuel*,[3] *Samuel*,[2] *Thomas*[1]), born in Berkeley Sept. 6, 1761 (twin with Silas); married Betsey,
daughter of Dea. Andrew Parker, of Barre.

Paul Tobey, private, on muster and pay roll of Capt. Abel
Babbitt's co., Col. John Hathaway's regt., for service at Rhode
Island on alarm from Aug. 1 to 7, 1780.

He removed to Chester, county of Windsor, Vt.;
sold to his brother Samuel Tobey, Esq., of Berkeley,
25 June, 1793, all his right in the estate of his
mother and in that of his deceased brother Silas
Tobey.

Paul Tobey of Chester, Vt., with his wife Betsey sold land
in Barre (Mass.), and their rights in the land set off as " thirds "
to Mary Parker, widow of the late Dea. Andrew Parker of
Barre, Oct. 9, 1794.

Andrew P. Tobey and Samuel Tobey of Cambridge joined
with Lincoln Whitcomb and Sarah, his wife, of Quechee, Vt.,
and Otis Cook of Chester, Vt., with Betsey his wife, in a quit-
claim deed of their rights in a tract of land in Barre, being the
share of their mother, Betsey Tobey, in the estate of her
father, Dea. Andrew Parker, late of Barre, Feb. 19, 1839.

Children:

239. i. Andrew Parker.[5]
     ii. Samuel.
     iii. Sarah; m. Lincoln Whitcomb.
     iv. Betsey; m. Otis Cook.

86

SYLVANUS[4] (*Thomas,[3] Samuel,[2] Thomas[1]*), born in
Sandwich June 19, 1741; married (published at Dartmouth—"of Sandwich"—April 18, 1763) Sarah,
daughter of Job Jenny. As Zaccheus Tobey of
Dartmouth had been appointed his guardian in 1758,
this may have been a reason for his removing to that
town. Was a cooper. He died at the comparatively
early age of 27. Job Jenny administered on his
estate Feb. 29, 1768, and was appointed guardian to
the son Sylvanus, a minor under 14 years of age.
This son received his portion of the property left by
the father Oct. 7, 1783, inheriting also that which belonged to his brother Thomas, "he being dead."

Children:

240. i. Sylvanus.[5]
    ii. Thomas. Enlisted at the age of "16"; arrived at
        Springfield July 30, 1780, for the term of 6
        months; *also*, enlisted for three years, June 5,
        1781, at Taunton, to be conducted to Springfield;
        in Capt. Hitchcock's co., Col. Joseph Hitchcock;
        age 18; occupation, blacksmith; residence, Dart-
        mouth.

87

THOMAS[4] (*Thomas,[3] Samuel,[2] Thomas[1]*), born in
Sandwich Jan. 5, 1745; married (published in Dartmouth Dec. 13, 1777) Patience Wing, "both of
Dartmouth." He was a sea-captain; commanded the
barque Grayhound; was lost on a voyage to France
about the year 1782.

Children:

241. i. Luke,[5] b. May 13, 1780.
242. ii. Elisha, b. 1781.

88

Seth[4] (*Thomas*,[3] *Samuel*,[2] *Thomas*[1]), born in Sandwich, Nov. 20, 1748.

Seth Tobey of Dartmouth, joiner, inventory of his estate was presented Oct. 7, 1783, by Benjamin Blossom, administrator.

93

Prince[4] (*Silas*,[3] *Gershom*,[2] *Thomas*[1]), born in Sandwich, March 9, 1736–7; (town record); died Sept. 6, 1803, "aged 65 years"; married first, Jan. 23, 1766, Mary Dillingham. He married second, in Boston, Dec. 8, 1783, Grace, daughter of Joseph and Abigail (Torrey) Webb, born June 14, 1737; she survived him and died Nov. 30, 1803, "aged 66 years."

"Prince Tobey, gentleman," of Sandwich, with his wife Grace, joined Nov. 5, 1796, with her family connections in a deed of land and buildings called "Borland's Row" in Boston, "which Ebenezer Woodward bought of Leonard Vassall Borland in 1784." The widow, in her will, dated Nov. 14, 1803, bequeathed her property to her sister Deborah Smith; her sister-in-law Deborah Webb, widow of her brother Nehemiah Webb, and to Hannah, daughter of Sarah Lewis, "who now lives with me."

94

Silas[4] (*Silas*,[3] *Gershom*,[2] *Thomas*[1]), born in Sandwich, March 20, 1739–40; married Emma ———. Mrs. Emma Tobey, aged 73, died in Sandwich, Sept. 9, 1823. [Nantucket Inquirer.]   See Revolutionary Record under No. 43.

Children "of Silas Tobey, Jr.":

	i.	Mary,[5] b. Aug. 20, 1770.
	ii.	Sarah, b. July 12, 1772.
251.	iii.	Simeon, b. July 2, 1774.

95

SIMEON[4] (*Silas,*[3] *Gershom,*[2] *Thomas*[1]), born in Sandwich, April 9, 1744. Simeon Tobey, mariner, of Sandwich, died before Nov. 9, 1773, when his widow Sarah was appointed administratrix.

96

STEPHEN[4] (*Silas,*[3] *Gershom,*[2] *Thomas*[1]), born in Sandwich, May 2, 1747; called "Junior" in Sandwich town records; married, Nov. 21, 1771, Rebecca Ellis. [See Revolutionary Rolls in Appendix and No. 56.]
Children:
  i. Ellis,[5] b. Sept. 6, 1772.
  ii. Elizabeth, b. Aug. 14, 1774.
  iii. Elizabeth, b. Nov. 5, 1776.
256. iv. Stephen, b. July 6, 1782.
257. v. Prince, b. July 14, 1785.
258. vi. Ebenezer Wing, b. March 25, 1788.
259. vii. Ellis, b. Jan. 6, 1791.

97

ELISHA[4] (*Ephraim,*[3] *Gershom,*[2] *Thomas*[1]), born in Sandwich, Jan. 2, 1738–9; died Feb. 23, 1808–9, at Alford, Mass.; married Susanna ———, who died at A., Feb. 8, 1821, in the 73d year of her age. He removed to Connecticut with his father and located at Sharon. Was a farmer and weaver. Was Capt. of the second Co. of the 14th Regt. Conn. Troops in Oct. 1780. [Conn. Records, Vol. I, p. 31.] Later (about 1792), he moved to Alford, Mass., where he spent the remainder of his life. Purchased a tract of 500 acres in the south part of the town, on a portion of which his grandson Elisha was living in 1885.

Children, born in Sharon, Conn.:

261. i. Jonathan.[5]
262. ii. Barnabas.
263. iii. Sylvanus.
264. iv. Heman.
265. v. Elisha.
266. vi. Ephraim.
267. vii. Benjamin.
     viii. Abigail; m. Erastus Hamline.
     ix. Harriet; m. Jonathan Elmore.

98

JESSE[4] (*Ephraim,*[3] *Gershom,*[2] *Thomas*[1]), born at Sharon, Conn., Jan. 26, 1740–1. Removed to Norfolk, Litchfield eo., Conn.

Children:

268. i. Abraham.[5]
269. ii. Jesse, b. in Norfolk, Conn., Aug. 14, 1772.
270. iii. Job Gibbs.
271. iv. Philo.
     v. Rehameradah, m. —— Bristol.
     vi. Anna.
     vii. Amanda; m. —— Babbitt.

99

GEORGE[4] (*Ephraim,*[3] *Gershom,*[2] *Thomas*[1]), born Sept. 2, 1745; married Abigail Knapp. Resided in Sharon and Norfolk, Conn.

George Tobey of Norfolk, Conn., made his will (filed in Probate Court of Berkshire co., Mass., July 8, 1823). Had estate in New Marlboro, Mass., valued at $269. Bequeathed to wife Abigail, sons Philander and George, daughters Abigail Rockwell and Martha Cowles, the daughter of a deceased son, and the heirs of deceased son Miles.

Children:

272. i. Bracy.[5]

273. ii. Miles.
274. iii. Philander.
275. iv. Josiah.
     v. Rebecca.
     vi. Martha; m. ——— Cowles.
     vii. Abigail; m. ——— Rockwell.
     viii. Lovicy.
     ix. Alta.
276. x. George, b. Aug. 28, 1785.

101

EPHRAIM[4] (*Ephraim,*[3] *Gershom,*[2] *Thomas*[1]), born in
Sharon, Conn., Aug. 16, 1755. He is believed to
have settled in Lebanon, Conn.; married Abigail
Doty. Removed to Alford, Mass.
Children:

277. i. John,[5] b. about 1779.
278. ii. George, b. about 1781.
     iii. Polly, b. Nov. 26, 1782.
     iv. Mercy, b. March 8, 1784.
279. v. Elisha.
280. vi. Roswell.
     vii. Asenath.
281. viii. Ephraim, b. Jan. 16, 1791.
     ix. Delia.
     x. Betsey.

102

GERSHOM[4] (*Gershom,*[3] *Gershom,*[2] *Thomas*[1]), born
about 1749; married Jan. 17, 1773, Innocent Ellis.
Resided in Sandwich.
Children:

283. i. Jonathan,[5] bapt. Nov. 14, 1773.
282. ii. Joshua, bapt. Oct. 1, 1775.

FIFTH GENERATION.

120

STEPHEN[5] (*Thomas,[4] Thomas,[3] Thomas[2], Thomas[1]*), born in East Yarmouth (now Dennis), June, 28, 1741; died June 29, 1820; married first, Mercy ———; "Marcy, wife of Stephen Tobey," was admitted to the church June 27, 1772. He married second, Mary, daughter of Ebenezer and Mary (Allen) Paine, born March 22, 1756. [Paine Family Records.] See Revolutionary Rolls in Appendix. He was appointed guardian of Molly Tobey, May 14, 1795.

The widow died in 1831, leaving the following will :

WILL OF MARY TOBEY.

I, Mary Tobey of Dennis in the County of Barnstable, do make & ordain this my last will & testament in manner & form following, viz: I give and bequeath to Mary Doane in the town of Harwich in the County of Barnstable my niece, all my estate both real & personal that I shall possess at my death, after my lawful debts is paid. And I appoint, nominate & constitute Nathaniel Doane of said County, sole executor of this my last will & testament, hereby revoking all other & former wills by me at any time heretofore made. In witness whereunto I have set my hand & seal this eight day of April A.D. one thousand eight hundred & thirty-one.

Signed, sealed, published & declared by the said testator Mary Tobey as and for her last will & testament, in the presence of us, who have subscribed our names as witnesses thereto in the presence of the said testator.

Lucy S. Buck.   her
Sally Y. Doane.   MARY X TOBEY
Nathaniel Doane 3rd.   mark

Proved October 31, 1831.

Child :
>MARY, called also Molly and Polly, baptized in private June 18, 1785. [Church Record.]

121

KNOWLES[5] (*Thomas,[4] Thomas,[3] Thomas,[2] Thomas[1]*), born in East Yarmouth (Dennis), May 22, 1744. He d. Sept. 13, 1807.

His will dated Sept. 5, 1807, probated March 15, 1808 ; bequeathed to brother Stephen and his wife Polly; to brother Samuel and his children, specifying one of them—Thomas, whom he appointed executor.

122

SAMUEL[5] (*Thomas,[4] Thomas,[3] Thomas[2], Thomas[1]*), born in East Yarmouth (now Dennis), April 1, 1746; was remembered in his father's will in 1787; his sons were legatees of his brother Knowles in 1807. He married in Falmouth, Oct. 17, 1765, Rebecca Hatch. Was a town officer in 1767.

Samuel Tobey, residence Falmouth, enlisted Jan 20, 1777, and served three years, till Dec. 31, 1779, in Col. Benjamin Tupper's regiment of the Continental Army; was at West Point, April 5, 1779. Was named in the account of money paid officers and men of that regiment in 1780 for depreciation of (currency) their wages.

Children:
301. i. Thomas,[6] b. 1766.
302. ii. John, b. Nov. 5, 1768. [Hist. Union, Me.]

123

SETH[5] (*Seth,[4] Thomas,[3] Thomas,[2] Thomas[1]*), born in Dennis, Nov. 18, 1769; baptized Nov. 26, 1769;

married Ruth ———; she was admitted to the church
June 29, 1806.

He resided on the ancient farm which had been his
father's grandfather's homestead, and transmitted it
to his son.

He died Jan. 21, 1829. We are fortunate in having his will.

WILL OF SETH TOBEY.

In the name of God, Amen. I, Seth Tobey, of Dennis
in the County of Barnstable do on this twentieth day of
December in the year of our Lord one thousand eight hundred & twenty-eight make & publish this my last will and testament in manner following, viz :

In the first place I give & bequeath to my two daughters
Polly Howes & Hellen Matthews the sum of fifteen dollars
each to be paid them by Executor hereafter mentioned in
twelve months after my decease ; I also give to my two daughters Nabby Tobey & Rebecca Tobey in equal shares the improvement of the South half of my dwelling house, and all the
moveable furniture therein.   Also the improvement of one good
cow, together with one half of all my real estate, so long as
they live unmarried ; but in case of marriage or death the improvement above mentioned ceases.   And in case of marriage
in lieu thereof, I give them the same amount in furniture or
money as my other two daughters have had that is now married
with the legacy of fifteen dollars each ; but in case one marries
or deceases & the other not, the one living or unmarried I give
the whole improvement of the cow above mentioned & she retains the improvement of one half of the above mentioned property.

Lastly. I give and bequeath to my only son Jonathan
Howes Tobey, all the remainder of my estate that may hereafter be found, both real, personal or mixed at his sole use and
disposal.   I also appoint him my said son sole executor of this
my last will and testament. In testimony whereof, I have
hereunto set my hand & seal the day & year above written.
Signed, sealed & published by the said Seth Tobey, declaring
this to be his last will & testament in the presence of us who

at his request were called as witnesses to the same & in his presence did hereunto subscribe our names.

Oren Howes.   SETH TOBEY (L.S.)
Enoch Howes.
Charles Bassett.

Proved March 10, 1829.   [Bk. 47, p. 438.]

Children:

    i.   Polly⁶; m. ——— Howes.
    ii.   Helen; m. ——— Matthews.
303. iii.   Jonathan Howes, b. in 1794.
    iv.   Abigail (Nabby).
    v.   Rebecca.

130

ZIMRI,⁵ (*Silas,⁴ Ebenezer,³ John,² Thomas¹*), born at Falmouth, June 10, 1767; died Dec. 7, 1824, at Charleston, S. C.; married in Falmouth, Oct. 22, 1794, Nancy Wing, born at Sandwich, April 20, 1772, died at Falmouth, Feb. 8, 1855. He was a sea captain, "beloved and lamented; lived and died in peace with all mankind."

He left no will. Administration was granted to William Nye of Falmouth, February 8, 1826.

The Inventory shows real estate valued at $919, consisting of dwelling house and outbuildings (homestead at Falmouth) $700, and right and interest in the homestead of the late widow Bethiah Tobey in Falmouth, $167; also a pew in the West Congregational meeting house. Allowance was granted to the widow Nancy of $205.25, which was all the personal property.

Children:

    i.   ʻRebecca,⁶ b. Aug. 25, 1796.
307. ii.   John, b. March 28, 1799.
308. iii.   Silas, b. March 12, 1801.
309. iv.   Joseph, b. Feb. 8, 1803.
    v.   Alvin, } b. May 25, 1805; { d. June 9, 1806.
310. vi.   Reuben, }

vii. Sarah, b. Feb. 29, 1808.
311. viii. Henry, b. March 8, 1811.
      ix. Frances (Fanny), b. Sept. 2, 1813; d. Jan. 15,
           1891.

131

SILAS[5] (*Silas*,[4] *Ebenezer*,[3] *John*,[2] *Thomas*[1]), born in
Falmouth, April 21, 1776; married in Boston, May
27, 1804, Waitstill Felt.

Silas Tobey of Boston, cordwainer, deceased. Waitstill Tobey, the widow, administered and gave bonds
April 8, 1812, Otis Morton and Benjamin Felt sureties; the latter was appointed guardian to said Tobey's
sons under 14 years of age, namely James and Willard, April 20, 1812. Dower of land set off to the
widow.

The widow married second, Francis Parland, of
Boston, and sold land, out of which her "thirds" had
been reserved, July 23, 1813; Mr. Parland bought
back the land from the purchaser.

Children:

312. i.   James.[6]
313. ii. Willard.

132

JOSIAH[5] (*John*,[4] *Eleazer*,[3] *John*,[2] *Thomas*[1]), born in
Sandwich, Dec. 1, 1761; died at Pawlet, Vt., in 1843,
" aged 81 "; married Lydia Baker, born about 1763,
died in 1825, " aged 62." He removed to Falmouth,
thence about 1783 to Pawlet, Vt. Was a deacon of
the Baptist church; selectman 1803 and 1804. [Hist.
Pawlet].

Children:

315. i.   John[6].
316. ii.   Josiah.
317. iii. Zeno, d. in 1836, aged 32.

iv. Mercy; m. David Downs, of West Haven, Vt.
v. Betsey.
vi. Hannah.
vii. Lydia.

133

JOHN[5] (*John,*[4] *Ebenezer,*[3] *John,*[2] *Thomas*[1]), born in
Sandwich, Dec. 31, 1766; settled at Falmouth; died
March 21, 1849; married Patience ——, who died in
May, 1855. He was a town officer at various times.

Children:

318. i. Russell,[6] b. ——, 1797.
319. ii. Isaiah Nye.
iii. Mercy, b. Nov. 15, 1803; m. Jan. 14, 1830, Daniel
Hall of Dennis.
320. iv. John, b. April 5, 1807.
v. Patience, b. Dec. 21, 1813.
321. vi. Charles, b. May 1, 1816.
vii. Remember Nye.

134

REUBEN[5] (*John,*[4] *Eleazer,*[3] *John,*[2] *Thomas*[1]), born
in Sandwich, Feb. 3, 1769; removed to Pawlet, Vt.;
was one of the very early members of the Baptist
Church and one of the selectmen of the town, 1816–
1818. [Hist. Pawlet].

135

THOMAS HOWES[5] (*John,*[4] *Eleazer,*[3] *John,*[2] *Thomas*[1]),
born in Sandwich Oct. 1, 1770; died in 1825. Deacon
of the church. Married in Falmouth, March 7, 1799,
Thankful Crowell.

He was appointed administrator of the estate of his
mother Mercy Tobey, late of Sandwich, Dec. 17,
1807.

WILL OF THOMAS H. TOBEY.

In the name of God Amen. I Thomas H. Tobey of Sandwich in the County of Barnstable and State of Massachusetts. being at present weak in body but of sound mind, memory and understanding do make and publish this my last will and testament in manner and form following, to wit :

1st. I give and bequeath unto my beloved wife Thankful Tobey, the use and improvement of one half of all my real estate during the time she shall continue my widow and also during the said term the use of all my indoor household furniture. And also I give unto her all the property that came by her father to dispose of as she may think best and for the children I do give and dispose the custody and instruction of them and each of them unto my loving wife until such time as they and either of them respectively shall obtain the age of twenty-one years.

2dly. I give and bequeath unto my son Freeman C. Tobey the sum of one thousand dollars to be paid him on his becoming of full age and also my wearing apparel.

3dly. I give and devise all my Estate both real and personal wheresoever the same may be, consisting of lands, buildings, livestock, farm utensils, notes of hand and book debts,* he allowing his Mother the improvement of one half of my real estate and paying out the legacy in this my will given and finding for my Sister Rebecca Tobey fire wood and provisions according to the Will of her Father. Also paying my just debts, funeral charges and the charges of settling my estate and performing every condition in this my will mentioned. Furthermore I give and bequeath unto said Watson F. Tobey all my household goods after the improvement of my wife.

Finally. I nominate and appoint my loving wife Thankful Tobey sole Executrix of this my last Will and testament. In witness whereof I have hereunto set my hand and seal this twenty-ninth day of July in the year of our Lord one thousand eight hundred and twenty-five.   THOMAS H. TOBEY.

Signed, sealed, published and declared by the above named Thomas H. Tobey for his last will and testament in the presence

---

* He undoubtedly intended to say here " to my son Watson F. Tobey."

of us who have hereunto subscribed our names as witnesses thereto in the presence of the said Testator and of each other.

Clark Cornish.
Lot Adams.
Temperance Tobey.

Proved Nov. 8, 1825.　　　[Bk 45, p. 87.]

Children:
322. i. Freeman Crowell, b. May 8, 1806.
323. ii. Watson Ford, b. Feb. 10. 1809.

136

ELEAZER[5] (*John,*[4] *Eleazer,*[3] *John,*[2] *Thomas*[1]), resided in Falmouth; married Sally ———.
Children:
　　i. Hannah,[6] b. Dec. 21, 1804.
324. ii. Silvanus, b. Sept. 14, 1806.

137

JAMES[5] (*John,*[4] *Eleazer,*[3] *John,*[2] *Thomas*[1]), born in Sandwich, Jan. 4, 1778; married Dec. 2, 1804, Temperance Crowell of Falmouth. He died Dec. 15, 1855.
Child:
325. Josiah,[6] b. Aug. 31, 1808.

138

BENJAMIN[5] (*Seth,*[4] *Seth,*[3] *Nathan,*[2] *Thomas*[1]), born in Sandwich, Feb. 27, 1750; m. first, Aug. 4, 1774, Zeruiah Fish. He married second, at Wareham, Jan. 4, 1810, Sarah, daughter of Jeremiah Bumpus and widow of Anselm Swift. He was a resident of Sandwich some years; followed the sea; became a captain. Had a packet, running to Boston. Removed there after a time. Purchased land in Shirley, Worcester Co., in 1807, and made his home there for a short time; sold the land in 1811 and returned to Boston. Loaned

money on mortgages in 1812, one of which he released
after removing to Wareham, where he made his home
in 1815.

He was a private in Capt. Ward Swift's company,
allowed pay for secret expedition to Rhode Island in
Oct., 1777; *also* seaman on muster and pay roll of the
officers and crew of the state brig Hazard, Capt. John
F. Williams, July 10 to 14, 1778.

He and his wife Sarah made a deed of gift of certain lands to "their two youngest daughters, Sarah
Augusta and Abigail Ann Perry," April 21, 1823.

Children:

    i.   Hepzibeth,⁶ b. in Sandwich, Aug. 10, 1777; m. in
           1793, David Fearing.

326. ii.   Curtis, b. in Sandwich, July 26, 1779.

    iii. Abigail, b. in Sandwich, Oct. 25, 1781; died early.

    iv. Sarah Augusta, b. May 16, 1811; m. Sept. 9, 1829,
           Hamden K. Pratt, of Bridgewater.

    v.   Abigail Ann Perry, b. June 24, 1817.

140

WILLIAM⁵ (*Joseph,⁴ Nathan,³ Nathan,² Thomas¹*),
born in Sandwich, Mass., Sept. 9, 1759; removed to
Whitefield, Me. He married Mary Sylvester, of
Harpswell, Me., born May 21, 1761, died in Somerville, Me., Nov. 22, 1845. He was a tanner and shoemaker. He removed about 1807 to Jefferson, Me.;
bought a tan-yard and carried on the business of
making leather and boots and shoes. He was a soldier in the Revolution and drew a pension after the
war. He died Aug. 22, 1835. See Revolutionary
Rolls in Appendix.

Children:

    i.   William,⁶ b. in Whitefield, Me., June 20, 1783;
          was drowned May 25, 1795.

    ii. Susannah, b. Jan. 31, 1785; m. John Powell; d.
        Oct. 16, 1811.

329. iii. Joseph, b. July 14, 1787.
  iv. Mary, b. June 4, 1789; m. James Mason; lived in the vicinity of Sebec, Me.
330. v. Elijah, b. Sept. 4, 1791.
331. vi. Benjamin, b. Dec. 28, 1793.
332. vii. William, b. Sept. 24, 1796.
  viii. Abigail, b. July 2, 1798; m. Dec. 11, 1728, Samuel Trask (his first wife); had 4 children; lived at Chelsea, Me.; d. July 22, 1836.
  ix. Celia, b. May 1, 1801; d. Jan. 11, 1893; m. (1) Oct. 11, 1824, William Perham, who d. in Cuba; she m. (2) Aug. 2, 1842, John Trask. Child: Roselia Trask, b. Aug. 28, 1843; m. Feb. 9, 1862, Greenwood C. Smith, who d. June 12, 1892, and she m. Nov. 4, 1893, Henry Smith, a brother.
333. x. James, b. May 20, 1803.
334. xi. George, b. Sept. 8, 1805.

141

BARNABAS[5] (*Joseph,*[4] *Nathan,*[3] *Nathan,*[2] *Thomas*[1]), born in Sandwich, March 20, 1761; married in Falmouth, Sept. 26, 1781, Thankful Parker. Received a piece of land by the will of Barnabas (son of Gershom) Tobey in 1763, and was a legatee of his grandfather in 1787.

Barnabas Tobey was a private on muster and pay roll of Capt. Job Crocker's Co., Col. Nathan Sparhawk's regt., from July 2 to Dec. 12, 1777; service in Rhode Island and sundry places in Massachusetts; *also*, private in Capt. Joseph Palmer's Co. from May 16 to Nov. 16, 1779, stationed at Falmouth; *also*, on muster and pay roll of Capt. Matthias Tobey's co., Col. (late Colonel) Hallet's regt., from July 29 to Nov. 2, 1780; *also*, private on muster and pay roll from July 20 to Sept. 28, 1781, raised by vote of Falmouth for defence of town in Barnstable county; *also*, on a warrant to pay officers and men, borne on a roll bearing date Oct. 2, 1782; warrant drawn in favor of selectmen of Falmouth.

7

142

LEWIS[5] (*Joseph,[4] Nathan,[3] Nathan,[2] Thomas[1]*), born
in Sandwich, June 17, 1763; married first, at Rochester, Sept. 7, 1786, Abigail Bassett of R.; married
second, at Dartmouth (New Bedford), May 17, 1795,
Rebecca Ingraham of New Bedford.   He was a sea
captain.   He bought land in "New Bedford village"
14 Aug., 1795; bought another tract "the 12th day of
the 4th month," 1796, and sold land there 21 May, 1798.
    Children:

335. i.   Rodolphus H.,[6] son of Lewis and Rebecca Tobey,
          b. at New Bedford, Feb. 22, 1813 [Macy Gene-
          alogy].
336. ii. George.

143

TIMOTHY[5] (*Joseph,[4] Nathan,[3] Nathan,[2] Thomas[1]*),
born in Sandwich, Sept. 19, 1765; died Jan. 26, 1856;
married Patience Fish.   Lived and died on the farm
afterward occupied by his son Ansel.
    Children:

      i.   Nancy,[6] b. Nov. 24, 1795.
337. ii.   Nathan, b. Aug. 29, 1797.
     iii. Rebecca, b. Aug. 10, 1799.
338. iv.   Lewis, b. Sept. 4, 1801.
339. v.   Henry, b. Oct. 9, 1803.
340. vi.   Ansel, b. Feb. 27, 1806.
     vii. Celia, b. July 21, 1808.
341. viii. Joseph, b. April 10, 1810.
     ix.   Caroline, b. April 19, 1812.
342. x.   Charles, b. July 9, 1815. .

144

SYLVANUS[5] (*Joseph,[4] Nathan,[3] Nathan,[2] Thomas[1]*),
born in Sandwich, June 4, 1769; married Celia ———.
He was a blacksmith.   He made his will Oct. 28, 1813;

it was probated Nov. 9, following. He gave all his property to his wife Celia and daughter Sally.

Child:

Sally.⁶

149

WILLIAM⁵ (*William,⁴Samuel,³ Jonathan,² Thomas¹*), born in Sandwich about 1768; married Nancy Bennett.

Removed to Nantucket. About the year 1826 he removed to Boston. He was a sea-captain.

Children:

    i.   Mary⁶, b. April 28, 1795; m. Aug, 15, 1816, Robert Francis, born Oct. 24, 1791; removed to Barnstable, thence to Newington, Conn.

        Children :

          1. Charlotte Francis,⁷ b. July 11, 1817; m. Elisha Fairfield, of Middletown, Conn.

          2. Ann Francis, b. Nov. 17, 1818; d. March 14, 1832.

          3. Mary Francis, b. Nov. 2, 1820; m. Oct. 18, 1843, John Wm. Humphrey, of New Britain, Conn., b. March 14, 1820; whose dau. Martha Ann Humphrey, b. March 11, 1849, m. June 1, 1870, Algernon A. Aspinwall, of Washington.

          4. Lydia Francis, b. Nov. 5, 1823; m. John Webster, of Newington, Conn.

          5. Harriet Francis, b. Nov. 5, 1823; m. Levi S. Wells, of New Britain, Conn.

          6. Joseph Francis, b. Nov. 4, 1828.

          7. Charles B. Francis, b. Nov. 20, 1830.

          8. Valina Ann Francis, b. Jan. 5, 1833; m. Baltis Sigsbee, of Quincy, Del.

          9. Robert Francis, b. Oct. 17, 1835.

    ii. Harriet Francis; m. Truman Ripley Hawley, of Boston.

359. iii. Charles.

360. iv. George W.

     v. Edwin; d. unm.

150

TRISTRAM[5] (*William,[4] Samuel,[3] Jonathan,[2] Thomas[1]*), born August, 1774; married Clarissa, daughter of Paul and Rebecca Handy, born March, 1780, died June 29, 1860 (pub. at Falmouth March 9, 1800). He removed to Nantucket; died Feb. 5, 1854.

Children:

	i.	Lucy,[6] b. in Sandwich, Sept. 23, 1802; m. John Pitts.
	ii.	Elizabeth, b. in Sandwich, March 4, 1805; m. Archibald Ward, of New Bedford.
361.	iii.	Anselm H., b. in Sandwich, May 17, 1808.
	iv.	Caroline, b. Nov. 25, 1810.
362.	v.	Albert H., b. in Sandwich, March 14, 1813.

151

ARCHELAUS[5] (*William,[4] Samuel,[3] Jonathan,[2] Thomas[1]*), born in Sandwich, about the year 1782; married Sarah, daughter of Hezekiah Lambert, born about 1784, died March 1, 1869. They sold land in Sandwich, April 18, 1807, and afterward resided in Attleboro, Mass., and Cumberland, R. I., and spent their last days in Smithfield, R.I. He died Feb. 27, 1850.

Children:

362a.	i.	Betsey,[6] b. Oct. 8, 1804; m. Samuel Sweetland.
362b.	ii.	Sophronia, b. Sept. 7, 1806; m. Daniel Bowen Fish.
363.	iii.	William, b. June 20, 1810.
364.	iv.	George A., b. about 1812.
365.	v.	James Hail, b. about 1817.
366.	vi.	Joseph, b. about 1821.
367.	vii.	Samuel, b. about 1824.

152

FRANKLIN[5] (*William,[4] Samuel,[3] Jonathan,[2] Thomas[1]*), born in Sandwich; married at New Bedford,

Oct. 13, 1805, Phebe Jenne. He was a sea-captain,
and died in a brief time after his marriage. His estate was settled in February, 1807, his widow administering. She married second, Elisha Tobey (No.
242).

159

ZENAS[5] (*Matthias,[4] Samuel,[3] Jonathan,[2] Thomas[1]*),
born about 1771; went with his father in his youth to
Machias, and resided the remainder of his life at the
Port.

160

ELISHA[5] (*Matthias,[4] Samuel,[3] Jonathan,[2] Thomas[1]*),
born in Sandwich about 1773; married first, Hannah
Phinney; she died May 17, 1827, aged 47 years; he
married second, Sarah Wilson, who died April 6, 1861,
aged 76 years. He was a carpenter. He went as a
child to Machiasport, Me., with his father, and spent
his life there. He died Dec. 20, 1855, aged 83 years.

Children:

368. i.   Samuel.[6]
ii. Hannah, b. Nov. 14, 1801; m. March 31, 1823,
William Sanborn, b. Aug. 8, 1799; they removed
to California; he d. in Watsonville, Oct. 14, 1864;
Mrs. Sanborn d. Oct. 22, 1846. See Sanborn
Genealogy for children.
369. iii. Elisha.
iv. Betsey, m. Samuel Small.
v.   Jane, b. May 6, 1809; m. John F. Sanborn, b.
Aug. 25, 1807. See Sanborn Genealogy for
children.
370. vi. Charles, b. Sept. 17, 1812.
vii. Mary, m. Charles W. Gates.

161

MATTHIAS[5] (*Matthias,[4] Samuel,[3] Jonathan,[2] Thomas[1]*), born in Sandwich, 1774; removed as a boy with

his parents to Machias, Me.; married Pamelia Anderson. He resided in Machiasport.

Matthias Tobey appears as a private on a pay abstract of Capt. Simeon Fish's company, Col. Freeman's regiment, for 5 days' service on alarm at Falmouth, September, 1779, by order of Brigadier Otis. Young as he was at the time, this person is doubtless Matthias Tobey, Jr.

Child:

Temperance,[6] m. Benjamin Crocker.

163

STEPHEN[5] (*Stephen*,[4] *Samuel*,[3] *Jonathan*,[2] *Thomas*[1]), born in Lee, Dec. 20, 1782; married there, July 7, 1805, Miriam Dickinson.

164

NATHANIEL[5] (*Stephen*,[4] *Samuel*,[3] *Jonathan*,[2] *Thomas*[1]), born in Lee, Feb. 17, 1788; married at Lee, Oct. 18, 1813, Polly Bassett, hailing from Unidella, N. Y., to which he had removed.

175

LEMUEL[5] (*Thomas*,[4] *Jonathan*,[3] *Jonathan*,[2] *Thomas*[1]), born in Rochester, July 20, 1781; died at New Bedford, June 27, 1850; married (intention in New Bedford, Dec. 7, 1805) Elizabeth (Betsey) Fales, daughter of Thomas Baylies and Elizabeth (Fales)* Richmond, born in Dighton, Oct. 14, 1783, died at Lakeville, March 28, 1855 ; administration of her estate was granted to Ebenezer Nye, Jr., July 3, He sold (his wife joining in the deed) Dec. 8, 1838, to Ebenezer and Francis Nye and Job T. Tobey of Rochester, " land and real estate which belonged to my late father Thomas Tobey, which is situated in the village of

* Elizabeth Fales was daughter of Judge Samuel Fales of Taunton.

Mattapoisett," etc. He was a sea captain. He resided some time at Mattapoisett, removing in later
years to New Bedford.

Children:

381. i.   Charles Richmond,⁶ b. in Dighton, April 21, 1806.
382. ii. Henry Fales, b. May 24, 1808.
     iii. Theodore, b. Aug. 18, 1810; d. Oct. 5, 1854.
     iv. Matthew, b. March 26, d. Aug. 15, 1813.
     v.   Elizabeth Fales, b. Feb. 19, 1816; d. June 19, 1894;
          m. May 15, 1836, Amos K. Crowell. No children.
     vi. Maria, b. Sept. 2, 1818; d. April 13, 1876 ; m.
          Dec. 29, 1842, her cousin, Job Townsend Tobey.

176

ISAAC SMITH⁵ (*Thomas,⁴ Jonathan,³, Jonathan,²
Thomas¹*), born Jan. 19, 1785; married Rachel ——.
Resided in Rochester. Sold land there in 1812, his
wife Rachel signing the deed with him. He and his
son Job T. were legatees in the will of his father in
1829.

Child:

383. Job Townsend,⁶ b. about 1816.

187

STEPHEN⁵ (*Joshua,⁴ Cornelius,³ Samuel,² Thomas¹*),
born in Sandwich, May 6, 1755. He was living at the
date of his father's will in 1794. He married in New
Bedford, March 11, 1798, Almy Bennett. She was a
daughter of Edward Bennett of Fair Haven, who bequeathed $25.00 to his "daughter, Amity Tobey" in
his will dated 16 Jan., 1808, and proved 3 Nov. 1812.
For further account see No. 384.

He was private on muster and pay roll of Capt. Joshua
Tobey's co., Nov. 20, 1775; served 1 month, 13 days; roll
sworn to in Middlesex Co., Jan. 18, 1776.

"Stephen Tobey" appears in a list of men belonging to

Sandwich; age 25 years; enlisted Feb. 1, 1777; term of enlistment during war; joined Capt. Killam's co., Col. Putnam's
(5th) regt.; list dated at West Point, Jan. 10, 1781. He
was enlisted into the Continental Army from the Barnstable
company of Col. Nathaniel Freeman's (1st) regt., and joined
Capt. Benjamin Brown's co. of Col. Putnam's regt.; *also*, on
pay accounts of Capt. Gardner's co., same regt., for service
from Jan. 1, 1777, to Dec. 31, 1779, claimed by Attleborough,
but awarded by committee for settling disputes between towns
to Sandwich. [Compare with No. 56.]

188

NATHAN[5] (*Joshua,*[4] *Cornelius,*[3] *Samuel,*[2] *Thomas*[1]),
born in Sandwich, Feb. 1, 1757; married in Rochester,
Sept. 2, 1792, Lucy Thatcher of Wareham, where he
had gone to reside.   She died April 26, 1802.

Nathan Tobey, seaman, on portledge bill of the officers and
crew of the sloop Republic, Capt. John Foster Williams, Aug.
26 to Nov. 18, 1776; *also*, Nathan Toby, Jr., private on
muster and pay roll of Capt. Simeon Fish's co. of Col. Freeman's regt., Sept. 8, 1778; service on alarm at Dartmouth
and Falmouth; *also*, private on pay abstract of Capt. Simeon
Fish's co of Col. Freeman's regt., for 5 days' service, marched
on alarm at Falmouth, Sept. 1779, by order of Brigadier Otis.

He learned the trade of tailor, and removed to Brookfield, where he bought a tract of land July 2, 1782,
and sold it April, 17, 1784.   He removed to Wareham and was a trader there in 1793; removed to Lee,
where he spent the rest of his days.   He died about
the last of September, 1805; Roland Thatcher administered on his estate.

Children:

i.   Eliel,[6] b. at Wareham, May 26, 1793; d. at Lee,
      Dec. 29, 1809, aged 16; "the last member of
      the family." [Lee Records.]
ii.   Joshua, b. do. June 13, 1795; d. May 10, 1796.

189

LEMUEL[5] (*Joshua*,[4] *Cornelius*,[3] *Samuel*,[2] *Thomas*[1]), born at Sandwich, May 12, 1760, married in Boston, June 22, 1787, Martha Williams, daughter of Rev. Abraham Williams, of Sandwich. Was a sea-captain; commanded large vessels and went on long voyages to the East Indies and elsewhere. Later he removed to Farmington, Me., where he died.

"Lemuel Toby" was a marine, on muster and pay roll of the ship Mars, Capt. James Nevins, from April 18 to June 12, 1781: roll dated at Boston.

Children:*

385. i. Lemuel,[6] b. March 31, 1788, at Sandwich.
386. ii. Robert William, b. Sept. 21, 1789, at Sandwich. Died young.
387. iii. Charles Henry, b. May 7, 1791, at Sandwich. He transacted business in Northampton and Hadley, still residing in Farmington, Me.; 7 Feb., 1867, being unmarried, he quitclaimed land which had belonged to Erastus Smith of H.
388. iv. William W., b. at Farmington, Me., in 1796.
      v. Caroline Williams, b. July 19, 1800; d. May 6, 1826; m. Nov. 7, 1818, Asa Abbott, b. in Sidney, Me., Nov. 7, 1793; d. at Farmington, Me., Feb. 16, 1863.

Children:

   1. Martha Caroline Hephzibah Abbott, b. Sept. 18, 1819; m. May 9, 1837, Samuel Belcher, Esq., of Farmington.

   Children:

      (1) Samuel Clifford Belcher, b. Mar. 20, 1839; m. Jan. 19, 1869,

---

* Märtha Catherine Tobey, b. in Farmington, Me., Sept. 16, 1820; m. April 21, 1842, George Sproul of Waldoboro, Me., b. April 23, 1800. [Sproul Family Record, in Gen. Adv., Sept., 1901,]

Ella Olive, daughter of Spaulding and Sarah (Rich) Smith of Wilton, Me.

(2) Anna Gill Belcher, b. 1841, d. 1842.

(3) Abbott Belcher, b. March 17, 1843.

(4) William Fuller Belcher, b. March 13, 1845; m. Oct. 6, 1869, Clara A. T., daughter of Daniel and Emily (Ela) Beedy.

(5) Fuller Belcher, b. Sept. 13,1852: d. June 24, 1852.

(6) Hamilton Abbott Belcher, b. Aug. 18, 1854.

(7) Mary Caroline Belcher, b. July 25, 1856; m. Oct. 24, 1878, James Hayes Waugh.

(8) and (9) d. in infancy.

2. Caroline Abbott, b. 1820, d. 1821.

3. Alexander Hamilton Abbott, b. Sept. 14, 1822; grad. Bowdoin College in the class of 1840; became principal of Farmington Academy. In 1849 he took the Little Blue Family School for Boys, which had been established by Rev. Samuel Phillips Abbott and made still more famous by having as its principal the distinguished minister and author Rev. Jacob Abbott. Under Mr. Alexander Hamilton Abbott the school grew in size and reputation; gathered many talented boys and fitted them for college or for business. Mr. Abbott was greatly valued by the community for his scholarly and friendly qualities, and his high character.

4. William Tobey Abbott, b. May 22, 1824; a merchant, resided in Farmington until 1854, when he removed to Fort Wayne, Ind.

190

CORNELIUS[5] (*Joshua,*[4] *Cornelius,*[3] *Samuel,*[2] *Thomas*[1]), born in Sandwich (not recorded), mentioned by his father in his will in 1794.

191

HEMAN[5] (*Cornelius,*[4] *Cornelius,*[3] *Samuel,*[2] *Thomas*[1]), born Dec. 11, 1763; resided in Sandwich. Married first, Elizabeth ——. She d. July 1, 1810. He married second, Sarah P——, who survived him. See Revolutionary Rolls in Appendix. He died in 1833.

WILL OF HEMAN TOBEY.

Be it remembered that I Heman Tobey of Sandwich in the County of Barnstable & State of Massachusetts Citizen do hereby make & ordain this my last Will and Testament, revoking all others.

And I hereby make the following disposal of my worldly goods after my decease, being now of sound & disposing mind & memory, viz : I give and bequeath to my Daughter Deborah, the sum of One thousand Dollars; to my Daughter Lucy the sum of One thousand Dollars; to my Grandson Sylvanus Nye son of my daughter Polly the sum of Five hundred Dollars when he shall arrive at the age of twenty-one years, in case he should arrive at that age. I give & bequeath to my children Thomas, Deborah & Lucy all my furniture in the house equally excepting my Clock, Desk & Book case, which I give to my son Thomas. I give and bequeath to my son Thomas all my real and personal estate of whatever name or nature forever provided he pays the above legacies. I hereby constitute & appoint my son Thomas sole Executor to this my last will & testament. In witness whereof I have hereunto set my hand and seal at said Sandwich, this fifth day of January in the year of our Lord eighteen hundred and thirty-three.

HEMAN TOBEY (L. S.)

114   TOBEY GENEALOGY.

Signed, sealed, published & declared by the testator for his
last will & testament in presenec of us

Melatiah Bourne.
Samuel Fessenden.
Ezra Tobey.

Proved May 1833.   Bk. 53, p. 235.

Children:

    i.   Deborah,⁶ b. May 26, 1789.
400. ii. Thomas Allen, b. Sept. 13, 1791.
  iii. Polly, b. Feb. 10, 1795; m. —— Nye.
  iv. Lucy, b. July 26, 1798.

192

MELITIAH⁵ (*Cornelius,⁴ Cornelius,³ Samuel,² Thomas¹*), born in Sandwich, Feb. 8, 1766; married in
Falmouth, Dec. 23, 1790, Mary, daughter of Stephen
and Hannah Crowell, born May 15, 1764, died July
11, 1845.   He died Nov. 28, 1851, aged 85 years 9
months.

Children:

  i. Lois,⁶ b. Sept. 12, 1791; d. Oct. 16, 1794.
  ii. Hannah, b. June 16, 1793; m. (1) June 23, 1814,
     Ebenezer Crocker 3d, of Barnstable; he d. July 1,
     1818.   She m. (2) May 30, 1819, Seth, son of
     Lemuel and Mary Pope, b. May 29, 1786, d.
     March 13, 1863.   She d. Feb. 3, 1885.   He was
     a farmer.

     Child of Ebenezer and Hannah (Tobey) Crocker:
     Ebenezer Crocker, b. Dec. 12, 1816; d. Jan. 24,
     1843.

     Children of Seth and Hannah (Tobey, Crocker) Pope:
     1. Charles Edward Pope, b. July 11, 1820; a far-
     mer; he m. Feb. 15, 1851, Harriet L. Bourne;
     she d. Feb. 11, 1902, aged 76 years, 10
     months, 8 days.

Children :

(1) Hannah Louise Pope, b. Dec. 15, 1851.
(2) Clarence Edward Pope, b. Sept. 24, 1856.
(3) Carrie Bourne Pope, b. Oct. 22, 1861.
(4) Charles Thomas Pope, b. Aug. 20, 1863.

2. Eunice Bourne Pope, b. April 13, 1822.
3. Ezra Tobey Pope, b. Aug. 27, 1825; m. Nov. 8, 1849, Abby S. Gibbs; she d. June 30, 1879, aged 52 years. He has been doorkeeper of the Mass. House of Representatives 20 years; resides in Sandwich.

Children :

(1) Francis Edward Pope, b. Aug. 24, 1850.
(2) Seth Freeman Pope, b. July 19, 1852; d. Jan. 28, 1884.
(3) Abby Gibbs Pope, b, March 16, 1854.
(4) Eben Crocker Pope, b. Dec. 31, 1855.
(5) Eugene Russell Pope, b. Sept. 28, 1857.
(6) Alice Estelle Pope, b. June 5, 1861.
(7) Annie Tobey Pope, b. March 1, 1863.
(8) Augustus Russell Pope, b. Oct. 12, 1866.
(9) Ezra Tobey Pope, Jr., b. March 2, 1868.

4. Francis Pope, b. March 6, 1828; a painter; resides in Boston. He m. Aug. 1, 1864, Augusta A. Davis; she d. July 30, 1894, aged 63 years.
5. An Infant, b. Aug. 20, 1830; d. soon.
6. Hannah Pope, b. Aug. 14, 1832.
7. Frederick Seth Pope, b. Sept. 19, 1834; newsdealer; resides in Sandwich; was postmaster 26 years. He m. Dec. 22, 1870, Martha E. Towle, of Great Falls, N. H.

Children :

(1) Frederick Seth Pope, Jr., b. Jan. 13, 1875; grad. Dartmouth Coll. 1897; superintendent of schools in Sandwich.
(2) Elsie Marie Pope, b. April 6, 1879; a school teacher.
(3) Ilda Towle Pope, b. April 7, 1883; studied at Bridgewater Normal School; is teaching (1902) at S.

401. iii. Ezra, b. Sept. 1, 1796.
402. iv. Joshua, } b. June 23, 1803; } d. Jan. 3, 1804.
     v. Elisha,
     vi. Mary Crowell, b. Aug. 7, 1806; m. May 26,1809,
         Rev. Warren Goddard, a Swedenborgian minis-
         ter, long at Brockton; she d. July 4, 1847.
     vii. Louisa, b. May 26, 1809, d. July 1, 1810.

193

JOSHUA[5] (*Cornelius,*[4] *Cornelius,*[3] *Samuel,*[2] *Thomas*[1]),
born in Sandwich, Aug. 5, 1772; married first—"of
Hudson, N. Y.",— at Wareham, March 19, 1796,
Hannah Fearing, of W. He married second, Dec. 1,
1799, Abigail, daughter of Thomas and Hannah (Stur-
gis) (Jennings) Bassett, born April 12, 1778. He
was then of Fairfield, Conn.

He resided at Farmington, Me., about two years,
and there his son Robert was born; returned for a
time to Sandwich, but later removed again to Hudson, N. Y., where he died Feb. 22, 1814, according to
the family record of his brother Melitiah.

Children:

    i. Mary (Polly)[6], b. Feb. 2, 1800; m. Nov. 27,
        1828, James H. Faunce; she d. June 3, 1869.

    Children:

        1. Abigail T. Faunce, b. Jan. 3, 1830; m. April
           29, 1852, James Thompson; she d. May 8,
           1854.
        2. Elizabeth Faunce, b. Aug. 8, 1831; d. June
           22, 1833.
        3. Joshua T. Faunce, b. Oct. 21, 1833; m. Oct.
           23, 1858, Harriet Thompson.
        4. Robert T. Faunce, b. Jan. 11, 1836; d. March
           5, 1857.

403. ii. Robert, b. Oct. 30, 1801.
404. iii. William, b. Sept. 24, 1807.
     iv. Abigail, b. May 4, 1811.

194

ELISHA[5] (*Cornelius,[4] Cornelius,[3] Samuel,[2] Thomas[1]*), born in Sandwich, Feb. 2, 1777; married first in Dorchester, April 16, 1801, Sally, daughter of John Humphreys, Jr., and Susannah Champney, his wife, born Oct. 6, 1781; she died Jan. 30, 1802. He married second, Elizabeth ———, who survived him and died Jan. 15, 1853, aged 73.

He was a tanner. He was drowned May 28, 1817.

Children:

   i.   Sally Humphrey,[6] b. Jan., 1802.
   ii. Elisha, b. Feb., 1805.
  iii. Jacob, b. Feb. 10, 1806; d. Aug. 1829.
  iv. Elizabeth Whittemore, b. Oct. 7, 1808.
   v. John Himan, b. April 6, 1809; d. Oct. 19, 1809.
  vi. John, b. May 5, 1811; d. Aug. 22, 1829.
 vii. Caleb, b. Dec. 6, 1813.
viii. Louisa Abigail, b. Jan. 24, 1816.
  ix. Lois McEven, b. Nov. 6, 1817.

195

LEMUEL[5] (*Elisha,[4] Cornelius,[3] Samuel,[2] Thomas[1]*), born Feb. 27, 1748–9. "Lemuel Tobey of Dartmouth and Elizabeth, daughter of Thomas and Thankful (Dillingham) Pope, were published Dec. 3, 1777, married Jan. 1, 1778."

Lemuel Tobey was 1st Lieutenant, on muster and pay roll of Capt. Thomas Crandon's company; enlisted July 15, 1775; served 5 months, 19 days. This is probably only a portion of the service he rendered. The title "gentleman," used by him in deeds, etc., after the Revolution, was based upon the fact of his having been a commissioned officer.

He exchanged with his brothers Elisha and William lands inherited from their father, Elisha, 1789–1791.

Lemuel of New Bedford, gentleman, with wife Elizabeth, sold land March 17, 1794, and in 1803. He afterward removed to Fairhaven. After his death the widow sold a house and lands to her son-in-law Thomas T. Terry.

Lemuel Tobey of Fairhaven made will March 25, 1820, probated Dec. 5 following; bequeathed to wife Elizabeth; son Elisha; daughter Sally, wife of Thomas Terry, blacksmith, of New Bedford; and to grandson Lemuel Terry. The widow Elizabeth made will March 4, 1824; probated Jan. 5, 1835; bequeathed to son Elisha; grandson Charles; daughter Sarah Terry; granddaughter Elizabeth Terry.

Children:

i.   Charles,ᵇ b. about 1779; d. in Dartmouth Jan. 19, 1811 [L]. He was a trader; his estate proved insolvent; his brother Elisha administered upon it March 5, 1811.

ii. Sally, b. Nov. 17, 1780; d. Dec. 20, 1835; m. in New Bedford, Sept. 19, 1802, Thomas T. Terry, b. Dec. 11, 1779, d. Dec. 27, 1827.

     Children :

     1. Elizabeth Pope Terry, b. June 2, 1803; d. Oct. 19, 1821.
     2. Thomas Pope Terry, b. July 6, 1805; d. March 18, 1883.
     3. Isaac Terry, b. July 25, d. Sept. 3, 1807.
     4. Lemuel Tobey Terry, b. Oct. 3, 1809; d. April 5, 1865.
     5. Charles Tobey Terry, b. March 28, 1811.
     6. Isaac Terry, b. July 15, d. July 25, 1813.
     7. Isaac Terry, b. Nov. 17, 1815; d. July 28, 1883.
     8. Sally Terry, b. Dec. 17, 1817; d. Sept. 3, 1822.

406. iii. Elisha, b. about 1784.

196

WILLIAM[5] (*Elisha,*[4] *Cornelius,*[3] *Samuel,*[2] *Thomas*[1]), born March 20, 1755-6; married in Boston April 15, 1782, Abigail Conant of Boston, who died Jan. 29, 1846, aged 83 years. She was a daughter of Samuel and Rebecca (Coffin) Conant of Charlestown, baptized June 20, 1762.

William Tobey of New Bedford, merchant, executor to the will of his father Elisha Tobey, late of New Bedford, sold, 11 Nov. 1797, land in Greenwich, Hampshire co., which had been conveyed by Cornelius Tobey to Elisha. [See Nos. 21 and 62.]

He was a merchant; he sold to his brother Lemuel, July 4, 1791, land which he had inherited from his father Elisha Tobey. He and his wife sold land in New Bedford, 2 June, 1790, to Mary Conant. He was the first postmaster of New Bedford, appointed in 1794, and served till 1806. [See Revolutionary Rolls in Appendix.] He died Jan. 5, 1833. His will, dated May 10, 1832, probated May 5, 1833, bequeathed his property to his wife Abigail, daughter Abby Parker, son William C., and his children William H., Frederick A. and Eliza; guardian was appointed for Eliza July 30, 1833. The widow Abigail made her will March 7, 1835, proved June 2, 1845, bequeathing to her daughter Abigail Parker and her son William C. Tobey.

Children:

    i.   Abigail,[6] m. June 9, 1812, Avery, son of John Avery Parker.

407. ii.   William C.

197

ELISHA[5] (*Elisha,*[4] *Cornelius,*[3] *Samuel,*[2] *Thomas*[1]), born in Dartmouth (New Bedford), Jan. 18, 1764; married July 16, 1784, Hannah Negus.

8

Elisha Tobey was a private on the muster and pay roll of Capt. Thomas Crandon's company, Col. John Hathaway's regiment, for service at Rhode Island on an alarm; service from Aug. 2 to Aug. 8, 1780, six days.

Elisha Tobey, private, on muster and pay roll of Capt. Isaac Pope's company, Col. Wm. Shepard's regiment (the 3[d] Mass. regiment), enlisted for 9 months, July, August, October, 1778; Jan. 5, 1779, on a certificate of service given by Capt. Isaac Pope, who certifies that the above-named Elisha Tobey, who was drafted into Capt. Nathaniel Hammond's co. in 1778, has now joined his company; also on rolls for March and April, 1779.

He was a joiner, and also (seems to be the same man) a mariner. Resided at New Bedford; sold his share of lands inherited from his father Elisha Tobey to his brother Lemuel, July 6, 1789, his wife Hannah signing with him; also to his brother William; bought land of Freeman Pope, Jan. 5, 1800.

Child:

> John,[6] b. Dec. 20, 1784; "John Tobey, son of Elisha and grandson of Doct. Elisha Tobey died in Jamaica." [Town record in 1802.]

198

Dr. CORNELIUS[5] (*Elisha,*[4] *Cornelius,*[3] *Samuel,*[2] *Thomas*[1]), born in Dartmouth, July 10, 1768; married Nancy ———.

He became a physician; resided in Freetown. After his death the widow administered on his estate, and Nov. 3, 1807, was appointed guardian of the children, Elizabeth W. and Frederick, being above the age of 14, and Elisha N. younger. She made her will Sept. 11, 1832, her son Frederick conveying his expected share of the estate to his sister the next day. Upon her death the document was admitted to probate Feb. 4, 1834, bequeathing her property to the three children.

Children:
i. Elizabeth Wilbore,* b. about 1792; m. Isaac Newton Hathaway.
   Children:
   1. Ann M. Hathaway; m. Gilbert Hinds.
   2. Frederick T. Hathaway.
   3. Elizabeth G. Hathaway.
   4. Harriet D. Hathaway.
   5. Irene Hathaway.
409. ii. Frederick, b. about 1794.
410. iii. Elisha Newcomb, b. about 1796.

199

ZACCHEUS[5] ($Zaccheus$,[4] $Zaccheus$,[3] $Samuel$,[2] $Thomas$[1]), born 1757; married (published in Dartmouth, Jan. 9, 1778) Mary Gifford. It is certain that he removed to Conway, and then to Butternuts, Otsego Co., N. Y.

Zaccheus Tobey of Conway, yeoman, sold, 22 Nov., 1790, to Peleg Gifford, now of Conway, lately of Sandwich, land and buildings in Conway.

Children, order not known:
412. Samuel.*   414. Christopher.
413. Levi.   415. Zaccheus.
     Deborah, m.   Harriet.
     James Sloane.*   Lucy.

201

ZOETH[5] ($Zoeth$,[4] $Zaccheus$,[3] $Samuel$,[2] $Thomas$[1]), born in Dartmouth, Sept. 15, 1764; married in New Bedford, Feb. 15, 1791, Sarah West, born July 7, 1770; (she survived him and married second, Peter Wheelock, and third, John Gray). He removed about 1792 to Wardsboro, Vt., and in 1799 to Calais, Vt., where he carried on a farm. From 1805 to 1810 resided in Eastern New York, but returned to Calais, where he spent the remainder of his life, dying March 16, 1812.

Children:
i. Elizabeth,* b. about 1791; m. in 1814, David Dag-

* Information of T. A. Sloane, of Colorado Springs, Colo., a grandson.

gett, b. 1778 in Charlton, Mass. Lived in Calais
and Montpelier, Vt. He d. in 1861; she in 1862.
Children :
1. Eli Daggett, b. 1815; d. young.
2. Polly W. Daggett, b. 1818; m. Isaac
   Chipman.
3. Maria K. Daggett, b. 1820; m. Thomas
   B. Muldoon.
4. Lyman Daggett, b. 1822; m. Mary E.
   Belding.
5. Avery T. Daggett, b. 1824; m. Mary J.
   Corwin.
6. David J. Daggett, b. 1827; m. Kate
   Reddy.
7. Delia F. Daggett, b. 1831; m. John R.
   Cooley.
8. Lizzie Daggett, b. 1833; m. John M.
   Gunnison.

419. ii.   Avery,[6] b. 1796.
     iii. Polly, b. 1798; m. first, in 1820, Alexander White.
           Children :
           1. Sarah Maria White, b. 1822.
           2. Amanda R. White, b. 1827, d. 1866. She
              m. second, Jeremiah Comins, b. in Charl-
              ton, Mass., in 1787; d. 1833; she d.
              1855.
420. iv.   Richard West, b. 1800.
     v.   Zoeth, Jr.; d. young.
421. vi.   Allen, b. 1805.

203

ELIJAH[5] (*Prince,*[4] *Zaccheus,*[3] *Samuel,*[2] *Thomas*[1]),
born in Dartmouth, Jan. 31, 1767; removed with his
father to Conway; married Sarah ———. Removed
to Ashfield.

He made his will April 3, 1813; it was proved Aug. 27,
1822. Bequeathed to his wife Sarah $600 in annual payments
of $100 each; his household furniture excepting his desk, mon-
eys on hand and other articles specified, and the use of his house
and lands while she should remain his widow. To his brothers

Elisha and Benjamin Tobey, and his sisters Deborah Faxon, Elizabeth Godard, Sarah Holloway and Pamelia Holloway, and to the heirs of his sister Jane Bond, two dollars each. His desk, when his wife shall cease to be his widow, to go to the eldest son of his brother Elisha; $50 to Lovina Lyon. The residue to The Massachusetts Baptist Missionary Society, committing it to the hands of Elders Jesse Hartwell of New Marlborough and Asa Todd of Chesterfield, whom he made executors of the will.

204

ELISHA[5] (*Prince,[4] Zaccheus,[3] Samuel,[2] Thomas[1]*), born in Conway, Feb. 22, 1779; went in 1792 to Philadelphia, Pa., where he remained till 1802, when he removed to Springfield, Mass. He was an ironworker, making at first fire-shovels and tongs, afterwards manufacturing firearms. He entered at length the service of the U. S. government; became an inspector, doing his office at Millbury, Ludlow, Chicopee, Middletown, Conn., and other places. Was a thorough mechanic. He was appointed deputy sheriff in 1812 by the first sheriff of Hampden county. Was a prominent Free Mason. He married first, Mrs. Mary Ann Gambier of Philadelphia, Pa.; she died in Springfield. He married second, Sophia Chapin Ferrey, granddaughter of Enoch Chapin, born April 8, 1788, died Aug. 24, 1859. In her will, dated 19 April, 1848, she bequeathed all her possessions to her son Josiah G. Tobey.

Mr. Elisha Tobey died June 29, 1840. His estate was administered upon, and guardianship of the two youngest children granted to his son-in-law Clark B. Stebbins.

Children:

422. i.   Joseph,[6] b. at Philadelphia, Pa., March 12, 1802.
    ii.   Jane, b. at Springfield, Feb. 4, 1804; m. Rev. Mr. Hyer of Carlisle, Pa.; a son, Wilbur Hyer, is a physician in Alabama.

iii. Margaret, b. Dec. 12, 1808; m. Clark B. Stebbins
      of Wilbraham; moved West; d. at Peoria, Ill.
423. iv. William.
     v. Mary A. C., b. Feb. 22, 1810; grad. Wilbraham
         Academy; became a teacher; d. at Memphis,
         Tenn.
424. vi. Henry, b. March 31, 1813.
    vii. Sophia Chapin, b. April 19, 1815; grad. Springfield
          Ladies' Seminary, and went South as a teacher;
          m. A. S. W. Goodwin, a successful manufacturer
          at St. Louis, Mo.
   viii. Elizabeth Godard, b. July 12, 1817; grad. Wilb.
          Acad.; taught at the South; d. in Springfield.
425. ix. Warren Delano, b. Jan. 24, 1819.
426. x.   George, b. Nov. 17, 1820.
427. xi. Josiah Godard, b. Sept. 4, 1822.
428. xii. Elisha, b. Jan. 26, 1826.
   xiii. Sarah, b. and d. in Sept., 1827.
    xiv. Sarah Elizabeth, b. Oct. 27, 1828; d. at St. Louis,
          Mo.
429. xv. Edward Everett, b. Oct. 17, 1832.

205

BENJAMIN[5] (*Prince,*[4] *Zaccheus,*[3] *Samuel,*[2] *Thomas,*[1]),
born in Conway, Jan. 23, 1781; married Deliverance
——. He resided at Conway. Bought and sold considerable land; was one of the executors of the estate
of his father; conveyed land in that capacity July 22,
1814, his wife Deliverance and his mother Jane signing the deed also.

"A child of Benjamin Tobey died May 25, 1813,
aged 3 days." [Conway record].

206

HERMAN[5] or HEMAN[5] (*Noah,*[4] *Zaccheus,*[3] *Samuel,*[2]
Thomas[1]), born in Ballston, Saratoga county, N. Y.;
the family after some years removed to Ohio.

Children:

430. i. William,' b. March 3, 1805.
431. ii. Henry, } b. June 6, 1810.
     iii. Melinda, }
     iv. Rosanna, b. March 12, 1812; m. Aaron Shirk.
        Children: 1. John Shirk. 2. Heman Shirk.
        3. Sarah Shirk. 4. Melinda Shirk.
432. v. Harlow, b. Nov. 12, 1819.
433. vi. Samuel, b. Dec, 16, 1821.
434. vii. Charles F., b. Jan. 29, 1823.
     viii. Emeline, } b. July 27, 1824.
     ix. Angeline, }
     x. Jane, b. Dec. 10, 1825; m. Alonzo Knox. Chil.:
        William Knox. Jane Knox. Priscilla Knox.
     xi. Amanda, b. June 10, 1828.

211

JOHN⁵ (*Jonathan,⁴ Jonathan,³ Samuel,² Thomas¹*),
born in Dartmouth, Aug. 31, 1779; died May 16,
1816; married (published in New Bedford, Aug. 10,
1804) Fanny, daughter of Capt. Levi and Molly
Rounsville; died Jan. 6, 1849. He was a carpenter;
resided at Freetown. Bought land in "Pocasset pur-
chase, so-called," 19 Feb. 1808. Bought land in New
Bedford in 1806 which the widow Fanny sold in 1829.
He made his will April 19; it was proved June 4,
1816; gave his estate to his wife Fanny, daughters
Nancy, Sally, Fanny and Mary, and son Rounsville.
The widow removed to Fall River, and sold New
Bedford land 4 Sept., 1821, and Freetown lands, 11
Feb., 1839.

Children:

   i. Nancy.⁶
   ii. Sally.
   iii. Fanny.
   iv. Mary.
435. v. Rounsville.

212

SILAS[5] (*Jonathan,*[4] *Jonathan,*[3] *Samuel,*[2] *Thomas*[1]), born in Dartmouth, Aug. 23, 1781; died "at Hudson, N. Y., March 17, 1816, aged 34 years" [Dart. rec.]; married Elizabeth (Betsey) Hardwick or Hendrick. Captain state militia, Columbia co., N. Y.

Child:

436. Silas,[6] b. 1813.

213

JONATHAN[5] (*Jonathan,*[4] *Jonathan,*[3] *Samuel,*[2] *Thomas*[1]), born in Dartmouth, July 12, 1787; married Hannah, daughter of Nathaniel and Hannah (Keene) Sears, born Jan. 23, 1792, died Aug. 12, 1872.

Mr. Sears was a man of energy and carried through some large enterprises. He owned a great deal of land and farmed on an extensive scale. He took the contract for and built the turnpike from Taunton; his house was the first stopping-place for the stages on the way out from New Bedford, a distance of seven miles from the center. Afterward he raised the bed of the road and much improved it, involving himself, however, in heavy litigation on account of the official obstructions placed in his way. His life was strenuous. He died Sept. 4, 1870.

Children:

i.   Stephen Sears,[6] b. Aug. 18, 1811; became a successful and intelligent man; did not marry; died March 28, 1874.

437. ii.   William Henry, b. June 18, 1813.

iii.   Hannah Sears, b. Nov. 1, 1815; m. May 5, 1833, George Vaughan, of Middleboro'; he d. March 19, 1875.

Children:

1. George Francis Vaughan, b. 1835.

2. Augustus Everett Vaughan, b. Nov. 14, 1837; res. in Watertown; a commercial traveller.

3. Hannah Othalia Vaughan, b. 1839; m. Jared
    Henry Beebe, of Springfield. Children: (1)
    J. Harry Beebe, (2) Arthur Franklin Beebe,
    (3) Albert Augustus Beebe.

iv. Emeline Harwick, b. May 23, 1818; m. Nov. 29,
    1838, Horatio, son of Nehemiah and Hannah
    Tinkham (Clark) Leonard, of New Bedford, b. in
    Middleboro July 10, 1816, d. July 4, 1880. The
    family reside at Malden.

Children:
1. Ellen Maria Leonard.
2. Horatio Herbert Leonard.
3. Stephen Henry Leonard.
4. Emma Jane Leonard.
5. Laura Anna Leonard.
6. Alice Tobey Leonard.
7. Clara Chatman Leonard.
8. Arthur Leonard.

438. v. Leonard White, b. Jan. 29, 1821.
      vi. Sarah, } b. Dec. 1, 1823; { d. March 29, 1826.
      vii. Alice, }   { d. in 1850.
      viii. Jane Frances, b. July 10, 1826; m. Samuel Ivers,
           of New Bedford.
      ix. Laura Ann Bartlett, b. Dec. 5, 1828; d. March 30,
           1849.
439. x. Jonathan Franklin, b, July 23, 1831.
      xi. Elizabeth Lewis, b. Nov. 30, 1833; d. Oct. 16,
           1841.

214

MARCHANT[5] (*Jonathan,*[4] *Jonathan,*[3] *Samuel,*[2] *Thomas*[1]), born in Dartmouth, April 3, 1791; married Maria Spring; she died in 1860.

He was a housewright in early and middle life.
Lived in Uxbridge till about 1833, when he removed
to Worcester; was a member of the school committee
there in 1837, and had other positions of trust. He
died July 24, 1839.

His will was made July 2, 1839, and was filed Aug. 6, 1839. He bequeathed his estate to his wife until her marriage or decease; then to be divided equally between his children, Sarah Ann, William Merchant, Maria Antoinette, Jane Eliza and Isaac Franklin. Emory Washburn, executor.

After a few years the widow returned to Uxbridge, and there died. Her estate was settled by P. Whitin Dudley at the request of the heirs, Oct. 30, 1860.

Children:

    i.   Sarah Ann[6]; m. in Worcester, Oct. 19, 1842, P. Whitin Dudley, of Uxbridge.

440. ii.   William Merchant.

   iii.   Maria Antoinette.

   iv.   Jane Eliza; b. 1833; d. in Boston, Jan. 6, 1904.

    v.   Isabella G., b. 1832; d. in Worcester, March 1, 1837.

441. vi.   Isaac Franklin, bapt. at Central Church, Worcester, Aug. 11, 1839.

215

WILLIAM ISAAC[5] (*Jonathan,[4] Jonathan,[3] Samuel,[2] Thomas[1]*), born in Dartmouth, July 6, 1793; died Aug. 1, 1825; married first, Nancy Taber; married second, Ruby Simmons; married third, —— Howland.

He was "lost at sea, in Lat. 36, 40 N. & Long. 67, 30 W." [Family record of his father.]

Child:

    i.   Eliza H.[6]; m. June 3, 1847, Harrison Loring, of Boston.

216

CORNELIUS[5] (*Jonathan,[4] Jonathan,[3] Samuel,[2] Thomas[1]*), born in New Bedford, May 26, 1796; married Ardinia Pollock. Removed to Cincinnati, O., and died there.

218

ABISHAI HUXFORD[5] (*Jonathan,[4] Jonathan,[3] Samuel,[2] Thomas[1]*), born in New Bedford, Sept. 5, 1804; died April 18, 1837; married Hannah Nye, daughter of Joseph and Hannah (Dillingham) Terry, born June 5, 1806; she died in Hyde Park, Feb. 10, 1887.

He was a tanner and currier and manufacturer of boots and shoes. Removed to Rochester about 1830.

Children:

  i.   William Isaac,[6] b. in Fairhaven, Jan. 26, 1827 ; died unmarried, about 1851.
  ii. Priscilla Juliette, b. Jan. 4, 1829; m. George Brayton. Child, Myra Merrill Brayton, b. Dec. 28, 1860, m. April 6, 1887, Charles Henry Morss, supt. of public schools at Medford. Children: (1) Edward Bond Morss, b. May 16, 1864, m. Mrs. Helen Nash; (2) Lucy Maria Tobey Morss, b. Oct. 13, 1868, d. Oct. 22, 1904.
  iii. Martha Burgess, b. May 14, 1831 ; d. Oct. 12, 1898.
  iv. Lucy Maria, b. Nov. 11, 1833.
443. v.   Joseph Terry, b. June 7, 1836.

219

Seth[5] (*Seth,[4] Jonathan,[3] Samuel,[2] Thomas[1]*), born about 1779; resided in Fairhaven. Stephen Merrihew administrator of his estate May 1, 1822.

220

EBENEZER WILLIAMSON[5] (*Seth,[4] Jonathan,[3] Samuel,[2] Thomas[1]*), born in New Bedford. Removed to Boston. Was a tailor; married Eunice ———.

222

SAMUEL[5] (*Samuel,[4] Eliakim,[3] Samuel,[2] Thomas[1]*), born [about 1773]; married in Jan. 1800, Caroline Martin, of Bristol, Me.; she died at Providence, R.I.,

July 16, 1842; "aged 74 years." He resided some time at Fairfield, Me.; died at Bristol, Me., March, 1814.

Children:

    i.   Martin,⁶ b. Jan. 1801; d. at Edenton, N. C., Feb., 1816, aged 16 years.

    ii.   Edward, b. May, 1802; died at Vassalborough, Me., Sept. 1812, aged 10 years.

445. iii.   William Henry, b. Feb. 13, 1804.

446. iv.   Samuel Boyd, b. Nov. 12, 1805.

223

ELIAKIM⁵ (*Samuel,⁴ Eliakim,³ Samuel,² Thomas¹*), born in Sandwich, Jan. 25, 1776; married first, Dec. 15, 1796, Experience Ellis, born July 23, 1776, died Sept. 6, 1814. He married second, Dorcas Clark of Norridgewock, Me.

He died Oct. 25, 1857.

Children (order not known):

    i.   Lydia.⁶

448. ii.   Heman, b. June 27, 1800.

        Cynthia, b. 1802.

449. iii.   Jonathan Ellis, b. 1804.

    iv.   Celia, b. 1806.

    v.   Elvira, b. 1809.

450. vi.   Edward.

451. vii.   John.

451ᵃ. viii.   George.

451ᵇ. ix.   Milton.

    x.   Lydia.

225

NATHANIEL⁵ (*Samuel,⁴ Eliakim,³ Samuel,² Thomas¹*), born in Fairfield, Me., in 1780; resided at Norridgewock, Me.; died in Boston, Dec. 31, 1870, aged 91; was buried at Fairfield.

Child:

452.   James H.,⁶ b. in Norridgewock, Me., June 14, 1810.

229

JONATHAN BURR[5] (*William,*[4] *Eliakim,*[3] *Samuel,*[2] *Thomas*[1]), born in Sandwich, May 30, 1794; married ———.

His children Hannah and William were legatees of his mother in 1828.
Children:

    i. Hannah.[6]
453. ii. William.

230

APOLLOS[5] (*Samuel,*[4] *Samuel,*[3] *Samuel,*[2] *Thomas*[1]), born in Berkley, Sept. 15, 1770; married Feb. 18, 1796, Hannah, daughter of Abel Crane, of Berkley, who made a deed of land to her May 23, 1800. She died Dec. 28, 1843.

He was a merchant; a man of unusual ability and worth; representative to the General Court (legislature) a number of years. He died in 1841.
Children:

454. i. Apollos,[6] b. April 9, 1798.
455. ii. Samuel, b. Dec. 4, 1799.
    iii. Eliza, b. Oct. 29, 1801; m. as his second wife, Dea. Barzillai Crane of Berkley, afterward of Assonet; d. at the age of 81.
456. iv. Charles Courtsworth Pinckney, b. June 10, 1803.
457. v. Caleb Strong, b. May 10, 1806.
    vi. Caroline Amelia.

231

ENOCH[5] (*Samuel,*[4] *Samuel,*[3] *Samuel,*[2] *Thomas*[1]), born in Berkley, Nov. 5, 1778; married, Nov. 21, 1801, Sarah (Sally), daughter of Ambrose and Philena Barnaby, of Freetown, born Oct. 31, 1780, died Oct. 8, 1820. [Barnaby Family.] He carried on extensive business. His trip-hammer, forge, blacksmith-shop, etc., were referred to in the deeds of adjacent properties.

He died before May 8, 1818, when his widow was appointed administratrix of his estate and guardian of the children; the lands, shop, houses and other real estate were appraised at $6,264.97. After the death of the widow, Rev. James Barnaby was appointed the children's guardian and administrator of her estate.

Children:

i. Sally.[*]
461. ii. Samuel Elam.
462. iii. Enoch.
   iv. William; he d. in his minority, and his estate was settled by Joseph D. Hathaway, July 5, 1833.
464. v. Jonathan Bowen.
   vi. Catherine; she d. Dec. 19, 1836, and Stephen Barnaby was administrator of her estate Jan. 3, 1837.

232

SILAS[5] (*Samuel*,[4] *Samuel*,[3] *Samuel*,[2] *Thomas*[1]), born in Berkley, March 21, 1787; grad. Brown University in 1807; married, Feb. 26, 1811, Betsey, daughter of Jabez Fuller, M.D., of Kingston, born Sept. 25, 1789, died June 17, 1878.

IN MEMORIAM. CAPTAIN SILAS TOBEY.

"Died of yellow fever, at Point Petre, Guadaloupe, Jan. 31, 1817, Capt. Silas Tobey, of Kingston, Plymouth County, Mass., aged thirty years, captain of the brig Prince Eugene, belonging to his father, Hon. Samuel Tobey of Berkley. Seldom does society receive a deeper wound, and the social and domestic circle a more distressing loss, than is inflicted by the untimely fate of the deceased. Endowed by nature with a clear and discriminating judgment, an ardent and open temper, which were matured, and improved by a liberal education and an extensive intercourse with mankind, he seemed peculiarly qualified to discharge the various duties, and participate in the numerous joys which spring from the civil and social relations. And those to whom he was known can testify how well, while he lived, he fulfilled the high expectations of his acquaintance, and how fully he gratified the joyous hopes of his relatives and friends. Alas! these fond hopes and expectations have become blighted only by his premature death. Though he had resided but a few years in Plymouth County, perhaps there never was an instance of a person of his age so soon attracting the notice of the virtuous and respectable, and enjoying general confidence and respect. . . . He passed through life with honor, and left behind him a name remembered with affection and respect. But while we lament his untimely fate as a loss to the community, we are aware there are those on this occasion whose loss is too great to be described, and whose sorrows are too deep and too sacred to be revealed.

"For him no more the blazing hearth shall burn,
Nor tender consort wait with anxious care;
No children run to lisp their sire's return,
Nor climb his knee, the envied kiss to share."

The widow married second, Phineas Sprague, being his second wife; his daughter, Hannah Brown Sprague, two years old at the time of his second marriage, became the wife of her son.

Child:

465. Edward Silas,⁶ b. April 5, 1813.

233

SILAS⁵ (*Timothy,⁴ Samuel,³ Samuel,² Thomas¹*), date and place of birth unknown. Residing in Conway, May 6, 1816, he sold a tract of land there. He removed to Caledonia, Genesee County, N. Y., and sold Sept. 26, 1819, a part of the farm which "his father Timothy Tobey" left at his decease to Samuel Tobey of Conway. The latter would appear to have been his brother. Later he removed to Oakfield in the same county, and sold a tract of land in Buckland, Mass., Sept. 6, 1843.

235

ALVAN⁵ or ALVIN⁵ (*Nathaniel,⁴ Samuel,³ Samuel,² Thomas,¹*) born in Berkley, May 20, 1778; graduated from Brown University in 1799; became a Baptist minister. Married Tirzah Hoar. He died in 1810.*
Child:
466. Alvan,⁶ b. at Wilmington, Vt.,April 1, 1808.

235a

NATHANIEL⁵ (*Nathaniel,⁴ Samuel,³ Samuel,² Thomas¹*), born January 4, 1784; married (published in Berkley, Jan. 1, 1806) Eunice Pierce. He removed to Caroline, Tompkins Co., N. Y.; residing there, Oct. 20, 1837, he and his wife Eunice sold land in Middleborough, Mass., formerly owned by his father, Nathaniel Tobey, late of Berkley, Mass.

237

WILLIAM⁵ (*Isaac,⁴ Samuel,³ Samuel,² Thomas¹*), born in Dartmouth, Feb. 23, 1773; married Zilpha Hall; was sometimes called Williams and sometimes William; had land in "that part of Conway which formerly belonged to Shelburne" and sold it Feb. 6, 1806, his wife joining with him in the deed. Sold other land in that vicinity in 1811. Mrs. Tobey died July 21, 1847, "aged 67 years, a native of Taunton." "Capt. William Tobey" died Dec. 30, 1852, "aged 80 years." [Conway Rec.]
Children, recorded at Conway:
　　i.　Ardelia,⁶ b. April 8, 1805.
　　ii.　Lydia Williams, b. July 5, 1806.
　　iii.　Ruth Emeline, b. Sept. 9, 1809.
　　iv.　Abigail Hall, b. June 3, 1811.
　　v.　Sarah Fisk, b. Feb. 22, 1813.
　　vi.　Rowena, b. Oct. 11, 1815.

* On presumptive grounds alone we place this family here.

vii. Mary Ann, b. Sept. 26, 1817.
viii. Fanny Dean, b. June 5, 1820; m. April 1, 1844,
     Daniel Rice.
" A child of William Tobey died Sept. 23,1817."

238

JOHN[5] (*Isaac,*[4] *Samuel,*[3] *Samuel,*[2] *Thomas*[1]), born
in Barre, Jan. 17, 1785; married first Sibyl —, who
died April 10, 1849, æ. 64; mar. second, July 5, 1849,
widow Eunice S. Forbes. He died before Sept. 30,
1850, when his widow asked that Samuel Tobey of
Buckland be appointed administrator; he was also appointed guardian to Sibyl A. and Edwin L. Tobey,
above the age of 14, and Josephine M. Carrier under
14, grandchildren and heirs of the deceased, May 15,
1860.

Charles H. Tobey with Olive N., his wife, of Byron,
Kent Co., N. Y., and John Williams Tobey, of Dover,
Cuyahuga Co., Ohio, joined with other heirs in a quit-
claim deed of their rights in the Carlton Farm in
Buckland (one half of which had been formerly men-
tioned in the inventory of John Tobey's estate),
April 3, 1860.

Children:
467. i. Charles H.[6]
468. ii. John Williams.

240

SYLVANUS[5] (*Sylvanus,*[4] *Thomas,*[3] *Samuel,*[2] *Thomas*[1]), was born about 1763.

He was a private on the muster and pay roll of Capt. Henry
James' company, service at Rhode Island on an alarm from
March 14th to 18th, 1781.

He was published at Dartmouth, May 22, 1785, to
Ruth Hammond. He learned the trade of housewright. Removed to Uxbridge; joined the church,
Dec. 3, 1786; bought land there, 2 May, 1789. Re-
9

moved to Bellingham; sold land in New Bedford to
Zaccheus Tobey of that place, June 23, 1788, his wife
Ruth also conveying her right of dower in the land.
Children:

469. i.   Thomas,* b. Jan. 4, 1788.
    ii.   Polly, b. Nov. 9, 1789; "a child of Sylvanus and
          Ruth Tobey," d. Feb. 18, 1790.
    iii. Sally, b. July 29, 1792.

241

LUKE[5] (*Thomas,*[4] *Thomas,*[3] *Samuel,*[2] *Thomas*[1]), born
in Fairhaven, May 13, 1780; married first, Nov. 3,
1805, Desire, daughter of Jethro Jenney of Acushnet,
born April, 1781; died July 19, 1818. They lived
some years in the old Jenney homestead. He married
second, Elizabeth, daughter of Samuel and Joanna
(Gilbert) Hathaway, born in Taunton, April 9, 1789.
He had two children that grew up by the first wife,
and five by the second. He resided in Acushnet.
He died Sept. 26, 1865. His will, dated Dec. 16,
1859, was proved May 4, 1866. He gave life use of
the estate to his wife, she to dispose of it to the children at her death according to her judgment.

Mrs. Elizabeth H. Tobey died April 12, 1876. She
made her will Oct. 2, 1874; bequeathed one half of
her pew in the Methodist Church to her grandchildren, the other half to the church; made bequests to
her daughter Charlotte A. Lewis and the children of
her late son Henry.
Children:

      i.   Phebe,* m. John Shaw of Fairhaven.
470. ii.   Thomas.
471. iii. Charles F.
     iv.   Charlotte Augusta, m. May 28, 1851, George N.
           Lewis, who d. at sea Sept. 6, 1854; she d. in
           Fairhaven, Nov. 12, 1892.

472. v. Henry A.
473. vi. Frederick.
474. vii. Nathaniel.

242

ELISHA,[5] (*Thomas,*[4] *Thomas,*[3] *Samuel,*[2] *Thomas*[1]),
born in Fairhaven in 1781; married in New Bedford,
April 7, 1808, Phebe, daughter of Jethro Jenney, sister of Desire, who married Elisha's brother Luke;
she was born in 1788; married first, Capt. Franklin
Tobey (No. 152) who died in 1807. She survived
her second husband, and died in 1868, aged 80 years
and two months.

Mr. Elisha Tobey was a carpenter and farmer; resided in Acushnet. He died Nov. 22, 1866, aged 85
years, 11 months and 16 days.

Children:

    i.   Celia J.,[*] b. in 1809; m. Nov. 12, 1845, Jethro
        Taber of Fairhaven, b. 1801, d. Aug. 22, 1872;
        she d. Nov. 17, 1881.

    ii.   Dorothy, b. 1812; m. Willard Mason, b. 1800, d.
        1855; she d. Dec. 9, 1878.

    iii. Maria Jenney, b. March 2, 1817; m. Nov. 1853,
        Asa Lothrop, of Yarmouth; he d. Dec. 19, 1879,
        aged 75 years, 22 days. She d. Dec. 26, 1902.
        Mrs. Lothrop kindly furnished many particulars
        relative to this branch in 1902.

475. iv. Elisha, b. 1821.

    v.   Patience, b. 1819; d, March, 1896; m. Capt. John
        Brayton of New Bedford; he d. at sea of heart
        disease. She m. (2) Capt. Edward Weeks of
        Nantucket.

    vi. Mary F., b. 1824; d. May 16, 1900; m. April 8,
        1846, Zenas Whittemore of N. B., who d. in
        1872, aged 75.

    vii. Phebe, b. 1826, d. of consumption July 25, 1860;
        m. Peleg Allen of Little Compton, R. I. He d.
        of consumption, March 23, 1867.

476. viii. Stephen, b. Nov. 10, 1828.
477. ix. Franklin.

261

JONATHAN[5] (*Elisha,*[4] *Ephraim,*[3] *Gershom,*[2] *Thomas*[1]), born in Sharon, Conn., in 1766. Removed to Alford, Mass., where he died June 12, 1832, " of cancer, aged 76 years." He married first, Polly Dyer; he married second, ——— Pratt; he married third, ——— Hatch; he married fourth, widow Anna (Hill) Dodge.

Children:

490. i. Jonathan Pratt,[6] b. Dec. 5, 1793.
491. ii. Augustus.
492. iii. Elisha L.
493. iv. William R.
    v. Harriet Sophronia, b. 1814; married Augustus R. Stoddard; died Dec. 25, 1842.

262

BARNABAS[5] (*Elisha,*[4] *Ephraim,*[3] *Gershom,*[2] *Thomas*[1]), born in Sharon, Conn.; married first, Lucinda, daughter of Dea. Joseph Lander of Sharon. He married second, Mrs. Abbie (Hurd) Pray.

He was one of the first members of the Protestant Episcopal Church of Sharon in 1829.

Children:

494. i. Erastus.[6]
495. ii. Henry.
496. iii. Albert.
497. iv. Heman.
498. v. Orville, b. (of second wife).
    vi. John E.; married, but left no children; resided in New York City, and was associated in business with Orville.

263

SYLVANUS[5] (*Elisha,*[4] *Ephraim,*[3] *Gershom,*[2] *Thomas*[1]), born March 16, 1773; died June 21, 1840;

married in Sharon, Conn., July 26, 1792, Irene, daughter of John Foster, born June 28, 1775, died in West Stockbridge, Mass., Jan. 9, 1855. He went with his father's family to Alford, Mass., where he was a farmer and merchant. Later he removed to West Stockbridge Center.

Children, born in Alford:

     i.   Clymena,[6] b. Feb. 9, 1793; d. 1873.

499. ii. Chester Field, b. July 30, 1795.

    iii. Alma, b. Nov. 27, 1798; d. July 25, 1841; m. Eli Barnes.

    iv. Selina, b. July 7, 1803; d. March 8, 1851; m. Ethan Van Dusan.

500. v.   John Foster, b. Dec. 2, 1811.

501. vi. Henry Marshall, b. May 16, 1816.

265

ELISHA[5] (*Elisha,[4] Ephraim,[3] Gershom,[2] Thomas[1]*), born in Sharon, Conn., Sept. 16, 1798; died at Morris, N. Y., April 22, 1877; married Lorania or Laura Hulburt; lived in Alford, Mass. Married second, Hannah B. ———, born Feb. 21, 1802, who died at Morris, May 22, 1890.

Children:

    i.   Louise[6]; m. ——— Kimball.

    ii. Angeline; m. ——— Benedict.

   iii. Whitfield; left no issue.

   iv. Harry.

266

EPHRAIM[5] (*Elisha,[4] Ephraim,[3] Gershom,[2] Thomas[1]*), born at Sharon, Conn., Dec. 20, 1774; died Jan. 24, 1812; married Zady Prindle, born April 5, 1777. She survived him, and married second, Sept. 13, 1813, Capt. Ebenezer Pope, of Great Barrington (by whom she had three children, John Pope, Harriet Pope and Seth Griswold Pope). She died Feb. 5, 1864.

Children:

i. Susan,⁶ b. March 20, 1800; d. Nov. 4, 1893.
ii. Zady, b. Jan. 21, 1802; d. Aug. 25, 1873; m. Nov. 14, 1821, Loring G. Robbins, b. 1797, d. 1886.

Children :

1. Mary Robbins.
2. Henry Tobey Robbins.
3. Eugene H. Robbins, b. Jan. 9, 1840; resides at Pittsfield, Mass.; firm of Robbins, Gamwell & Co., iron pipe, boilers, engines, etc.

502. iii. Egbert Prindle, b. Feb. 4, 1804.
503. iv. Henry Villars, b. March 18, 1806; d. Oct. 29, 1854; m. Elizabeth ――――; removed to Kentucky.
v. Mary Louise, b. April 3, 1808; d. June, 1884; m. ―――― Ball; child Mary Ball, m. Ed. Brainard.
vi. Elisha, b. June 15, d. Nov. 10, 1810.

268

ABRAHAM⁵ (*Jesse,⁴ Ephraim,³ Gershom,² Thomas¹*), born in 1766; married Jerusha Pomeroy. Settled at West Stockbridge; was a farmer; died Sept. 20, 1847, " aged 81 years "; administration of his estate Nov. 5, 1847. Jerusha died March 28, 1852, aged 80.

Children:

504. i. Pomeroy,⁶ b. Dec. 8, 1790.
505. ii. Hylon, b. March 31, 1793.
iii. Harlowe, b. Dec. 9, 1794; d. Oct. 13, 1798.
iv. Grove, b. Nov. 9, 1796; d. Oct. 18, 1798.
v. Minerva, b. Aug. 3, 1799.
506. vi. Frederick, b. Feb. 12, 1801.
507. vii. Abraham, b. 1805.
viii. Jerusha, b. 1807; m. ―――― Edwards, of West Stockbridge.
ix. Albert; died of yellow fever; unmarried.
508. x. Franklin.

269

JESSE[5] (*Jesse,[4] Ephraim,[3] Gershom,[2] Thomas[1]*), born in Norfolk, Conn., Aug. 14, 1772; married in Jay, N. Y., Submit Ward, born in Dover, Dutchess Co., N. Y., Aug. 3, 1780. Settled in Jay, N. Y., with a number of Connecticut people; owned two large farms in Champlain; " accumulated a fine property; built many good houses." He also speculated somewhat in New Hampshire lands. " Jesse Tobey, of Jay, Essex Co., N. Y., husbandman, for $590, sold 50 acres in Epsom, N. H., to Jonathan Yeaton, of the same, May 15, 1811; land was purchased of James Blake who had bought it of Thomas Jenness." [Exeter Deeds 193, 222.] He last lived in the brick house recently occupied by his granddaughter, Miss Anna H. Tobey. He was six feet high, energetic and forceful. Seven children lived to grow up and have families. He died May 29, 1848.

Children:

	i.	Clarinda,[6] b. April 8, 1799.
509.	ii.	Jesse, Jr., res. Jay, N. Y., d. æ 57 yrs.
	iii.	Laura.
	iv.	Lorinda.
	v.	Submit Ward.
	vi.	Anna.
510.	vii.	George Gibbs.
	viii.	Pierpont.
	ix.	Deliverance.
	x.	Caroline.
	xi.	Adeline.

270

JOB GIBBS[5] (*Jesse,[4] Ephraim,[3] Gershom,[2] Thomas[1]*), born about 1774; married (published at West Stockbridge, May 19, 1800) Electa Reese.

Child:

512. Franklin Reese,[6] b. July 4, 1802.

276

GEORGE[5] (*George,*[4] *Ephraim,*[3] *Gershom,*[2] *Thomas*[1]), born Aug. 23, 1785; married first, June 18, 1815, Aurelia Smith; she died May 12, 1819. He married second, April 16, 1820, Betsey White, who died Jan. 17, 1865.

Children:

520. i. John S.[6]
521. ii. Miles B., b. Feb. 20, 1821.
522. iii. George R., b. June 1, 1823.
523. iv. Starr, Dec. 18, 1825.
524. v. Philander, b. April 16, 1831.
     vi. Alta, b. in 1833.
525. vii. Acil, b. Jan. 9, 1838.
     viii. Emma E., b. June 18, 1841; m. Oct. 5, 1858, Morton P. Fitch.

281

EPHRAIM[5] (*Ephraim,*[4] *Ephraim,*[3] *Gershom,*[2] *Thomas*[1]), born in Lebanon, Conn., Jan. 16, 1791; died Sept. 1, 1844; married, Nov. 9, 1815, Lucy, daughter of Dr. Uriel and Deborah (Fay) Montague, (who removed from Sunderland, Mass., to New Hartford, N. Y., about 1798); she was b. Sept. 1, 1794, and died Sept. 1, 1844.

He resided at first in Canaan, Conn., and then removed to Madison County, N. Y.

Children:

     i. Delia Thirza (or Theresa[6]), b. Sept. 3, 1816; d. July 15, 1830.
526. ii. Henry Richmond, b. Sept. 1, 1818.
     iii. Lorenia M., b. Dec., 1820; d. March 25, 1862.
     iv. Lucy Ann., b. May 13, 1823; d. Dec. 7, 1866.
527. v. Uriel Montague, b. May 20, 1826.
     vi. Myron H., b. Nov. 16, d. Dec. 21, 1830.
     vii. Louise Theresa, b. Sept. 8, 1833; d. Jan. 21, 1883.
528. viii. Charles Clinton, b. Dec. 31, 1835.

SIXTH GENERATION.

302

JOHN[6] (*Samuel*,[5] *Thomas*,[4] *Thomas*,[3] *Thomas*,[2] *Thomas*[1]), born in Falmouth, Mass., Nov. 5, 1768; married first, June 13, 1791, Mary, daughter of George and Mary (Chase) West, born at Tisbury, Dec. 11, 1772, died Aug. 27, 1832. He married second, July 5, 1835, widow Melicent Wingate, daughter of Thomas Jones, an Englishman, born at Hancock, N. H., Aug. 17, 1796. He was a sea-captain; "retired from sea-going on account of great deafness." Settled at Union, Me., in 1791.

Children:

    i.   Rebecca,[7] b. Jan. 17, 1793; m. (1) Nov. 10, 1810, Calvin Chase, from Warwick, Mass., a storekeeper in Union, Me.; removed to Mirimachi, N. B., where he died; she m. (2) Thomas Chase, brother of Calvin, and lived at Warwick, Mass.

    Children:

        1. Mary Chase, b. Sept. 27, 1811; m. —— Martin; res. Hallowell, Me.
        2. William Witt Chase, b. Aug. 22, 1813.
        3. Alameda Chase; d. at Mirimachi.
        4. Emily Chase (child of Thomas and Rebecca).
        5. Elvira Chase.
        6. Almira G. Chase, b. Dec. 25, 1826; m. —— Woodbury; res. at Royalston.
        7. Edward Chase.
        8. Martha Chase.

    ii. Polly (alias Mary), b. Jan. 16, 1795; d. at Gardiner, Me., Nov. 5, 1831; m. John Palmer.

    Children:

        1. Gilman Palmer; m. Mary Brown, of Salisbury, Mass.; res. Lancaster, Mass.

2. John Palmer; d. young.
3. Nathaniel Tobey Palmer, M.D.; res. Brunswick, Me.; m. Mary Merritt, dau. of Capt. Wm. Curtis, b. May 8, 1812.
4. Mary Palmer; m. Richard Webster, of New Vineyard, Me.; removed to Hampton, Ill.
5. Eliza Jane Palmer; m. ――― Palmer.
6. Augustus Palmer; m. Mary Sanford; res. Bath, Me.
7. Dudley Palmer.
8. Harriet Palmer.

535. iii. Nathaniel, b. July 21, 1796.
    iv. Love, b. July 26, 1798; m. April 24, 1831, Seth Miller; she d. Nov. 28, 1838.
    v. Eliza, b. May 3, 1800; m. Nov. 13, 1818, John Stevens; d. June 5, 1837.
    vi. Jane West, b. May 25, 1802; m. Stephen Carriel, 1827.
    vii. Lydia, b. April 26, 1804; d. Feb. 12, 1835.
    viii. John, b. March 8, 1806; d. of consumption April 8, 1828.
536. ix. Edward, b. Feb. 19, 1808.
    x. Caroline, b. and d. 1810.
    xi. Harriet, b. July 8, 1811; m. Dec. 22, 1833, Wm. C. Jackson.
    xii. Caroline, b. June 10, 1813; m. in 1835, Leander Martin; res. Jefferson, Me.
537. xiii. Leander, b. Sept. 17, 1815.

303

JONATHAN HOWES[6] (*Seth*,[5] *Seth*,[4] *Thomas*,[3] *Thomas*,[2] *Thomas*[1]), son of Seth Tobey and Ruth, daughter of Capt. Jonathan Howes, was born in Dennis, in 1794. He lived on the ancestral farm, a quiet, useful life, training his children well; prepared them to go out into the world and accomplish larger things. Was much interested in town and school affairs. He was spared to a good age, dying Jan. 15, 1872. He married Rachel, daughter of Samuel Bassett, of Barn-

THE TOBEY FARM, DENNIS, MASS.

stable, and granddaughter of Capt. Elisha Bassett.
By the courtesy of his son, Mr. Frank Bassett Tobey,
we are able to present a remarkably realistic view of
the "old homestead" about which so many interesting
associations linger.

Children:

538. i.   Seth,⁷ b. 1827.
539. ii.   Charles, b. 1831.   ¹
540. iii. Frank Bassett, b. Sept. 15, 1833.

311

HENRY⁶ (*Zimri*,⁵ *Silas*,⁴ *Ebenezer*,³ *John*,² *Thomas*¹), born in Falmouth, March 4, 1811; died April
19, 1888; married Nancy D. ————; she died at
Lynn, April 29, 1871.

Children, born in Falmouth:

i.   Henry Jackson,⁷ b. Nov. 12, 1836; d. April 17,
      1837.
ii.   Alice Weston, b. April 6, 1838; d. April 23, 1839.
iii. Alice Weston, b. July 1, 1840; m. Jan. 1, 1860,
      Dr. John H. Mackie. [See Spooner Genealogy.]
iv.   Harriet Foster, b. April 9, 1843; d. at Georgetown,
      D. C., June 20, 1848.
v.   Julia T., b. Oct. 13, 1848.
544. vi.   John Henry, b. March 20, 1851.
vii. Marie Etta, b. April 18, 1853.

315

JOHN⁶ (*Josiah*,⁵ *John*,⁴ *Eleazer*,³ *John*,² *Thomas*¹),
born at Pawlet, Vt.; married Chloe, daughter of Dr.
Ithamar Tilden. Removed to Ohio about 1844.

316

JOSIAH⁶ (*Josiah*,⁵ *John*,⁴ *Eleazer*,³ *John*,² *Thomas*¹),
born in Pawlet, Vt., about 1800; married Lorette,
daughter of Joseph P. Upham. He was justice of
the peace twenty years. Had the title of Colonel.
Was held in high estimation; died in 1863.

Children:

    i.   Azro[7]; d. in 1857, aged 26.
    ii. Chipman J.; went West.
546. iii. George.

318

RUSSELL[6] (*John*,[5] *John*,[4] *Eleazer*,[3] *John*,[2] *Thomas*[1]), born in Falmouth in 1797; died in New Bedford, Oct. 19, 1884, at the house of his son Robert G. He married in Falmouth, Oct. 19, 1823, Roxanna, daughter of Noah Hatch, born in 1800. Went on whaling voyages when a young man; then settled on a farm in East Falmouth.

Children:

560. i.   Gilbert Russell,[7] b. Nov. 7, 1824.
    ii. Franklin, b. June 2, 1828; d. Jan. 19, ~~1829~~ *1656*,
561. iii. Thomas Nye, b. April 1, 1831.
562. iv. Robert Goodwin, b. Dec. 2, 1840.

560 a,

319

ISAIAH NYE[6] (*John*,[5] *John*,[4] *Eleazer*,[3] *John*,[2] *Thomas*[1]), married, in Falmouth, May 19, 1829, Jane A. Phinney, of Falmouth. Was captain of various whaling ships, and an enterprising voyager. He died June 7, 1891.

Children:

563. i.   Asa Phinney,[7] b. March 5, 1838.
    ii. William Foster, b. May 5, 1841; d. June 20, 1841.

320

JOHN[6] (*John*,[5] *John*,[4] *Eleazer*,[3] *John*,[2] *Thomas*[1]), born in Falmouth, April 5, 1807; married Lydia ———. Was captain of a whaler and made voyages to the North and South Pacific oceans.

Children :
564. i.   John A.', born July 31, 1839.
    ii.   Henrietta F., born Dec. 13, 1841.
    iii. George B., born June 1, 1846.
    iv. Ella M., born Aug. 9, 1848.

134

(Correcting article on page 99.)

Reuben⁴ Tobey, born in Sandwich, Mass., as stated in the former article, married Rebecca Weeks. He was noted for industry and economy and acquired a handsome property. Was one of the deacons of the Baptist church of Pawlet, Vt., to which he had removed. He removed in 1850 to Pittsford, N. Y., and died there in 1852. His wife died a few days afterward, aged 82.

Children of Reuben⁴ and Rebecca (Weeks) Tobey :
    i.   Arthur,⁶ m. Abigail, daughter of Seth Blossom, and moved to Pittsford, N. Y.
    ii.   Zenas, m. Ruth, daughter of Jacob Putnam, and removed to Mendon, N. Y.
    iii. Reuben, Jr., m. first, Betsey, daughter of Jacob Putnam, who d. in 1843; m. second, Salina Rogers, of Pittsford, N. Y.; 2 children by first wife.
    iv. Sally; m. Dea. Seth P. Stiles of Auburn, N. Y.; d. 1863, æ. 63.
    v.   Rebecca.
    vi. Emily; m. John Simonds; d. 1852, æ. 43.

323

WATSON FORD⁶ (*Thomas Howes,⁵ John,⁴ Eleazer,³ John,² Thomas¹*), born in Falmouth, Feb. 10, 1809; married ——.

Children :
566. i.   Thomas Howes,' b. June 24, 1834.
567. ii.   Watson Freeman, b. Jan. 12, 1837.
568. iii. Charles Warren, b. May 13, 1841.

148   TOBEY GENEALOGY.

325

JOSIAH[6] (*James,[5] John,[4] Eleazer,[3] John,[2] Thomas[1]*),
born Aug. 31, 1808; resided at Falmouth; married
first, ———; married second, ———; married "third,
at Wareham, March 25, 1858, Hepzibah F., daughter
of George and Bethiah Christie, and widow of ———
Sturtevant, æ. 36." [Wareham record.]
Children :

   i.   Elmira F.,[7] of Josiah and Sarah, b. in Sandwich,
       Feb. 6, 1843.
   ii. Sarah, " of Josiah and Hepsibeth," b. in Falmouth,
       Feb. 15, 1859.

326

CURTIS[6] (*Benjamin,[5] Seth,[4] Seth,[3] Nathan,[2] Thomas[1]*), born in Sandwich, July 26, 1779; died in 1832.
Resided in Wareham; married Dec. 27, 1804, Thirzah,
daughter of Moses Swift Fearing and his wife Keziah
Briggs, born Oct. 22, 1788. He was a man of affairs,
chosen town clerk in 1816, commissioned Justice of
the Peace in 1824, with the title of esquire. He built
a cotton factory " on a small brook running into Wewe-
wantil River, at a place called the Polls," in 1816,
and carried on business there with some degree of
success. He entered into partnership with his father
in law, Mr. Fearing, articles signed Dec. 3, 1814.
[Bristol Co. Deeds.]

The widow Tirzah married Walter D. Burbank of
Plymouth, at Wareham, Jan. 29, 1833.
Children:

     i.   Hope Briggs,[7] b. Feb. 17, 1806 ; m. Jan. 23, 1825,
        Phinehas Savery, Jr., of Wareham.
575. ii. Joshua Briggs, b. Feb. 9, 1807.
576. iii. Moses Swift Fearing, b. Oct. 17, 1810.
577. iv. Seth Fish, b. June 29, 1814.

329

JOSEPH[6] (*William,*[5] *Joseph,*[4] *Nathan,*[3] *Nathan,*[2] *Thomas*[1]), born in Whitefield, Me., July 14, 1787; married Martha Murray, born April 21, 1791; resided in Somerville, Me. (formerly called Patricktown). He died Dec. 17, 1860.

Children:

588. i. Charles,[7] } b. April 18, 1813.
589. ii. Erastus, }
590. iii. William Sylvester, b. June 6, 1815.
591. iv. Hanson, b. June 20, 1818.
    v. Emeline, b. March 2, 1821; d. Sept. 20, 1834.
    vi. Harriet L., b. July 2, 1823; d. Feb. 6, 1850.
    vii. Leander, b. March 16, 1826; d. Sept. 18, 1827.
592. viii. Leander, b. Aug. 17, 1828.
593. ix. Miles, } b. March 9, 1831; } m. Dec. 14, 1851, Anson B. Bowler; d. Nov. 20, 1862.
    x. Lydia, }

330

ELIJAH[6] (*William,*[5] *Joseph,*[4] *Nathan,*[3] *Nathan,*[2] *Thomas*[1]), born in Whitefield, Me., Sept. 4, 1791; married first, Hannah Parslee of Whitefield; married second, Mrs. Hannah E. Noble, " who brought him two children of her former husband, and bore him two more after he was sixty years old." He died Aug. 26, 1881.

Children:

i. Alonzo.[7]
ii. Orin.
iii. Nathan.
iv. Sheldon.
v. Ann.
vi. Hannah.
vii. Eliza.
viii. Sarah.
594. ix. Charles.
595. x. Elias Baxter.

331

BENJAMIN[6] (*William,*[5] *Joseph,*[4] *Nathan,*[3] *Nathan,*[2] *Thomas*[1]), born in Whitefield, Me., Dec. 28, 1793; married Mary Mason. Resided in Starks, Me. He died April 26, 1818.

332

WILLIAM[6] (*William,*[5] *Joseph,*[4] *Nathan,*[3] *Nathan,*[2] *Thomas*[1]), born in Whitefield, Me., Sept. 24, 1796; married Dec. 11, 1828, "Ezeruey" (Zeruiah) Edmonds, of Patricktown (now Somerville), Me.; she was born in Edgecomb, Me., June 24, 1810, and died May 20, 1881. He died July 4, 1882.

Mrs. Tobey and three of the children were members of the Baptist Church. He was a farmer and shoemaker, residing at Jefferson, Me.

Children:

    i.   Elvira Elizabeth,[7] b. Feb. 15, 1831; d. March 11, 1837.

    ii.   Harriet Adeline Gibbs, b. July 29, 1832; d. Oct. 25, 1863.

    iii. John William Edmunds, b. April 28, 1835, a house-carpenter; d. Dec. 16, 1865.

    iv. Anna Elizabeth Edmunds, b. Sept. 22, 1841; m. at Sidney, Me., June 30, 1874, Jesse Y. Burrill, who was born at Palmyra, Me., Dec. 17, 1847. They reside at North Whitefield, Me.

        Child:

           Hattie M. Burrill,[8] b. June 13, 1876; m. at Mapleton, Me., J. Fred Ricker. Child, Lena Addie Ricker, b. at Chapman, Me., Nov. 14, 1900.

    v.   A son, b. March 10, d. March 23, 1845.

333

JAMES[6] (*William,*[5] *Joseph,*[4] *Nathan,*[3] *Nathan,*[2] *Thomas*[1]), born in Whitefield, Me., May 20, 1803; married Susannah H. Jones. Resided at East Pittston, Me. He died Feb. 24, 1839. The widow moved to Milton.

Susannah H. Tobey, of Fairmount, in the township of Milton, made her will Oct. 10, 1867, proved Dec. 5, 1883. Bequeathed her estate to her daughter, Mary Jane Tobey; appointed William Phillips Walley of Boston, executor. Mrs. Tobey died at Athol, Jan. 25, 1882, and proceedings were also entered in the Probate Court of Worcester County to administer on her estate. The records convey the information that "the next of kin were Susan A. Thayer, wife of Andrew J. Thayer, of Athol, a daughter; Mary Jane Wheeler, wife of Oliver Wheeler, of Boston, a daughter; Georgiana Cate Hemenway, wife of Frank Hemenway, of Framingham, Fred Tobey Cate of San Francisco, Cal., Ralph Cate, of Peru, N. Y., a minor, said Georgiana, Fred and Ralph being children of Rebecca Celia Cate, a deceased daughter of the deceased Susannah; Gertrude V. Dale, of Boston, daughter of Eliza Antoinette Dale, a deceased daughter of the deceased Susannah. Mrs. Tobey (dau. of Sylvanus Jones) was born in Sandwich Dec. 7, 1799.

Children :

i. Susan Augusta[7] ; m. Andrew J. Thayer, of Athol.
ii. Rebecca Celia, b. about 1829 ; m. Ralph Cate, of South Boston ; d. at Peru, N. Y., March 27, 1868.
iii. Mary Jane, b. 1828; m. in Boston, Oct. 13, 1851, Walter D. Madocks, of Boston, b. at Ellsworth, Me., 1828; m. (2) in Boston, Aug. 1, 1880, Oliver Wheeler, of Boston, b. at Bowdoin, Me., 1824.
599. iv. James William, b. in May, 1836.
v. Elizᵃ Antoinette, b. 1834; m. in Boston, July 18, 1861, Franklin Dale, of Boston, b. at Walpole, N. H., 1832; she d. Aug. 22, 1869.
vi. Sarah, d. 1857.

334

GEORGE[6] (*William,[5] Joseph,[4] Nathan,[3] Nathan,[2] Thomas[1]*), born in Whitefield, Me., Sept. 8, 1805; married, Oct. 31, 1832, Mary Jane Perham, born in Warren, Me., Jan. 14, 1804; her brother William married Celia Tobey, George's sister. He was a tanner and shoemaker; lived on the Heald place in Jefferson, Me. He died April 21, 1841; she died Jan. 4, 1870.

Children:

600. i. Samuel Otis,[7] b. Aug. 28, 1833.

10

ii. Celia Abigail, b. Dec. 31, 1834; d. Sept. 22, 1856.
iii. Charles Sylvester, b. March 10, 1836; d. Feb. 12,
       1842.
iv. Fuller, b. Sept. 1, 1837; living, single, in 1902.
v.   Mary Elizabeth, b. March 11, 1840; m. April 17,
       1864, Francis Augustus Pinkham, b. in Hallowell,
       Me., Sept. 25, 1840; he enlisted in March, 1864,
       in Co. C, 31st Me. Inf.; saw considerable service,
       and was injured while at work on breastworks; he
       was discharged Aug., 1865; draws a pension.
       He lived in Gardiner, Me., 1865-7; removed to
       Aroostook County and resided in Silver Ridge,
       1868-1876, and in No. 1, Range 4, 1876-1886;
       returned in 1886 to Pittston, Me., where he still
       resides. A farmer.

Children:

1. Abby Frances Pinkham, b. May 9, 1866; m.
   June 7, 1891, Charles Otis Gerry, b. in Alton,
   Me., April 14, 1865; he was a carpenter;
   they res. in Hartford, Conn.
2. Charles Augustus Pinkham, b. March 31, 1869;
   blacksmith; res. Boothbay Harbor, Me.
3. Mary Lydia Pinkham, b. May 14, 1871; m.
   Oct. 28, 1894, Edward Grant Meader; res.
   Gardiner, Me.

   Children:

   (1) Bessie Elizabeth Meader, b. Oct. 23, 1897.
   (2) Grace Irene Meader, b. Oct. 17, 1899.
   (3) Georgia Edith Meader, b. Jan. 28, 1902.

4. Catherine Sidney Pinkham, b. Aug. 25, 1873;
   m. May 7, 1899, Everett Lindsey Caston, b.
   May 8, 1879; res. Hartland, Me.; one child,
   Otis Alphonso Caston, b. Feb. 3, 1900, at
   Hallowell, Me.
5. Frank Otis Pinkham, b. Sept. 14, 1876.
6. Elizabeth Celia Pinkham, b. Nov. 18, 1878.
7. George Edmund Pinkham, b. Jan. 28, 1880;
   R. R. man, Alleghany, Pa.
8. Rose Evelyn Pinkham, b. March 27, 1885.

335

RODOLPHUS H.[6] (*Lewis,*[5] *Joseph,*[4] *Nathan,*[3] *Nathan,*[2] *Thomas*[1]), born in New Bedford, Feb. 22, 1813; married, at Poughkeepsie, N. Y., March 28, 1843, Eveline Macy, born at Ghent, N. Y., March 12, 1821. [Macy Genealogy.]

336

GEORGE[6] (*Lewis,*[5] *Joseph,*[4] *Nathan,*[3] *Nathan,*[2] *Thomas*[1]), born in New Bedford.
Child:
Sarah[7]; m. in N. B., Dec. 21, 1848 (called in record "dau. of George Tobey" and granddaughter of Rebecca (Ingraham) Tobey), Samuel Leonard, Jr.

POSTSCRIPT.— We learn too late for insertion in its proper place on page 104 that Lewis' Tobey, No. 142, had children: Alice,[6] Sarah,[6] Lewis[6] and Franklin,[6] besides Rodolphus[6] and George,[6] whom we have mentioned on said page. We therefore add the son Franklin[6] below, giving him the serial number 336a.

336 a.

FRANKLIN[6] (*Lewis,*[5] *Joseph,*[4] *Nathan,*[3] *Nathan,*[2] *Thomas*[1]), born in 1806; died in 1862; married, in New Bedford, Oct. 18, 1831, Rebecca Wood, born in 1808, died in 1882. He was a merchant, some time a partner of Benjamin T. Ricketson.
Children:
603. i. Thomas W.,[7] b. 1832.
604. ii. Frank, b. 1834.
iii. Mary H., b. April 19, 1838; m. Jan. 11, 1864, Theodore E. Macy; residence New York city.
Children:
1. Mortimer Macy.
2. Florence Macy; m. Edward B. May.
3. Isabel Macy.
4. Marion Macy.
5. George Macy.

iv. Anna T., b. 1841; m. Charles J. Barclay, U. S. N.
Child:
Edith Barclay; m. Major C. O. Long, U. S.
Marine Corps.
v. Alice P., b. Dec. 2, 1843; m. Dec., 1864, Loum
Snow, of New Bedford, son of Loum Snow and
Abby Harris Easton (Mowry), of Smithfield, R. I.,
b. Aug. 5, 1840.
Children:
1. Loum Snow, Jr., b. Oct. 27, 1865.
2. Alice T. Snow, b. March 4, 1867.
3. Agnes Snow, b. April 30, 1868.
4. Richard S. Snow, b. Dec. 15, 1869.
5. Jeannie Snow, b. Nov. 30, 1871.

605. vi. John L., b. April 11, 1847.

339

HENRY[6] (*Timothy,[5] Joseph,[4] Nathan,[3] Nathan,[2] Thomas[1]*), born in Sandwich, Oct. 9, 1803; married, in
Boston, Oct. 20, 1831, Sarah P., daughter of Daniel
and Rebecca (Stimpson) Rea. He was a "master
mariner," *i.e.* a sea-captain; his home was in Sandwich. He died, and administration of his estate was
granted Jan. 13, 1835. The widow married second,
May 9, 1836, Samuel Nye, of Sandwich.
Child:
Sarah,[7] b. in Boston, 1834; m. in Sandwich, Dec. 24,
1856, Henry C. Goodspeed, of New York, b. in Barnstable in 1835.

340

ANSELL[6] (*Timothy,[5] Joseph,[4] Nathan,[3] Nathan,[2] Thomas[1]*), born in Sandwich, Feb. 27, 1806; died in
1895, "aged 89 years"; married Mehitable ———.
He was a farmer; occupied the farm where his father
had spent his life.

Children:

i. Elizabeth,[7] b. March 3, 1835; m. Jan. 24, 1855, Braddock E. Fish.
ii. Mary Ann, b. Aug. 20, 1836.
iii. Susan, b. Oct. 25, 1838; d. Sept. 9, 1839.
iv. Emily C., b. Sept. 29, 1839.
v. Vesta M., b. 1843; m. in Boston, Oct. 14, 1880, Peleg T. Brown, b. in Scituate, 1836, son of John and Clarissa Brown; res. Sandwich.
609. vi. Nathan Lewis, b. Nov. 6, 1845.

341

JOSEPH[6] (*Timothy,[5] Joseph,[4] Nathan,[3] Nathan,[2] Thomas[1]*), born in Sandwich, April 10, 1810; died in Boston, of consumption, March 21, 1863. He learned the trade of carpenter. Removed to Boston and entered into partnership with Elijah Smith and John W. Tinkham, and carried on an extensive business in house-building and real estate.

He married, at New Bedford, Sept. 16, 1833, Sarah, daughter of Christopher and Charity Slocum, born in New Bedford, died in Boston, July 30, 1887, aged 72. He made his will Jan. 28, 1863, adding a codicil Feb. 19th, bequeathing his estate to his wife Sarah S. and his sons William M. and Joseph H. Tobey.

Children:

i. Carrie R.,[7] b. 1838; d. of consumption, June 14, 1859.
610. ii. William M.
611. iii. Joseph H.

359

CHARLES[6] (*William,[5] William,[4] Samuel,[3] Jonathan,[2] Thomas[1]*), born at Nantucket about 1798; married. Became a captain of a whaling ship not far from the age of 21. Was master of the ship "Lady Adams" which sailed away from Nantucket, but never re-

turned, and her fate was not known. He left one
child who grew to be a woman of rare qualities; married Judge Henry A. Scudder, of Boston, Mass., and
Washington, D. C.; died in 1893.

360

GEORGE W.[6] (*William,[5] William,[4] Samuel,[3] Jona-
than,[2] Thomas[1]*), born in Nantucket about 1801;
married in Boston, Aug. 17, 1826, Mary Vial Barrett.
She died about 1880; was buried at Fairfield, Conn.
Made his home in New London, Conn. He died in
San Francisco, Cal., about 1850.
Children:

612. i.   Charles Bennett,[7] b. Sept. 18, 1828.
     ii.   Agnes W., b. 1835; m. March 6, 1853, William
           Hayes. No children.
     iii. Mary Louisa, b. at Hudson, N. Y., March 31, 1838;
           d. Jan. 12, 1874; m. Dec. 21, 1858, Sturges
           Raymond, Jr., b. at Greenfield, Conn., Nov. 27,
           1825, d. Nov. 4, 1868; res. Southport, Conn.
           Children :
           1. Addie L. Raymond, b. Nov. 17, 1859; d.
              Aug., 1872.
           2. William H. Raymond, b. Sept. 21, 1861;
              d. July 26, 1864.
           3. Finette B. Raymond, b. Feb. 13, d. Dec.
              23, 1864.
           4. Mary B. Raymond, b. Jan. 13, 1869.
     iv.   George W., b. June 10, 1843; served in the 84th
           N. Y. Vol. Inf. in the War of the Rebellion; was
           killed at Groveton, Aug. 30, 1862.

361

ANSELM H.[6] (*Tristram,[5] William,[4] Samuel,[3] Jonathan,[2] Thomas[1]*), born in Sandwich, May 17, 1808;
married first, Eliza Jenks; married second, Eloise M.

Resided some years at Nantucket, to which he had gone as a child with his father. Removed to New Bedford. Was a dentist. He made his will July 9, 1870; proved Feb. 3, 1871; bequeathed his property to his wife Eloise M.; to his daughter Sarah J., wife of George Emerson of Melrose, and to Mr. Emerson; to grandson Walter C. Macy.

Children:

 i. Sara J.,[7] b. at Nantucket, April 28, 1833; m. first, Dec. 1, 1854, John W. Macy; residence, Melrose. [Macy Genealogy.] Child: Walter C. Macy. She m. second, George Emerson of Melrose.

 ii. Samuel Jenks, b. in January, d. in July, 1835.

362

ALBERT H.[6] (*Tristram,*[5] *William,*[4] *Samuel,*[3] *Jonathan,*[2] *Thomas*[1]), born in Sandwich, March 14, 1813; married at New Bedford, April 13, 1834, Nancy, dau. of John and Nancy (Little) Irish of Little Compton, R. I.; she died June 26, 1894, aged 87 years, 3 mos. Resided at Nantucket. He died April 8, 1877.

Children:

613. i. Benjamin G.,[7] b. 1836.
614. ii. Albert.
615. iii. Horace, b. Aug. 13, 1846,

362 a

BETSEY[6] (*Archelaus,*[5] *William,*[4] *Samuel,*[3] *Jonathan,*[2] *Thomas*[1]), born Oct. 8, 1804; married Samuel Sweetland, born Aug. 11, 1802, son of Aretas and Huldah Sweetland of Pawtucket, R. I., a very skilful mechanic; resided at Providence, R. I., died Dec. 29, 1884; she died Jan. 14, 1887.

Children: Mary Elizabeth, Anna, Imogene and Nathan Sweetland; of these, Anna married Otis S. Clapp, now city engineer of Providence.

362 b

SOPHRONIA⁶ (*Archelaus,⁵ William,⁴ Samuel,² Jonathan,²
Thomas¹*), born Sept. 7, 1806; married Dec. 1, 1828, Daniel
Bowen Fish, born March 3, 1804, at Rehoboth; resided at
Providence, R. I.; died Feb. 25, 1867; she died Aug. 2,
1889.

Children:

1. Sarah Jane Fish, b. Oct. 17, 1829; d. June 20, 1846.
2. Eleanor Frances Fish, b. May 22, 1834; m. Samuel Pyke,
   who d. in 1904. Children: (1) Jane Collins Pyke, b.
   July 3, 1857; m. Rev. Gibbs Braislin; d. April 30, 1904.
   (2) James Tobey Pyke, b. Dec. 2, 1858. (3) Ella
   Frances Pyke, b. July 3, 1863: d. Oct. 22, 1864.
3. James Tobey Fish, b. Aug. 17, 1836; m. Aug. 30, 1869,
   Jennie Nevins, who d. July 21, 1881. Child: Earl
   Hamilton Fish, b. Feb. 21, 1873; d. 1904.
4. Abbie Harding Fish, b. Jan. 5, 1839; m. Nov. 20, 1862,
   Samuel Gorham. Children: (1) Frederick P. Gorham,
   b. April 29, 1871; m. June 24, 1896, Emma J. Lapham.
   (2) Howard Bowen Gorham, b. Feb. 10, 1876,; m. June
   1, 1905, Helen A. A. Whittemore.
5. William Henry Fish, b. Jan. 3, 1841; d. April 17, 1868.
6. Martha Potter Fish, } b. Apr. 2, 1843, { d. July 22, 1865.
7. Marion Porter Fish, } { d. Dec. 26, 1843.

363

WILLIAM⁶ (*Archelaus,⁵ William,⁴ Samuel,³ Jonathan,² Thomas¹*), born June 20, 1810; married at
North Providence, R. I., March 29, 1836, Sarah Ann,
daughter of Lemuel and Sarah (Smith) Angell, born
Sept. 8, 1816, died Feb. 17, 1883.

He was a blacksmith, taught the trade to three of
his brothers.

He removed to Greenville, in the town of Smithfield, R. I., about 1856, and opened a store of general
merchandise, which he carried on till he resigned it
into the care of his son Oscar in 1875.

He died Feb. 18, 1894.

Children:

616. i.   Oscar Angell,⁷ b. Jan. 10, 1837.

   ii. Sarah Amanda, b. Sept. 15, 1839 ; d. July 31, 1861 ;
       m. in Boston, Sept. 15, 1857, Ethan C. Thornton,
       b. 1830. Child : Leland A. Thornton, b. 1861.
617. iii. William Henry, b. Sept. 15, 1842.
   iv. Ellen Frances, b. Aug. 3, 1844 ; m. George Albert
       Southwick. Child : Oscar Howard Southwick.
618. v. James Edwin, b. Oct. 18, 1848.

364

GEORGE A.[6] (*Archelaus,*[5] *William,*[4] *Samuel,*[3] *Jonathan,*[2] *Thomas*[1]), born about 1812; married Ann ———, and had children; resided many years in Georgiaville, in the town of Smithfield, R. I.; afterwards was proprietor of a restaurant in Providence; removed to Iowa.

Children:

    i. Frank.[7]   iii. Charles.
    ii. Stephen.   iv. Henry.

365

JAMES HAIL[6] (*Archelaus,*[5] *William,*[4] .*Samuel,*[3] *Jonathan,*[2] *Thomas*[1]), born about 1814; became a Baptist minister; served churches at Manton, R. I., and elsewhere; purchased land at Nayatt, in Barrington, R. I., and made a home there. He died at Providence, at the house of his daughter, Mrs. Dennis O'Reilly, Jan. 2, 1878. He married Harriet ———, who survived him, and afterward removed with her daughter to Woonsocket, R. I., where she died about 1903. Dennis O'Reilly was afterward in business at Woonsocket, R. I.

366

JOSEPH[6] (*Archelaus,*[5] *William,*[4] *Samuel,*[3] *Jonathan,*[2] *Thomas*[1]), born about 1816; married at North Providence, R. I., March 23, 1845, Eliza, daughter of

11

Nicholas Steavens of Smithfield, R. I.   He died Aug. 24, 1893; she died Sept. 17, 1888.

367

SAMUEL[6] (*Archelaus,*[5] *William,*[4] *Samuel,*[3] *Jonathan,*[2] *Thomas*[1]), born about 1818; married ~~first, in Providence, R. I., May 20, 1840, Susan Hunt; married second~~, Betsey P., daughter of Samuel and Ruth (Tinkham) Walden of Gloucester, R. I. She died at Worcester, Nov. 11, 1896, aged 71. He was a blacksmith; resided at Providence and Gloucester, R. I. He died Feb. 19, 1899.

Children:

628. i.   Walter.[7]
~~629. ii.   Samuel Edwin, b. 1850.~~
630. iii.   Willard A., b. 1852.
    iv.   Ella M., b. 1855; m. July 21, 1872, George H. Brown, son of Vincent and Susan Brown.

368

SAMUEL[6] (*Elisha,*[5] *Matthias,*[4] *Samuel,*[3] *Jonathan,*[2] *Thomas*[1]), born at Machiasport, Me., in October, 1799; died March 26, 1873; married Nancy Burton Robinson, born Oct. 4, 1808, died in 1884.   [See No. 630 *et seq.*]

370

CHARLES[6] (*Elisha,*[5] *Matthias,*[4] *Samuel,*[3] *Jonathan,*[2] *Thomas*[1]), born in Machias, Me., Sept. 17, 1812; died May 11, 1875; married Aug. 27, 1837, Lydia, daughter of William and Lydia (Albee) Gardner, born July 11, 1818, died Feb. 5, 1898. He followed the sea a number of years; was in the employ of the Whitneyville and Machiasport R. R., on their lumber wharves, some twenty years. He afterward worked as a painter, and lost his life by the fall of a staging on which he was at work.

Children:

i. Judith Ann,[7] b. Sept. 11, 1838; m. May 14, 1860, Harlan Evander Plummer of Harrington, Me., a master mariner. He d. in hospital at Philadelphia, Pa.

Children:

1. Asenath Monson Plummer, b. April 4, 1861; m. June 26, 1881, Willard D. Coffin of Harrington, Me.

Children:

(1) Adelaide Geneva Coffin, b. Aug. 24, 1884.
(2) Alice May Coffin, b. Oct. 29, 1887.
(3) Grace Augusta Coffin, b. Nov. 10, 1889.
(4) John Leslie Coffin, b. Aug. 1, 1891.
(5) Charles Alphonso Coffin, b. July 7, 1899.

2. Adelaide Geneva Plummer, b. Sept. 6, 1870.

ii. Adeline, b. Oct. 1, 1840; m. June 4, 1876, Edward Wallace Shackford of Eastport, Me., master mariner. No children.

634. iii. James Osbert, b. March 19, 1844.

381

CHARLES RICHMOND[6] (*Lemuel,[5] Thomas,[4] Jonathan,[3] Jonathan,[2] Thomas[1]*), born in Dighton, April 21, 1806; died at San Francisco, Cal., Oct. 30, 1850; married at New Bedford, June 1, 1838, Maria Patey, daughter of Lemuel and Rachel (Bailey) Robbins, born at Plymouth, January 28, 1819, died at New Bedford, April 6, 1895.

Charles Richmond Tobey was born in Dighton, and became a sailor while still a youth. His son, who has assisted in the compilation of this book, refers to the fact that both his maternal uncles were whalers; that his father and uncle Henry were also whalers, his uncle Theodore being also a sailor, but in the merchant service. Like many another sailor, however, Mr. Charles Richmond Tobey joined the gold seekers who went in 1849 in large numbers from New Bedford and vicinity to California. There he met his death.

Another who knew him says : " I never heard any one speak of him but in the highest praise, and remember many times hearing people say he was the best man they ever knew."

One who was with him when he died said : " He was one of the best men God Almighty ever made."

" Never impatient, never railing at fortune, which treated him none too well."

Children:

i. Harriet Newell,[7] b. April 5, 1843.
ii. Thomas Richmond, b. Sept., 1844; d. April 10, 1845.
iii. Susan Maria, b. April 5, 1846; d. Oct. 30, 1879.
635. iv. Charles Robbins, b. Sept. 8, 1847.
636. v. Rufus Babcock, b. May 6, 1849.

382

HENRY FALES[6] (*Lemuel*,[5] *Thomas*,[4] *Jonathan*,[3] *Jonathan*,[2] *Thomas*[1]), born May 24, 1808; married July 26, 1831, Mary Nye of North Falmouth. Resided at North Falmouth and afterward at New Bedford. He died Sept. 10, 1884.

Captain Henry Fales Tobey went on his first whaling voyage at the age of fifteen, and, although successful, in 1858 accepted the position of mate on the Wamsutta, one of the daily line of steamers running from New Bedford to New York. During the Civil War he was in command of one of the ships composing the Stone Fleet, which was sunk in Charleston Harbor for blockade purposes. Later he was in command of the Hen and Chickens Lightship, until his health compelled him to relinquish the service. Capt. Tobey was a man of many friends, and was especially fond of children. He was a typical sailor, generous to a fault.

Children, born at North Falmouth:

i. Rebecca H.[7]; resides in Fall River.
ii. Frances N., b. March 27, 1840.
iii. Lemuel Thomas, b. Sept. 6, 1842; "lost in Chesapeake Bay, Nov. 29, 1874, in attempting to save a wrecked vessel, while employed on the New

York and Wilmington Steamship line." [From the memorial stone in the cemetery at North Falmouth, Mass.]

638. iv. Henry Fales, Jr., b. May 21, 1848.

383

Job Townsend[6] (*Isaac Smith,[5] Thomas,[4] Jonathan,[3] Jonathan,[2] Thomas[1]*), born in Rochester; married in New Bedford, Dec. 29, 1841, his cousin Maria, daughter of Lemuel (No. 175) Tobey, born Sept. 2, 1818, died April 13, 1876. Resided in Rochester, and later in Lakeville. He was an efficient and enterprising man, highly regarded by those with whom he came in contact. He died at Lakeville Feb. 11, 1892, aged 80 years, 1 month, 17 days.

Children:

i. Elizabeth Fales,[7] b. Jan. 17, 1847; d. Feb. 14, 1896; m. Dec. 27, 1869, Thomas Wells Clark of Boston, b. in Middleborough in 1844, son of Willard and Boadicea T. Clark.

Children:
1. Louis Wells Clark, b. Nov. 6, 1870; m. Aug. 29, 1895, Caroline Fairfield Warren.
2. Amy Citoyenne Clark, b. April 2, 1874.
3. Bessie Fales Clark, b. March 26, 1876.
4. Richmond Tobey Clark, b. Dec. 21, 1877.
5. Rufus Wilton Clark, b. June 20, 1882.

ii. Martha, b. May 7, 1849.
iii. Mary Lincoln, b. July 3, 1851.
iv. Rachel Maria, b. June 14, 1854.

388

William W.[6] (*Lemuel,[5] Joshua,[4] Cornelius,[3] Samuel,[2] Thomas[1]*), born in Farmington, Me., in 1796; married in Boston, Sept. 8, 1854, Jane, daughter of John and Alice Rogers, born in St. John, N. B., in 1832. He joined with Edward A., Sarah A. E., and Horace Williams, 21 Aug., 1866, in quitclaiming land which had been Erastus Smith's to Sylvester Smith, in consideration of the care the latter had taken of Erastus. Wife Jane Rogers Tobey joined in the deed.

"William W. Tobey, dry goods merchant, formerly of 1084 Washington St., Boston, but now of St. John, N. B., out of business," made will April 23, 1870, proved Aug. 14, 1876; bequeathed to his "wife Jane (formerly Rodgers)" all his estate.

400

THOMAS ALLEN[6] (*Heman,[5] Cornelius,[4] Cornelius,[3] Samuel,[2] Thomas[1]*), born in Sandwich, Sept. 13, 1791; married Hannah ———.

Children:

    i.   Nancy,[7] b. Feb. 4, 1817; m. Henry Wing; son Henry T. Wing res. New York City.

    ii.   Hannah, b. Feb. 10, 1820.

    iii.   Mary Nye, b. May 12, 1822; m. Sept. 24, 1843, George Giddings of Ipswich; residence, Newton.

    iv.   Elizabeth A., b. July 24, 1824; m. (as his second wife) Henry Wing of East Sandwich.

    v.   Heman, b. March 31, 1827; merchant in Boston; d. unm; administration of his estate granted Oct. 30, 1856, to Henry Wing.

643. vi.   Henry Davis, b. March 16, 1831.

401

EZRA[6] (*Melitiah,[5] Cornelius,[4] Cornelius,[3] Samuel,[2] Thomas[1]*), born in Sandwich, Sept. 1, 1796; married Elizabeth (Betsey), daughter of Stephen and Elizabeth Bassett, b. Sept. 5, 1799; died at N. Bridgewater, Feb. 25, 1866.

Children:

    i.   Mary,[7] b. April 6, 1820; m. June 6, 1847, Rufus Kimball of North Bridgewater.

644. ii.   Melitiah, b. April 22, 1822.

iii. Martha Bassett, b. March 2, 1824.
645. iv. Ezra, b. June 2, 1826.
646. v. Charles Nye, b. May 26, 1828.
    vi. Elizabeth Bassett, b. Sept. 20, 1830; m. Dec. 26, 1853, Ephraim T. Belcher of Randolph.
   vii. Hannah, b. Dec. 28, 1832; m. Sept. 27, 1853, Owen Field of North Bridgewater.
647. viii. William Henry, b. April 11, 1840.
   ix. Jeanette Augusta, b. Sept. 28, 1842.

402

JOSHUA[6] (*Melitiah,*[5] *Cornelius,*[4] *Cornelius,*[3] *Samuel,*[2] *Thomas*[1]), born in Sandwich, June 23, 1803; married Nov. 8, 1824, Martha, daughter of William and Martha (Freeman) Fessenden, born in 1842, died Sept. 22, 1846. He died March 4, 1841.
Children :

    i. Nancy Fessenden,[7] b. Oct. 10, 1825; m. Robert Bailey.
   ii. Louise, b. Jan. 26, 1827; m. Oct. 25, 1846, William H. Marston of Sandwich.
   Children :
      1. Charles Henry Marston.
      2. William Warren Marston.
  iii. Triphosa Colton, b. Dec. 3, 1828; m. Benj. F. Gibbs of Wareham.
   iv. Mary Warren, b. Jan. 24, 1831; m. Sept. 16, 1850, William E. Brigham of Marlboro.
   v. Ellen Goodwin, b. May 15, 1833; died.
   vi. Lydia Russell, b. Oct. 17, 1835; m. May 15, 1853, William E. Brigham (second wife).
  vii. Charles Henry, b. March 3, 1837; died in his youth.
648. viii. Joshua Fessenden, b. June 25, 1840.

403

ROBERT[6] (*Joshua,*[5] *Cornelius,*[4] *Cornelius,*[3] *Samuel,*[2] *Thomas*[1]), born in Sandwich, Oct. 30, 1801; married first, Nancy Ball Fessenden, who was born Aug. 16,

1804, and died Nov. 16, 1841. He married second, at Falmouth, Sept. 8, 1842, Elizabeth C. Eldred of that place, who died Nov. 8, 1847, aged 37. He married third, March 23, 1848, Melinda Naomi Wells, who died Dec. 1, 1894.

He was in the employ of the Sandwich Glass Company from 1825 .till he retired in 1886. He died Nov. 12, 1892, aged 91 years and 13 days.

Children:

    i.   William Robert,[7] b. Nov. 12, 1827, d. Aug. 30, 1828.

649. ii.   Gustavus Bassett, b. May 18, 1832.

    iii.   Isabella Graham, b. April 23, 1835, d. Dec. 25, 1855.

650. iv.   William Robert, b. Oct. 27, 1841.

404

WILLIAM[6] (*Joshua*,[5] *Cornelius*,[4] *Cornelius*,[3] *Samuel*,[2] *Thomas*[1]), born in Sandwich, Sept. 24, 1807; died at sea on the ship *Herald*, coming from Charleston, S. C. He was a carpenter, and went South winters to work at his trade.

406

ELISHA[6] (*Lemuel*,[5] *Elisha*,[4] *Cornelius*,[3] *Samuel*,[2] *Thomas*[1]), married in New Bedford, April 7, 1808, Lydia Swift. Merchant in Fairhaven; bought land there in 1813; called "Elisha Tobey, Second."

May 1, 1822, he sold all his share in the real estate left in the will of his father, Lemuel Tobey, late of Fairhaven; June 7, 1822, the same was re-conveyed to Lydia. He died in Fairhaven, May 18, 1859.

Children:

    i.   Charles,[7] mentioned in his grandmother's will in 1824; d. in 1854, and his estate was administered by Elisha Tobey of Fairhaven.

657. ii. Elisha, b. April 22, 1822.
    iii. Elizabeth P., d. March 31, 1885, at Acushnet, leaving a will dated Jan. 8, 1884, proved May 1, 1885, making her niece Sophia M. Hart her principal heir, with legacies to Lemuel T., Francis C. and Herbert Terry, Caroline M. Martin, Eliza P. Goodale and others.

407

WILLIAM C.^{6} (*William*,^{5} *Elisha*,^{4} *Cornelius*,^{3} *Samuel*,^{2} *Thomas*^{1}), born in New Bedford, 1789; married Eliza, daughter of Col. George Claghorn. He became a sea-captain; died at Rochester, Jan. 4, 1847, aged 58.

Children:

660. i. William Henry,^{7} b. Dec. 11, 1810.
    ii. Frederick Augustus; d. at Cambridge, Sept. 7, 1875, æ. 62, 7, 14.
    iii. Elizabeth H.; her brother William H. was appointed her guardian, Nov. 2, 1847.

409

FREDERICK^6 (*Cornelius*,^{5} *Elisha*,^{4} *Cornelius*,^{3} *Samuel*,^{2} *Thomas*^{1}), born about 1794. Became a housewright. He removed to Columbus, Muscogee county, Georgia. He sold, Sept. 12, 1832, to his brother-in-law, Isaac Newton Hathaway of Freetown, one half of the real estate of which his mother, Mrs. Nancy Tobey, had been the owner, which portion she had bequeathed to him by her will dated 11 September, 1832. [Bristol Co. Deeds.] He also joined with his sister Elizabeth W. Hathaway, widow, in the conveyance of certain lands in Freetown, April 10, 1847.

413

LEVI^6 (*Zaccheus*,^{5} *Zaccheus*,^{4} *Zaccheus*,^{3} *Samuel*,^{2} *Thomas*^{1}), born in Susquehanna co., Pa., Feb. 27, 1820; married ———.

Child:

Sarah M.,[7] b. Feb. 9, 1863; m. Clarence Egbert
Wellman, b. in Triangle, Broome co., N. Y.,
Aug. 28, 1854. Son: Horace Levi Wellman,
b. in Sheldon, Ia., Dec. 27, 1883.*

419

AVERY[6] (*Zoeth,[5] Zoeth,[4] Zaccheus,[3] Samuel,[2] Thomas[1]*), born near Montpelier, Vt., in 1796; removed
to Russellville, Ill., about 1825; married Sally Norton.
Child:
669.	Savell.[7]

420

RICHARD WEST[6] (*Zoeth,[5] Zoeth,[4] Zaccheus,[3] Samuel,[2] Thomas[1]*), born 1800; married first, 1822, Lydia,
daughter of Edmund Tucker, born 1803, died 1844;
he married second, Hannah C. (Dodge) Kelton.

He was a farmer, hotel-keeper and mill-owner at
Calais, Vt., E. Montpelier, Walden, and Royalton,
Vt.; died at Calais in May, 1874.
Children:

    i.   Delia Irene,[7] b. 1823; m. Thomas Bell; residence,
        Heil's Grove, R. I.

    Children :

        1. Abbie W. Bell, b. 1856.
        2. Arthur Bell, b. 1864.

670. ii.   William Elliot, b. 1825.
     iii.   Phebe Roxanna, b. 1828; m. 1854, Amos W.
         Eddy of Walden, Vt.

    Children :

        1. Emma L. Eddy, b. 1855, d. 1875.
        2. Marcia M. Eddy, b. 1857.
        3. Nellie M. Eddy, b. 1862.
        4. Edmund W. Eddy, b. 1870.

671. iv. Orvis S., b. 1832.
672. v.   James K., b. 1845.

* Information of Mrs. Mary Louise Wellman Loomis.

421

ALLEN[6] (*Zoeth*,[5] *Zoeth*,[4] *Zaccheus*,[3] *Samuel*,[2] *Thomas*[1]), born about 1805; married Elvira Ellis. He was a farmer; resided at Calais, Vt.
Children:
673. i.   Elbridge A.,[7] b. 1847.
674. ii. Martin D., b. 1853.

422

JOSEPH[6] (*Elisha*,[5] *Prince*,[4] *Zaccheus*,[3] *Samuel*,[2] *Thomas*[1]), born in Philadelphia, Pa., March 12, 1802; lived at Conway, Mass., in his boyhood; became a merchant, residing at Middletown, Conn.
Children:
i.   Sarah[7]; m. Daniel S. Camp.
ii.   Jane; m. Dr. Burke.
iii. Nellie; m. Edward Cutts of Port au Prince.
iv.   Joseph Delano; d. unm.
v.   Frank; deceased.

425

WARREN DELANO[6] (*Elisha*,[5] *Prince*,[4] *Zaccheus*,[3] *Samuel*,[2] *Thomas*[1]), born in Springfield, Jan. 24, 1819; graduated at Wilbraham Academy.

Became a merchant at Warren; removed to Rochester, N. Y., where he died before May 22, 1860, when administration of estate he had owned in Berkshire co., Mass., was granted to George Tobey.

426

GEORGE[6] (*Elisha*,[5] *Prince*,[4] *Zaccheus*,[3] *Samuel*,[2] *Thomas*[1]), born in Springfield, Nov. 17, 1820; died at Blandford, Dec. 21, 1898; married first, in Dec., 1843, Lucina, daughter of Luther and Rachel (Chase) Stoddard of Chicopee, born Feb. 12, 1825, died May 24, 1866; married second, June 12, 1867, Mrs. Lucy

Davis (Gould) Pratt of Longmeadow, daughter of
Benjamin and Hannah (Powers) Gould, born Jan. 23,
1832; she survived Mr. Tobey, and resides in Springfield.

He graduated at High School; entered the U. S.
Armory at Springfield in 1843; was inspector of contract work in the manufacture of arms for thirty-four
years at Middletown, Conn., and other places. Removed to Blandford in 1877, and resided on a farm
the rest of his life.

Children:

690. i.   Frank Gerry,[7] b. Jan. 15, 1847.
     ii.   Elizabeth Lucina, b. Aug. 10, 1850; m. Harry
          Cornelius Mayher.
691. iii. William Henry, b. Sept. 5, 1869.

427

JOSIAH GODDARD[6] (*Elisha,[5] Prince,[4] Zaccheus,[3]
Samuel,[2] Thomas[1]*), born in Springfield, Sept. 4, 1822;
died at St. Louis, Mo.

Was a dry goods merchant; entered the U. S. army
in the Civil War; served on surgeons' staff.

428

ELISHA[6] (*Elisha,[5] Prince,[4] Zaccheus,[3] Samuel,[2]
Thomas[1]*), born in Springfield, Jan. 26, 1826; in later
life wrote his name Elisha H. Tobey.

Was in railroad supply business. Served in the
Civil War; rose to the rank of colonel; commanded
his regiment at Petersburg, Va. He died at Waukegan, Ill., July 11, 1886.

429

EDWARD EVERETT[6] (*Elisha,[5] Prince,[4] Zaccheus,[3]
Samuel,[2] Thomas[1]*), born in Springfield, Oct. 17, 1832;
died at Chicago, Ill.

Removed to Memphis, Tenn.; was auditor of The
Louisville & Memphis R. R. Entered the Union army
at opening of the war; was wounded at the battle of
Shiloh; recovered, and led his company at Vicksburg,
where he was again wounded. Received the rank of
colonel by brevet. He married Harriet Whittledon,
who survived him and resided in Memphis (1902).
Child:

> Edward[7]; d. in 1902.

430

WILLIAM[6] (*Heman,*[5] *Noah,*[4] *Zaccheus,*[3] *Samuel,*[2]
Thomas[1]), born March 3, 1805; married Ada Amanda
Brooks, who was born May 21, 1810, near Geneva,
N. Y. Removed in 1832 to York township, Union
county, Ohio. Had a log-cabin home, a mile and a
half from the nearest neighbor, with Indians and wild
animals all about. Fearless and full of faith, they
lived on and brought up their family.
Children:

696. i. John Elbert,[7] b. 1835.
ii. William, b. in 1845; enlisted in the Federal Army
in 1861, was taken sick and came home on a fur-
lough, and died.
697. iii. Henry Archibald, b. April 6, 1852.

431

HENRY[6] (*Heman,*[5] *Noah,*[4] *Zaccheus,*[3] *Samuel,*[2] *Thomas*[1]), born June 6, 1810; married ———.
Children:

i. Harlow.[7]
ii. Emeline.

172

432

HARLOW[6] (*Heman,*[5] *Noah,*[4] *Zaccheus,*[3] *Samuel,*[2] *Thomas*[1]).
Children:
  i. Charles.[7]
  ii. Orton.
  iii. Emily.
  iv. Jane.

433

SAMUEL[6] (*Heman,*[5] *Noah,*[4] *Zaccheus,*[3] *Samuel,*[2] *Thomas*[1]), born Dec. 16, 1821.

434

CHARLES F.[6] (*Heman,*[5] *Noah,*[4] *Zaccheus,*[3] *Samuel,*[2] *Thomas*[1]), born Jan. 29, 1823; died Aug. 17, 1891; married June 30, 1847, Mary Jane Strong, born Sept. 5, 1829, still living (1905), in fairly good health.
Children:
  i. Melinda M.,[7] b. June 20, 1849; m. Sept. 26, 1867, Uriah Cook, now a dealer in fine sheep at Lunda, O.
    Children:
    1. Arch T. Cook, b. July 22, 1868.
    2. Fred W. Cook, b. April 4, 1871.
    3. Harry S. Cook, b. June 20, 1873.
  ii. Mary, b. May 22, 1851; d. Aug., 1892; m. Sept., 1869, John M. Lane.
    Children:
    1. Omer Lane, b. July 22, 1870.
    2. Estella Lane, b. March 1, 1872.
    3. Elvesta Lane, b. Dec. 3, 1875.
    4. Forest Lane, b. June 17, 1885.
  iii. Virginia F., b. March 4, 1854; m. May 3, 1873, William L. Morse.
    Children:
    1. Charles H. Morse, b. Sept. 1, 1875.
    2. Guy I. Morse, b. July 25, 1882.
701. iv. William A., b. March 27, 1858.
702. v. Edward C., b. Oct. 15, 1870.

436

SILAS WARREN[6] (*Silas,[5] Jonathan,[4] Jonathan,[3] Samuel,[2] Thomas[1]*), born at Hudson, N. Y.; married Alida S. Miller. [Am. Ancestry, II.] He bought land in Freetown (Mass.), in 1862 of Stephen S. Tobey, and sold it in 1873, his wife, Alida S., joining in the deed. He died in 1884.

Child:

    Silas Warren.[7]

437

WILLIAM HENRY[6] (*Jonathan,[5] Jonathan,[4] Jonathan,[3] Samuel,[2] Thomas[1]*), born in New Bedford, June 18, 1813; married first, Sept. 2, 1838, Hannah Howland; after her death he married second, Sept. 15, 1844, Elizabeth Folger, daughter of Edward and Judith (Folger) Hussey, of Nantucket. She died at Cambridge March 13, 1895, aged 74 years, 8 months.

He was an accountant quite a portion of his life, but became a travelling salesman. Lost his life in a railroad accident at Yarmouth Junction, Feb. 16, 1882.

Children:

    i.   Elizabeth Howland,[7] b. May 31, 1845; m. John Ireland, of Watertown.

    ii.   Helen Amelia, b. March 31, 1846; m. Charles A. Macomber, of West Bridgewater.

    iii.   Edward W., b. June 19, 1849; d. July 22, 1851.

704.   iv.   Warren Price, b. March 27, 1851.

    v.   Alice Gardner, b. Sept. 4, 1852; d. June 19, 1856.

    vi.   Mary Folger, b. Dec. 26, 1853; m. Eben Guerrier.

    vii.   Edward Hussey, b. Sept. 3, 1856; d. in infancy.

705.   viii.   Harrison Loring, b. Dec. 31, 1858.

    ix.   William Henry, b. Dec. 3, 1859; d. in infancy.

    x.   Another child was born and died very soon; dates unknown.

438

LEONARD WHITE[6] (*Jonathan,[5] Jonathan,[4] Jonathan,[3] Samuel,[2] Thomas[1]*), born in New Bedford, Jan. 29,

1821; married, in New York city, Jane Anne Oakley, who survived him. He was a capable and fortunate business man; residing most of his mature life in New York, and died there about 1877. Administration of so much of his estate as was in Bristol County, Mass., was granted Nov. 2, 1877, to Charles W. Bonney.

439

JONATHAN FRANKLIN[6] (*Jonathan*,[5] *Jonathan*,[4] *Jonathan*,[3] *Samuel*,[2] *Thomas*[1]), born in New Bedford, July 23, 1831; married first, in Boston, Oct. 15, 1852, Abby Whiton, daughter of Charles and Fanny (Farrington) Houghton, born in Hillsborough, N. H., Jan. 21, 1834, died Jan. 1, 1876. He married second, May 3, 1876, Alice May, daughter of Joseph Frederick and Lucy (Sprague) Milner, born in Boston, July 17, 1858.

He was a complete machinist and engineer, with detailed knowledge of all branches of the subject; often entrusted with critical and important matters. Resided at Watertown, having a church home at Eliot Congregational Church in Newton for the latter part of his life. Had some Western life in earlier days. He died Dec. 2, 1902. Mrs. Alice May Tobey resides in Watertown.

Children:

    i.   Abby Elflida,[7] b. July 31, 1855; m. April 16, 1877, Augustus Dean, son of Samuel Bridge and Adelaide Augusta (Jones) Dean, b. Aug. 6, 1855. He is in the advertising department of the Boston Herald; resides at Melrose.

    Children :

      1. Marion Dickson Dean, b. May 9, 1878.
      2. Adelaide Louise Dean, b. March 12, 1881.

    ii. Arthur Franklin, b. Oct. 9, 1879; is a commercial traveler for a Boston dry goods house; resides with his mother in Watertown (near Newton).

443

JOSEPH TERRY[6] (*Abishai Huxford,*[5] *Jonathan,*[4] *Jonathan,*[3] *Samuel,*[2] *Thomas*[1]), born at Rochester, June 7, 1836; married at New Bedford, Jan. 23, 1862, Ruth Soule, daughter of Ebenezer and Ruth S. (Cardy) Ryder, born in New Bedford, Jan. 23, 1840. His father died when he was 9 months old; at twelve he began to work away from home as opportunity offered; at eighteen, went to St. Albans, Vt., and learned the watchmaker's trade, after which he established himself at New Bedford, where he has continued ever since, enlarging his business to include sportsman's goods, etc.

Children:

i. Walter Mason,[7] b. Dec. 12, 1862; became a seaman; was lost at sea in the Gulf Stream, Dec. 12, 1895, after 16 years of service.

ii. Frank Clinton, b. Nov. 9, 1865; was afflicted with a spinal trouble from birth; was always delicate; became an artist of much ability; d. at home Nov. 9, 1892.

iii. Charles Wyman, b. March 20, 1867; learned the trade of machinist, and entered into the study of all connected with it very eagerly till he rose to the grade of a designer and builder of machinery. He married, Feb. 26, 1902, Hattie Swift, daughter of David S. R. and Adaline Hand Durfee, of New Bedford. He resides at Fairhaven; is master mechanic and superintendent of the Atlas Tack Mfg. Co.'s eyelet department.

445

WILLIAM HENRY[6] (*Samuel,*[5] *Samuel,*[4] *Eliakim,* *Samuel,*[2] *Thomas*[1]), born in Bristol, Me., Feb. 13, 1804; married first, at Bristol, Jan. 21, 1825, Nancy A. Johnston, who died at Gardiner, Me., Dec. 3, 1833, aged 31 years. He married second, Nov. 15, 1837, Mrs. Lucy L. Weston; she died in Sept., 1843; they

12

had no children. He married third, in East Machias, Me., June 2, 1845, Mrs. Mary Gardner (Kellar) Ames, daughter of Capt. John and Susan (Phinney) Kellar, who was born in Thomaston, Me., Jan. 11, 1814, and married first, Jan. 21, 1831, Capt. Alfred Ames, who died July 28, 1841.

Mr. Tobey lived in Bristol, Me., until 1827, when he went to Vassalborough, Me., where he remained till 1833, when he removed to Gardiner, Me., and engaged in the lumber business. Here his wife died. After that he went West and studied medicine at Cincinnati, O. In 1837 he returned to Bristol, Me.; in 1840 settled at St. Stephens, N. B., where his second wife died. In 1845 he removed to East Machias, Me. He went to California in 1849 or 1850 on the schooner " Oriental "; returned by the way of the Isthmus of Panama the next year; died of heart failure April 21, 1854. His wife survived him into the present century, spending her last days in the suburbs of Boston.

Children:

i. Sarah Lockwood,[7] b. at Bristol, Me., July 12, 1826; m. at East Machias, Me., Jan. 14, 1849, Josiah Harris; she d. July 18, 1899.

Children :

1. Clara Fairbanks Harris, b. at Cutler, Me., Oct. 26, 1849; now living at East Machias, Me.
2. Anna Harris, b. at Cutler, Me., Oct. 18, 1853; d. Nov. 8, 1853.
3. Edward Tobey Harris, b. at E. Machias, Me., March 10, 1856; m. at Hastings, Wis., Oct., 1880, Cora, dau. of Dea. Nathan and Mary (Williams) Bacheller, b. at Whitneyville, Me.; res. Bellevue, Mich. Child: Bertha C. Harris, b. at Minto, N. Dak., July 7, 1885.
4. William Page Harris, b. at E. M., Oct. 25, 1859; m. at Minneapolis, Minn., Jan., 1884, Mary E. Worthley, of Houlton, Me.; res.

Bellevue, Mich. Child: Clinton Pope Harris, b. in Stone Co., N. Y., Nov. 7, 1891.

5. Linnie Sarah Harris, b. at E. M., Jan. 15, 1868; educated at Washington Academy; author of "Bertha's Summer Boarders," "The Young Capitalist," and other works.

ii. Caroline Martin, b. at Vassalborough, Me., Aug. 23, 1828; m. at Waterville, Me., Rev. James Hector Humphrey, who was b. at Orwell, Mass., Aug. 19, 1819, and d. at Eureka, Kan., in Jan., 1872. A minister of the M. E. church; volunteered in the Civil War; rose to be lieut.-colonel; after the war lived in Missouri 5 years, then removed to Kansas; d. from the effects of service in the war.

Children:

1. Steadman Humphrey, b. in Illinois before 1860; d. 1880.
2. Anna Humphrey, b. in Kansas, May 29, 1867; m. John Aller; res. Corwin, Kan. Child: Gladys Aller, b. March, 1895.

iii. Edward Martin, b. at Gardiner, Me., July 12, 1830; d. at sea, between San Francisco and Australia, in 1852.

iv. Susan Kellar, b. at E. Machias, May 9, 1846; res. Brookline.

v. Alfred H., b. at E. M., Dec. 14, 1847; d. Aug. 12, 1869.

446

SAMUEL BOYD[6] (*Samuel,*[5] *Samuel,*[4] *Eliakim,*[3] *Samuel,*[2] *Thomas*[1]), born in Bristol, Me., Nov. 12, 1805; died at Providence, R. I., June 23, 1867; married first, Nov. 13, 1828, Sarah, daughter of Benoni and Phebe Lockwood; she died June 5, 1833, aged 31 years and 6 months. He married second, Jan. 29, 1835, Sarah, daughter of John and Lydia Fry of Bolton, Mass.; she survived him, and died May 25, 1894.

He removed to Providence, R. I., during his boyhood; was educated at Plainfield, Conn., and Burlington, N. J.; studied medicine with Dr. Mauran in Providence, and took full course of lectures at Philadelphia, where he received the degree of M. D., March 27, 1828. He entered into practice in partnership with his preceptor, after a time continuing by himself. Was a member and minister of the Society of Friends, an officer of The Yearly Meeting School; a trustee of Brown University from 1835, and chancellor from 1854 till his death. Was successful in business as in professional pursuits, and aided in building up some of the most prosperous manufacturing establishments in the city. Was one of the originators of the Rhode Island Hospital and one of the trustees of the Butler Hospital for the Insane; also vice-president of the Dispensary, and commissioner of the "Dexter Donation." He was greatly honored and beloved.

Children:

	i.	William Benoni,[7] b. Sept. 9, 1829; d. Dec. 6, 1830.
706.	ii.	William Benoni, b. Nov. 17, 1830.
707.	iii.	Samuel Boyd, Jr., b. Dec. 6, 1831.
708.	iv.	John Fry, b. Nov. 29, 1835.
	v.	Edward, b. June 5, 1838; d. July 29, 1839.
709.	vi.	Thomas Fry, b. Sept. 30, 1840.
	vii.	Sarah Caroline, b. Feb. 8, 1844.
	viii.	Lydia Anna, b. Oct. 30, 1846; d. Dec. 2, 1899.

448

HEMAN[6] (*Eliakim,*[5] *Samuel,*[4] *Eliakim,*[3] *Samuel,*[2] *Thomas*[1]), born in Fairfield, Me., June 27, 1800; married Feb. 1, 1829, Eliza Leighton of Ripley, Me. Resided at Oldtown, Me. He died in February, 1882.

Children:

John Heman.	710. Samuel Leighton, b. in Oldtown,
William.	Oct. 6, 1834.

Edwin.   Augustus.
Celia.   Sarah.
                711. Merritt.

452

JAMES H.⁶ (*Nathaniel*,⁵ *Samuel*,⁴ *Eliakim*,³ *Samuel*,²
*Thomas*¹), born in Norridgewock, Me., June 14, 1810;
died in Boston, May 6, 1865.

452 a

WILLIAM⁶ (*William*,⁵ *Samuel*,⁴ *Eliakim*,³ *Samuel*,²
*Thomas*¹), born in Waterville, Me., in 1814; married
second, at Charlestown, Nov. 22, 1858, Sarah E.,
daughter of John and Rebecca Gilling, born in Boston in 1836.

453

WILLIAM⁶ (*Jonathan Burr*,⁵ *William*,⁴ *Eliakim*,³
Samuel,² *Thomas*¹), born about 1820. Received a
legacy from his father's mother in her will of 6 Feb.,
1828.

454

APOLLOS⁶ (*Apollos*,⁵ *Samuel*,⁴ *Samuel*,³ *Samuel*,²
*Thomas*¹), born in Berkley, April 9, 1798; married
first (published Oct. 14, 1820), Caroline Bryant of
New Bedford. Married second, Lois Bryant. "Lois,
widow of Apollos Tobey and daughter of Gamaliel
Bryant, died, aged 31 years." [Providence Journal,
Dec. 21, 1829.] Died before May 7, 1822, when his
widow was appointed administratrix of his estate.
  Children:
  i.   Edward⁷; said to have died abroad before reaching
       the age of 20 years.
  ii. "Apollos, son of Rev. Apollos Tobey of Berkley,
       aged 24 years, died at New Bedford." [Provi-
       dence Journal, March 4, 1822.]

455

SAMUEL[6] (*Apollos,[5] Samuel,[4] Samuel,[3] Samuel,[2] Thomas[1]*), born in Berkley, Dec. 4, 1799; died in Philadelphia, Pa., Dec. 25, 1876; married Nov. 18, 1840, Mary Beveridge, daughter of Benjamin and Mary (Howell) Jones of Philadelphia, Pa., born Feb. 18, 1814, died Oct. 26, 1887.

He was a merchant in New Bedford (Tobey and Hathaway) in dry goods trade, and also sending out whale-ships and dealing in oil till 1848. He removed to Philadelphia, and, with his brother and partner Caleb Strong Tobey, purchased the first machines invented in the United States for the manufacture of envelopes; carried on the business on 5th St., near Walnut, until 1876.

Children:

   i.   Helen,[7] d. in 1842.
   ii. Mary Howell, b. Dec. 9, 1843.
  iii. Caroline Jones, b. May, 1849; d. Oct. 6, 1853.
  iv. Harriet Jones, b. Sept. 30, 1854; m, Jan. 27, 1891, in the Votive church, Vienna, Austria, Charles Maria de Roth, at that time in the Austrian army.

Child:

     Herbert Carl M. de Roth, b. in Florence, Italy, Feb. 9, 1892.

456

CHARLES COURTSWORTH PINCKNEY[6] (*Apollos,[5] Samuel,[4] Samuel,[3] Samuel,[2] Thomas[1]*), born in Berkley, June 10, 1803; married first, Mary ———. He married second, Emeline, daughter of James and Eliza Snow, born in New Bedford, Jan., 1813, died in Boston, May 17, 1877. He died in Boston, "of old age," Dec. 18, 1874.

Children:

i. Lizzie P.,[7] b. 1838; m. in Boston, March 10, 1860, Willard W. Codman, son of W. W. and Elizabeth T. Codman, of Boston, b. 1837.

ii. James Snow, b. Nov. 19, 1843.

iii. Sarah A., b. Sept. 26, 1845; m. in Boston, Nov. 23, 1869, James A. Kingman, of Boston, piano tuner, b. in Winchester, N. H., in 1842.

iv. Winfield Scott; d. Feb. 4, 1848.

457

CALEB STRONG[6] (*Apollos,[5] Samuel,[4] Samuel,[3] Samuel,[2] Thomas[1]*), born in Berkley, May 10, 1806; died in Philadelphia, Pa., March 7, 1876; married, in New Bedford, Oct. 26, 1831, Ruth Swift, daughter of William and Ruth (Swift) Ross,* born in New Bedford, Feb. 20, 1807; she died Jan. 17, 1876.

He spent many years in New Bedford in mercantile life, dealing in dry goods and also handling the products of whale fishery in which his firm (Tobey and Hathaway) were engaged. With his brother Samuel he removed in 1848 to Philadelphia, Pa., and manufactured envelopes and paper bags, seed bags, tobacco bags, etc. He was a man of the highest moral principle and of an amiable but firm character; a member of the First Unitarian Church in Philadelphia; domestic in his tastes, belonging to no clubs. The death of his wife brought a weight upon his system, a general breaking down, from which he could not rally; and he died in two months.

Children:

i. Francis McCoun,[7] b. Oct. 6, 1832; d. of croup, Jan. 6, 1838.

ii. Laura Hathaway, b. April 20, 1840; has contributed valuable information for this book.

* William Ross was a son of James Ross, born in Alniss, Perthshire, North Britain, Jan. 24, 1757, died in New Bedford, Mass., Oct. 24, 1809. Ruth Swift was born at the Head of Acushnet river, New Bedford, in 1766, and died July 28, 1838.

iii.　Sarah Coffin, b. Oct. 24, 1844; m. Jan. 9, 1873,
　　　John Goodheart Rothermel, son of Peter Frederick
　　　Rothermel, artist; residence, Swarthmore, Pa.
　　Children :
　　　　1.　Laura Tobey Rothermel, b. March 16, 1874; d.
　　　　　Jan. 22, 1892.
　　　　2.　Caroline Gertrude Rothermel, b. June 21, 1477.
　　　　3.　Bessie Green Rothermel, b. Dec. 2, 1880.
720. iv.　Frank Ross, b. in Philadelphia, Pa., Jan. 19, 1847;
　　　unmarried.　Mr. Tobey is president of the Allison
　　　Manufacturing Co. ; a director of the West End
　　　Trust Co., and identified with other large interests.

461

SAMUEL ELAM[6] (*Enoch,[5] Samuel,[4] Samuel,[3] Samuel,[2] Thomas[1]*), born in Berkely about 1803.　Was a
blacksmith.　Removed to "Flowerfield in the county
of St. Joseph and state of Michigan."　Was living
there May 9, 1835, when he and his brother Jonathan
B. (still a resident of Berkely) sold one 1/16th interest
in certain lands in Bristol County, Mass.　Sold his
right in the estate of his sister Catherine, situated in
Fall River, Mass., Jan. 30, 1838.　[Bristol Co. Deeds.]

464

JONATHAN BOWEN[6] (*Enoch,[5] Samuel,[4] Samuel,[3]
Samuel,[2] Thomas[1]*), born in Berkely about 1810.　Removed after May 9, 1835, to "Flowerfield in the
county of St. Josephs, state of Michigan"; was a
blacksmith there when he joined with his brother
Samuel E. in conveying all rights to estate of his deceased sister Catherine in 1838.

465

EDWARD SILAS[6] (*Silas,[5] Samuel,[4] Samuel,[3] Samuel,[2]
Thomas[1]*), born in Kingston, April 5, 1813; married
in Boston, April 5, 1841, Hannah Brown, daughter of

EDWARD SILAS TOBEY.

Hon. Phineas and Hannah (Brown) Sprague,* born
in Duxbury, July 28, 1821, died Jan. 4, 1898. After
a long and eminently successful and useful life, Mr.
Tobey died March 29, 1891. He was a man of strong
religious principle, of sterling integrity, generous and
benevolent, and of gracious and courtly manner. He
was a total abstainer from intoxicants, and an active
promoter of the Temperance reform; he was an ardent Christian of the Orthodox school, a man of faith
and works well blended. We quote from *The Boston
Journal* of March 30, 1891, the following account of
the leading events of his life and the estimation in
which he was held.

Hon. Edward S. Tobey, well known as a former Postmaster
of Boston, died suddenly last evening at his home on Harris.
Street, Brookline. Pneumonia was the cause of death.

Mr. Tobey was born at Kingston, Mass., April 5, 1813.
He was a son of Silas Tobey of Berkley, and grandson of Hon.
Samuel Tobey, also of Berkley, Judge of the Court of Common
Pleas of Taunton. Mr. Tobey began his education in the
school on Mason Street, Boston, and finished it in the High
School at Duxbury. He had originally intended to enter Har-
vard College, but ill-health forced him to change his plans.
He received the honorary degree of A.M. from Dartmouth
College in 1861. In 1830, on his return from a voyage to
Spain, he re-entered the counting-room of his stepfather, who
was the senior partner of the old established firm of Phineas &
Seth Sprague, extensively engaged in foreign and domestic
commerce as shipowners. There he continued until 1860,
having been taken into the firm in 1833. In 1838 he was
chosen Director in the United States Insurance Company of
Boston. In 1839 he was chosen Director of the Commercial
Bank, and was a Director in the Union Bank in Boston from

* Mr. Tobey was descended on his mother's side from Dr. Samuel Fuller of
the Mayflower; from John Alden and Priscilla Mullens. Mrs. Tobey was descended from Francis Sprague who came to Plymouth in the Anne in 1623,
and from William Sprague of Charlestown, who was a son of Edward Sprague,
of Upway, Dorsetshire, England. In another line she was descended from
Capt. Myles Standish, the redoubtable defender of Plymouth colony, and also
from John Alden and Priscilla Mullens, as her husband was.

1842 to 1866. He was also a member of the Board of Managers of the Suffolk Savings Bank. He was one of the founders of the Boston Board of Trade, and was Vice-President of the Board in 1859, and President in '61, '62 and '63. In 1861 he became a Director in the Union Steamship Company, and Chairman of its Building Committee for the construction of two iron steamships of 2000 tons each. They were built by Harrison Loring of South Boston, and were named the Mississippi and the Merrimac. They were to run between Boston and New Orleans, but were prevented from so doing by the outbreak of the war.

He was one of the Trustees of Dartmouth College for eight years, and was the first to contribute to the Webster professorship. He was for several years a Trustee of Bradford Academy, and a generous giver to its funds.

He was appointed by President Grant a member of the first Board of Commissioners on Indian Affairs; remained in the board three years; declined the offer of the appointment of Commissioner of Indian Affairs.

He was also a Director in the Boston and Southern Steamship Company, and Chairman of its Building Committee for the construction of two iron steamships, the South Carolina and the Massachusetts, which were also built by Harrison Loring, and sold to the United States Government. During the war Mr. Tobey was appointed by Gov. Andrew a member of the Committee on Harbor Defences. As President of the Board of Trade, he received a confidential telegram from Secretary of War Stanton requesting the appointment of three persons to confer with others from New York, Philadelphia and Washington to devise the most effectual method of destroying the rebel ram Merrimac. The Boston delegation consisted of Mr. Tobey, ex-Mayor Lincoln and Mr. J. C. Converse. In 1861 he was one of three delegates, appointed in behalf of the Board of Trade, to meet delegates from the Boston, New York and Philadelphia banks, Chamber of Commerce of New York and Board of Trade of Philadelphia, in Washington, to confer with Secretary Chase and Congress as to the financial policy to be adopted by the Government. In 1861 Mr. Tobey became President of the Boston Young Men's Christian Association. As Chairman of its Army Committee, he was actively engaged in co-operation with the United States Christian Commission.

Through the agency of this committee supplies in aid of sick and wounded soldiers were distributed to the value of $1,000,000. Soon after the close of the war he became one of the 100 corporators of national asylums for soldiers, located at Hampton, Va., Dayton, O., and Togus Springs, Augusta, Me.

In 1866 Mr. Tobey was elected to the Massachusetts Senate. In 1875 he was appointed Postmaster of Boston by President Grant. He was reappointed by President Hayes, and again by President Arthur. He brought to the duties of his office a long business experience, and fully believed that they should be administered on business principles. The increase in the volume of business during his administration is measurably indicated by the increase of gross receipts in money from $940,000 to $1,550,000.

Mr. Tobey was the first President of the Fall River Steamboat Company. He was the first Treasurer of the Russell Mills, Plymouth, Mass., a successful duck manufacturing company, and had continued in that office since 1854. He held official relations to many educational, religious and philanthropic institutions, among which were the Congregational Association, American Missionary Association, Boston Missionary Society, American Peace Society, Discharged Soldiers' Home, Pilgrims' Society, Dartmouth College, Bradford Academy, Historic Genealogical Society and Webster Historical Society. In 1871, as President of the Pilgrims' Society, he was concerned in deciding upon the memorial to the Pilgrims' observance of their first Sabbath in America, which was spent on Clark's Island, Duxbury. In 1861, when the founding of the present Institute of Technology was under consideration by the Legislature, Mr. Tobey was one with others to address the Legislative Committee in its behalf, and it was through his personal influence that Dr. William J. Walker became interested in the projected institute, and gave for its establishment the large sum which secured the legislative grant of land for the institution. Mr. Tobey held official relations to the institute for several years.

Mr. Tobey was a member of Mt. Vernon Church, Boston, from the first year of its foundation, 1842, under the pastorate of Rev. Dr. Kirk. He was Treasurer of the society for 18 years, and for several years Chairman of the Prudential Committee. In April, 1883, he moved to Brookline, and entered into church relations with the Harvard Church. Mr. Tobey leaves a widow, three sons and two daughters.

Children, all but the youngest, born in Boston:

i. Elisabeth Sprague,[7] b. Jan. 10, 1842. Miss Tobey has made her life tell in the family circle and beyond those limits. In 1884 she was elected president of the Mass. Woman's Christian Temperance Union, as the successor of Mrs. Mary A. Livermore, and was re-elected for six annual terms. Declining another term, she gave herself entirely to the work to which she felt divinely called, that of evangelism. For fourteen years she conducted special services in connection with churches of various denominations in each of the New England states, auxiliary to the pastors. In these services it is estimated that many hundreds began the better life in response to Miss Tobey's appeals and efforts. One particular experience of great interest was her preaching in the Orthodox Congregational Church of Berkley, of which her great-great-grandfather, Rev. Samuel Tobey, was pastor a century and a half before.

ii. Cornelius Sprague, b. Oct. 15, 1843; d. March 14, 1848.

iii. Alice Sophia, b. May 6, 1846; m. Dec. 14, 1865, George W. Ware, Jr., son of George W. and Amanda Mildred (Rand) Ware, b. in Boston, Oct. 3, 1837; studied at Andover and Middlebury; grad. Amherst Coll. 1859, and Harvard Law School 1861; hon. A.M. Harvard Univ. 1862, Middlebury 1868. He was a counsellor at law in Boston. He d. Feb. 12, 1890.

Child:

Alice Mildred Ware, b. Sept. 12, 1866; d. Feb. 21, 1867.

iv. Hannah Brown Sprague, b. June 25, 1848; m. in Boston, Dec. 21, 1871, George Hay Stuart, Jr., son of George Hay Stuart, Esq. (the distinguished merchant and philanthropist, founder and president of The United States Christian Commission in the war of the Rebellion), and Mrs. Martha Kyle (Dennison) Stuart, b. in Philadelphia, Pa., Feb. 11, 1849. They reside at Ardmore, Pa.; he is connected with the Philadelphia agency of The International Mercantile Marine Company; is an elder in the Presbyterian church and active in various philanthropic enterprises.

Children:

1. George Hay Stuart, 3d, b. in Boston, Oct. 12, 1872; is assistant treasurer of the Girard Trust Co. of Philadelphia.
2. Edward Tobey Stuart, b. in Chestnut Hill, Pa., Oct. 19, 1876; is assistant treasurer of the Cambria Steam Co. of Philadelphia.
3. Elizabeth Sprague Stuart, b. in Chestnut Hill, Pa., Aug. 19, 1878.

   v. Amelia, b. April 7, 1851; d. July 6, 1861.
723. vi. Phineas Sprague, b. Dec. 19, 1853.
   vii. Edward Silas, b. Sept. 29, 1855: d. July 23, 1902. Was private secretary to his father from the beginning of his term as postmaster of Boston till 1884, when he was appointed assistant postmaster; later, for several years, until his death, he was supt. of the collection department of the N. E. Telegraph and Telephone Co. of Boston. He was a member of the Sons of the Revolution and the Society of Colonial Wars. He was a member of the Pennsylvania Society of the Sons of the Revolution.
724. viii. Sidney Berkeley, b. Nov. 1, 1858.
   ix. Arthur Waddington, b. Feb. 12, 1861; d. in Kansas City, Mo., Dec. 16, 1898. He resided some years at Philadelphia, Pa.; went to Kansas City on an engagement in Telephone business, and died there of pneumonia.
   x. Miriam Amelia, b. in Nantasket, July 23, 1863.

466

ALVAN[6] (*Alvan*,[5] *Nathaniel*,[4] *Samuel*,[3] *Samuel*,[2] *Thomas*[1]), born in Wilmington, Vt., April 1, 1808; married in Charlestown, Aug. 20, 1835, Elizabeth, daughter of Chester and Elizabeth (Watts) Adams, born March 5, 1812, died in So. Berwick, Me., May 11,

1897.   He was graduated at Amherst College in 1828, and at Andover Theological Seminary in 1831; received the degree of D.D. from Dartmouth in 1867; was ordained at Durham, N. H., pastor of the Congregational Church, Nov. 20, 1833; remained till 1871, and was then pastor and emeritus at So. Berwick till his death, Sept. 20, 1874.

Children:

    i.   Sarah Adams,[7] b. in Charlestown, Aug. 20, 1836; m. Oct. 25, 1860, Rev. Jonas Atwood Bates, of Granby.

    ii. Elizabeth Watts, b. Jan. 26, 1839.

    iii. Mary Webb, b. Dec. 18, 1841; d. Oct. 6, 1899, unmarried.

    iv. Martha Tirzah, b. Dec. 14, 1843.

468 a

SAMUEL[6] (*John*,[5] *Isaac*,[4] *Samuel*,[3] *Samuel*,[2] *Thomas*[1]), born and resided in Buckland.   Settled his father's estate; was a mechanic.

Child:

    Lizzie,[7] b. Jan. 4, 1862.

470

THOMAS[6] (*Luke*,[5] *Thomas*,[4] *Thomas*,[3] *Samuel*,[2] *Thomas*[1]), born in Acushnet; married Sept. 7, 1834, Rebecca Brayton.   He died in 1857.   David Brayton was appointed administrator of his estate, April 7, 1857, and Loum Snow was appointed guardian of the children May 5th following.

Children:

    i.   Eliza B.,[7] b. Sept. 4, 1836; m. March 23, 1859, Capt. Charles H. Pierce, of Acushnet, b. Feb. 24, 1830, d. Oct. 1, 1876.

Children :
   1. Henry C. Pierce, b. March 20, 1860 ; m. May
      3, 1881, Lillian M. Tripp, b. Feb. 23, 1861.
   2. William T. Pierce, b. Dec. 3, 1865.
730. ii. Charles H.
731. iii. George B.
   iv. Alice B., b. Dec. 31, 1844.
732. v. John B.
   vi. William J. ; d. Aug. 22, 1847.

471

CHARLES F.[6] (*Luke,[5] Thomas,[4] Thomas,[3] Samuel,[2] Thomas[1]*), born in Acushnet (Fairhaven) in 1822; married Sept., 1846, Sarah D. Thatcher. They died in San Francisco, Cal.

Child, born in Fairhaven:
   Elizabeth N.,[7] b. July 15, 1848.

472

HENRY A.[6] (*Luke,[5] Thomas,[4] Thomas,[3] Samuel,[2] Thomas[1]*), born in Acushnet; married Helen M. Chandler. His children were remembered in the will of his mother, in 1876. He died in San Francisco, Cal., March 4, 1873.

Children:
   i. Henry H.,[7] b. Aug. 9, 1857.
   ii. Ella Frances, ⎱ b.Aug. 29,1858 ; ⎰ d. April 8, 1859.
   iii. Mary Helen, ⎰   ⎱ d. Aug. 12, 1863.
   iv. Emma Juliette, b. July 27, 1860.

473

FREDERICK[6] (*Luke,[5] Thomas,[4] Thomas,[3] Samuel,[2] Thomas[1]*), born in Acushnet; married Mary Chandler, a sister of his brother Henry's wife. Removed to California.

475

ELISHA[6] (*Elisha,*[5] *Thomas,*[4] *Thomas,*[3] *Samuel,*[2] *Thomas*[1]), born in Fairhaven, " in 1821 "; married at Providence, R. I., in Sept., 1845, Mrs. Jane Loring, daughter of John and Bitha [Bethia] T. (Binney) Gould and widow of Rev. Joel Knight; she was born in Hull, Feb. 22, 1812, died in New Bedford, April 7, 1852. He was a painter by trade, but going West about 1850 he became a farmer, and bought and sold real estate profitably. Returned East. He married second, Love Butler of Edgartown; he married third, Sophia ———. Died at Haverhill, Oct. 14, 1896.

Children:

735. i.   Elisha Franklin,[7] b. May 30, 1846.

   .ii.   Jane Gould, twin with the above; d. Sept., 1846.

   iii.   Mary Bitha, b. March 31, 1849 ; m. in Waukon, Ia., Aug. 6, 1864, Alanson Pratt, b. in Maine, Sept. 6, 1840. Res. Waterloo, Ia.

   Children :

     1. Edward Wilson Pratt, b. Sept. 8, 1865.

     2. Clara May Pratt, b. Nov. 25, 1868.

     3. Cora Mabel Pratt, b. Feb. 29, 1876.

     4. Frederick Archer Pratt, b. May 5, 1879.

     5. Roy Gerald Pratt, b. June 11, 1885.

476

STEPHEN[6] (*Elisha,*[5] *Thomas,*[4] *Thomas,*[3] *Samuel,*[2] *Thomas*[1]), born in Acushnet, Nov. 10, 1828; died Jan. 27, 1885; married Phebe Sampson.

Child:

Francelia,[7] b. in New Bedford, Dec. 16, 1859.

477

FRANKLIN[6] (*Elisha,*[5] *Thomas,*[4] *Thomas,*[3] *Samuel,*[2] *Thomas*[1]), born in New Bedford " in 1828 "; married first, June 24, 1851, Phebe, daughter of Peleg and Ruth Potter, who was born in Westport in 1831, and died Oct. 1, 1879. He married second, Mrs. Etta (Hayden), widow of John Long. He was a plumber; resided some years at Fairhaven; removed to New Bedford, and carried on business (firm of Tobey and Coggeshall). He died Nov. 12, 1884. His son Franklin, Jr., administered on the estate and gave bonds, with John B. and George F. sureties, Dec. 5, 1884. Allowance made to the widow Etta H., Feb. 6, 1885.

Children, born in Fairhaven:

737. i.   John B.,[7] b. June 4, 1853.
738. ii. Franklin, Jr., b. Nov. 1, 1854.
739. iii. George Frederick, b. Jan., 1858.
     iv. Adelaide F., b. Oct., 1859.
     v.   Mary S.; d. Nov. 12, 1878.

490

JONATHAN PRATT[6] (*Jonathan,*[5] *Elisha,*[4] *Ephraim,*[3] *Gershom,*[2] *Thomas*[1]), born Dec. 5, 1793; married at Great Barrington, April 19, 1819, Nancy Lester, b. May 16, 1803.

Children:

     i. Louise E.[7]; d. at 19 years of age.
750. ii. Henry Augustus, b. Oct. 12, 1821.

492

ELISHA L.[6] (*Jonathan,*[5] *Elisha,*[4] *Ephraim,*[3] *Gershom,*[2] *Thomas*[1]); married at Alford (published Oct. 22, 1837) Charlotte M. Barrett. Residence, Alford.

Children:

     i. George,[7] b. 1841; d. Sept. 10, 1843, "aged 2 y., 2 m. and 18 d."
753. ii. George B., b. June 17, 1845.
     13

493

WILLIAM R.[6] (*Jonathan,[5] Elisha,[4] Ephraim,[3] Gershom,[2] Thomas[1]*), married in Alford, Oct. 13, 1841, Hannah L. Barrett.
Children:
   i. Alphonso.[7]
   ii. Nettie; m. Walter Crego.

494

ERASTUS[6] (*Barnabas,[5] Elisha,[4] Ephraim,[3] Gershom,[2] Thomas[1]*), born in Sharon, Conn.; married Ann Meriam of Brookfield, Conn. He died in Hamilton, Can., in 1849.
Children:
   i. Mary J.[7]; d. in infancy.
   ii. William Barnabas; a druggist; m. Emeline E. Robinson; residence, Syracuse, N. Y.
     Children:
      1. William R.
      2. Florence.

495

HENRY[6] (*Barnabas,[5] Elisha,[4] Ephraim,[3] Gershom,[2] Thomas[1]*); resided at Hudson, N. Y.; kept a hotel at the steamboat landing; m. Sophia ——; died Oct. 18, 1840.
Children:
    Chloe.[7]   Mary Sophia.
    Jane.   Julia Frances.

496

ALBERT[6] (*Barnabas,[5] Elisha,[4] Ephraim,[3] Gershom,[2] Thomas[1]*), born in Canaan, Conn.; married Emily Howes, born in Sullivan co., N. Y.

Child:

Elisha C.,[7] b. at Amina, N. Y.; d. at Westfield,
Feb. 4, 1897, æ. 67, 8, 13.

497

HEMAN[6] (*Barnabas,*[5] *Elisha,*[4] *Ephraim,*[3] *Gershom,*[2]
Thomas[1]); married Hannah Boland of Sharon, Conn.;
she died May 14, 1835. He died Aug. 25, 1873.

Children:

    i.   Horace N.,[7] b. March 18, 1821; d. Sept. 16, 1822.
758. ii. Horace M., b. Dec. 25, 1822.
759. iii. Henry S., b. June 8, 1824.
    iv. Harriet B., b. July 22, 1826; m. first, Joseph
        Hagadorn, of Poughkeepsie, N. Y.; m. second,
        Benjamin Sherow, of Washington Wallow; she
        d. Oct. 17, 1896.
    v.   Sophronia E., b. Oct. 17, 1828; m. March 26, 1856,
        Luther Eaton, of Kent, Conn. Has contributed
        family records.
    vi. Mary Jane, b. Aug. 27, 1831; d. May 6, 1832.
    vii. Sophia Ann, b. March 27, 1833; d. Dec. 21, 1834.
    viii. Norman, b. Jan. 4, d. July 8, 1835.

498

ORVILLE HURD[6] (*Barnabas,*[5] *Elisha,*[4] *Ephraim,*[3]
Gershom,[2] *Thomas*[1]), child of Barnabas by second wife.
Went when a young man to New York; went into
the business of curing, preserving and packing meats
on an extensive scale; also started that business in
Chicago, Ill., where he built the first house for the
business, which he carried on in both cities.

Children:

760. i.   Edwin.[7]
    ii. Elizabeth.
    iii. Abby.
761. iv. William.
762. v. John.
    vi. Ellen; res. Chicago, Ill.
763. vii. Frank Hurd, b. in Chicago, Ill., in 1852.

499

CHESTER FIELD[6] (*Sylvanus,[5] Elisha,[4] Ephraim,[3] Gershom,[2] Thomas[1]*), born in Alford, July 30, 1795. Married (published at West Stockbridge Oct. 24, 1830), Maria Taylor. She died Dec. 11, 1852; he married second, Sept. 12, 1854, Oladine Burkhardt, who died May 1, 1897. He resided at West Stockbridge and later at Egremont; was a farmer and merchant. He died Aug. 6, 1878.

Children:

    i. Antoinette,[7] m. —— Ives.

765. ii. Lester S., b. Feb. 8, 1839.

500

. JOHN FOSTER[6] (*Sylvanus,[5] Elisha,[4] Ephraim,[3] Gershom,[2] Thomas[1]*), born in Alford, Dec. 2, 1811; removed to West Stockbridge Center, and was a leading member of the church at that place. He married Lois French, who died Jan 11, 1884. He died Jan. 7, 1884. No children.

501

HENRY MARSHALL[6] (*Sylvanus,[5] Elisha,[4] Ephraim,[3] Gershom,[2] Thomas[1]*), born in West Stockbridge, May 16, 1816. He was town clerk in 1839; member of the Mass. Legislature 1840–1841 ; removed to Greenwich, N. Y.; married first, at G., Oct. 2, 1844, Elizabeth, daughter of Abram and Sarah (Adams) Burrill, born in Salisbury, N. Y., March 15, 1823; died Feb. 11, 1855. He married second, Nov. 13, 1856, Katharine, daughter of James and Sylvia Moor, born in Schaghticoke, N. Y., Oct. 11, 1817. He removed in 1867 to Oneonta, N. Y., where he and his son were engaged in dry goods business until his death April 27, 1879.

The widow died Jan. 30, 1885.

Child:

770. Albert Burrill,[7] b. Oct. 1, 1845.

502

EGBERT PRINDLE[6] (*Ephraim,[5] Elisha,[4] Ephraim,[3] Gershom,[2] Thomas[1]*), born at Alford, Feb. 4, 1804; married July 25, 1828, Sally, daughter of Bethuel and Betsey (Arnold) Seely, of Farmington, Conn., born Aug. 21, 1806; she died Aug. 1, 1869.

Resided at Great Barrington; was a blacksmith. He died May 16, ~~1869.~~ *1854.*

Children:

775. i.   Charles Henry.[7]
776. ii.   Edwin,   } b. Feb. 15, 1834.
777. iii. Edward, }

504

POMEROY[6] (*Abraham,[5] Jesse,[4] Ephraim,[3] Gershom,[2] Thomas[1]*), born in West Stockbridge, Dec. 8, 1790; married ———.

Children:

   i.   Edward.[7]
   ii. Sophia.

505

HYLON[6] (*Abraham,[5] Jesse,[4] Ephraim,[3] Gershom,[2] Thomas[1]*), born in West Stockbridge, March 31, 1793; married March 20, 1816, Florella Hitchcock.

"Capt. Hylon Tobey died Nov. 9, 1822, aged 29 years and 8 months . . . became a Mason Nov. 22, 1814." [Town Record.]

Children:

   i.   George.[7]
   ii.   Clarissa.
   iii. Mary.

506

FREDERICK[6] (*Abraham,[5] Jesse,[4] Ephraim,[3] Gershom,[2] Thomas[1]*), born in West Stockbridge, Feb. 12, 1801; married ———.
He died at Canaan, N. Y.
Child:

> Jane,[7] died in Canaan, N. Y.

507

ABRAHAM[6] (*Abraham,[5] Jesse,[4] Ephraim,[3] Gershom,[2] Thomas[1]*), (called also Abram), born in West Stockbridge in 1805; married Feb. 3, 1829, Clarinda, daughter of Nathaniel and Nancy (Hammond) Lathrop, born Feb. 6, 1805, in Canaan, N. Y., died April 2, 1878.

He resided at West Stockbridge. Was a thrifty farmer, prominent in town affairs and well known throughout the adjoining towns.

Was elected captain of militia March 17, 1829, and resigned Jan. 11, 1833. He died May 28, 1875.

Children:

i.   Egbert Morgan,[7] b. Oct. 31, 1830; d. Feb. 12, 1831.
ii.   Jeanette Elizabeth, b. Jan. 23, 1832; m. Oct. 12, 1852, Robert H. McLellan, of Troy, N. Y. She d., s. p., in March, 1896.
iii.   Henry M., d. at the age of sixteen.
iv.   Mary M., b. Sept. 20, 1838; m. Sept. 20, 1858, Charles E. Platt, of Waterbury, Conn.; res. at Great Barrington.
780. v.   Edwin Jerome, b. Jan. 8, 1842.
781. vi.   Theodore Pomeroy, b. Jan. 16, 1844.

508

FRANKLIN[6] (*Abraham,[5] Jesse,[4] Ephraim,[3] Gershom,[2] Thomas[1]*), born at West Stockbridge; married Elizabeth ———.

⁕ Children:

    i.   Amelia,⁷ m. ——— Vasey.
    ii. Ellen, b. at W. Stockbridge, Dec. 2, 1843; m.
        ——— Halsey.
    iii. Frances, b. Jan. 22, 1849; m. ——— Baldwin.
    iv. Sarah, m. ——— Vasey.
    v.   Mary, d. unmarried.

509

JESSE⁶ (*Jesse,⁵ Jesse,⁴ Ephraim,³ Gershom,² Thomas¹*), born in Jay, N. Y., about 1800; died there at the age of 75 years.

510

GEORGE GIBBS⁶ (*Jesse,⁵ Jesse,⁴ Ephraim,³ Gershom,² Thomas¹*), born in Jay, N. Y., 1811; died 1894; married Harriet B., daughter of Isaac and Martha (Barber) Finch, born in Jay, N. Y., died in Boston, Oct. 25, 1892, aged 88 years, 10 months, and 21 days.

Children:

        i.   Anna Hortense,⁷ b. March 3, 1841.
782. ii. George Gibbs Finch, b. 1843.
       iii. Frances Martha, b. 1845; m. Charles H. Jones,
           lumber manufacturer; res. Tacoma, Wash.
783. iv. Walter Henry, b. Dec. 2, 1847.
784. v.   Carter McVene, b. Nov. 15, 1849.
       vi. Harriet Submit, b. 1851; m. Jerome Stickney, a
           dentist; res. Ausable Forks, N. Y.

517

ZALMON⁶ (*Miles,⁵ George,⁴ Ephraim,³ Gershom,² Thomas¹*), born⁕ at Norfolk, Conn., July 27, 1791; married first, Margaret C. ———; married second, in Upton, Mass., March 21, 1833, Sophronia Baker. He graduated at Brown University in 1817; resided in

---

⁕ Statistics respecting his father, Miles, are lacking, and we have no article upon him; but in the will of George, No. 99, on page 92, *ante*, it is to be noticed that there is a bequest to "the heirs of his deceased son Miles."

Providence till about 1836; was ordained pastor of
the Baptist church at Bristol, R. I., in March, 1836,
and remained there three years; had pastorates at
Warwick and Pawtucket, R. I., and spent the latter
part of his life at Warren, R. I. He died Sept. 17,
1858, " aged 67 years, 1 month and 21 days," specified
as " son of Miles and Abigail," and " born in Norfolk."
Child:

> Zalmon Augustus,[7] was married by his father at
> Providence, R. I., Nov. 21, 1853, to Rowena C.
> Wood.

520

JOHN S.[6] (*George,[5] George,[4] Ephraim,[3] Gershom,[2]
Thomas[1]*), born ———; married in 1841 Caroline
Prescott. He died in 1866.
Children:

i. Sophronia.[7]
ii. Irene.

524

PHILANDER[6] (*George,[5] George,[4] Ephraim,[3] Gershom,[2] Thomas[1]*), born April 16, 1831; married Martha ———. Resided at Sheffield.
Children (incomplete list):

i. Irene,[7] b. in 1857; m. March 8, 1876, Silas Rote
(son of Leonard and Elizabeth), b. in Sheffield in
1849.
ii. Nellie E., b. in 1861; m. at Sheffield, March 11,
1885, Frederick E. Bartholomew (son of Henry
A. and Sabrina) of Canaan, Conn., b. in 1860.

526

HENRY RICHMOND[6] (*Ephraim,[5] Ephraim,[4] Eph-
raim,[3] Gershom,[2] Thomas[1]*), born Sept. 1, 1818; died
May 27, 1897; married ———.
Child:

Clara L.,[7] m. ——— Stearns.

NATHANIEL TOBEY, OF UNION AND WALDOBORO, ME.

527

URIEL MONTAGUE⁶ (*Ephraim,⁵ Ephraim,⁴ Ephraim,³ Gershom,² Thomas¹*), born May 20, 1826. Residence, Sauk Center, Minn.; a merchant.

528

CHARLES CLINTON⁶ (*Ephraim,⁵ Ephraim,⁴ Ephraim,³ Gershom,² Thomas¹*), born Dec. 31, 1835. A merchant at Sauk Center, Minn.

SEVENTH GENERATION.

535

NATHANIEL⁷ (*John,⁶ Samuel,⁵ Thomas,⁴ Thomas,³ Thomas,² Thomas¹*), born in Union, Me., July 21, 1796; married first, March 5, 1820, Hannah, daughter of George and Barbara (Hoffses) Miller; she died June 10, 1848; he married second, Betsey, daughter of Jacob and Margaret (Kuhn), widow of Jacob Miller, born Nov. 10, 1814, died Nov. 14, 1900.

He resided at Union, Jefferson and Waldoboro; died March 22, 1879.

Children:

i. Almeda,⁸ b. July 9, 1821, d. Sept. 24, 1847; m. Robert Langer of Bath, Me.

ii. Eben Stone, b. Aug. 17, 1822, d. April 11, 1845; was mate of ship "Union," and d. at New Orleans, La.

iii. James Riley, b. Oct. 25, 1823, d. Dec. 8, 1846; mate of ship "Lapland," and d. at New Orleans, La.

iv. Mary Jane, b. Sept. 25, 1824, d. in infancy.
v. Elijah Miller, b. Dec. 24, 1825, d. in 1850; captain of a ship, sailed to Honolulu, H. I., and d. there.
vi. Mary Jane, b. Mar. 18, 1827, d. in infancy.
vii. John, b. Sept. 12, 1828, d. in July, 1846.
viii. Rebecca Morse, b. Sept. 22, 1829, d. July 10, 1839.
800. ix. Thomas West, b. Nov. 10, 1830.
801. x. Nathaniel, Jr., b. Feb. 2, 1832.
xi. William Jackson, b. Nov. 25, 1833.
802. xii. Albert Rice, b. Feb. 10, 1835.
xiii. Galen Horace, b. Feb. 10, 1836.
xiv. Rebecca Chase, b. April 6, 1856; m. Nov. 14, 1874, Alton J. Hall.
Children :
1. Inez C. Hall, b. Feb. 28, 1876; m. July 12, 1899, Charles A. Damon, of Reading.
2. Margaret E. Hall, b. Nov. 8. 1878.
3. Ella B. Hall, b. Nov. 16, 1880.
4. H. Graham Hall, b. March 26, 1897.

536

EDWARD[7] (*John*,[6] *Samuel*,[5] *Thomas*,[4] *Thomas*,[3] *Thomas*,[2] *Thomas*[1]), born in Union, Me., Feb. 19, 1808; married Eliza Gilchrist; resided in Montville, Me.; died " about 1886." The widow died in 1896.

537

LEANDER[7] (*John*,[6] *Samuel*,[5] *Thomas*,[4] *Thomas*,[3] *Thomas*,[2] *Thomas*[1]), born at Union, Me., Sept. 17, 1815; m. Harriet Bagley, who died in 1882. Resided at Montville, Me.; died in June, 1890.

538

SETH[7] (*Jonathan Howes*,[6] *Seth*,[5] *Seth*,[4] *Thomas*,[3] *Thomas*,[2] *Thomas*[1]), born in Dennis; married in Boston, June 2, 1853, Lucinda D., daughter of

CHARLES TOBEY.

Thomas N. Kingsbury, born in Boston 1832, died June 14, 1861.

He studied law with Hon. Robert Rantoul, and was admitted to the bar. Was for many years clerk of the Municipal Court of Boston. He died at Dennis at the old family homestead, Sept. 15, 1883, " aged 59," says town record.

Child:

> Charles Kingsbury,⁸ b. Oct. 31, 1856; d. May 6, 1860.

538 a.

RUTH,⁷ daughter of Jonathan Howes,⁶ born in 1826. married in Dennis, May 14, 1857, Asa Shiverick, Jr. (his third marriage).

BETSEY,⁷ daughter of Jonathan Howes,⁶ died in Dennis, unmarried, aged 52 yrs., 5 mos. and 4 days, April 12, 1881.

539

CHARLES⁷ (*Jonathan Howes,*⁶ *Seth,*⁵ *Seth,*⁴ *Thomas,*³ *Thomas,*² *Thomas*¹), born in Dennis in 1831. He left his native town in the opening of his manhood and betook himself to the expanding young city of Chicago. He opened a furniture store on State Street, south of Van Buren, in the year 1856, his place of business being 20 by 60 feet. The following year his brother Frank Bassett Tobey came to help the enterprise onward, and the brothers rose rapidly to the front rank of the business. Doing all their work, economizing as well as pushing forward, they were able to weather the severe financial panic of those years and to advance in every way. Though burned out in the fearful conflagration of 1871, they improvised a salesroom and made gains replace their losses,

soon having much larger business than before. The
Tobey Furniture Company was organized in 1875,
Charles being president and Frank B. manager.

Charles died in September, 1888, honored and lamented. He was unmarried.

540

FRANK BASSETT[7] (*Jonathan Howes,*[6] *Seth,*[5] *Seth,*[4]
Thomas,[3] *Thomas,*[2] *Thomas*[1]), born at Dennis, Sept.
15, 1833; worked on the farm in summer and attended
school winters till 18 years old; then was clerk in
the Post Office and village store. As a very young
voter he wrote the call for the first convention of the
infant Republican party in his native town. Went
to Chicago in 1857 and put himself in the service of
his brother, whose partner he soon became in the business described above. In 1890 the firm doubled the
capacity of their ware-rooms, making their floor space
143,000 square feet in lieu of the 1000 of their first
store. The firm has trade all over this country and
somewhat abroad.

Mr. Tobey is president of the Trustees of Rush
Medical College, of the Society for Ethical Culture,
and treasurer and a director of the Illinois Children's
Home and Aid Society. He retains the old homestead at Dennis and has built and maintains a very
large and famous hotel at the seashore in the town,
which bears the aboriginal name of Nobscussett
House.

Mr. Tobey has entered the Illinois Society of Sons
of The American Revolution on the basis of the services of his great-grandfather (Lieut. Seth Tobey,
1716–1801), and of his maternal ancestors, Capt. Jonathan Howes and Capt. Elisha Bassett.

Mr. Tobey has been a liberal helper of the making
of this book.

FRANK BASSETT TOBEY.

544

JOHN H.[7] (*Henry,*[6] *Zimri,*[5] *Silas,*[4] *Ebenezer,*[3] *John,*[2] *Thomas*[1]), born in Falmouth, March 20, 1851; died at Taunton, unmarried, Jan. 23, 1889.

546

GEORGE[7] (*Josiah,*[6] *Josiah,*[5] *John,*[4] *Eleazer,*[3] *John,*[2] *Thomas*[1]), born in Pawlet, Vt., about 1835; married Laura, daughter of John C. Bishop.

560

GILBERT RUSSELL[7] (*Russell,*[6] *John,*[5] *John,*[4] *Eleazer,*[3] *John,*[2] *Thomas*[1]), born in Falmouth, Nov. 7, 1824; grad. Union College, Schenectady, N. Y., in 1846; married at S., Eliza Campbell; became a hardware commission merchant in New York city. Died Feb. 27, 1862.

Child:

> Lizzie Russell[8]; m. James Reagles, M.D., surgeon U. S. Army.
>
> Children :
>
> 1. Gilbert Russell Reagles.
> 2. James Reagles, Jr.

560 a

FRANKLIN HATCH[7] (*Russell,*[6] *John,*[5] *John,*[4] *Eleazer,*[3] *John,*[2] *Thomas*[1]), born in Falmouth, married there Dec. 5, 1853, Aurelia W., daughter of Oliver and Grace Holmes, born in 1829. He followed the sea, and rose to be mate of the ship "Spartan". He died in the Pacific Ocean Jan. 19, 1856, and was buried at Pitcairn's Island.

561

THOMAS NYE[7] (*Russell,[6] John,[5] John,[4] Eleazer,[3] John,[2] Thomas[1]*), born in Falmouth, April 1, 1831; married Nov. 17, 1853, Alice J., daughter of Benjamin and Alice Aikin, born in 1832. He was a wheelwright. He died at East Falmouth, Aug. 4, 1862.
Child:

> Abby,[8] m. Mr. Edson.

562

ROBERT GOODWIN[7] (*Russell,[6] John,[5] John,[4] Eleazer,[3] John,[2] Thomas[1]*), born in East Falmouth, Dec. 2, 1840; married at Saugerties, N. Y., Oct. 20, 1875, Amelia Ann Kuypers, daughter of Samuel and Joanna Amelia (Kuypers) Davis, born Aug. 7, 1837, died in Boston, April 29, 1905.

After a youth of work on the farm and study in the public schools, he went at 18 to the city of New York and learned business in the establishment of his oldest brother. Upon the death of the latter Robert settled the estate. In the War of the Rebellion he was appointed clerk in the office of his mother's brother, Col. Albert D. Hatch, of New Bedford, and had the experience of writing out the document calling for a draft, being himself drafted, rejected by the surgeon for physical disability, and making out the certificate of discharge; thus doing all his country required of him, though without performing a soldier's part. He remained in the Provost Marshal's office till it was discontinued. He then spent several years in the hardware importing house of G. W. Albertus in New York; returning to New Bedford was clerk of the Mt. Washington Glass Co. 12 years; was in the auditing department of the Thompson-Houston Electric Co. till consolidation with the Edison Company in

1895; since that time he has been clerk of the Board of Gas and Electric Light Commissioners. He is a member of Emmanuel Congregational Church, Roxbury, and a Knight Templar in the Boston Commandery.

Children, born in New Bedford:

i.   Joanna Amelia,[8] b. Sept. 3, 1876; m. in Boston, July 20, 1905, Lemuel Du Bois, a hardware merchant at Ellenville, N. Y.

ii.   Matthew Julien, b. Dec. 1, 1877; grad. Harvard Univ. 1901; now with the Burroughs Adding Machine Co., New York city.

iii.   Lilly Allen, b. April 30, 1880.

563

ASA PHINNEY[7] (*Isaiah Nye,[6] John,[5] John,[4] Eleazer,[3] John,[2] Thomas[1]*), born at Falmouth, March 5, 1838; died at Waquoit, Dec. 29, 1901; married April 1, 1859, Eliza Jane, daughter of William and Mary Loring (Bradford) Hyer, born in Providence, R. I., Aug. 22, 1840.

He was a wheelwright; carried on the carriage business at Mansfield a few years. Kept a hotel in Waquoit 35 years, during 20 of which he was tax collector for the town. Was representative to the General Court in 1885.

Child:

Minnie Jane,[8] b. 28 April, 1862; m. Nov. 1, 1882, Robert King Runyon, of Newark, N. J.; he d. Nov. 8, 1889. After his death the widow studied medicine, graduating from the Women's Medical College of New York; practised some time there, but is now (1905) resident physician of the women's department of Oberlin University, where her daughter, Ruth Humphrey Runyon, b. March 5, 1885, is a student.

564

JOHN ALBERT[7] (*John,[6] John,[5] John,[4] Eleazer,[3] John,[2] Thomas[1]*), born in Falmouth, Jan. 31, 1839; married at Mansfield, July 2, 1869, Phebe A., daughter of John and Caroline Webb, born in 1847.

After a youth on the farm he learned the trade of carriage maker and worked at New Bedford. In the Civil War he enlisted in company I, 3d Mass. Vol. Infantry, Sept. 22, 1862, and served at Plymouth and Newbern, N. C., and elsewhere; was mustered out June 26, 1863. In 1865 he removed to Mansfield, and carried on the business of carriage making. In 1881 he removed to East Falmouth and took a farm. Since 1901 he has been tax collector of Falmouth.

Children:

803. i.   William Albert,[8] b. April 24, 1871.
     ii.   Minnie Izana, b. Jan. 24, 1874; m. Dec. 31, 1891, Frederick Kelley Swift, of Sagamore (Sandwich), son of Charles D. and Bethia (Kelley) Swift.
           Child:
           Phebe Webb Swift, b. Jan. 24, 1904.

565

GEORGE B.[7] (*John,[6] John,[5] John,[4] Eleazer,[3] John,[2] Thomas[1]*), born in Falmouth, June 1, 1846; married at Somerville, Oct. 21, 1874, Hattie M., daughter of Ahira and Jane Carver, born in Vermont in 1853. He was at that time a milkman.

575

JOSHUA BRIGGS[7] (*Curtis,[6] Benjamin,[5] Seth,[4] Seth,[3] Nathan,[2] Thomas[1]*), born in Wareham, Feb. 9, 1807; married at Middleboro (published at Wareham, Aug. 30, 1835), Susanna Keith, daughter of Isaac and Naomi (Keith) Pratt, born Jan. 15, 1811, still living as we go to press at the ripe age of ninety-four years. She is a lineal descendant of Rev. James Keith, the Scotchman who came over to New England on finishing his education at Aberdeen and was the pastor of the infant church at Middleboro. Among the intermarrying families in her lineage were those of Edson, Washburn, Conant and Bryant, worthy lines of the old Pilgrim stock.

Mr. Tobey entered into the cotton manufacturing business in early life but afterwards turned his attention to the iron business in the line of the manufacture of nails. He was a clear-headed and far-sighted man, advancing promptly with the improvements in the art, and carried the business forward with marked success. His son has followed in the same occupation. The industry has been of much value to the people of Wareham as well as to the manufacturers themselves. Besides this attention to the making of good articles for good money Mr. Tobey became a sagacious investor and was entrusted with responsibilities for the public. He was chosen president of the Wareham Bank and of the Savings Bank, occupying the positions upwards of a score of years; was a director in railroad and mining enterprises, cotton and other factories and other industries. His policy was honest and strong, brave in times of depression but invariably redeeming his promises and upholding the credit of the institutions for which he stood. He was also an excellent public speaker and took part in important public movements to some degree; and was liberal toward objects which commended themselves to his judgment. He died of anemia Dec. 25, 1870.

Children:

    i.   Gerard Curtis,* b. Oct. 16, 1836; Harvard University, A.B. 1859, LL.B. 1860; a banker in Wareham and Boston.

14

ii.   Horace Pratt, b. Jan. 4, 1838; Harvard Univ. A.B.
      1858; president of the Tremont Nail Company.
iii. Theodore F., b. March 31, 1840; d. at Cohasset,
      Aug. 26, 1877.
805. iv. George O., b. Oct. 27, 1841.

576

Moses Swift Fearing[7] (*Curtis,[6] Benjamin,[5] Seth,[4]
Seth,[3] Nathan,[2] Thomas[1]*), born in Wareham, Oct. 17,
1810; married in Rochester in December, 1835, Judith
K., daughter of David Peckham, born in 1813.

He was a merchant in Wareham; fitted out vessels
for their voyages to some extent; had other interests.
Removed to Boston; was agent of the Tremont Nail
Company; also agent for the Bennington Crockery
Co.   He died of heart disease, Feb. 22, 1879.   The
widow made her home in the Brighton district of Bos-
ton in her latter days, passing away Aug. 7, 1883.
Her daughter still resides there.
Children:

i.   Tirzah Isabella,[8] b. Aug. 24, 1836.
ii.   Austin King, b. July 15, 1839; died.
806. iii. Austin Burnell, b. Aug. 20, 1843.

577

Seth Fish[7] (*Curtis,[6] Benjamin,[5] Seth,[4] Seth,[3] Nathan,[2] Thomas[1]*), born in Wareham, June 29, 1814;
married June 27, 1837, Lucina Gibbs, of Middleborough, born June 29, 1816; died Dec. 15, 1901.

He was a farmer, residing at South Wareham.   He
died from the effects of a railroad accident, July 6,
1891.
Children:

807. i.   Curtis, Jr.,[8] b. April 4, 1838; d. in San Francisco,
          Cal., March 10, 1905.
ii.   Elizabeth Thatcher, b. April 3, 1840; m. at Ware-
      ham, April 6, 1864, Duane L. Bliss, son of

William and Lucia M. Bliss of Savoy, a resident
of Gold Hill in the Territory of Nevada, 30 years
old, his second marriage. They removed to the
Pacific Coast. Mr. Bliss is president of The
Lake Tahoe Railway and Transportation Company, with headquarters at San Francisco, Cal.
Children:
1. William T. Bliss, b. Aug. 23, 1865.
2. Charles T. Bliss, b. July 20, 1867.
3. Hope L. Bliss, b. Jan. 19, 1870.
4. Walter D. Bliss, b. Aug. 23, 1872.
5. Duane L. Bliss, Jr., b. May 15, 1874.
6. Frederick K. Bliss, b. June 13, 1883.

808. iii. Walter Danforth, b. May 7, 1842.
iv. Susanna Pratt, b. March 5, 1845. Resides on the
old place.
v. Tirzah F., b. Oct. 9, 1847; d. Nov. 18, 1848.
vi. Emma T., b. Dec. 7, 1852; d. Jan. 21, 1854.

589

ERASTUS[7] (*Joseph,*[6] *William,*[5] *Joseph,*[4] *Nathan,*[3]
Nathan,[2] *Thomas*[1]), born in Somerville, Me., April 18,
1813, twin with Augustus; married first Jane Dudley;
married second, Oct. 30, 1850, Abigail Clark. He
died May 27, 1851.
Children:
i. George H.[8]; was Major of the 16th U. S. Inf.; died
in Texas.
ii. Joseph, died at Elmira, N. Y., from the effects of
injuries received in a railroad collision.

591

HANSON[7] (*Joseph,*[6] *William,*[5] *Joseph,*[4] *Nathan,*[3] *Na-
than,*[2] *Thomas*[1]), born in Somerville, Me., June 20,
1818; resided there; married Lydia H.
Child:
Frank D.[8]; m. in Providence, R. I., March 3, 1870,
Lucy J. Martin.

593

ALONSO[7] (*Elijah,[6] William,[5] Joseph,[4] Nathan,[3] Nathan,[2] Thomas[1]*), born in Jefferson, Me., June 23, 1826; married Hannah Elizabeth Welch; was a ship-joiner; died July 1, 1868.
Children:

    i.   Ida A.[8], b. 1853, m. at Newburyport, Sept. 14, 1877, Charles R. Smith, a druggist, son of Samuel and Elizabeth Smith.

    ii. Charles Albert, b. Jan. 23, 1863.

    iii. Sumner B., b. "at West Washington, Me.," 1864; m. at Newburyport, Aug. 22, 1883, Carrie I., daughter of Cyrus and Rhoda A. Fowler, b. Seabrook, N. H., in 1874. Child: Hannah Lizzie,[9] b. at Salisbury, Jan. 28, 1886.

    iv. A son, b. Feb. 8, 1866.

    v. Lillian F., b. in 1869, m. at Haverhill, Nov. 21, 1894, George F. Leighton, son of John E. and Adelia A. (Tilton) Leighton.

    vi. George Albert, b. Aug. 27, 1874.

595

ELIAS BAXTER[7] (*Elijah,[6] William,[5] Joseph,[4] Nathan,[3] Nathan,[2] Thomas[1]*), born in Somerville, Me., "a son of Elijah and Mrs. Hannah E. (Noble) Tobey." He resided at Winthrop Centre, Me., in 1899.
Children:

    i.   Fred R.[8]

    ii. William A.

    iii. Charles O.

    iv. H. E.

596

HARRY[7] (*Benjamin,[6] William,[5] Joseph,[4] Nathan,[3] Nathan,[2] Thomas,[1]*), born in Whitefield, Me., married in Providence, R. I., Sept. 23, 1862, Susan E. Woodbridge.

600

SAMUEL OTIS[7] (*George,[6] William,[5] Joseph,[4] Nathan[3] Nathan,[2] Thomas[1]*), born in Jefferson, Me., Aug. 28, 1833; married Feb. 9, 1865, Hannah Etta Hodgkins, born May 12, 1845. He lives on the old farm; he and his family are associated with the Baptist church of the town.

Children:

810. i.   Orin F.[8], b. Aug. 20, 1866.
811. ii. George W., b. Sept. 22, 1867.
     iii. West C., b. May 1, 1869.
812. iv. Charles S., b. Sept. 6, 1870.
     v.   Mary Ella, b. Dec. 26, 1878; m. June 26, 1901,
          Forest Atwood Flagg. Child: Beatrice Flagg.
     vi. Ellen Weeks, b. July 28, 1880.
     vii. Miranda Hall, b. March 23, 1882.

605

JOHN LEWIS[7] (*Franklin,[6] Lewis,[5] Joseph,[4] Nathan,[3] Nathan,[2] Thomas[1]*), born in New Bedford, April 11, 1847; married at Middleboro, Feb. 16, 1884, Rebecca E., daughter of Roger and Mary Kennedy, born at St. John, N. B., in 1864. He died at Middleboro, Sept. 4, 1895.

Child:

815.   Franklin[8]; resides at Brockton.

611

JOSEPH H.[7] (*Joseph,[6] Timothy,[5] Joseph,[4] Nathan,[3] Nathan,[2] Thomas[1]*), born in 1848; married first, April 16, 1874, Catherine E., daughter of Robert and Elizabeth Hanwell, born in England in 1854, died in Boston, March 8, 1875. He married second, May 1, 1881, Adeline, daughter of William and Bridget Boyson, born in Dorchester in 1853. A machinist; resides in Boston.

612

CHARLES BENNETT[7] (*George W.,[6] William,[5] William,[4] Samuel,[3] Jonathan,[2] Thomas[1]*), born in Boston, Sept. 18, 1828; married at Brooklyn, N. Y., Oct. 3, 1855, Frances Matilda, daughter of Bennett and Locada (Gullifar) Hyde, born in Brooklyn.

He resided in Brooklyn and in Glen Cove, N. Y. He was captain of Company C, in the 84th regiment N. Y. Vol. Inf. in the War of the Rebellion; was severely wounded at the second battle of Bull Run, Aug. 31, 1862. He died at Glen Cove, N. Y., Jan. 8, 1904.

Children:

820. i.   Bennett Hyde,[8] b. in Brooklyn, N. Y., July 8, 1856.
     ii. Terena, b. Nov. 16, 1859; m. Feb. 22, 1898, William E. Hatton, son of John Hatton, who served in the War of the Rebellion.
     iii. Augusta White, b. Jan. 24, 1864; m. Dec. 29, 1897, Ebenezer Storer, a descendant of Lieut. Ebenezer Storer of Revolutionary fame.
          Children :
          1. Frances Storer, } b. Nov. 17, 1899.
          2. Naomi Storer, }

613

BENJAMIN G.[7] (*Albert,[6] Tristram,[5] William,[4] Samuel,[3] Jonathan,[2] Thomas[1]*), born in Nantucket in 1836; married there, Dec. 19, 1858, Sarah E., daughter of William and Lydia Gifford, born in 1840.

Child:

825. Herbert A.,[8] b. Sept. 2, 1867.

614

ALBERT I.[7] (*Albert,[6] Tristram,[5] William,[4] Samuel,[3] Jonathan,[2] Thomas[1]*), was born, and resided, in Nantucket. He married Elvira ———.

Children:
i. Clara Bell,[8] b. Jan. 8, 1861; d. Aug. 10, 1864.
ii. Albert I.
iii. Jane M.
iv. Harry A., b. in 1877; m. Sept. 27, 1897, Edith M., daughter of George H. and Mary E. (Spencer) Hamblin.
v. Edith M.; m. Ezra M. Horton, of Burlington, Vt. Child: Robert Wyman Horton, b. in 1878.

616

OSCAR ANGELL[7] (*William,*[6] *Archelaus,*[5] *William,*[4] *Samuel,*[3] *Jonathan,*[2] *Thomas*[1]), born in Smithfield, R. I., Jan. 10, 1837; married June 12, 1861, Addie, daughter of William Fenner and Abby (Winsor) Brown, born March 15, 1837. He was educated in the public schools of Smithfield and at Wilbraham Academy. Was some years in the general store of his father; three years manager of a store at Hebronville, Mass., kept by B. B. and R. Knight, cotton manufacturers; succeeded his father in the store in Greenville, R.I., in 1875. Has been postmaster also for more than twenty years; member of the town council of Smithfield three years, and town clerk since 1871.

Mr. Tobey has rendered very efficient assistance to the editor in compiling the statistics of the descendants of Archelaus.[5]

Children :
i. Jessie Howard,[8] b. April 28, 1862, in Hebronville, Mass.; m. Henry Farnam Smith; has resided in Smithfield ever since her marriage, Mr. Smith being assistant postmaster and deputy town clerk.
Children :
1. Harold Tobey Smith, b. Sept. 6, 1887.
2. Helen Sumner Smith, b. June 23, 1891.
3. Jessie Ethelyn Smith, b. Sept. 7, 1898.

ii. William Edgar, b. Dec. 16, 1863; graduate of
Mowry and Goff's English and Classical School,
Providence, R. I.; with Stone, Carpenter and
Wilson, architects, Providence, and with others in
the same line in New York City; a draughtsman
for some time with a firm in Central Falls, R. I.,
and drew the plans for the construction of two
large copper refining plants; with the Raritan
Copper Works and the Delamar Copper Co.,
Perth Amboy, N. J.; is now a partner in the
Geo. W. Mercer Construction Co. of Perth
Amboy.

iii. Charles Sumner, b. Jan. 6, 1866; d. Nov. 29, 1887;
unm.; grad. M. and G. Class. School; was clerk
in the wholesale dry goods house of Hartwell,
Richards & Co., Providence, three years before
his lamented death.

iv. Jennie Lester, b. June 8, 1874; graduate of the
English High School and the State Normal
School, Providence, and is now a teacher in a
grammar school there.

617

WILLIAM HENRY[7] (*William,[6] Archelaus,[5] William,[4]
Samuel,[3] Jonathan,[2] Thomas[1]*), born in Smithfield,
R. I., Sept. 15, 1842; married, 1865, Emma F. Cook.
Is bookkeeper and paymaster of the Lonsdale Manu-
facturing Company at the village of Lonsdale, R. I.
Has held various town offices in the town of Cumber-
land, R. I.

Children:

Robert Irving.[8]   George Angell.
Harold.   Sallie Ethel.

618

JAMES EDWIN[7] (*William,[6] Archelaus,[5] William,[4]
Samuel,[3] Jonathan,[2] Thomas[1]*), born in Smithfield,
R. I., Oct. 18, 1848. He was educated in the public

schools of Smithfield, and at Lapham Institute, North
Scituate, R. I., under Thomas L. Angell, principal.
Studied medicine with Doctor Clapp of Pawtucket,.
R. I.; took a course of training in Mass. General
Hospital, Boston. Practised at Central Falls, R. I.,
building up a large and successful practice. He died ·
July 28, 1891.

628

WALTER L.⁷ (*Samuel,⁶ Archelaus,⁵ William,⁴ Jona-*
than,³ Samuel,² Thomas¹), married Annie McAlpin
of Lincoln, R. I. Resided at Providence, R. I., where
his widow still lives.
Child:

> Elvah Elsie,⁸ b. Oct. 26, 1871.

630

WILLARD A.⁷ (*Samuel,⁶ Archelaus,⁵ William,⁴*
Samuel,³ Jonathan,² Thomas¹), born in Providence,
R. I., in 1852; married Feb. 23, 1873, Henrietta A.
Saltonstall, born in 1853; she died Dec. 1, 1893.
Children:

> i. Earl Preston,⁸ b. Dec. 28, 1880.
> ii. Ethel Frances, b. July 4, 1883.

631

HORATIO⁷ (*Samuel,⁶ Elisha,⁵ Matthias,⁴ Samuel,³*
Jonathan,² Thomas¹), born in Machiasport, Me., about
1820. Was a fine penman, accountant and salesman
and clean, upright young man, managing the business
of an uneducated but shrewd merchant and shipbuilder,
in the fifties, when the writer (C. H. P.) was a boy
at Machias. A son, William Berton Tobey, is superintendent of a cloth mill at South Berwick, Me.
Records have failed to arrive in time to be printed here.

633

GEORGE LORING[7] (*Samuel,[6] Elisha,[5] Matthias,[4] Samuel,[3] Jonathan,[2] Thomas[1]*), born at Machiasport, Me., June 17, 1853; married at Boston, July 14, 1880, Abbie A., daughter of Capt. Aaron W. and Angeline Grant of Machiasport, born July 16, 1855.

He was educated at the public schools of his native town, at Washington Academy in East Machias and at Waterville Classical Institute; graduated at Bowdoin Medical School, June, 1879. He entered upon the practice of medicine at Shrewsbury at once, removing thence to Lancaster in December, 1880, and in February, 1896, to Clinton, where he now resides.

Children:

    i.   George Loring,[8] Jr., b. June 3, 1881; M.D. Harv. Univ. 1903; in practice in Boston.

    ii.   Guy Davis, b. in July, 1883; insurance agent and stock broker at Clinton and Boston.

    iii.   Harold Grant, b. Dec. 22, 1884.

634

JAMES OSBERT[7] (*Charles,[6] Elisha,[5] Matthias,[4] Samuel,[3] Jonathan,[2] Thomas[1]*), born in Machiasport, Me., March 19, 1844; married July 28, 1867, Lauretta Eliza, daughter of George and Eliza (Seavy) Harmon.

He followed the sea for two years; then learned the trade of cooper. Enlisted Feb. 22, 1864, in Co. B, 31st Me. Vol. Inf.; participated in all the engagements of the regiment; was promoted to sergeant; was mustered out after Lee's surrender. Returned to his native place and worked at his trade. Was with the U. S. Coast and Geodetic Survey two years. Has been postmaster, selectman, assessor, clerk and justice of the peace. Is a merchant.

Children:

    i.   Nina Etta,[8] b. Aug. 27, 1868; d. Aug. 17, 1869.

ii.   Celia Philena, b. Nov. 22, 1871.
iii. A son, b. Feb. 4, d. 5, 1883.

635

CHARLES ROBBINS[7] (*Charles Richmond,*[6] *Lemuel,*[5] *Thomas,*[4] *Jonathan,*[3] *Jonathan,*[2] *Thomas*[1]), born in New Bedford, Sept. 8, 1847; married Abbie Delia, daughter of George Gilbert Huddy, born Jan. 26, 1854. He was a tinsmith; worked several years at Whitman. Made friends extensively; was a member of Plymouth Rock Lodge of the Knights of Pythias. Died very suddenly, of heart disease, on his way home from the postoffice in the evening of Dec. 12, 1898.

Child, by adoption:

Nina Whitney,[8] b. July 31, 1883.

636

RUFUS BABCOCK[7] (*Charles Richmond,*[6] *Lemuel,*[5] *Thomas,*[4] *Jonathan,*[3] *Jonathan,*[2] *Thomas*[1]), born in New Bedford, May 6, 1849; married first, June 21, 1882, Caroline Mary, daughter of Henry Oscar and Avis J. (Eaton) Gifford, born Oct. 3, 1852, died April 3, 1890. He married second, at Quincy, May 12, 1892, Genevieve Rebecca, sister of his former wife, born at Monkton, Vt., Oct. 11, 1854. He had business experience at New Bedford, at Kingston, and afterward in the store of R. H. White & Co., Boston. He then fitted for college at Phillips Academy, Andover, and was graduated from Amherst in 1877 and from Andover Theological Seminary in 1880. Received the degree of A.M. from Amherst College in 1881. Was ordained pastor of the Congregational Church at Harwich, Nov. 30, 1880, and remained there until 1883, when, imbued with the missionary spirit, he went to Helena, Montana; there he completed the organization of a church and continued as pastor till

1885.   He also had brief pastorate at Carrington, S. D., and Ashburnham, Mass.

From Ashburnham he was called, in 1888, to the position of associate pastor of Berkeley Temple, Boston, with Rev. Chas. A. Dickinson. His unusual abilites as an organizer and worker found in the work of this institutional church fuller opportunity for their best expression. Practical, yet possessed of liveliest sympathies, he worked among the young people, the poor, the unfortunate, to whom the work of this church made its strongest appeal; and much of the success of this new departure in religious effort in Boston was due to his wise direction of the department coming under his special care.

Desiring a wider field for his abilities, or rather, realizing the wider field outside the church in which he might extend his usefulness, in 1895 he resigned from his position and organized the Memorial Trust. This philanthropy and charity found the scope of its efforts in its motto: *Nihil humani alienum,* "Nothing that pertains to humanity is foreign to me;" and the range of its helpfulness may almost be said to be the varied needs of the poor, the perplexed, the unfortunate in a cosmopolitan city, its assistance being sought not only by individuals but by kindred philanthropies.

Besides the Memorial Trust, Mr. Tobey was the founder of The Ingleside, a successful work for homeless and untrained girls (now under other direction), and of The Boston Floating Hospital, a work which has attracted attention not only at home but abroad, and whose beneficence will always be associated with his name. Unique in its character and work it is, perhaps, one of the most helpful of Boston's noble list of philanthropies.

As to this Tobey Genealogy it is proper to say that Mr. Tobey began many years ago to feel a strong affection for the family connections of that father who was not spared for him to know; and he gathered a good deal of information on the subject from that personal motive. At length he conceived the scheme of bringing into existence this genealogy, and has contributed freely of money and time to make it a success.

The writer of this article (C. H. P.) testifies to the fervent spirit which has characterized the whole undertaking, and trusts the family at large will not forget the debt due to Rufus Babcock Tobey for this work.

REV. RUFUS BABCOCK TOBEY, A. M., AND HIS DAUGHTER
AVIS CAROLINE.

Mr. Tobey's home is at Quincy.
Child:
Avis Caroline,⁸ b. May 3, 1893.

644

MELITIAH⁷ (*Ezra,⁶ Melitiah,⁵ Cornelius,⁴ Cornelius,³ Samuel,² Thomas¹*), born in Sandwich, April 22, 1822; married Caroline E., daughter of Stephen and Caroline (Larkin) Fessenden, born in Windham, N. H., May 10, 1832, died in Brockton, Nov. 28, 1891. Mr. Tobey was in the furniture business in Brockton.
Child:
Abby F.,⁸ b. at N. Bridgewater, July 3, 1857.

647

WILLIAM HENRY⁷ (*Ezra,⁶ Melitiah,⁵ Cornelius,⁴ Cornelius,³ Samuel,² Thomas¹*), born in Sandwich, April 11, 1840; married first, Helen M.———. Resided in Brockton. He married second, at Bradford, June 24, 1889, Mrs. Hattie F. Greenleaf, born in 1849.

648

JOSHUA FESSENDEN⁷ (*Joshua,⁶ Melitiah,⁵ Cornelius,⁴ Cornelius,³ Samuel,² Thomas¹*), born in Sandwich, June 25, 1840; married Cordelia, daughter of Zenas and Almira Brett, of North Bridgewater, born in 1840, died Nov. 14, 1892. He is a merchant; after carrying on business in several towns he settled down for a permanent home in Harwich.
Children:
850. i.   Charles Fessenden,⁸ b. at Palmer, July 25, 1861.
     ii. Fred Almon, b. at Abington, Jan. 24, 1863; d. in infancy.
     iii. Martha Louise, b. Jan. 28, 1864; d. in infancy.
     iv. Joshua Lincoln; d. in infancy.
     v.   Fred Keith, b. Jan. 2, 1867; d. Sept. 5, 1889.

220   TOBEY GENEALOGY.

vi.   Lillian Alma, b. at Wellfleet, Sept. 9, 1868; m.
      Oct. 10, 1889, Fred W. Sargent.
vii. Phosa Colton, b. at Provincetown, May 19, 1871.
851. viii. George Beebe, b. May 17, 1873.
ix.   Avis Louisa; m. Frank Bostock, of Brockton.
x.   Cordelia Brett; m. Nov. 22, 1899, Edward Lyman
      Perkins, of Brockton, son of Stillman S. and
      Mary I. (Curtis) Perkins, b. in 1869.
852. xi. Jesse Cook, b. May 2, 1877.
xii. Lulu Bartley, b. July 29, 1878.
xiii. Nannie Mayo, b. Feb. 16, 1880.
xiv. Arthur Wilkinson.
xv.   Harry Wolcott, b. at Harwich, Aug. 8, 1884.

649

GUSTAVUS BASSETT[7] (*Robert,[6] Joshua,[5] Cornelius,[4]
Cornelius,[3] Samuel,[2] Thomas[1]*), born in Sandwich,
May 18, 1832; married in Sandwich, May 7, 1856,
Amy Estella, daughter of Henry Vose and Louisa
Chapouil Spurr, born in Cambridge, March 16, 1835.
He went in 1849 to Worcester to learn the business
of copper-plate printing, but abandoned it on account
of its unhealthfulness; removed to Buffalo, N. Y., and
entered a hat and cap store, where he remained till
1862, when he went to New York and engaged in the
wholesale hat and cap business. Resides (1902) in
Brooklyn, N. Y.
Children:
i.   Louise Estelle,[8] b. at Buffalo, N. Y., June 11, 1858;
      d. in Brooklyn, N. Y., June 8, 1875.
ii.   Ethel Marguerite, b. in Brooklyn, N. Y., March 20,
      1878; m. June 18, 1901, Samuel Eugene Giber-
      son, son of Capt. Samuel Giberson, a veteran of
      the Civil War.

650

WILLIAM ROBERT[7] (*Robert,[6] Joshua,[5] Cornelius,[4]
Cornelius,[3] Samuel,[2] Thomas[1]*), born in Sandwich,

Oct. 27, 1841; died at Westfield, Dec. 31, 1872, of typhoid fever; married Oct. 19, 1870, Lucy Emma, daughter of Mather and Caroline (Chapouil) Hayward, born in Cambridge, March 4, 1847. As a boy he was educated in the public schools of Sandwich; in early manhood, in New York city, entered the dry goods business and removed in 1870 to Westfield, Mass., where he continued in the same line.

Child:

860. i. William Hayward,⁸ b. June 27, 1872.

660

WILLIAM HENRY⁷ (*William C.,*⁶ *William,*⁵ *Elisha,*⁴ *Cornelius,*³ *Samuel,*² *Thomas*¹), born in New Bedford, Dec. 11, 1810; removed to Providence, R. I., and later to Rochester, N. Y. Was an apothecary; he married in Providence, at the Congregational Church on the West side, Oct. 18, 1829, Lucy Worth Fuller, born in New Bedford. He died at Rochester, N. Y., Sept. 22, 1864.

Children:

    i. Lucy Anne.⁸
862. ii. William Henry Augustus.
    iii. Nathaniel.

670

WILLIAM ELLIOT⁷ (*Richard West,*⁶ *Zoeth,*⁵ *Zoeth,*⁴ *Zaccheus,*³ *Samuel,*² *Thomas*¹), born 1825; married 1853, Martha F. Martin, who died 1878. Residence, Calais, Vt.

Children:

    i. Anna C.,⁸ b. 1856; drowned 1873.
    ii. Lydia M., b. 1859.

671

ORVIS S.⁷ (*Richard West,*⁶ *Zoeth,*⁵ *Zoeth,*⁴ *Zac-*

222 TOBEY GENEALOGY.

cheus,[3] *Samuel,*[2] *Thomas*[1]), born 1832; married 1859, Nancy M. Hargin. Residence, Hammond, Wis.
Children:
- i. Jennie B.,[8] b. 1863.
- ii. Alpa A., b. 1866.
- iii. Lena J., b. 1867.
865. iv. James K., b. 1870.

672

JAMES K.[7] (*Richard West,*[6] *Zoeth,*[5] *Zoeth,*[4] *Zaccheus,*[3] *Samuel,*[2] *Thomas*[1]), born 1845; married Mary C. Robinson; lives in Calais, Vt.
Children:
- i. Lelia M.,[8] b. 1873.
- ii. Laura C., b. 1875.
- iii. Clara Leone, b. 1879.

673

ELBRIDGE A.[7] (*Allen,*[6] *Zoeth,*[5] *Zoeth,*[4] *Zaccheus,*[3] *Samuel,*[2] *Thomas*[1]), born at Calais, Vt., in 1847; married Katy Doty, who died in 1879. He is a physician, residing at Warren, N. H.
Child:
870.   Allen.[8]

690

FRANK GERRY[7] (*George,*[6] *Elisha,*[5] *Prince,*[4] *Zaccheus,*[3] *Samuel,*[2] *Thomas*[1]), born Jan. 15, 1847; married, Jan. 21, 1875, Ednah Dow, daughter of Retire Parker of Exeter, N. H., born May 2, 1846.

He is a merchant (F. G. Tobey & Co., hatters, glovers and hosiers) in Springfield; has been in business on Main Street since April, 1870. Is a member of South Congregational Church, of the local Historical Society, the Sons of the American Revolution, the

Knights Templar, and several clubs; a director in the Springfield National Bank, etc.
Children:

i. Mary Lucina,⁸ b. Jan. 21, 1877; d. Nov. 12, 1886.
ii. Hathorne Parker, b. Dec. 5, 1879; d. Jan. 23, 1884.

691

WILLIAM HENRY⁷ (*George*,⁶ *Elisha*,⁵ *Prince*,⁴ *Zaccheus*,³ *Samuel*,² *Thomas*¹), born Sept. 5, 1869; married in Brookline, July 5, 1892, Georgia Anna, daughter of Alexander and Sophia (Goodrich) Rogers, born at Hopkinton, N. H. He resides in Concord, N. H.
Child:

George Roger,⁸ b. July 13, 1901.

696

JOHN ELBERT⁷ (*William*,⁶ *Heman*,⁵ *Noah*,⁴ *Zaccheus*,³ *Samuel*,² *Thomas*¹), born in York, Union Co., O., in 1835.
Children:

875. i. Edward J.⁸
ii. Jennie May, b. Sept. 16, 1863; m. April 3, 1884, David Sargent Danforth, son of Jeremiah Morrow and Mary Ann (Smith) Danforth, b. Jan. 24, 1861. Resides near Marysville, O.
Children:

1. Grace May Danforth, b. Feb. 18, 1885.
2. Thomas Dwight Danforth, b. Aug. 22, 1889.
3. Florence Marguerite Danforth, b. Jan. 12, 1894.

697

HENRY ARCHIBALD⁷ (*William*,⁶ *Heman*,⁵ *Noah*,⁴ *Zaccheus*,³ *Samuel*,² *Thomas*¹), born in York, Union Co., O., April 6, 1852; married, in 1881, Minnie, daughter of Jacob S. and Eleanor Conklin, born in Sidney, O., Sept. 15, 1857, died Aug. 19, 1902.
15

His early days were spent on the farm in York and afterward at Mt. Victory, Hardin Co., O., where his father carried on a shoe shop. Then he worked at the carpenter's trade, going to school winters. Then peddled pumps for a firm at Kenton. With his earnings he went to Ohio Wesleyan University at Delaware, O., for three months at one time and six at another. Studied medicine with Dr. William Watt at Kenton, and, by his father's loans, was enabled to go to Miami Medical College at Cincinnati, O., where he graduated in 1875. He practised at Sidney, O., two years, there meeting the lady (just out of High School and about to enter Delaware University) who was destined to be his wife. Was assistant physician at the Columbus State Hospital three years. In 1884 he entered upon private practice again at Lima, O.; thence, two years later, he was called, without making application for the position, to be Superintendent of the Toledo State Hospital, over which he still presides. Of its more than 1700 patients two thirds live without any screens to their windows and walk out in the open air to their meals; more than sixty buildings are on the place, without a fence around the grounds, probably one third of the patients going and coming about the grounds as they please. The Doctor's mottoes are: "Love your neighbor as you love yourself," and "Don't look past the man to see the lunatic, but rather look past the lunatic to see the man."
Children:

    i.   Helen C.,[8] b. at Dayton, O., Aug. 5, 1883.
    ii. Alice B., b. at Lima, O., Dec. 19, 1884.
    iii. Clara Louise, b. at Toledo, O., June 18, 1889.

701

WILLIAM A.[7] (*Charles Firman*,[6] *Heman*,[5] *Noah*,[4] *Zaccheus*,[3] *Samuel*,[2] *Thomas*[1]), born March 27, 1858; married in 1882, Flora Dally. He is a farmer at West Mansfield, O.

Children:
  i.   Eva,⁸ b. Sept. 18, 1885.
  ii. Lula, b. Oct. 1, 1887.

702

EDWARD C.⁷ (*Charles Firman,⁶ Heman,⁵ Noah,⁴ Zaccheus,³ Samuel,² Thomas,¹*) (born Oct. 15, 1870; married April, 1901, Margaret Stine. Works in a grain elevator at Waldo, O.
Children:
  i.   A daughter,⁸ b. and d. in 1902.
  ii. Verell, b. July 3, 1903.
  iii. Raymond, b. Aug. 1904.

704

WARREN PRICE⁷ (*William Henry,⁶ Jonathan,⁵ Jonathan,⁴ Jonathan,³ Samuel,² Thomas¹*), son of William H. and Elizabeth F. (Hussey) Tobey, and grandson of Jonathan and Hannah (Sears) Tobey, was born at New Bedford, Mass., March 27, 1851. At the age of 15 years he went on a whaling voyage to the Indian Ocean, and returning in 1869 learned the trade of a printer, following this occupation for 21 years, and then went into the manufacture of advertising calendars and specialties in New Bedford. He married, at New Bedford, Sept. 30, 1873, Louisa P., daughter of Martin L. and Mary E. (Sanderson) Hathaway of New Bedford.
Children:
  i.   Beulah Louise,⁸ b. March 29, 1876; m. June 17, 1903, J. Herbert Smith of New Bedford, bookkeeper Mechanics National Bank of New Bedford, son of Joseph B. and Marietta (Kirk) Smith.
  ii. William Henry, b. Jan. 27, 1879; d. accidentally Aug. 29, 1891.
  iii. Elizabeth Hathaway, b. Aug. 11, 1889.
  iv. Warren Price, Jr., b. Dec. 21, 1892.

705

HARRISON LORING[7] (*William Henry,*[4] *Jonathan,*[5] *Jonathan,*[4] *Jonathan,*[3] *Samuel,*[2] *Thomas*[1]), was born at New Bedford, Dec. 31, 1858. He followed the sea in his younger days and then entered the employ of the New York, New Haven & Hartford Railroad and rose to the position of engineer. Married Helen M. Beal of Plymouth.
Children:
    i.   Charles H.,[8] b. Aug. 6, 1884.
    ii.   Bertha L., b. April 28, 1887.
   iii. Albert L., b. July 1, 1888; d. Oct. 24, 1893.
   iv. Marion B., b. June 23, 1890.
    v. George, b. and d. July 3, 1893.
   vi. Lester I., b. Jan. 16, 1895.
  vii. Mabel B., b. June 30, 1899.

706

WILLIAM BENONI[7] (*Samuel Boyd,*[6] *Samuel,*[5] *Samuel,*[4] *Eliakim,*[3] *Samuel,*[2] *Thomas*[1]), born in Providence, R. I., Nov. 17, 1830; married, in August, 1856, Elizabeth Faxon. Resided at Oakland, California. Died Dec. 1, 1888.
Children:
    i.   Mary Adeline,[8] b. in Providence, R. I., July 3, 1860; m. Dec. 2, 1903, Thomas Nelson Hastings, of Walpole, N. H.
   ii. Caroline Gardiner, b. Oct. 9, 1865; m. Oct. 9, 1889, Harrison Parker Bridge, of St. Louis, Mo.; he d. Aug. 25, 1895.
       Child:
          Harrison Gardiner Bridge, b. Oct. 21, 1892.

707

SAMUEL BOYD[7] (*Samuel Boyd,*[6] *Samuel,*[5] *Samuel,*[4] *Eliakim,*[3] *Samuel,*[2] *Thomas*[1]), born in Providence, R. I., Dec. 6, 1831; died Jan. 30, 1898. Was an accountant, spent most of his life in New York city. Did not marry.

708

JOHN FRY[7] (*Samuel Boyd,[6] Samuel,[5] Samuel,[4] Eliakim,[3] Samuel,[2] Thomas[1]*) born in Providence, R. I., Nov. 29, 1835; died there Oct. 5, 1882; married, June 20, 1860, Adeline Chandler Rhodes; she survived Mr. Tobey and died Nov. 15, 1883.

He was graduated from Brown University, A.B., 1855; Harvard Law School, LL.B., 1861; practised law in Providence, R. I.; clerk of the senate 1859–1861; justice municipal court 1861-2; member Common Council 1866-9; reporter of decisions of Supreme Court 1868-1874; member R. I. House of Representatives 1877-8 and 1880-2; alderman 1879; judge advocate general 1881-2. He was 1st Lieut. and Adjutant of the 10th Regt. R. I. Vol. Inf. in the War of the Rebellion, commissioned May 26, 1862, mustered out with regiment Sept. 1, 1862.

709

THOMAS FRY[7] (*Samuel Boyd,[6] Samuel,[5] Samuel,[4] Eliakim,[3] Samuel,[2] Thomas[1]*), born in Providence, R. I., Sept. 30, 1840; grad. Brown Univ., A.M., 1859; LL.B., Harvard Univ., 1861; married Aug. 2, 1881, Marie Rebecca, daughter of Col. Charles W. Wingard, U. S. Army, and his wife Henrietta E. (Shoemaker) Wingard. He enlisted in company D., 10th R. I. Vol. Infantry, May 29, 1862, and was chosen sergeant; was commissioned captain 7th regt. Sept. 4, 1862, major Jan. 7, 1863; served at Fredericksburg, Va., and in Kentucky and Mississippi. Resigned Feb. 9, 1864. Afterward entered the regular army; was commissioned 2d lieut., 14th U. S., Infantry, May 3, 1865;

1st lieut. same month; captain 1874; and major 1904.
Resides in Washington, D. C. (1905).

710

SAMUEL LEIGHTON[7] (*Heman,*[6] *Eliakim,*[5] *Samuel,*[4]
Eliakim,[3] *Samuel,*[2] *Thomas*[1]), born in Oldtown, Me.,
Oct. 6, 1834; died at South Norridgewock, Me., Nov.
12, 1870; married July 5, 1862, Mary Augusta French.
Child:

> Grace,[8] b. March 23, 1864; m. June 27, 1888,
> at Andover, Mass., Philip Tillinghast Nicker-
> son. She has contributed helpfully to the gene-
> alogy of this branch of the family.
> Children:
> 1. Martha Nickerson, b. March 22, 1889.
> 2. Philip Nickerson, b. April 6, 1890; d.
>   Jan. 30, 1895.

711

MERRITT G.[7] (*Heman,*[6] *Eliakim,*[5] *Samuel,*[4] *Elia-
kim,*[3] *Samuel,*[2] *Thomas*[1]), born in Norridgewock, Me.,
in 1856; married in Boston, March 12, 1895, Emma
A., daughter of George and Mary E. Currier, born in
Newburyport in 1866. He is a druggist; resides at
Amesbury.

723

PHINEAS SPRAGUE[7] (*Edward Silas,*[6] *Silas,*[5] *Samuel,*[4] *Samuel,*[3] *Samuel,*[2] *Thomas*[1]), born in Boston,
Dec. 19, 1853; died April 17, 1886; married in Boston, Sept. 21, 1876, Anne, daughter of James R.
and Susan H.(Bancroft) Bayley, born in Winchester,
Nov. 15, 1853; died Feb. 16, 1884. He was some-
time a member of the firm of Lockwood, Brooks &
Co., booksellers, in Boston.
Children:

880. i.   Reginald Sprague,[8] b. in Boston, June 28, 1877.
   ii. Leslie, b. July 26, 1879.
   iii. Eliot Lester, b. Nov. 1, 1880.

724

SIDNEY BERKELEY[7] (*Edward Silas,*[6] *Silas,*[5] *Samuel,*[4] *Samuel,*[3] *Samuel,*[2] *Thomas*[1]), born in Boston, Nov. 1, 1858; married in Boston, Nov. 3, 1879, Minerva Bucklin, daughter of Edward Augustus and Dorcas (Greene) Kelley, born in Providence, R. I., June 23, 1858.

He has resided in Boston until recently when he has removed to Providence, R. I.

Child:

881.   Berkeley Greene,[8] b. Providence, R. I., Jan. 10, 1881.

730

CHARLES H.[7] (*Thomas,*[6] *Luke,*[5] *Thomas,*[4] *Thomas,*[3] *Samuel,*[2] *Thomas*[1]), born in New Bedford about 1840; married Susan M. Tripp.

Children:

  i.   Carrie E.[8], b. at Middleboro, July 24, 1874; m. there Dec. 16, 1891, Charles Melvin Leonard, son of Charles E. and Martha E. (Holmes) Leonard, b. in 1861.

  ii.   Minnie B., b. June 5, 1876.

731

GEORGE B.[7] (*Thomas,*[6] *Luke,*[5] *Thomas,*[4] *Thomas,*[3] *Samuel,*[2] *Thomas*[1]); married June 19, 1865, Miriam, daughter of Freeman and Ardra (Allen) Hathaway, born June 8, 1844.

He became a merchant in New Bedford.

735

ELISHA FRANKLIN[7] (*Elisha,*[6] *Elisha,*[5] *Lemuel,*[4] *Eliakim,*[3] *Samuel,*[2] *Thomas*[1]); born in New Bedford, May 30, 1846; married March 20, 1871. Ann Louisa Baker, born in Providence, R. I., Feb. 22, 1856.

He was a druggist in Providence; removed to Des
Moines, Ia.

Child:

> Ida Louisa,⁹ b. in Fairfax, Ia., March 4, 1873;
> m. at Des Moines May 18, 1893, William Per-
> lie Morse, son of Darwin L. and Hattie A. (Ba-
> ker) Morse, b. in Topeka, Kan., Nov. 17, 1868;
> residence Chicago, Ill. (1898).

737

JOHN BRAYTON⁷ (*Franklin,⁶ Elisha,⁵ Thomas,⁴
Thomas,³ Samuel,² Thomas¹*), born in Fairhaven June
4, 1853; married in South Dartmouth, Nov. 19, 1885,
Flora T., daughter of Ephraim and John Ellis, born
in 1864.

He became a sea captain; died of typhoid fever,
Oct. 19, 1896. Mrs. Tobey married second Charles
L. Kirkland.

738

FRANKLIN⁷ (*Franklin,⁶ Elisha,⁵ Thomas,⁴ Thomas,³
Samuel,² Thomas¹*), born in Fairhaven, Nov. 1, 1854;
married June 15, 1879, Susan Foster, daughter of
Elisha and Sarah Bunker, born March 15, 1858.

He was educated in the public schools of New Bedford. He resides (1905) at Kingston, N. Y., where
he has been for ten years superintendent of the Gas
and Electric Company.

Children:

i. Olive Bunker,⁸ b. Nov. 20, 1882.
ii. Bessie Louise, b. July 6, 1884.
iii. Elihu Franklin, b. Aug. 3, 1886.
iv. James Phillip, b. Nov. 14, 1889.

739

GEORGE FREDERICK[7] (*Franklin,[6] Elisha,[5] Thomas,[4] Thomas,[3] Samuel,[2] Thomas[1]*), born in Fairhaven, Jan., 1858; married first, Emma Case; married second, Mrs. Mattie, widow of John Case. He is a plumber, was for some years with Tobey & Coggeshall, afterward with Coggeshall & Maxfield, of New Bedford. Resides at Kingston, N. Y.

750

HENRY AUGUSTUS[7] (*Jonathan Pratt,[6] Jonathan,[5] Elisha,[4] Ephraim,[3] Gershom,[2] Thomas[1]*), born Oct. 12, 1821; married April 17, 1856, Angeline Amanda Rice. Residence Great Barrington.

Children:

    i.   Louise Angie,[8] b. Dec. 20, 1857.

885. ii.   Pratt Lorenzo, b. Nov. 25, 1863.

753

GEORGE B.[7] (*Elisha L.,[6] Jonathan,[5] Elisha,[4] Ephraim,[3] Gershom,[2] Thomas[1]*), born at Alford, June 17, 1845; married Celeste Harrington; married second, Loretta Jones.

Children:

886. i.   Leroy E.

    ii.   Leda, "of George B. and Loretta (Jones) Tobey," m. at Alford, Feb. 22, 1900, Herbert Stoddard. [State transcript of town records.]

758

HORACE M.[7] (*Heman,[6] Barnabas,[5] Elisha,[4] Ephraim,[3] Gershom,[2] Thomas[1]*) born Dec. 25, 1822; married Ann Brown, of Salt Point. N. Y., and resides there.

759

HENRY S.[7] (*Heman,*[6] *Barnabas,*[5] *Elisha,*[4] *Ephraim,*[3] *Gershom,*[2] *Thomas*[1]), born June 8, 1824; married Eliza Seabury, of Poughkeepsie, N. Y. He died April 13, 1860.

Children:

    i.   Heman A.,[8] m. and had children.
    ii. Clara, d. in her girlhood.
890. iii. Arthur G.
    iv. Catherine, m. George Mooney, of Poughkeepsie,
           N. Y., res. (1899) in Brooklyn, N. Y.
           Children :
              1. George Mooney.
              2. Estelle Mooney.

763

FRANK HURD[7] (*Orville Hurd,*[6] *Barnabas,*[5] *Elisha,*[4] *Ephraim,*[3] *Gershom,*[2] *Thomas*[1]), born in Chicago, Ill., in 1853.

Child :

    Orville Hurd,[8] a subscriber, residing in 1904, at
    200 W. 57th Street, New York city.

765

LESTER S.,[7] (*Chester Field,*[6] *Sylvanus,*[5] *Elisha,*[4] *Ephraim,*[3] *Gershom,*[2] *Thomas*[1]), born Feb. 8, 1839; died July 5, 1869.

Children:

    i. Annie.[8]
    ii. Charlotte.

770

ALBERT BURRELL[7] (*Henry M.,*[6] *Sylvanus,*[5] *Elisha,*[4] *Ephraim,*[3] *Gershom,*[2] *Thomas*[1]), born in Greenwich, N. Y., Oct. 1, 1845; married Feb. 18, 1874, in Homer, N. Y., Carrie Eliza, daughter of Rufus and Harriet O.

ALBERT BURRELL TOBEY.

(Hart) Edwards, born in Virgil, N. Y., April 12, 1849. Graduated at Eastman Business College, New York city. Spent some years in Henry, Illinois, and in 1867 settled at Oneonta, N. Y., and engaged in dry goods business (the largest establishment in that line between Albany and Binghamton). He is a member and trustee of the First Presbyterian Church; president of the local Y. M. C. A.; member of the Board of Health; director in the Building and Loan Society; active in all local improvements. Under his presidency the Y. M. C. A. built a large building and dedicated it free from debt. He is a commissioner of Auburn Theological Seminary; was a delegate to the General Assembly in 1902.

Children:

i. Henry Edwards,⁸ b. Jan. 11, 1875; grad. Oneonta Normal School 1894; Amherst College, A.B., 1898; New York Law School, LL.B., 1900; admitted to the bar 1900. In practice in New York; residence, Brooklyn. A director of the India Rubber and Gutta Percha Insulating Co., Yonkers, N. Y., and of the League Publication Co., New York. Member Delta Upsilon College fraternity; a Free Mason and Royal Arch Mason; also member of the University Club of Brooklyn.

ii. Katherine Hart, b. March 10, 1885; graduated Oneonta High School 1902; member of the class of 1907 at Wellesley College.

775

CHARLES HENRY⁷ (*Egbert Prindle,⁶ Ephraim,⁵ Elisha,⁴ Ephraim,³ Gershom,² Thomas¹*), born in West Stockbridge, Jan. 14, 1830; married first, Oct. 11, 1853, Maria B. Scofield, of Westfield; she died Oct. 26, 1895, and he married second, Feb. 17, 1902, at St. Augustine, Fla., Mrs. Frances A. Lindley. He settled at Eau Claire, Wis., and afterward removed to Sparta, Wis.; he died May 17, 1905.

234

Child:

> Charles Egbert,[8] b. July 31, 1858; m. at Sparta, Wis., Oct. 16, 1888, May Thayer.

776

EDWIN[7] (*Egbert P.*,[6] *Ephraim*,[5] *Elisha*,[4] *Ephraim*,[3] *Gershom*,[2] *Thomas*[1]), born (twin with Edward) Feb. 15, 1834. Married May 4, 1863, Adelaide Grace Rockwell Stevens, of Great Barrington. He was a tanner; carried on the business at Suffield, Conn., from 1875 to the close of his life. Was a warden of Calvary (Episcopal) Church, and a faithful, earnest worker in whatever he undertook. He died Aug. 2, 1897; Mrs. Tobey died Jan. 15, 1902.

Children:

    i.   Grace Treat,[8] b. March 10, 1865; is a member of the Daughters of the American Revolution.

   ii.   Edwin Seeley, b. Feb. 7, 1879; d. April 24, 1905.

777

EDWARD[7] (*Egbert P.*,[6] *Ephraim*,[5] *Elisha*,[4] *Ephraim*,[3] *Gershom*,[2] *Thomas*[1]), born Feb. 15, 1834; graduated at Westfield Normal School in 1859. Served in the 49th Mass. V. I. in the War of the Rebellion. Married April 15, 1867, Sarah E. Sawtelle, born in Hallowell, Me. He resided in Milbury, Pittsfield and Cambridge. He died May 13, 1878.

Child:

> Edward Nelson,[8] b. at Millbury, July 16, 1871; grad. Harvard Univ. 1896, Harvard Medical School 1900. Physician at Somerville.

780

EDWIN JEROME[7] (*Abraham*,[6] *Abraham*,[5] *Jesse*,[4] *Ephraim*,[3] *Gershom*,[2] *Thomas*[1]), born in West Stockbridge, Jan. 8, 1842; married Oct. 4, 1870, Marion E., daughter of John and Mary Hixon Brooks, of Canaan,

N. Y., born March 27, 1847. Mr. Tobey was a partner in the flour and feed mills at Rockdale in 1870 and 1871; returned to West Stockbridge and to the Tobey homestead farm on which he has continued ever since. Was an assessor for many years and has held other town offices. He is a deacon of the Congregational Church.

Children:

894. i.   Frederick Clinton,⁸ b. Sept. 3, 1871.
    ii.   Theodore Lathrop, b. Nov. 28, 1872; d. in infancy.
895. iii. George Edwin, b. Dec. 8, 1873.
    iv. Mary Elizabeth, b. Feb. 19, 1875.
    v.   Sarah Kellogg, b. April 12, 1877; d. in infancy.
    vi. Charles, b. Aug. 23, 1882; d. in infancy.
896. vii. Albert Abram, b. Oct. 29, 1883.

781

THEODORE POMEROY⁷ (*Abraham,⁶ Abraham,⁵ Jesse,⁴ Ephraim,³ Gershom,² Thomas¹*), born in West Stockbridge, Jan. 16, 1844; died May 8, 1881; married Isadore, daughter of Chauncey and Electa Smith, of Canaan, N. Y. He was a partner in the Rockdale Mills; then partner with L. Moffat in a store in W. Stockbridge; then removed to Pittsfield where he was in company with H. Teeling in a large cracker bakery.

Children:

    i.   Jessie Lathrop,⁸ b. Sept. 6, 1868; m. at Canaan, N. Y., Feb. 3, 1891, Fred A. Cooley. Res. Pittsfield.
    ii. Clara Flint, b. June 16, 1870; m. first, at Pittsfield, Nov. 15, 1892, Francis K. Matterson; m. second, F. L. Peck; res. Providence, R. I. (Gifford & Peck).
    iii. Florence Smith, b. Dec. 12, 1873; res. Providence, R. I.
    iv. Margaret Edith, b. Oct. 1, 1877; m. June, 1903, Edwin Young, Providence, R. I.

782

GEORGE GIBBS FINCH[7] (*George Gibbs*,[6] *Jesse*,[5] *Jesse*,[4] *Ephraim*,[3] *Gershom*,[2] *Thomas*[1]), born at Jay, N. Y., March 4, 1843; married Matilda Weston. Resides at Burlington, Vt.; is a lime and lumber manufacturer.
Children:

   i.   Anna Grace.[8]
   ii.   Jesse Weston; grad. University of Vermont, A.B., 1900; Harvard Univ. Law School, LL.B., 1903; is a lawyer in New York city.
   iii.   Lucille.

783

WALTER HENRY[7] (*George Gibbs*,[6] *Jesse*,[5] *Jesse*,[4] *Ephraim*,[3] *Gershom*,[2] *Thomas*[1]), born in Jay, N. Y., Dec. 2, 1847; married Sept. 24, 1884, Mary, daughter of Alfred and Lucy Ann (Kingsland) Baber, born March 3, 1853.

He was graduated from the New York Homœopathic Medical College in 1874; practised four years at Keesville, N. Y.; removed to Boston where he now resides, having his residence and office at 173 Newbury Street.
Children:

   i.   Mary Baber,[8] b. June 2, 1886.
   ii.   Harriet Finch, b. Sept. 13, 1887.
   iii.   Walter Philip, b. April 3, 1891.

784

CARTER MCVENE[7] (*George Gibbs*,[6] *Jesse*,[5] *Jesse*,[4] *Ephraim*,[3] *Gershom*,[2] *Thomas*[1]), born in Jay, N. Y., Nov. 15, 1849; graduated from the Homœopathic Medical College, N. Y., 1877; married Ruth, daughter of William James and Henrietta Taylor (Alton) Abrams, born Feb. 6, 1863. Is in practice at North Granville, N. Y.

EIGHTH GENERATION.

800

NATHANIEL[8] (*Nathaniel,[7] John,[6] Samuel,[5] Thomas,[4] Thomas,[3] Thomas,[2] Thomas[1]*) was born in Union, Me., Feb. 2, 1832. Resided some years at Thomaston, Me.; removed with his wife and one child to Mississippi in 1859; then to Texas in 1872, and to Carlsbad, N. M., in 1901. He married in May, 1853, Sarah E. Hinkley, of Warren. Mr. and Mrs. Tobey wrote from Carlsbad in 1902.

Children:

  i. Minnie L.,* b. in Thomaston, Me., Oct. 27, 1856; m. in May, 1875, Paul F. Erb, of Galveston, Tex., and resides at Dallas, Tex. He is a cotton dealer.

  Child:

    William Tobey Erb, b. July, 1881.

  ii. William Stone, b. in Chatawa, Miss., Aug. 15, 1860.

  iii. Natalie S., b. in Chatawa, Miss., March 13, 1863; d. Aug. 8, 1864.

  iv. Hattie French, b. in Thomaston, Me., Jan. 26, 1865; m. in April, 1885, James Pope Cole, of Galveston, Tex., who d. Jan. 26, 1898. She res. at Carlsbad, N. M.

801

ALBERT RICE[8] (*Nathaniel,[7] John,[6] Samuel,[5] Thomas,[4] Thomas,[3] Thomas,[2] Thomas[1]*), born at Jefferson, Me., Feb. 10, 1835; married April 6, 1872, Emma Potting. Removed to Thomaston, Me., then to San Francisco, Cal., where he died Oct. 18, 1888.

Children:

   i.   Bert West[9] ; d. young.
  ii.   Sadie, b. June 22, 1875; m. Thomas Inman, M.D.
 iii.   Albert B. ; d. young.
 iv.   Emma, b. Sept. 30, 1881.
  v.   Bertie, b. Jan. 29, 1885.
 vi.   Olive, b. March 17, 1886; d. young.

802

THOMAS WEST[8] (*Nathaniel,[7] John,[6] Samuel,[5] Thomas,[4] Thomas[3] Thomas,[2] Thomas[1]*), born at Jefferson, Me., Nov. 10, 1830; married Aug. 20, 1863, Evelyn H. Wyllie, of Warren, Me.; she died Feb. 14, 1867. Resided at Thomaston, Me. He died Sept. 20, 1875.

Child:

1903   Katherine Libby,[9] b. Jan. 26, 1866; m. Aug. 27, 1888, William H. Gross, a marble manufacturer, of Lee.

804

WILLIAM ALBERT[8] (*John A.,[7] John,[6] John,[5] John,[4] Eleazer,[3] John,[2] Thomas[1]*), born in Mansfield in 1871; married March 29, 1904, Lottie May Colby, of Gardiner, Me.

Child:

     John,[9] b. in Falmouth, March 7, 1905.

805

GEORGE O.[8] (*Joshua Briggs,[7] Curtis,[6] Benjamin,[5] Seth,[4] Seth,[3] Nathan,[2] Thomas[1]*), born in Wareham, Oct. 27, 1841; married July 12, 1871, Blanche Henry, daughter of Lucius Henry and Lydia Clark (Morse) Waterman, born Dec. 23, 1850. Among her ancestors she can count the noble William Bradford, one of the constituent members of the Pilgrim Church at Scrooby, England, and in Leyden, Holland, a passen-

ger on the Mayflower, long governor and the finest
historian of the Plymouth Colony; Thomas Prence,
another of the governors of that colony; Edward
Gray, Richard Warren, and others of note.

Mr. Tobey entered into the service of the United
States in the crisis of the Rebellion. He served in
the navy.

He resides in Wareham.

Children:

   i.   George Oakes,⁹ Harv. Univ., A.B. 1898, LL.B.
       1902; in the practice of law at Wareham and
       New Bedford.

   ii.   Alice Virginia.

806

Austin Burnell⁸ (*Moses Swift Fearing,⁷ Curtis,⁶
Benjamin,⁵ Seth,⁴ Seth,³ Nathan,² Thomas¹*), born in
Wareham, Aug. 20, 1843; married Feb. 13, 1873,
Helen Aurelia, daughter of Stephen Gibson and Lucy
Smith (Tinker) Barker, born in Belvidere, Ill.

Mr. Tobey served in the Federal army in the War
of the Rebellion in the Fourth Massachusetts Infantry. The regiment was sent to the Department of
the Gulf, and did duty in the Mississippi and Red
River valleys. He was appointed hospital steward
and had important duties. When sick and taken
prisoner he still kept the care of United States fellow
prisoners who were sick; succeeded in maintaining
pleasant relations with the Rebel officers in control,
and was duly exchanged after a time. After the war
he became a partner in the Banking and Brokerage
firm of Irving A. Evans & Co., of Boston. Later was
agent of the National Fast Color Eylet Co.

Resides in Cambridge.

Child:

      Gerard Burnside,⁹ b. Dec. 24, 1873, d. May 28,
      1874.

16

807

CURTIS[8] (*Seth Fish,*[7] *Curtis,*[6] *Benjamin,*[5] *Seth,*[4] *Seth,*[3] *Nathan,*[2] *Thomas*[1]), born in Wareham, April 4, 1838; died in California, March 10, 1905. He was proprietor* of the Metropolitan Foundry in San Francisco, having his residence at Menlo Park.
Child:

Curtis, Jr.[9]; San Francisco, Cal.

808

WALTER DANFORTH[8] (*Seth Fish,*[7] *Curtis,*[6] *Benjamin,*[5] *Seth,*[4] *Seth,*[3] *Nathan,*[2] *Thomas*[1]), born in Wareham, May 7, 1842; married Oct. 17, 1865, Sally Lothrop, daughter of Daniel Baxter, of Hyannis; she died Oct. 15, 1886. He married second, Oct. 21, 1902, Mary Moore, daughter of R. T. Lincoln, of New York city.

He is a capitalist and business man of San Francisco; vice-president of the Lake Tahoe Railway and Transportation Co., associated with his brother-in-law, Mr. D. L. Bliss. Resides at Palo Alto, Cal.
Child:

Ada Elizabeth,[9] b. April 11, 1867; d. Nov. 14, 1899.

810

ORIN F.[8] (*Samuel Otis,*[7] *George,*[6] *William,*[5] *Joseph,*[4] *Nathan,*[3] *Nathan,*[2] *Thomas*[1]), born in Jefferson, Me., Aug. 20, 1866; married Aug. 9, 1890, Mrs. Anna Belle Doe. See has two children by former marriage. He is a merchant in Randolph, Me., in the firm of Moore and Tobey.

811

GEORGE W.[8] (*Samuel Otis,*[7] *George,*[6] *William,*[5] *Joseph,*[4] *Nathan,*[3] *Nathan,*[2] *Thomas*[1]), born in Jeffer-

---

* We regret that particulars of his successful life have failed to reach us, although we have made repeated efforts to secure them.

son, Me., Sept. 22, 1867; married May 21, 1896, Emma Blanche Linscott. He lives on a farm in Jefferson.

Children:

   i.   Carl Weeks,⁹ b. Sept. 5, 1897.
   ii. Dorris Adelaide, b. July 18, 1900.
   iii. Arad West, b. Nov. 6, 1901.

812

CHARLES S.⁸ (*Samuel Otis*,⁷ *George*,⁶ *William*,⁵ *Joseph*,⁴ *Nathan*,³ *Nathan*,² *Thomas*¹), born in Jefferson, Me., Sept. 6, 1870; married June 26, 1896, Emma Belle Scallon, of Hallowell, Me. He is a house carpenter; resides at Oakland, Me.

Child: Esther Marion,⁹ b. July 3, 1897.

820

BENNETT HYDE⁸(*Charles B.*,⁷ *George W.*,⁶ *William*,⁵ *William*,⁴ *Samuel*,³ *Jonathan*,² *Thomas*¹), born in Brooklyn, N. Y., July 8, 1856; married April 14, 1877, Harriet Barnes Newell, born in New Haven, Conn., June 30, 1857; she is a descendant of Captain Simeon B. Newell of Revolutionary fame. (See Historical Records, Hartford, Conn.)

Mr. Tobey is manager of the New York agency of several manufacturers of fine carpets.

Child:

Marguerite Naomi,⁹ b. in Brooklyn, March 19, 1888.

825

HERBERT A.⁸ (*Benjamin G.*,⁷ *Albert*,⁶ *Tristram*,⁵ *William*,⁴ *Samuel*,³ *Jonathan*,² *Thomas*¹), born in Nantucket and resides there; a painter and afterward a druggist's clerk. He married April 20, 1890, Lydia G., daughter of Oliver C. and Ellen M. Hatch, born in 1866.

Children:
  i.   Evelyn S.,* b. March 1, 1891.
  ii. Louise, b. July 15, 1893.

850

CHARLES FESSENDEN[8] (*Joshua Fessenden,*[7] *Joshua,*[6] *Melitiah,*[5] *Cornelius,*[4] *Cornelius,*[3] *Samuel,*[2] *Thomas*[1]), born at Palmer, July 25, 1861, married Arletta Campbell, of Akron, O.; resides in Cleveland, O.

851

GEORGE BEEBE[8] (*Joshua Fessenden,*[7] *Joshua,*[6] *Melitiah,*[5] *Cornelius,*[4] *Cornelius,*[3] *Samuel,*[2] *Thomas*[1]), born at Provincetown, May 17, 1873; married in Boston, June 1, 1899, Lillian F., daughter of Frederick and Nellie (Snow) Dodge, of Roxbury, born at Ashland in 1875.
Resides in Dorchester (Boston).

852

JESSE COOK[8] (*Joshua Fessenden,*[7] *Joshua,*[6] *Melitiah,*[5] *Cornelius,*[4] *Cornelius,*[3] *Samuel,*[2] *Thomas*[1]), born in Provincetown, May 2, 1877; married Edith L. Smith, of Brockton.
Resides in Dorchester.

853

ARTHUR WILKINSON[8] (*Joshua F.,*[7] *Joshua,*[6] *Melitiah,*[5] *Cornelius,*[4] *Cornelius,*[3] *Samuel,*[2] *Thomas*[1]), born in Harwich; married Minerva S. Handien, of Dennis. He is associated in business with his father in Harwich.

860

WILLIAM HAYWARD[8] (*William Robert,*[7] *Robert,*[6] *Joshua,*[5] *Cornelius,*[4] *Cornelius,*[3] *Samuel,*[2] *Thomas*[1]),

born in Westfield, June 27, 1872; married at Chicago,
Ill., May 3, 1900, Myra Estelle, daughter of Newton
Herbert and Clara (Lane) Bates, born at Chicago,
Jan. 19, 1876. He made his home in Chicago in
1894, entering the dry goods commission business;
became in 1897 Western manager for J. H. Lane &
Company of New York city. Resides at Evanston,
Ill.
Has taken much practical interest in the compila-
tion of this genealogy.
Child:
    Newton Hayward,⁹ b. July 4, 1903.

862

WILLIAM HENRY AUGUSTUS⁸ (*William Henry,*⁷
*William C.,*⁶ *William,*⁵ *Elisha,*⁴ *Cornelius,*³ *Samuel,*²
*Thomas,*¹), born in New Bedford, March 1, 1835;
married at Cambridge, Nov. 21, 1870, Catherine R.
Stone, daughter of John R. and Mary Arrington, of
Salem. Resides at New Bedford.

875

EDWARD J.⁸ (*John Elbert,*⁷ *William,*⁶ *Heman,*⁵
*Noah,*⁴ *Zacheus,*³ *Samuel,*² *Thomas*¹), resides in Union
County, O.
Children:
    i.   Edwin.⁹
    ii. Henry Archibald.
    iii. A daughter.

880

REGINALD SPRAGUE⁸ (*Phineas Sprague,*⁷ *Edward
Silas,*⁶ *Silas,*⁵ *Samuel,*⁴ *Samuel,*³ *Samuel,*² *Thomas*¹),
born in Boston, June 28, 1877; married Nathalie
Alexander, of New York city.

He is in the service of the Commission House of
Henry W. Peabody of New York; was for four years
the representative of the house in South Africa.
Child:

Edmund Sprague,⁹ b. in 1897.

881

BERKELEY GREENE⁸ (*Sidney Berkeley*,⁷ *Edward
Silas*,⁶ *Silas*,⁵ *Samuel*,⁴ *Samuel*,³ *Samuel*,² *Thomas*¹),
born at Providence, R. I., Jan. 10, 1881; married at
Agawam, Sept. 23, 1905, Laura Pyne, daughter of
Frederick William and Mary Sophronia (Pyne) Clark,
born in Agawam, April 23, 1883.

He has a position in the Deep River, Conn., office
of Pratt, Read & Co. of New York city, manufacturers
of Ivory goods, etc.

885

PRATT LORENZO⁸ (*Henry Augustus*,⁷ *Jonathan
Pratt*,⁶ *Jonathan*,⁵ *Elisha*,⁴ *Ephraim*,³ *Gershom*,²
*Thomas*¹), born Nov. 25, 1863; married June 16, 1889,
Ellen Adell Potter; residence Great Barrington.
Children:

  i.   Henry Pratt,⁹ b. May 12, 1890.
  ii. John Reuben, b. Jan. 6, 1892.
 iii. Helen Adell, b. July 3, 1893.

886

LEROY E.⁸ (*George B.*,⁷ *Elisha L.*,⁶ *Jonathan*,⁵
Elisha,⁴ *Ephraim*,³ *Gershom*,² *Thomas*¹), born at Alford, 1874; married at Great Barrington, Nov. 15,
1898, Lelia M., daughter of Parker L. and Delia
(Duncan) Stoddard.

890

ARTHUR G.⁸ (*Henry L.,⁷ Heman,⁶ Barnabas,⁵ Elisha,⁴ Ephraim,³ Gershom,² Thomas¹*), born in Poughkeepsie, N. Y., married Oct. 27, 1874, Florence Deyo, of Highland, N. Y. Is editor of a newspaper in Poughkeepsie, N. Y.

Children:

   i.   Arthur Nichols,⁹ b. June 4, 1876; d. March 4, 1882.
   ii.   Clara Eliza, b. Feb. 11, 1878; d. April 24, 1882.
   iii.   Earle Deyo, b. Dec. 22, 1883; Princeton Univ., class of 1905.
   iv.   Florence Emma, b. June 7, 1895.

894

FREDERICK CLINTON⁸ (*Edwin J.,⁷ Abraham,⁶ Abraham,⁵ Jesse,⁴ Ephraim,³ Gershom,² Thomas¹*), born in W. Stockbridge, Sept. 3, 1871. He graduated from the Mass. Agricultural College at Amherst in the class of 1895. Was a teacher in three different preparatory schools (for college) till 1901, when he returned to his native place and engaged with his brothers in the manufacture of lime at a point south of the village of West Stockbridge, under the firm name of Tobey Brothers.

895

GEORGE EDWIN⁸ (*Edwin Jerome,⁷ Abraham,⁶ Abraham,⁵ Jesse,⁴ Ephraim,³ Gershom,² Thomas¹*), born in West Stockbridge, Dec. 8, 1873; married first, in Belmont, Sept. 12, 1900, Gertrude A., daughter of Sylvester C. and Alice (Locke) Frost of Belmont, born July 4, 1872, died July 27, 1902. He married second, in Ashburnham, Jan. 6, 1904, Mary Ella, daughter of Albert and Ella (Locke) Needham, born April 8, 1877.

Child:

   i.   Charles Sylvester,⁹ born July 4, 1902.

896

ALBERT ABRAM[8] (*Edwin Jerome,*[7] *Abraham,*[6] *Abram,*[5] *Jesse,*[4] *Ephraim,*[3] *Gershom,*[2] *Thomas*[1]), born in West Stockbridge, Oct. 29, 1883; married in Great Barrington, Oct. 12, 1904, Laura Wallace, daughter of Frank and Ida R. Dillon, born in Yonkers, N. Y.

PART SECOND

JAMES OF KITTERY, ME., AND HIS DESCENDANTS

JAMES TOBEY OF KITTERY, ME., AND HIS DESCENDANTS.

1

JAMES[1] TOBEY was in Kittery, in the district of Maine, at a very early day, probably by the year 1665. The earliest date when a grant of land was made to him from the town (in its regular distribution to settlers) is June 24, 1687. But there is mention in the records of the county court for the year 1669 of a witness in the case of Mary Green, named "Katherine Tobee." Mr. Stackpole (in the admirable History of Kittery) suggests this may have been the first wife of James Tobey. At all events after 1687 the records of the town make frequent mention of the man and his sons. He was the father of quite a large family, some of whom were of age in 1688, indicating that James was adult as early as 1665 certainly; this would carry his own birth back to the neighborhood of 1640, we may estimate. The term "old" which was applied to him at the time of his tragic death in 1705 might have been used concerning a man of sixty or upwards. No very close approximation to his age can be made from these data, it will be seen.

He was evidently a farmer by occupation, whether bred to that or to some other avocation. His social position is shewn by the term "yeoman" used in his deed of land to his sons. He belonged to that grand middle class of Englishmen who gave to our country the most earnest, adventurous, aspiring materials for the founding of a nation. Unquestionably he was a native of England, since the very small number of persons in New England in the colonial period who were Scotch, Irish or of other nationality were so mentioned in the town and county records with great particularity. But we find no trace of the former residence of the man nor of his relatives in any document of the period. He was a man of energy and character, well esteemed in his community, lamented at his death. The very imperfect records of the town deny us details such as we desire; but there is good evidence of his worth in the upright and reputable character of his children.

He married before 1659 a wife who bore him the children who reached maturity before the close of the century. It may be entirely reasonable to suppose that she was the "Katherine" of whom mention has already been made. But she died, and the widower found a second consort in the person of a widowed neighbor, Ann Hanscomb, whose husband, Thomas Hanscomb, had been a worthy citizen of the town. She survived Mr. Tobey and was living in 1720 when the Hanscomb estate was finally divided.

The Indians came down on the settlements of the valley of the Piscataqua and other neighboring districts of New Hampshire and Maine very fiercely and with hawk-like swiftness; many of the people were captured, a larger number shot or tomahawked.

On one of the most savage of these raids the diary of Pike tells us that "Old James Tobey of Kittery and his son James were killed," along with others. The particulars are not given. It was a sad cutting off of valuable members of the infant settlement, a mournful experience for the Kittery people in general and the Tobey family in particular.

So sudden a death gave no time for the making of a will. But the kind father had already anticipated the close of life, and had bestowed the principal portion of his estate on his sons. We have the deeds on record by which he conveyed part of his lands, and another deed made after his death by the remaining children in transfer of other property. To these documents we are indebted for a number of facts of importance about the family, as will be seen by careful reading of those we here present.

James Tobey, Senior, gave his son Stephen four acres of land in Kittery, May 7, 1695; and in the autumn following made the deed of gift which we present in full below:

DEED OF JAMES TOBEY, SENIOR.

"Know all by these presents that I James Tobey Senr, of the town of Kittery in ye County of York yeoman, for divers good causes and considerations me hereunto moving, but especially for ye love I bear unto my two sons John and William Tobey Have given granted Alienated and confirmed, And doe by these presents ffreely give grant Alienate Enfeoff and confirm all my housing and lands lying in ye Township of Kittery, that is to say my house & house lot and all my other lands Excepting ye four acres of land which I have given unto my Sonne Stephen Tobey whereon his house now Standeth Alsoe I give unto my two sons John and William Tobey whereon all the Timb^r wood & woods and und^r wood trees standing lying or growing on ye above mentioned p^{r}mises as alsoe all priviledges appertinances high wayes Easmt^s of what kind soever unto ye s^d John & William Tobey their heires and Assigns for ever Alsoe I doe freely give unto my two sons John Tobey and William my Stock of cattle to them & their heires forever/To say two oxen three steeres four cows three heifers one Bull twelve Sheep three sows and one Mare/ To have and to Hold all ye above house and housing lands Appertinances, priveledges Stock of cattle, above mentioned to the onely use benefit and behoofe of them the s^d John and William Tobey their heires and Assigns for ever/ Equally to be Devided between them the s^d John and William Tobey aboves^d Yeelding and paying yearly and every year unto me ye s^d James Tobey Senr, during my

Naturall life the one halfe part of all y⁰ Increase of y⁰ above Specified Stock of cattle & one halfe part of the produce of y⁰ fruites of y⁰ Earth as corn apples Cyder butter cheese and all whatsoever y⁰ sᵈ plantation produceth. And also convenient Roome in my now dwelling house I do reserve for my own use during my naturall life Alsoe I doe freely give unto my two sons John Tobey and William Tobey all my household goods to them and their heires for ever excepting my bed and furniture which I give unto my daughter Mary Tobey, viz all my woollen & Linnen and Pewter & brass & Iron & vessels of wood I doe freely give unto my sᵈ Sons / Always provided and to be understood that my said Sons John & William Tobey doe well and truly pay render of couse to be paid unto me y⁰ sᵈ James Tobey Senʳ y⁰ halfe Increase above mentioned during my Naturall life And at my Decease to pay five shillings in money to my son Stephen Tobey & one heifer to my Son James Tobey And to my two sons Richᵈ and Isaac Tobey five pounds each And to my Daughter Mary my younger daughter ten pounds one halfe in money and the other halfe in currant pay. And furthermore I y⁰ said James Tobey doe covenant with y⁰ sᵈ John and William Tobey that y⁰ p'mises are free from all manner of incumbrance whatsoever and y⁰ peaceable possession thereof to maintain against all manner of psons whatsoever /

Witness my hand & Seal this Second day of Septembʳ One thousand Six hundred Ninety & five—

In presents of us

Richard Rogers

Mercy Gowen

Richard Carter

The signe of

JAMES .T. TOBEY (his) (Seal)

Acknowledged 16 Sept. 1695.

In 1702 he sold to Stephen one half of a grant of 20 acres which had been granted to him May 16, 1694.

After Mr. Tobey's death his son Stephen administered on the estate, presenting his account 11 February, 1705–6. The following transfer took place afterward:

Richard Tobey of Portsmouth, with his wife Martha; Isaac Tobey, of Kittery; John Paul, of Kittery, and his wife Margaret; with Mary Tobey, of Kittery, sold to their brother Stephen Tobey, of Kittery, Dec. 16, 1706, all their rights in lands formerly owned by their father, James Tobey late of Kittery, deceased. [York Deeds, vii, 63.] Nearly twenty years later Mary, having married Robert Jordan and removed to Falmouth, quitclaimed all her possible interest in these lands to her brother Isaac.

Children, birth-dates wanting:

2. i.   Stephen,' b. probably about 1665.
    ii. James; deposed at Dover, giving his age such as to indicate that he was born about 1667; was killed by the Indians at the same time as his father.
3. iii. John.
4. iv. William.
5. v.   Richard.
6. vi. Isaac.
    vii. Margaret; m. John Paul.
    viii. Mary; m. in 1706, Robert Jordan, second son of Rev. Robert Jordan, the pioneer minister of Richmond Island, later a resident of Portsmouth, by his wife Sarah, daughter of Mr. John Winter, another important pioneer. Mary, wife of Robert Jordan, Senior, of Falmouth, in the county of York, sold 12 Feb., 1735-6, to Isaac Tobey of Portsmouth, in the province of New Hampshire, all her right and title [to lands] in Kittery. [York Deeds 17, 271.]

SECOND GENERATION.

2

STEPHEN[2] (*James[1]*), born probably about 1665; married in Dover, N. H., Nov. 29, 1688, Hannah, daughter of Charles and Mary Nelson (formerly of Kittery, but then of Newington, N. H.). He was a juryman in 1690 and 1691. He was a shipwright. His home was in Kittery. He received a gift of land from his father, Sept. 16, 1695, and bought another tract of the administrator of John Green's estate, Jan. 13, 1695–6. He had still another piece from his father in 1702.

"In company with Joseph and Matthew Libbey, Daniel Fogg and Joseph Hammond he purchased in Dec. 1699, the Bay Land or Knowles purchase (in what is now the town of Eliot), extending from Frank's Fort to Watts' Fort by the river, fronting on the river at the Long Reach, then back to Marsh Hill. His portion of the shore was set off on the southeast side of the lot."

He built vessels at Mast Cove. With his wife Hannah he sold, May 16, 1701, land which he had formerly purchased in the above-mentioned partnership.

He was one of the founders of the (Congregational) church in the North Parish of Kittery (now Eliot), in 1721.

He signed his name "*Stephen Tobey*" as witness to the will of his father-in-law, Charles Nelson, 7 Aug., 1688, and to a deed of land to Jacob Smith, May 16, 1701. He conveyed lands to his sons Samuel, John and Stephen Jr., in 1735, and to Stephen, Jr.,

JAMES: SECOND GENERATION.

in 1743. May 7, 1737, he joined with two neighbors,
"all above the age of 70," in testimony relative to a
resident in Kittery "60 years ago." [York Deeds,
20, 31.] His wife Hannah joined with him, 19 Oct.,
1748, in deeding all his personal and moveable estate,
and his rights in Berwick derived from Charles Nelson,
to his son Stephen, Jr.

   Children:

	i.	Katherine,³ b. Oct. 25, 1689.
7.	ii.	Samuel, b. Jan. 31, 1692.
8.	iii.	James, b. Oct. 21, 1694.
9.	iv.	John, b. Jan. 2, 1699.
10.	v.	Stephen, b. Jan. 3, 1702.
	vi.	Hannah, b. Jan. 10, 1705–6; m. (1) Jan. 7, 1724–5, Robert Staples; m. (2) Nov. 16, 1757, Nathaniel Libbey.

3

JOHN² (*James¹*), born as early as 1668; signed,
"John Tobey," as a witness, in the will of Charles
Nelson, in 1688; received with his brother William,
in 1695, a deed of land from their father [see full text
ante]; also had a grant of land in Kittery in 1699.
Either he or his nephew John is several times
mentioned as a landholder in Kittery. Perhaps the
person the town clerk intended by "John Tobe," who
was published Oct. 31, 1735, to Leah Smart, he "of
Kittery," she "of Derim" [Durham?], may have been
this man or a son of his; but nothing further has been
learned about them.

4

WILLIAM² (*James¹*), born at date to us unknown,
but probably about 1670; resided in Kittery up to the
year 1695 at least, when he and his brother John received a joint deed of their father's homestead and
chattels, on condition of paying him half the income
and paying bequests to brothers and sisters.

17

5

RICHARD[2] (*James*[1]), born about 1676; removed to Portsmouth, N. H., and married Martha, daughter of Samuel Heard of Dover, N. H. Evidence of this relationship appears in a deed of Richard and Martha, March 3, 1717–8, quitclaiming all right in the estate of her father Samuel and her brother John Heard, to her uncle Tristram Heard and her brother Samuel Heard. [N. H. Deeds, XII., 576.] Martha was "received into yᵉ Covenant and baptized" in the Portsmouth church, July 14, 1708. Their children were duly baptized in infancy, as the records, fragmentary though they are, show us.

Richard was a cordwainer or shoemaker, a busy man; when elected constable, that is tax collector, in 1720, he preferred to pay the stated fine rather than perform the duties of the office. Chosen one of the "Tything men," whose duty it was to preserve order in meeting, he accepted the trust, in 1721 and 1722. He accumulated some property, and we have deeds showing how it was disposed of by him and by his heirs. He had some land in the new plantation of Barrington, not far away, and this he sold in 1738–9. That he was a member of the church is shown by the fact of his election to the duty of aiding in maintaining the decorum of the house of God. He passed away not far from the year 1746, perhaps; his wife was named among the members of the church at the ordination of Rev. Samuel Langdon, in 1747.

His children scattered from the homestead before his death in some cases, the remainder soon after.

He performed military duty in the critical time of the Indian wars.

"Richard Tobey" is mentioned among Portsmouth men who served Aug. 30 to Sept. 10, 1708, in "A List of Souldiers Names : and Time they Served att her Majesties ffourt Wᵐ and

Mary: at New Castle in the province of New Hampshire, New England 1708."
" Rich�ᵈ. Tobey " is enrolled as "from Coll. Vaughans," in " A Muster Roll of the Souldiers under My Command in A Scout 1712" filed by Capt. James Davis. [N. H. State Papers.]

He conveyed half of his house in Portsmouth to his son Isaac, Jan. 10, 1735. This was sold by the son after the death of his father.

Isaac Tobey of Portsmouth, cordwainer, sold to Edward Brooks of Portsmouth, mariner, April 11, 1741, half his dwelling house in P., formerly belonging to his father Richard Tobey of Portsmouth. Signed by "Isaac Tobey" and Elizabeth his wife.

Solomon Staples of Kittery, Me., shipwright, and Martha, his wife; John Walden of Portsmouth, shipwright, and Lydia, his wife; Abigail Toby of Portsmouth, single woman and spinster; Samuel Tobey of Portsmouth, turner, and Mary Tobey of Portsmouth, single woman and spinster, sold to Edward Brooks of Portsmouth, mariner, Aug. 2, 1746, all their title in " the late Mansion House and Garden thereto belonging that was the Mansion House and Garden of Richard Tobey late of Portsmouth aforesaid Cordwainʳ Deceased Father of the Said Martha, Lidia, Abigail, Samuel and Mary.

Mary Toby Widow, Samuel Toby Chairmaker, William Tobey Mariner, John Knight Labourer, & Sarah his wife, John Toby Labourer, John Jones Mariner, & Polly his wife, all of Portland in the county of Cumberland, Mass., sold for £7–10 to Jacob Waldron of Portsmouth, Merchant, all their right to a house & lot in Portsmouth on High street. [The date is wanting, but the deed was acknowledged Dec. 13, 1788, and recorded at Exeter March 18, 1789.]

From the church records and these deeds we can make out the list of children, though it is manifestly imperfect.

Children:

19. i.   Samuel.³
    ii. Martha; received to the church in July, 1715; m. Solomon Staples, b. June 20, 1705.

20. iii.   William, bapt. Sept. 30, 1711.
21. iv.   Isaac, bapt. Jan. 31, 1713–4.
    v.   Catherine, bapt. Jan. 15, 1715–6.
    vi.   Experience, bapt. December, 1717.
    vii.   Lydia, bapt. Nov. 29, 1719; m. John Walden.
22. viii.   John.
    ix.   Sarah; m. John Knight of Portland.
    x.   Abigail, living, single, in Portsmouth in 1746.
    xi.   Mary (Polly); single in 1746; m. John Jones of Portland before 1788.

THIRD GENERATION.

7

SAMUEL[3] (*Stephen,*[2] *James*[1]), born June 30, 1692; married, Dec. 29, 1720, Mary, daughter of John and Mary (Diamond) Spinney; her mother was widowed and married second, —— Burnham of Kittery; in her will, Dec. 4, 1733, she made bequest to her "daughter Mary Tobey." Samuel and Mary joined in deeds of land with other Spinney heirs in 1732 and 1749, and sold land inherited from her father Nov. 6, 1761. After her husband's death she sold other tracts 18 May, 1773. Samuel, John and Stephen made a division of a tract they had owned together in Berwick, 5 May, 1767. He gave to his son Samuel, 3 Aug. 1762, his homestead farm and certain other lands, to be possessed after the death of himself and wife.

  Children:
    i.   Abigail;[4] m. April 10, 1752, William Fernald.
25. ii.   William, bapt. Aug. 2, 1730.
    iii.   Mary, bapt. Nov., 1734.
26. iv.   Samuel, "2ᵈ," b. in 1734.
27. v.   Nathaniel, b. Sept., 1742.

9

JOHN³ (*Stephen*,² *James*¹), born Jan. 2, 1699; married Elizabeth, daughter of James and Mary (Tetherly) Staple. They were published 9 Nov. 1723. She died in Sept., 1769. He was a farmer. He and his wife sold, 15 March, 1755, her interest in the estate of her deceased father, James Staple. He died Dec. 6, 1778, bequeathing his property to his daughters Mary Foster and Hannah Tobey and his son John; will proved Jan. 4, 1779.

Children:

    i.   Mary,⁴ b. Nov. 22, 1727 ; m. Nov. 15, 1753, Parker Foster.

    ii. Hannah, b. Sept., 1729 ; d. June 23, 1814.

33. iii. John, b. Nov. 12, 1733.

10

STEPHEN³ (*Stephen*,² *James*¹), born in Kittery, Me., Jan. 2, 1702; married first, Oct. 25, 1726, Anne, daughter of Peter and Mary (Lang) Staples. After her death he married second, Nov. 30, 1749, Margaret, daughter of Daniel and Margaret (Gowen) Emery. He resided on his father's homestead. He acquired land in "Pudding Hole Common" in partnership with Richard Rice, and sold it 14 March, 1747. He and Margaret sold, 27 Jan. 1752, land in Berwick inherited from her father, Daniel Emery. He died about 1788.

Stephen Tobey of Kittery, yeoman, bought land in Falmouth, Me., Oct. 16, 1765, and sold it July 7, 1787.

The widow Margaret made her will 16 Sept. 1788, proved 20 April, 1795, bequeathing to her "son in law" Stephen Tobey, daughter Lois Kelley, Nathaniel Gerrish, Thomas Claridge, and Ann Claridge, Elizabeth Avery and her own brothers and sisters.

Children:

i.   Eunice,⁴ bapt. in May, 1729; m. Aug. 23, 1750, Jonathan Gerrish.

ii.   Hannah, bapt. Aug. 2, 1730.

iii.   Anna, bapt. Nov., 1732; m. Thomas Claridge.

34. iv.   Stephen, bapt. Feb., 1734–5; m. (1) (published Nov. 12, 1762) Sarah Dennett; m. (2) Oct. 26, 1786, Mary Rogers. He died childless, leaving a will dated 12 April, proved 15 May, 1800, bequeathing his property to his wife Mary, sisters Anne Claridge, Lois Kelley, Martha Ham and Eunice Gerrish; to Stephen Claridge of Newfield, son of Thos. Claridge, and to Thalas Black. His widow d. in 1814.

v.   Lois, bapt. Dec. 9, 1739; m. Nov. 28, 1759, William Kelley, of Dover, N. H.

vi.   Martha, bapt. Sept., 1742; m. —— Ham.

19

SAMUEL³ (*Richard*,² *James*¹), born in Portsmouth, N. H.; married Mary, daughter of Samuel and Sarah (Cotton) Pickering, of Portsmouth. Her mother was a daughter of Benjamin Cotton, and Samuel Tobey with Mary, his wife, sold their rights in the Cotton estate April 4, 1749, detailing the relationship.

Samuel was a turner and chair-maker. He " recognized his baptismal covenant " and was received to full communion in the church March 5, 1748–9. He was a worthy and valuable citizen. He served in the Colonial Wars.

Samuel Tobey is in a list of men in Abraham Trefethen's company of men drawn from Col. Moore's regiment at Canso, April 15, 1745, and served to July 9, 1745, "in the late expedition against Louisbourg". He petitioned with some of his comrades July 11, 1747, for "smart money as compensation for their sufferings and the want of the necessities and comforts [of life] in the late expedition to Louisbourg." He reported "41 days in which he had no rum and 9 that he had no bread; 15 gallons of molasses for 6 men for the whole time and no butter and no sugar."

He was one of the inhabitants of Portsmouth who petitioned for a grant of land for a township at " Winnepissioky," Nov. 17, 1748. He also signed a petition the same year for a township on the Merrimac river.

A list of the men under the command of Capt. Job Clement a " Gard for Rochester and Barrenton," N. H., April 7, 1748, includes Samuel Tobey, "monthman."

He removed about the year 1753 to Portland, Me., having sold real estate to George Massey, Feb. 10, 1753, his wife joining in the deed; and on the 24th of the same month he sold "part of the mansion house of his honoured father, Richard Toby, late of Portsmouth." His name is on the tax-list in Portland for the year 1766;—a poll-tax of 5s., 6d.

Samuel Tobey of Portland, turner, bought land on Fore St., May 7, 1799.

In the very fragmentary records of Portland's early history which remain since the destructive fire of 1866, we find only a few items relating to the family. We have no clue to the time of death of either Samuel or Mary, nor full knowledge about his children. Two were baptized at Portsmouth, the name of the second being omitted; it is practicable to identify both of these; we simply write down the somewhat indefinite records regarding the others born in Portland. Mrs. Abbie S. Merrill told of the son John who became a Revolutionary soldier and had a pension, and the daughter Abigail who married Mr. McKnight.

Children:

45. i.   William,⁴ bapt. at Portsmouth, N. H., July 15, 1750.
46. ii. Samuel, believed to be the child "of Samuel Tobey" who was bapt. at Portsmouth, N. H., March 15, 1752.

47. iii. John, "a child of ———— Tobey," bapt. at Portland, Oct. 9, 1757.
iv. "A child of ———— Tobey," bapt. July, 1759.
v. "A daughter of ———— Tobey," bapt. June 15, 1766.
vi. "A child, drowned" at Portland, Me., in "Sept.,
1766."
vii. Abigail, "Nabby, of Samuel Tobey," bapt. July 24,
1768 ; m. ———— McKnight.
viii. "A child, one year old, died in April, 1769."

20

WILLIAM³ (*Richard,² James¹*) born in Portsmouth,
N. H., baptized Sept, 30, 1711; became a sea-captain.
Lived in Portland, Me., certainly in his later years,
being there at the signing of the family deed of the
old homestead in Portsmouth in 1788, as we have
seen on a previous page. It has been inferred that
he married; yet no wife's right of dower was conveyed
along with his own right in the deed above mentioned.
He may have been widowed before that date. He
was at the time 77 years of age, as we see by reference to the date of his baptism.

William Tobey of Falmouth, mariner, bought land on the
Northerly side of the lane that leads to Mariner's Spring, June
18, 1783, and sold it Sept. 11, 1784.

21

ISAAC³ (*Richard,² James¹*), born in Portsmouth,
N. H., baptized Jan. 31, 1713–4; married at Hampton, N. H., Jan. 13, 1736–7, Elizabeth Page. His
father had already given him half of his house in Portsmouth,— Jan. 10, 1735. This, as we have seen in the
article on the father, Isaac and Elizabeth sold in 1741.
He learned his father's trade of cordwainer. He removed to Hampton Falls, N. H. He was called into
the service of the country, in the French and Indian
War, as we see from the following petition; for al-

though it was not granted it is evidence of the facts there stated.

"Isaac Tobey of Hampton Falls," in a petition dated Jan. 15, 1760, stated "That your petitioner was a soldier in the service of this Province, the Summer Past, That while he was in the Service at Sarratoga he had his Gun Stolen." He asked for an allowance for the same. The petition was marked " dismissed"; but was filed without any controverting of the statements it contained. Only the Province could not see the way clear to recompense the man for the lost piece. [New Hamp-State Papers.]

Children:

50. i. Richard.[4]
51. ii. William.
52. iii. Samuel Brooks, b. about 1748.
53. iv. Page, b. in 1750.

FOURTH GENERATION.

25

WILLIAM[4] (*Samuel,[3] Stephen,[2] James[1]*), born in Kittery, bapt. Aug. 2, 1730; married first, —; married second, May 8, 1777, Hannah Remick.

He was a sea-captain. Bought land in Kittery, part of the Mitchell homestead, 6 July, 1767. His father sold him land at Simmons' brook, 13 Sept. 1768; this deed he assigned to John Tobey, Jr., for a consideration, 16 May, 1770.

He died before Nov. 29, 1791, when claims were filed against his estate, Stephen Hanscom administrator; the liabilities exceeded the property.

Division of the estate of William Tobey, late of Kittery, was made 30 April, 1808, between Josiah Tobey (with his wife Elizabeth), William Tobey, John Woodman and Andrew Tobey of Kittery. Josiah Tobey, Jr., was one of the witnesses.

Children:

97. i.   Josiah,* b. about 1771.
98. ii.   William, b. about 1773.
     iii. A daughter who m. John Woodman.
99. iv.   Andrew, b. about 1778.

26

SAMUEL[4] (*Samuel,[3] Stephen,[2] James[1]*), born in Kittery, Me., in 1734; married (published March 17, 1764) Mary, daughter of Stephen Paul; she was born in 1738 and died Nov. 20, 1801. He conveyed certain lands in Kittery and Berwick for the term of his own life to his son James, 26 May, 1806.

Children:

100. i.   Stephen,* baptized with the two following April 22, 1770.
      ii.   Abigail; m. 15 Nov., 1789, David Libbey.
101. iii. James, b. June 22, 1769.
      iv.   Samuel, bapt. June 27, 1772; d. young.
      v.   William, bapt. Aug. 14, 1774; d. young.
      vi.   Sarah, } twins; { d. Sept. 25, 1817.
      vii. Mary, }   { d. young.
102. viii. John, bapt. July, 1780.
      ix.   William, b. 1782; d. Oct. 17, 1801.
103. x.   Samuel, } b. 1785; {
      xi.   Mary,   }   { m. 10 Aug. 1807, Isaac Spinney.

27

NATHANIEL[4], (*Samuel,[3] Stephen,[2] James[1]*), born at Kittery in Sept., 1742; married (published June 11, 1768) Anne Tapley of Pepperell Borough.

33

JOHN[4] (*John,[3] Stephen,[2] James[1]*), born Nov. 12, 1733; married (published 10 Oct., 1767) Anne, daughter of James and Elizabeth (Fernald) Fogg, born 2

March, 1739.   He died between the 16th July, 1779,
when he bought the rights of his sister in their father's
estate and the setting off of his sister Mary Foster's
portion of their father's estate, one half — "he having
left no male heir"—May 3, 1802.   John, Jr.'s daughter Elizabeth was appointed administratrix of his
estate Sept. 24, 1801.

Children:

   i.   Elizabeth,⁵ b. 6 Nov., 1768; m. 28 Dec. 1802,
       Ezra Libby (his second wife).

  ii.   Anna, b. Aug. 19, 1772; m. Joseph Staples.
       They sold, 28 Nov. 1806, that portion of a tract
       of land which had once belonged to John To-
       bey and his brothers Samuel and Stephen, and
       had been assigned to John in their division,
       Dec. 22, 1742, and had descended to Anna by
       inheritance.

45

WILLIAM⁴ (Samuel,³ Richard,² James¹), born in
Portsmouth, N. H., baptized July 15, 1750; removed
with his father to Portland, Me.   He was married in
Falmouth by Rev. Dr. Deane, Sept. 9, 1773, to Tabitha
Brackett; he married, July 17, 1785, Mitty (Submit)
Cox.   "William Tobey's wife died of consumption June
10, 1784" tells us of Tabitha's death, although the record states the woman's age at "88"; but the second
marriage makes it evident that the woman who died
was Tabitha; and as we also have record of the death
of "a child of William Tobey," dying "of consumption" in October, 1783, at the age of one year, the
writer believes that the record of the wife's age should
read 33, which clearly applies to this case.   Tabitha
Tobey was admitted to the First Church, Aug. 21,
1774, and the children were baptized in due time.
Mrs. Submit Tobey died after bearing at least five
children, and "Capt. William Tobey of Portland"

married, June 1, 1813, Mercy, daughter of Richard
Tobie of New Gloucester (No. 50). She outlived
him and died in Levant, Me., Oct., 1863. [Rev. A.
Titus.] He built a house on Hampshire street, in
Portland. He was a sea captain, an intelligent, efficient man.

William Tobey of Portland, yeoman, bought land in Portland Nov. 16, 1786.

William Tobey and Submit, his wife, in her right, joined
with Elizabeth, relict of Benj. Stevens, Sally Cox, Moses Cox
and others, in a quitclaim deed of land May 28, 1800.

William Tobey, mariner, mortgaged his house and land on
Hampshire St., Portland, to Sally Sanborn of Portland, single
woman, Oct. 26, 1812; discharged, paid April 26, 1818, as
by her signature in the margin.

The loss of the town records and most of the other
early documents of Portland—among the ravages of
the great conflagration—compels us to construct the
list of children of this large and important family from
the records of the First Church and from private
sources. By dint of minute inquiries and scrupulous
care we have a list which we hope contains no errors.
Much of the information regarding this family came
from Mrs. Martha Abigail Sanborn Merrill of Searsport, Me., who died in 1902, aged 90 years, and from
Mrs. Martha A. Robinson, of Portland, Me.

Children:

     i.   Mercy,[5] bapt. Sept. 18, 1774.
     ii.   Tabitha, bapt. June 16, 1776; m. Jonathan Stevens.
     iii. Mercy, bapt. Nov. 16, 1777; m. Joseph Stevens.
110. iv. Edward ("Ned"), bapt. July 30, 1780.
     v.   Eunice, bapt. May 26, 1782.
111. vi. William, bapt. May 28, 1786.
112. vii. Robert, bapt. Oct. 7, 1787.
113. viii. Lemuel, b. about 1789.
     ix. Lucy; m. Capt. George Loring.
     x.   Enoch.
114. xi. Marcia, b. 1814; m. George Fessenden.

46

SAMUEL[4] (*Samuel,[3] Richard,[2] James[1]*), born in Portsmouth, baptized March 15, 1752; removed with his father to Falmouth, later called Portland, Me., and June 16,1774, he was married to Abigail (Nabby) Cox by Rev. Dr. Deane. He died April 14, 1822; "Nabby Tobey, consort of Mr. Samuel Tobey, died Oct. 23, 1815, aged 63 years." [Gravestones in Eastern Cemetery.] He and his wife were received into full communion in the First Church, April 2, 1775.

Samuel Tobey, Jr., of Portland, chairmaker, was one of several trustees (apparently) who received a deed of land in Portland, April 10, 1807.

Samuel Tobey, corporal, on muster and pay roll of Capt. Joseph Noyes' co., from July 11 to Dec. 31, 1775; served 6 months, 5 days; stationed at Falmouth.

Samuel Tobey, Jr., matross, on a return of Capt. Abner Lowell's co., return of muster made by Col. Peter Noyes, Aug. 11, 1777; stationed at Falmouth, Cumberland co. Samuel Tobey appears in a return of men enlisted into the Continental army from Cumberland co. of Col. Peter Noyes' (1st) regt.; dated Nov. 20, 1778; res. Falmouth; term of enlistment 3 years; joined Capt. Skillings' co., Col. Francis' regt.

Daniel Tobey with wife Eliza, and Bailey Pierce with wife Eliza, residing in Frankfort in the county of Hancock, sold land in Portland which had descended to Daniel Tobey and Eliza Pierce from their father Samuel Tobey, late of Portland, under date of June 11, 1822.

Nathaniel Mitchell and Eunice his wife, and Eliza Pierce, of Boston; Josiah Hayden and Dorcas his wife, of Braintree; with Daniel Tobey and Eliza his wife, of Frankfort in the county of Waldo sold their interest. Nov. 24, 1847.

Children:

 i. Mary,[5] bapt. April 30, 1775.

115. ii. Samuel, bapt. Jan. 5, 1777.

 iii. Nabby, bapt. Nov. 22, 1778.

 iv. Dorcas, bapt. May 6, 1781; m. Josiah Hayden, of Boston.

v.   Eunice, bapt. Jan. 9, 1785; m. Nathaniel Mitchell.
116. vi. Charles, bapt. Oct. 21, 1787.
     vii. Eliza, m. Bailey Pierce.
117. viii. Daniel.

47

JOHN[4] (*Samuel,*[3] *Richard,*[2] *James*[1]), born in Portland, baptized Oct. 9, 1757; grew up and took his place among the defenders of the infant nation in the Revolution; testimony to this service and to the pension he afterward received came from his grand niece, Mrs. M. A. S. Merrill.

John Tobey, private, on muster and pay roll of Capt. John Lane's co., from June 17 to Nov. 1, 1775, and from Nov. 1 to Dec. 31, 1775; served 2 months, 5 days; roll dated at Cape Ann; res. Falmouth; *also*, private on a return of Capt. Samuel Darby's co., Col. John Bailey's regt. in service at Valley Forge, Jan. 25, 1778; residence Falmouth; *also*, private, on muster and pay roll of Capt. Simeon Fish's co., Col. Freeman's regt., from Sept. 11 to Sept. 12, 1779; served on alarm at Falmouth 2 days; *also*, in a list of the men enlisted into the Continental Army out of the 1st Cumberland co., regt., Col. Peter Noyes; belonging to Falmouth; enlisted for 3 years; *also*, in a statement of continental balances with rank of private, in Col. Bailey's regt.; engaged 3 years; *also*, John, private, on a warrant to pay officers and men on a roll bearing date, March 17, 1784, of Capt. Thompson J. Skinner's co.; *also*, on an account against the U. S. by the Commonwealth of Massachusetts for amounts paid officers and men of Col. John Bailey's regt., on account of depreciation of their wages for the first three years service in the Continental Army from 1777 to 1780; account exhibited by committee on claims in behalf of Massachusetts against U. S., Sept. 21, 1887.

50

RICHARD[4] (*Isaac,*[3] *Richard,*[2] *James*[1]), married at Seabrook, N. H., April 28, 1768, Jemima Haskell. [Town Record.] He was a respected citizen of the little town; chosen to serve on the county grand jury in 1778 and 1780; elected a member of the board of selectmen in 1778 and continued in the office several years. Chosen one of the assessors in 1788.

He and his brothers have the distinction of being the first of the Kittery family to sign their name "Tobie," so far as records show, and their descendants have religiously adhered to the example set them in this respect.

"Richard Tobie of Seabrook, N. H., yeoman, and Jemima, his wife, sold for $200 to Jemima, wife of Edward Melcher of Kensington, N. H., land on the highway to Kensington, Nov. 4, 1788.

The spirit of adventure which led older men of the family to seek new fields for enterprise led him to the central district of Maine, whither many of the most vigorous sons of Massachusetts and New Hampshire were in those days removing. He found a spot which attracted him in New Gloucester in Cumberland county, Maine, and thither he removed.

Richard Tobie of New Gloucester, Massachusetts Bay, gentleman, sold to Willard Emery of Hampton Town, N. H., gentleman, for £6, 4 acres in Mossey Swamp in Hampton Town, it being the land that was Anthony Emery, Esquire's, Sept. 18, 1789. To this the wife's signature is not appended; probably she was in Maine and the possibility of her demanding the right of dower seemed too small for the grantee to require her signature.

He was born June 26, 1740, and died in New Gloucester Oct. 8, 1827,

OBITUARY.

Died in New Gloucester (Me.) Oct. 8, 1827, Mr. Richard Tobie. At the commencement of the Revoluntary War the deceased was appointed an officer under the Continental Congress, which office he sustained until a short time before the close of the war, when he relinquished it, and was chosen a

lieutenant in a volunteer company. Shortly after this the news
of peace came, and they did not leave the town of Hampton
Falls, N. H. In 1789 he removed to New Gloucester, Me.,
where by industry and frugality he acquired a valuable property; in 1799 he was baptized and joined the Baptist church
in that town, of which he was a worthy and exemplary member till the time of his death. He was kind and affectionate in
his family and beloved by all who knew him; he retained his
reason till the last, and would discourse upon events which took
place sixty or seventy years ago with surprising accuracy. His
memory was strong and retentive. His descendants were
thirteen children, sixty-nine grandchildren and twenty-four
great grandchildren, in all one hundred and six, ninety-one
of whom were living at the time of his death.

Children, the first nine recorded on the town book
of Seabrook, N. H.:

118. i.   Richard,[5] b. Jan. 23, 1769.
119. ii. Jonathan, b. Oct. 6, 1770.
     iii. Sarah, b. Sept. 20, 1772; m. John Starbird.
     iv. Mercy, b. Aug. 1, 1774; m. (1) June 1, 1813,
          Capt. William Tobey, of Portland; m. (2) Oct.
          25, 1821, William H. Pierce. She died in Le-
          vant October, 1863.
     v.   Elizabeth (Betsey), b. July 16, 1776; m. Oct. 3,
          1797, Job Lurvey.
     vi. Dolley, b. May 8, 1778; d. unmarried.
     vii. Marthey (Martha) (Patty), b. March 16, 1780; m.
          Aug. 29, 1807, Levi Hersey.
120. viii. William, b. June 18, 1782.
     ix. Abigail, b. Jan. 27, 1785; m. March 9, 1815,
          Aaron Bray, of Poland, Me,
     x.   Jemima, b. in New Gloucester, Me., May 13, 1787;
          m. Stephen Cobb.
121. xi. Thomas Haskell, b. Sept. 17, 1789.
122. xii. Ezra, b. April 13, 1793.
123. xiii. Levi, b. Aug. 30, 1795.

51

WILLIAM[4] (*Isaac,*[3] *Richard,*[2] *James*[1]), born in
Hampton Falls, N. H. We may naturally suppose

him to be the William Tobey, of Poplin, N. H., joiner,
who bought 125 acres of land in the township of Not-
tingham, parish of Deerfield, N. H., for £102, May 3,
1774. His son William Tobie, of Deerfield, husbandman, sold an undivided half of this tract "which my
honoured father William Tobey deceased bought of
Josiah Bartlett," Oct. 1, 1792; and Nathan Tobie of
Deerfield, husbandman, sold the other half, specifying
his relationship, etc., Nov. 19, 1792.

Children:

124. i. William.[5]
125. ii. Nathan, bapt. at Hawke, N. H. (now Danville),
         Aug. 23, 1772.
     iii. Hulda, bapt. at H., Nov. 14, 1773.

52

SAMUEL BROOKS[4] (*Isaac,[3] Richard,[2] James[1]*), born at
Hampton Falls, N. H., in 1749 (as by record of death);
removed when a boy to Weare, N. H., and was "bound
out" to Jonathan Dow. On reaching his majority
he married Elizabeth, daughter of Lieut. Samuel Cald-
well. He set up house-keeping on the highest hill in
town, since called by his name. Kept store and farmed.
His wife shared the hardships and toils of rough
pioneering. She survived him, and died Aug. 19,
1848, aged 99 years, 2 months and 8 days. Their
house was a hospitable establishment. He was often
a town officer, and several terms representative to the
Legislature; became very wealthy, considerably in-
fluential; was distinguished alike for ability, hospi-
tality, excessive drinking and an ungoverned temper.
The history of Weare gives these facts and many
details.

He had no children. Adopted Mrs. Tobie's niece,
Bessie McNeil, who afterward married a Mr. Mudge;
the daughter of this couple, Esther, married Nathan
Philbrick and inherited the Tobie farm.

18

272   TOBEY GENEALOGY.

Among the deeds of Samuel Brooks Tobie on record
are two of importance, genealogically: April 16, 1773,
he sold a lot of land in Hampton which he had purchased in 1772; Sept. 30, 1778, he sold a lot in Bow
which had been given to him by his "Aunt Manton."
[Exeter Deeds, 117, 195.]
He died Jan. 31, 1836, aged 87 years.

53

PAGE⁴ (*Isaac,*³ *Richard,*² *James*¹), born in Hampton Falls, N. H.   Settled in Falmouth, Me.   He
was a housewright; bought land June 11, 1772.
Married a wife named Betty, who joined him in a
deed July 22, 1774.   He removed to North Yarmouth,
Me., and sold his Falmouth land May 16, 1794.   He
served in the Revolution, as the following extracts
from the Mass. Archives show.

Page (Tobie), on a billeting roll of Capt. John Worthly's
co., Col. Edmund Phinney's regt., from May 8 to July 11,
1775; served 64 days; res. Falmouth, Me.

Page appears on a receipt dated Cambridge, Feb. 20, 1776,
for pay for Nov. and Dec. 1775, signed by himself and others;
received of lieutenant Crispus Graves.

Page (Toby), private, on a pay abstract of Capt. William
Cobb's co., Col. Jonathan Mitchell's regt. mileage sworn to at
North Yarmouth, Nov. 26, 1779; res. New Casco.   Detach-
ment raised in Cumberland Co., for services on Penobscot expedition; reported as having first drawn rations at Falmouth
and as discharged there; and as marching July 8 to Aug. 30,
1779.

In a Descriptive List of Men received in the County of Cumberland to serve in the army of the United States, printed in
"Old Times in North Yarmouth," vol. 3, p. 338, we find:

"Page Tobie, 32 years old, 5 ft. 8 in. high, of dark com-
plexion, with gray eyes, black hair; a housewright, residence
Falmouth" (Me.), enlisted for F. for 3 years May 31, 1782,
in Morrill's company, Illsley's regiment.   On the back of the
paper he signed a promise June 3, 1782, that he would deliver

himself, Joshua Wescott, Cato Frost and Dublin Titcomb to
Major Pettingill at Boston in the most expeditious manner.
Other soldiers endorsed similar promises on the paper."

FIFTH GENERATION.

97

JOSIAH[5] (*William,[4] Samuel,[3] Stephen,[2] James[1]*),
born in Kittery, Me., about 1771; married Oct. 8,
1791, Elizabeth Sayward, who died Oct. 25, 1838,
aged 68 years. He died Sept. 24, 1856, aged 85.
He was a fisherman, and later a sea captain.

He and his wife joined with his brother William Tobey and
Miriam his wife, and William Seaward also of Kittery in quit-
claim deed of all their interest in the estate of their grandfather
Clement Dearing, late of Kittery, intestate, March 16, 1801,
" said Elizabeth, William and Miriam being children and representatives of our mother Mary who was a daughter of said
intestate." This was Clement Dearing, Jr., who married Miriam, daughter of Benjamin and Joanna (Ball) Hutchins. Josiah and Elizabeth mortgaged land and all rights in the estate
of his father William Tobey, late of Kittery, deceased, Jan.
26, 1813.

Child:
196.   Josiah Jr.,[6] b. about 1792.

98

WILLIAM[5] (*William,[4] Samuel,[3] Stephen,[2] James[1]*),
born in Kittery, Me., about 1773; married (published
Aug. 9, 1794) Miriam Sayward. William Tobey (the
same, I suppose) married April 22, 1816, Lucy Woodman.

Child:

197.   William, Jr.,⁶ b. about 1795.

99

ANDREW⁵ (*William,*⁴ *Samuel,*³ *Stephen,*² *James*¹), born in Kittery, Me., about 1778, married (published at Kittery, Oct. 13, 1799) Eunice Edgerley, of Alton, N. H.

He was a sea captain; with wife Eunice bought land in New Durham, N. H., Jan. 8, 1805, and sold it Dec. 18, 1811.

100

STEPHEN⁵ (*Samuel,*⁴ *Samuel,*³ *Stephen,*² *James*¹), born in Kittery, Me., in 1765; baptized with two younger children April 22, 1770; married in Kittery, July 8, 1792, Sally (Sarah), daughter of Capt. Dependance and Catherine (Leighton) Shapleigh, born 28 Feb., 1773.

He was a carpenter; removed to Maryland Ridge in the town of Wells.

He made his will 1 Aug., 1844, bequeathing his property to his wife Sarah, sons Stephen, Samuel and William, daughters Polly Paul, Betsey Raitt and Sally Blaisdell.

Children:

198. i.   Stephen.⁶
199. ii.   Samuel, b. 179ö.
    iii.   Polly, m. —— Paul.
    iv.   Betsey, b. 22 Sept., 1802; m. James Raitt, of Portsmouth, N. H.

    Children:

    1. Daniel G. Raitt, b. 8 July, 1822.
    2. Jeremiah Raitt, b. 3 April, 1824.
    3. James Raitt, b. and d. in 1826.
    4. Sarah E. Raitt, b. 21 Oct., 1827.
    5. Stephen T. Raitt, b. 25 Oct., 1829.

6. Caroline D. Raitt, b. 2 Nov., 1832; d. 18 Feb.,
   1874.
7. Armine D. Raitt, twin with Caroline, d. 28 June,
   1867.
8. James W. Raitt, b. 2 Nov., 1835.
9. John B. Raitt, b. 7 March, 1838.
10. George K. Raitt, b. 23 April, 1841.

 v. Sally, m. —— Blaisdell.
200. vi. William, b. 1814.

101

JAMES[5] (*Samuel,*[4] *Samuel,*[3] *Stephen,*[2] *James*[1]), born
in Kittery, Me., June 22, 1769; married Nov. 9, 1792,
Hannah, daughter of James and Hannah (Bartlett)
Shapleigh, born June 24, 1771, died June 24, 1861.
He died Dec. 26, 1846.

Children:

i. Lydia,[6] b. April 28, 1793; m. May 20, 1815, Nathaniel Adams of Newington, N. H., b. May 25,
1793, d. Oct. 3, 1861; she d. Aug. 20, 1861.

Children:

1. James T. Adams, b. March 22, 1817; d. Aug.
   19, 1850.
2. Matilda S. Adams, b. Oct. 14, 1818.
3. Lydia Adams, b. Oct. 3, 1820; d. Oct. 30,
   1820.
4. Nathaniel D. Adams, b. Nov. 5, 1824.
5. Mary J. Adams, b. Oct. 13, 1828.
6. John W. Adams, b. Feb. 24, 1834.

ii. Olive, b. July 16, 1794; m. April 4, 1813, Richard, son of Samuel and Elizabeth (Yeaton) Shapleigh, b. May 30, 1794, d. Oct. 11, 1740; she d.
Oct. 22, 1874.

Children:

1. Albert Shapleigh, b. ——, d. April 14, 1819.
2. William Shapleigh, b. July 16, 1814, d. March
   27, 1815.

3. Mary P. Shapleigh, b. May 17, 1817, d. Jan. 2, 1837.
4. Jane, b. Jan. 27, 1819, d. Feb. 23, 1826.
5. Elizabeth Y. Shapleigh, b. March 9, 1821, d. Feb. 5, 1837.
6. Hannah T. Shapleigh, b. March 20, 1823.
7. John Shapleigh, b. March 17, 1825.
8. Olive J. Shapleigh.
9. Albert Shapleigh.
10. Richard H. Shapleigh.
11. Sarah F. Shapleigh.
12. Mary E. Shapleigh.

iii. Abigail, b. May 6, 1798; m. Oct. 29, 1822, Asa Brooks; he d. May 20, 1872, aged 74 years, 9 mos. She d. Aug. 2, 1884.
Children :

1. Hannah T. Brooks, b. May 14, 1824, m. William G. Cole.
2. John Wesley Brooks, b. Oct. 3, 1825.
3. Isabel Brooks, b. Jan. 23, 1828.
4. James William Brooks, b. April 7, 1830.
5. Angeline Brooks, b. April 3, 1834, m. Nov. 7, 1858, Joseph B. Remick.

iv. Isabel Shapleigh, b. June 3, 1800; m. Feb. 22, 1821, James Knowlton, who d. June 16, 1880; she d. Jan. 11, 1895.
Children :

1. Nathaniel Knowlton, b. Jan. 4, 1822; d. Oct. 4, 1867.
2. Isabel Knowlton, b. March 1, 1824; m. 26 Nov., 1849, Jefferson Raitt.
3. Mary Knowlton, b. Sept., 1826, d. 1828.
4. Mary T. Knowlton, b. April, 1828, d. July 6, 1848.
5. James H. Knowlton, b. Oct. 30, 1831.
6. Hannah A. Knowlton, b. July 15, 1834; m. June 8, 1858, Charles Daniels.
7. Lucy J. Knowlton, b. Feb. 8, 1837, m. Nov. 14, 1859, John D. Frost.

8. Sarah E. Knowlton, b. Dec. 6, 1840, m. Aug. 25, 1864, Myrick L. Hatch.
9. George W. Knowlton, b. Feb. 10, 1843.

201. v. James Shapleigh, b. Sept. 25, 1801.
   vi. Mary Paul, b. May 7, 1805; m. Dec. 10, 1827, Oliver Paul. She d. Oct. 10, 1879.

Children:
1. Caroline A. Paul; m. Marshall W. Post.
2. Ann Mary Paul, b. March 9, 1833, d. Oct. 31, 1857.
3. Olive J. Paul, m. Albion K. L. Bedell.
4. Charles E. Paul.
5. William Albert Paul.
6. James Wesley Paul.

202. vii. William, b. Nov. 17, 1807.

103

SAMUEL[5] (*Samuel*,[4] *Samuel*,[3] *Stephen*,[2] *James*[1]), born in 1785; married, Nov. 27, 1806, Lucy, daughter of James and Mary (Dixon) Paul. Resided in Kittery (now Eliot). They joined with other heirs in a quitclaim deed of property inherited from her father, 27 Nov., 1811; they sold another tract to her brother James Paul, 7 Feb., 1814. His estate was administered upon by his widow Lucy, who sold land and a shop to James in 1840, and other land to William in 1846.

Children:

207. i. Samuel,[6] b. May 16, 1807.
208. ii. Stephen, b. May 4, 1808.
   iii. Mary, b. May 29, 1809; d. Jan. 9, 1864.
209. iv. Alexander, b. Oct. 7, 1810.
   v. Catherine, b. Feb. 14, 1812; d. Nov., 1892.
   vi. Lucy A., b. Feb. 25, 1813; d. Nov. 23, 1843; m. March 15, 1835, Bartholomew Berry.
   vii. Sarah, b. April 11, 1815; d. Feb. 12, 1843.
210. viii. James, b. Nov. 29, 1816.
   ix. Abigail, b. Aug. 4, 1818; d. 1829.

x.   William, b. Sept. 29, 1819; m. Lydia Kinnear of Rye, N. H.; no children; d. Dec. 30, 1900.

xi.   Caroline, b. Oct. 30, 1822; d. Sept. 13, 1895; m. Daniel Neal.

Children:

1. Caroline A. Neal, b. Sept. 4, 1846; m. April 28, 1868, John Somerby of Portsmouth, N. H. Child: Hattie Caroline Somerby, b. April 8, 1869; d. Nov. 28, 1895.
2. William Oliver Neal, b. March, 1848; d. 1851.
3. Ida Frances Neal, b. March 21, 1852.
4. Alice Jane Neal, b. Oct. 7, 1856; d. 1871.
5. Francis Herbert Neal, b. March 14, 1858.

xii.   Jane A., b. March 22, 1825; d. Aug. 28, 1897; m. James Reed.

Children:

1. Emma A. Reed, b. Sept. 5, 1845; m. Oct. 9, 1864, Vivaldi S. Reed of Newburyport, Mass.

    Children:

    (1) Elmer G. Reed, b. Aug. 11, 1865; m. Dec. 22, 1885, Carrie M. Bayley.

    (2) Ina M. Reed, b. Feb. 4, 1871; m. Oct. 20, 1890; d. Nov. 20, 1900.

2. Edgar E. Reed, b. March 20, 1848; m. Dec. 2, 1872, Mary E. Mahoney. Child: Ethel May Reed, b. March 13, 1874.

211. xiii.   Oliver Paul, b. Feb. 26, 1826.

xiv.   Olive Augusta, b. March 30, 1828; d. 1869; m. H. Sefton of Harrison, O.; no child.

113

LEMUEL[5] (*William,*[4] *Samuel,*[3] *Richard,*[2] *James*[1]), born in Portland, Me., about 1787; married Sarah (familiarly called Sally), daughter of Capt. Paul Sanborn; she was born in 1787; her father served in the Revolution, and had a pension from 1818. Lemuel

Tobey became a sea-captain; served in the war of 1812, for which he drew a pension in later years. Resided in Portland, Me. Was lost at sea, off Cape Hatteras, in 1830.

Lemuel Tobey of Portland, mariner, bought of John Knight, yeoman, for $480, July 8, 1818, a lot of land with buildings on the northwesterly side of Fore Street, near land which Knight sold Sept. 30, 1813, to Samuel Tobey, Jr. This tract he mortgaged the same day; he paid the notes, and the mortgage was discharged Nov. 22, 1822. Another deed is on record signed by Lemuel and Sarah; final date Nov. 23, 1819. He retained lands, the rental of which, in later years, afforded some revenue to his widow.

Children:

  i.   Submit Cox,* b. in April, 1814; m. first, Mr. Davis; m. second, John H. Russell of Portland, Me. She d. Feb. 9, 1896, leaving her husband, and two children, Lemuel T. Davis and Susan A. Davis.

230. ii. William, b. Jan. 9, 1817.

 iii. Martha Abigail Sanborn, b. 1822; m. George Merrill. Resided at Searsport, Me.

  Children :

    1. George L. Merrill. Res. Dixfield, Me.
    2. Eugene Merrill. Res. Portland, Me.
    3. Frank Merrill. Res. California.
    4. Abbie Merrill; m. Rufus Fowler. Res. Brooklyn, N. Y.

  iv. Sarah, m. Benjamin Flint,* son of Capt. Joseph and Sarah (Jones) Flint of Damariscotta, Me., b. July 22, 1833.

  Child :

  Charles R. Flint.

* Capt. Joseph Flint was son of Dr. Thomas Flint and his wife, Lydia, daughter of John (Benjamin, Benjamin, Joseph) Pope of Danvers, Mass., who removed from North Reading to Damariscotta, Me. He was a surgeon in the Revolutionary War, was once captured on a privateer and carried to England, a prisoner. Capt. Joseph Flint was a captain of militia in the War of 1812, and was stationed at Fort Edgecomb, Me.

114

ENOCH⁵ (*William,⁴ Samuel,³ Richard,² James¹*), born in Portland, Me., in 1799, and resided there; died in August, 1845; married and had eight children, one of whom, Mr. Edward Howard Tobey, was living in New York City in 1899.

Enoch Tobey of Portland, cooper, bought land and buildings in Portland, Sept. 17, 1823.

Enoch G. Tobey, of Portland, bought land there, June 1, 1869.

118

RICHARD⁵ (*Richard,⁴ Isaac,³ Richard,² James¹*), born in Seabrook, N. H., Jan. 23, 1769; married, June 23, 1790, Betsey, daughter of Clement Fickett of Falmouth, born June 6, 1768, died Nov. 28, 1870, aged 101 years, 5 months and 22 days. He lived on the place his father had formerly occupied, on Tobie Hill, in New Gloucester, which came to be one of the finest farms in the town.

Children:

	i.	Ruth R.,⁶ b. Nov. 19, 1791; m. (1) —— Wilson; m. (2) —— Winchester; she d. Oct. 30, 1886, at East Corinth, Me.
	ii.	Betsey, b. Oct. 23, 1793; m. in 1818, Moses Stinchfield, and resided in Corinth, Me., but d. in Elgin, Ill., Jan. 31, 1886.
240.	iii.	Nathaniel Haskell, b. Oct. 5, 1795.
241.	iv.	Richard Brooks, b. March 10, 1797.
242.	v.	Clement Fickett, b. Aug. 13, 1799.
	vi.	Almira, b. Aug. 19, 1801; d. Aug. 13, 1802.
243.	vii.	Christopher Columbus, b. Jan. 20, 1803.
244.	viii.	George Washington, b. Nov. 7, 1805.
	ix.	Mary Ann, b. Dec. 13, 1807. Resided in Corinth till a few years ago she made her home in Bangor, Me., where she is still living (1905).
	x.	Daniel D. L., b. Aug. 22, 1809; d. Jan. 22, 1810.
245.	xi.	Daniel Lewis, b. March 5, 1811.

119

JONATHAN L.[5] (*Richard*,[4] *Isaac*,[3] *Richard*,[2] *James*[1]),
born in Seabrook, N. H., Oct. 6, 1770; married Feb.
13, 1800, Lydia, daughter of Edward Parsons.
He resided in New Gloucester; died April 20, 1814.

He left a will which was among those destroyed in the great
fire at Portland; his widow, Lydia, and brother Richard Tobie,
Jr., as executors of the will, sold a tract of land Aug. 15,
1817, Richard Tobie and Job Haskell being witnesses.

Children:

246. i.   Edward Parsons,[6] b. Oct. 13, 1800.
247. ii. Samuel, b. Dec. 28, 1802.
     iii. Jonathan, b. Nov. 14, 1804; d. unmarried.
248. iv. Elbridge, b. Dec. 6, 1806.
     v.   Lydia Parsons, b. June 20, 1808; d. unmarried.
     vi. Elisha, b. May 11, 1811; d. unmarried.

120

WILLIAM[5] (*Richard*,[4] *Isaac*,[3] *Richard*,[2] *James*[1]),
born at Seabrook, N. H., June 18, 1782; married Aug.
29, 1807, Sarah (Sallie) daughter of Aaron Bray of
Poland, Me., where they resided.

He bought land in Poland, March 30, 1820. He
conveyed lands to his son Joshua A., April 9, 1837,
and to William A., May 20, 1842. Other deeds are
on record.

Children:

249. i.   Joshua A.,[6] b. July 20, 1807.
     ii.   Harriet J., b. March 21, 1809; m. at Medford, Oct.
           11, 1852, Asahel Gilbert (his second marriage).
250. iii. William A., b. in 1811.
251. iv.   Thomas.
252. v.   Daniel B.
253. vi.   Jonathan.
     vii. Adeline; m. —— Bray.
     viii. Lydia, m. —— Byram.

ix. Sarah E.; m. May 13, 1843, Daniel A. Taylor;
     res. Mechanic Falls, Me.; d. in Medford, Mass.,
     1896.
  Children:
     1. Sarah Ada Taylor, b. Nov. 12, 1844; m. James
        Temple.
     2. George A. Taylor, b. Feb. 22, 1845.
     3. Georgiana Taylor, b. July 31, 1847; m. C. F.
        Merrill.
     4. Charles Sumner Taylor, b. June 18, 1864; m.
        Lizzie Talmer.
 x. Mary A., b. 1829; m. at Medford, Sept. 18, 1850,
     Mitchell Aiell, of Medford, b. in 1823.

121

THOMAS HASKELL,[5] (*Richard*,[4] *Isaac*,[3] *Richard*,[2]
James[1]), born in New Gloucester, Me., Sept. 17, 1789;
married first, March 14, 1816, Lucy, daughter of William and Dorcas (Bennett) Pickett. William Pickett
was a soldier in the Revolution. Mrs. Tobie died in
Boston, Jan. 10, 1828. He married second, April 14,
1831, Mary, daughter of John Harris, born Sept. 17,
1796, and died April 20, 1872. In the War of 1812
he rendered a brief service at Portland, Me., then
marching to Plattsburg, N. Y., for some further duty.
He was a school teacher in his young manhood.
Several years of his early life were spent in Boston
and here his daughters by the first wife were born.
He returned to New Gloucester, Me., where he spent
the rest of his life. He died Sept. 27, 1875.
  Children:
     i. Lucy,[6] b. in Boston, May 17, 1820; m. June 14,
         1840, James Merrill, of New Gloucester, Me.,
         son of William (William, Edmond, James, Nathan, Abel, Nathaniel), of the Newbury line, b.
         May 18, 1815, d. June 19, 1896. He was a selectman, assessor and justice of the peace, an
         honored citizen of New Gloucester.

JAMES MERRILL, ESQ.

Children :
1. George Henry Merrill, b. May 23, 1841; res.
   long near Boise city, Ida., a miner, not married. He d. Oct. 6, 1902.
2. Thomas Tobie Merrill, b. Dec. 13, 1842; m.
   Nov. 12, 1873, in Boston, Abby F., dau. of
   Chester D. Pratt, of Weymouth. He was a
   soldier in the Civil War; is a commercial traveler, res. Rockland.
   Children :
   (1) Fannie Louise Merrill, b. Dec. 15, 1875;
       d. Nov. 22, 1882.
   (2) Walter Stanley Merrill, b. Nov. 1, 1880;
       grad. Harv. Univ. 1903; is a partner of
       Mr. Yagi, a Japanese merchant in New
       York city, who was a classmate (firm of
       Yagi & Merrill, American and Japanese
       commission merchants).

3. Elvira L. P. T. Merrill, b. Dec. 16, 1844; m.
   Dec. 25, 1865, Mr. (afterward Reverend)
   Samuel F. Pearson, b. in Roxbury, July 16,
   1844, at that time a business man in Boston.
   In 1873 he became interested in the "Reform
   Club" movement, an advocate of total absti-
   nence for the individual and prohibition for the
   state.   In 1878 he established a Gospel Mission
   in Portland, Me., which became a headquarters
   for charity and reform work. He was not only
   active in Maine and the other states of this
   Union but went abroad and lectured throughout
   the British Isles under the auspices of the British
   Temperance Society, securing 100,000 pledges.
   He was ordained to the ministry at Old Orchard, Me., Aug. 6, 1879. His work consisted
   largely of expositions of the fearful miseries
   caused by ardent spirits, and the administering
   of the pledge. His lectures "Seven Years in
   Hell," and "Man Inside Out" he delivered
   hundreds of times with telling effect. In 1900
   he was elected sheriff of Cumberland County,

Me. He enforced the law impartially, heroically against a combination of desperate criminals and their "respectable" allies, but won the admiration and respect of all while driving the criminals to their dens. He died amidst his labor, Aug. 6, 1902, of Bright's disease. His wife had died Jan. 4, 1901, just after his entrance on his office, leaving him the brave charge "Be a good sheriff." She was an ardent supporter of all the Mission work, doing many self-denying acts for the needy. The lives of both Mr. and Mrs. Pearson were literally given to the city of Portland "in Jesus' Name."

Children :

(1) Mary Frances Pearson, b. in New Gloucester, Me., Oct. 9, 1866; d. May 17, 1869.

(2) Evangeline Pearson, b. Jan. 27, 1869; she entered most efficiently into the Gospel Mission work, leading the singing with her cornet in many hundred meetings, playing in the quartette which led the singing at several annual meetings of The Women's Christian Temperance Union, and assisting her parents greatly in their foreign and home work. She m. Aug. 28, 1902, Frederick Davenport Swazey, a business man of Portland, Me.

4. James K. Polk Merrill, b. Feb. 17, 1847; was a soldier in the Civil War in Co., H., 7th Me. Vol. Inf., transferred to the 1st Veteran Vol. regt. He died at Fairfax Hospital, Va., July 14, 1865, from disease brought on by long marches from Petersburg, Va., to Washington, D. C., after the surrender of the Confederate forces—so eager were the "boys in blue" to reach their Northern homes. He was buried in New Gloucester, Me.

5. Martha Hersey Merrill, b. April 11, 1849; m. October 27, 1870, Van B. Bray, who was b. in Phillips, Me., April 20, 1833; he

MRS. LUCY (TOBIE) MERRILL.

res. in Deering, Me., a merchant, some years;
was an honest and a noble man. He served
in the Civil War; d. at Portland, Me., Jan.
4, 1904.

> Child : James Melzar Bray, b. Nov. 8, 1873;
> m. in Milford, Sept. 18, 1905, Marion
> L. Tompkins. He is superintendent of the
> Granite quarries of Milford.

6. Lucy Tobie Merrill, b. July 16, 1851; m. Dec.
11, 1872, Rev. Anson Titus, son of Anson
and Almira (Sabine) Titus, b. in Phelps, N.Y.,
June 21, 1847, a Universalist clergyman and
widely honored genealogist. To him we are
indebted for very many particulars respecting
the descendants of Richard Robie of New Gloucester and all the story of this special branch.
He was graduated from the Theological department of St. Lawrence University, Canton, N.Y.,
in 1872. He has had pastorates at Charlton,
Weymouth, Amesbury and Natick, Mass., and
for three years at Towanda, Pa. In recent
years he has been doing antiquarian service,
collaborating with historians in the preparation
of local and general history, and in the deter-
mining difficult genealogical questions. He is
a member of several leading Historical societies,
a lecturer on American history, a frequent con-
tributor to the Universalist Quarterly; resides
in Somerville. Mrs. Titus has been much interested in the cause of Woman's Suffrage,
Women's Christian Temperance Union Work,
and the Daughters of Maine Club of Somerville.

> Children :

>> (1) Anson Merrill Titus, b. in New Glou-
>> cester, Me., April 8, 1875; grad.
>> Tufts Coll. 1898; is a civil engi-
>> neer in the employ of Richardson &
>> Burgess, contractors and builders,
>> Washington, D. C.

(2) Marian Lucy Titus, b. in Weymouth,
Nov. 10, 1880; Tufts Coll., A.B.,
and Class Day poet 1902, A. M.
1903; member of B.K.; teacher
of English in the David Prouty
High School, Spencer, 1903–5.

7. Ezra Tobie Merrill, b. Feb. 6, 1854; m. June
28, 1886, Minnie L., daughter of Bradley O.
Wood, of Haverhill. He is a contractor and
builder; res. since 1893 in Somerville.

   Children:

     (1) Charles Edward Merrill, b. in Ware,
       Oct. 11, 1887.

     (2) Frank Wood Merrill, b. in Temple-
       ton, Nov. 21, 1889.

     (3) Pauline Merrill, b. in Athol, April 2,
       1892.

     (4) Herbert Cummings Merrill, b. in
       Somerville, July 1, 1894.

8. Charles Winslow Merrill, b. Oct. 2, 1856; m.
Cecilia ———; res. La Fayette, Colo.; a
carpenter and builder. His wife was a widow,
with children by former husband.

8. Frank Herbert Merrill, b. Jan. 23, 1859; m.
Aug. 1, 1883, in Foxcroft, Me., Abby S., dau.
of Samuel Foxcroft of New Gloucester Me.,
great grand dau. of Rev. Samuel Foxcroft,
first minister of N. G., and gr. dau. of Col.
Joseph Ellery; she was b. Dec. 16, 1857, d.
April 5, 1896, in Pomona, Cal., where the
family had been living some time.

   Children:

     (1) Joseph Foxcroft Merrill, b. June 3,
       1884.

     (2) Louise Foxcroft Merrill, b. Sept. 13,
       1888.

ii.   Martha H.*, b. in Boston, Dec. 25, 1822; m. Oct.
23, 1848, Elisha Pote Merrill. They resided in
New Gloucester, Me. She died Dec. 9, 1853,

and he died Dec. 13, 1855, æ. 31 years. They
had one child, Frederick Twombly Merrill, who
died at the age of two years.

iii. Elvira E. La Fayette, b. in Boston, May 14, 1825,
was one of the babies whom the French general
La Fayette kissed when visiting Boston that year,
and bore his name as a memorial of that fact.
She m. in Boston, Dec. 25, 1853, John Sherburne Tuttle, b. in Effingham, N. H., June 7,
1824. He was a contractor and builder in Chelsea; a soldier in the Civil War; d. at the Soldiers' Home in Chelsea, April 25, 1897; buried
at New Gloc., Me. She d. at Newton, Jan. 15,
1883.

Children:

1. Anson Burlingame Tuttle, b. Nov. 17, 1856;
m. July 4, 1882, Sadie E. Clark. Resides at
Everett.
Child: Anson Clark Tuttle, b. Aug. 13, 1883.

2. John Mallalieu Tuttle, b. Oct. 17, 1861; m.
Nov. 18, 1891, at Salina, Kan., Delia Purington, b. at Lincoln, Vt., Dec. 12, 1872. He
is a jeweler.

Children:

(1) Herbert Purington Tuttle, b. Nov.
21, 1892.
(2) Jessie Elvira Tuttle, b. July 2, 1894.
(3) Ralph Mallalieu Tuttle, b. Feb. 10,
1896.
(4) Leon Anson Tuttle, b. Nov. 1897.
(5) Fred Dewey Tuttle, b. May 1, 1899.
(6) Gertrude Florence Tuttle, b. in 1901.

3. William Henry Tuttle, b. Sept. 13, 1868; res.
in Kansas; editor of a newspaper.

iv. Thankful Hobbs, b. in New Gloucester, Me., Feb.
20, 1832; m. June 10, 1858, Charles G.Morrill.
She d. June 27, 1873.

Children:

1. Walter Morrill.

19

      2. Clarence Morrill.

      3. A daughter who d. æ. 7 yrs.

  v. Mary Clarissa, b. Aug. 26, 1834; m. (1) Oct. 24, 1860, Benjamin A. Lunt; he d. Dec. 13, 1864, and she m. (2) Aug. 13, 1871, Joseph L. Brown.

Children :

      1. Henry A. Lunt, b. July 22, 1861.

      2. Benjamin Lunt, d. in boyhood.

      3. John (posthumus) was brought up by his uncle Samuel Lunt; is a druggist in Freeport, Me.

      4. Ezra Brown; resides in Poland, Me.

  vi. Rosilla Merrill, b. Oct. 20, 1836; m. May 2, 1858, John O. Harris; she d. Feb. 12, 1863. Res. New Gloucester, Me.

Children :

      1. Mary Ardilla Harris, b. July 4, 1859.

      2. Annie R. Harris, b. Feb. 11, 1861; d. aged 2 yrs.

  vii. Ardilla H., twin of Rosilla Merrill; m. April 10, 1853, Silas H. Churchill, b. Jan 19, 1817, d. Oct. 4, 1898. She d. Feb. 2, 1903.

Children, b. in Raymond, Me. :

      1. Frederick Tobie Churchill, b. April 15, 1854; m., 1889, Laura Very of Danvers. Res. New Gloucester, Me.

      Children :

          (1) Cecil Very Churchill, b. 1890.

          (2) Velma D. Churchill, 1894.

      2. Rosilla Tobie Churchill, b. Nov. 2, 1855; d. Sept. 16, 1858.

      3. Walter Churchill, b. May 8, 1858; m. March 19, 1884, Ida L. Blodgett, of Colebrook, N.H.; he is a merchant in Berlin, N. H. The sons are (1905) attending Dartmouth College.

      Children ;

          (1) Peleg W. Churchill, b. July, 1885.

          (2) Wendell H. Churchill, b. Oct., 1889.

          (3) Sally Churchill, b. Oct. 1895.

4. Leroy Churchill, b. July 16, 1860; m. Alice A.
   Atherton, of Colebrook, N. H., where he was
   postmaster for a number of years. He d. in
   Minot, Me., Oct. 7, 1892, æ. 32 yrs.

   Children:

      (1) Eva Hammond Churchill.
      (2) Blaine Leroy Churchill.

5. Wendell A. Churchill, b. April 20, 1863; m.
   and res. in Colorado.

122

EZRA[5] (*Richard*,[4] *Isaac*,[3] *Richard*,[2] *James*[1]), born
in New Gloucester, Me., April 13, 1794; died July
14, 1875; married first, May 24, 1821, Nancy, daughter of Thomas Witham, of New Gloucester, born Nov.
19, 1801, died May 7, 1838. He married second,
July 18, 1839, Eliza, daughter of Silas Estes, of Falmouth; she was born June 1, 1805, and died July 9,
1893. Resided in New Gloucester some years; then
removed to North Yarmouth, Me., where he died.
His will, full of thoughtful bequests, was dated Feb.
10, and probated Sept. 3, 1875.

Children:

254. i.   Ezra Levi,[6] b. July 5, 1826.
    ii.   Persis Temple, b. Aug. 27, 1831; d. Feb. 24,
        1855.
   iii.   Electa Ann Beebe Nancy, b. March 21, 1837; d.
        March 28, 1857.
   iv.   Sarah Eliza Temperance, b. Jan. 21, 1843; m. Feb.
        28, 1866, Charles F. Plant; she d. Oct. 16,
        1873.

        Child:

        Persis Temple Plant, b. Oct. 28, 1868; m.
        Joseph McLean; res. Raymond, Me. Child:
        Margaret McLean.

123

LEVI[5] (*Richard*,[4] *Isaac*,[3] *Richard*,[2] *James*[1]), born in New Gloucester, Me., Aug. 30, 1795; married Feb. 15, 1830, Lydia Cummings, daughter of William Proctor, born April 10, 1811, died Feb. 17, 1887.

He removed in 1845 to Windham, Me., and in his later years removed to Charlestown, Mass., died Oct. 19, 1886. His body was carried to North Windham, where he had been held in very high esteem.

Children:

  i. Rhoda Louisa,[6] b. in Windham, Me., in 1835; m. in Boston, Jan. 16, 1860, Marshall Lombard of Cumberland Mills, Me., b. in Standish, Me., in 1842; she d. Oct. 19, 1893. Res. at Standish, Me., and removed to Mapleton, Aroostook county, Me.

    Children:

    1. Charles Lombard; d. æ. 21 years.
    2. William Lombard; d. æ. 18 years.
    3. Adelbert Lombard; m. Eva Pomeroy. Child: Ruth Marie Lombard, b. 1903.
    4. Hattie Lombard; m. Frank Condon.

    Children:

      (1) William Marshall Condon.
      (2) Winifred Louise Condon.
      (4) Charles Adelbert Condon, b. Oct. 19, 1903.

  ii. Lucretia; res. Charlestown, Mass.
 iii. Hannah Elizabeth; d. in infancy.
 iv. Juliette Elizabeth; d. æ. 12.

124

WILLIAM[5] (*William*,[4] *Isaac*,[3] *Richard*,[2] *James*[1]), born in Hawke, now Danville, N. H.; removed to Deerfield, N. H., where he was a farmer in 1792, when he and his brother Nathan sold a tract of land which they had inherited from their father. We have no account of his family.

125

NATHAN[5] (*William,*[4] *Isaac,*[3] *Richard,*[2] *James*[1]), born in Hawke, now Danville, N. H., baptized Aug. 23, 1772; was brought up in Deerfield, N. H., till he reached mature years; removed to Montville, Me., and spent the remainder of his life there. Was a farmer.

Nathan Tobie of Deerfield, husbandman, sold to Joseph Hilton, Esq. of D., land with buildings thereon, Nov. 19, 1792. Nathan Tobie, cordwainer, of Candia, N. H., bought, Aug. 25, 1798, land in Candia and sold the same, buildings included, Oct. 6, 1800; his wife Eleanor signed the deed of sale.

Children:

261. i.   Nathan.[6]
262. ii. Joseph C.
263. iii. Jonathan.
264. iv. David.
265. v.   Ira Wadleigh.

SIXTH GENERATION.

196

JOSIAH, JR.[6] (*Josiah,*[5] *William,*[4] *Samuel,*[3] *Stephen,*[2] *James*[1]), born in Kittery, Me., about 1792; married first, March 23, 1820, Miriam Lewis; married second, April 4, 1844, Sarah Flanders.

He was a sea-captain, residing in Kittery; died about 1872.

Children (list in family Bible):

300. i.   William,[7] b. Dec. 31, 1820.
301. ii. Josiah, b. Dec. 25, 1822.
     iii. Mary Elizabeth, b. April 18, 1824.

302. iv. Augustus, b. March 28, 1826; m. Nov. 1, 1848,
          Eunice D. Patch. His son Augustus, Jr., was
          drowned from schooner Eldorado with six others
          in Gloucester Bay, Aug. 24, 1873. [Gloc. rec-
          ord.]
303. v.   Samuel Lewis, b. June 9, 1828.
     vi. Malinda, b. Sept. 8, 1830.
304. vii. John, b. Jan. 7, 1832.
305. viii. Charles, b. Feb. 28, 1835.
306. ix. Thomas, b. March 1, 1837.

197

WILLIAM, JR.[6] (*William*,[5] *William*,[4] *Samuel*,[3] *Stephen*,[2] *James*[1]), born in Kittery, Me., about 1795; married first, April 10, 1819, Temperance Mitchell; married second, Oct. 29, 1825 (called "William Tobey, 3d") Caroline Perkins.

Elizabeth Mitchell, of Kittery, for love and affection to her great grand-daughter, Mary Elizabeth Tobey of the same, daughter of William Tobey the third of Kittery and Caroline Tobey his wife, and for the sum of $395, paid by the said William Tobey, conveyed to him all her real estate in Kittery July 6, 1836, in consideration of care and consideration of herself for the rest of her life. This property was sold Dec. 2, 1848, by Caroline with Mary E., wife of John Peak, of Boston, to Jonathan Gunnison of Kittery, Me., the women holding the property independently of their husbands.

Child:
Mary Elizabeth,[7] b. about 1820; m. John Peak.

198

STEPHEN[6] (*Stephen*,[5] *Samuel*,[4] *Samuel*,[3] *Stephen*,[2] *James*[1]). Resided in Wells, Me. He made his will Nov. 5, 1872, proved Feb. 18, 1873; bequeathed his estate to his wife Isabella and his daughter Mary Ann, wife of Daniel Page.

201

JAMES SHAPLEIGH[6] (*James*,[5] *Samuel*,[4] *Samuel*,[3] *Stephen*,[2] *James*[1]), born in Kittery, Me., Sept. 25, 1801; married Oct. 30, 1826, Mary Jane, daughter of Capt. Josiah and Martha Kelley (Parry) Remick. She died Sept. 27, 1884. He died Dec. 19, 1887. Children:

i. Ellen Augusta,[7] b. Aug. 11, 1828; m. Jan. 1, 1852, Joseph Fogg Kennard.

Children:

1. George Herbert Kennard; m. Emma Sweetland.
2. Walter Clarence Kennard; m. Sept. 18, 1895, Nettie B. Hough, b. Nov. 4, 1865.
3. John Parry Kennard.

ii. Martha Jane, b. Feb. 28, 1831; m. (1) Dec. 24, 1848, Charles W. Walker, of Portsmouth, N. H.; he d. May 4, 1860. She m. (2) Oct. 6, 1864, Charles W. Stimson, of Kittery: he d. May 25, 1895.

Children:

1. Charles William Walker, b. Jan. 12, 1852; m. Emma Hayes.
2. James Tobey Walker.
3. Mary Alice Walker; m. (1)——— Wilson; m. (2) ——— Chamberlain.
4. Annie Stimson.
5. Nellie Stimson.
6. Albert Stimson.

iii. Hannah Shapleigh, b. Nov. 26, 1833; d. June 14, 1836.

iv. Annie Shapleigh, b. May 3, 1836; m. June 15, 1875, Richard H. Shapleigh.

319. v. Martin Parry, b. Jan. 15, 1840.

202

WILLIAM[6] (*James*,[5] *Samuel*,[4] *Samuel*,[3] *Stephen*,[2] *James*[1]), born Nov. 19, 1807; married Dec. 18, 1827,

Polly Goodwin, born Sept. 4, 1811, died Dec. 4, 1887. He died Aug. 6, 1865.

Children:

320. i.   James William,[7] b. May 4, 1830.
     ii.   Rozan C. (Rosa Ann), b. April 11, 1832; m. Richard H. Shapleigh.

Children:

         1. Elmore Shapleigh, b. 1851, d. 1852.
         2. Ida E. Shapleigh, b. Sept. 3, 1861; m. Dec. 3, 1885, Benjamin Symonds.
         3. Harry Shapleigh, b. June 1869, d. Jan. 19, 1874.

321. iii.   John Goodwin, b. Jan. 29, 1834.
     iv.   Henry C., b. Sept. 4, 1836; d. July 9, 1838.
     v.   Olivia Matilda, b. March 25, 1838; d. Sept. 28, 1841.
322. vi.   Henry C., b. March 11, 1840.
     vii.   Olivia M., b. Nov. 11, 1843; m. Jan. 22, 1865, John M. Lydston.

Children:

         1. Alice M. Lydston, b. Oct. 22, 1865; m. May 15, 1887, G. B. Kirkpatrick.
         2. Walter C. Lydston, b. Oct. 1, 1869; m. Dec. 11, 1895, Sadie B. Ellenwood.

323. viii. Franklin O., b. Feb. 10, 1845.

207

SAMUEL[6] (*Samuel,*[5] *Samuel,*[4] *Samuel,*[3] *Stephen,*[2] *James*[1]), born May 16, 1807; married, Nov. 12, 1829, Mary Hammond, daughter of Samuel and Sarah (Staples) Dixon, born Feb. 3, 1800. He was a ship-carpenter. Resided in Eliot, Me. He died April 25, 1858, leaving a will dated 8 April, 1858, in which he made bequests to his widow and each of his children, five of whom were still in their minority; Ichabod Cole, executor.

Children:

i.   Mary Abigail,[7] b. Sept. 30, 1830; m. Jan. 6, 1852, Samuel A. Remick; d. Oct. 4, 1860.
Children :
1. Myron E. Remick, b. in June, 1853; d. unm. Jan. 23, 1878.
2. Lucy Ella Remick, b. Oct., 1855; m. in 1875, Frederick Thomas Browne.
3. Edgar W. Remick, b. in 1857; m. Dec. 27, 1879, Annie L. Welch of Eliot, Me.
4. Antoinette Remick; m. Eben Randall of Medford, Mass.

330. ii. Nathaniel Dixon, b. Feb. 21, 1833.
iii. Helen Marr, b. March 1, 1835 ; m. Sept. 21, 1858, Henry A. Cann.
Children :
1. Alice A. Cann, b. May 27, 1859; m. Jan. 22, 1880, Joseph Trowbridge of Charlestown.
2. Helen Louise Cann, b. Dec. 13, 1863 ; m. June 20, 1887, Charles G. Greeley of East Boston.

iv. Olive Jane, b. Sept. 23, 1836 ; d. May 7, 1841.
v.   Sarah Adelaide, b. Jan. 13, 1839 ; m. Sept. 8, 1861, Paschal M. Langton.
Children :
1. George M. Langton, b. Jan. 2, 1863 ; d. Oct. 25, 1874.
2. Elmer E. Langton, b. Aug. 30, 1864; m. Oct. 18, 1888, Carrie L. Bartlett of Eliot.
Children :
(1) Viola L. Langton, b. April 22, 1890.
(2) Helen M. Langton, b. May 18, 1892.
(3) Ora Frances Langton, b. Feb. 9, 1894.
3. Aletta S. Langton, b. June 8, 1866 ; m. Dec. 25, 1899, Fred. W. Leach of Moultonboro, N. H.
4. Clarence A. Langton, b. June 19, 1873 ; m. June 10, 1897, Edith L. Orr of Syracuse, N. Y.

Child :
Muriel C. Langton, b. Nov. 13, 1900.
331. vi. Samuel Augustus, b. Oct. 23, 1841.
332. vii. William Wallace, b. April 2, 1844.
viii. Elethea Ober, b. Feb. 21, 1848.
ix. Clara Frances, b. Feb. 6, 1850 ; m. April 25, 1905,
William Henry Wallace of Boston; salesman in
a wholesale millinery store.

208

STEPHEN[6] (*Samuel,[5] Samuel,[4] Samuel,[3] Stephen,[2]
James[1]*), born May 4, 1808; married, Oct. 12, 1834,
Jane Hobbs of Charlestown, Mass., formerly of Hin-
ton, England. He learned the business of shipbuild-
ing; became foreman of a shipyard, and after seventeen years of that experience, went into business in
company with Daniel Littlefield of Portsmouth, N. H.,
their yard being located on Noble's Island. The firm
built large vessels, chiefly clipper ships, and their
reputation was very high. Some thirty-five great
vessels went from their hands to sail in all oceans.
The island was sold to a railroad corporation in 1877;
the partnership was dissolved, and Mr. Tobey retired
from active business. He resided on Islington Street,
in what was known as the Ball place. He had a large
circle of friends, being kindly, genial and unobtrusive;
was a member of Piscataqua lodge of Odd Fellows.
Mrs. Tobey died in 1867, after which he made his
home with his daughter, Mrs. E. D. Coffin, till his
death in December, 1892.
Children:
i. Martha J.,[7] b. March 1, 1836; m. April 29, 1857,
Frank Martin of Portsmouth, N. H.
Children :
1. Clarence H. Martin, b. Aug. 15, 1858; d. May 5,
1889.

    2. Frank H. Martin, b. Dec. 21, 1859; d. Oct.,
       1860.
    3. Arthur F. Martin, b. Aug. 3, 1863; m. Aug.,
       1889, Mary E. Weeks.
    4. George E. Martin, b. July 3, d. Sept. 20, 1865.
    5. Helen C. Martin, b. July 21, 1875.

ii. Annie M., b. April 1, 1838; m. Dec. 2, 1856,
    Robert Mitchell of Kennebunk, Me.
  Children :
    1. Helen E. Mitchell, b. Sept. 29, 1857 ; m. Sept.
       27, 1882, Gilbert Jessup of Tracy, Minn.
    2. Carrie G. Mitchell, b. Dec. 2, 1858 ; d. Oct. 9,
       1861.
    3. Katie E. Mitchell, b. April 3, 1860 ; d. Oct. 2,
       1861.
    4. Samuel L. Mitchell, b. Sept. 7, 1863 ; d. Feb.
       27, 1883.
    5. Robert L. Mitchell, b. Feb. 6, 1865 ; m. Feb. 1,
       1894, Nina E. Rand of North Hampton, N. H.

iii. Helen A., b. Feb. 6, 1840; m. Oct. 12, 1858,
    Edward D. Coffin of Portsmouth, N. H.
iv. Katie A., b. Dec. 2, 1843 ; m. in 1862, Howard A.
    Dunyan of Portsmouth, N. H.; d. May 2,
    1864.
v. George E., b. Nov. 24, 1848 ; d. July 19, 1867.

209

ALEXANDER[6] (*Samuel,[5] Samuel,[4] Samuel,[3] Stephen,[2] James[1]*), born Oct. 7, 1810; married in 1837 Clarissa, daughter of James and Mary (Kennard) Paul. He died June 14, 1844. She married second, Dr. William Hanscom.

Children:

333. i.   George,[7] b. Aug. 8, 1838.
334. ii. Edwin, b. June 10, 1840.
     iii. Albert H., b. Feb. 22, 1844; d. July 9, 1865.

210

JAMES[6] (*Samuel,[5] Samuel,[4] Samuel,[3] Stephen,[2] James[1]*), born Nov. 29, 1816; married Mary Tucker. Resided in Portsmouth, N. H. He died Aug. 17, 1882.

Children:

i. Lizzie G.,[7] b. Oct. 19, 1848; m. Sept. 16, 1868, Robert G. Norton of Portsmouth, N. H.

Child:

Bessie L. Norton, b. Oct. 16, 1872.

ii. Lucy A., b. Sept. 7, 1856; m. May 31, 1876, Charles H. Peabody of Andover, Mass.

Children:

1. Lizzie W. Peabody, b. Oct. 19, 1877; m. Harry T. Marks of Lynn, Mass.
2. Mary E. Peabody, b. Nov. 14, 1878.
3. Hattie E. Peabody, b. March 1, 1881; m. March 26, 1898, George H. Crossan of Lynn.
4. Ruth M. Peabody, b. June 19, 1890.

iii. Emma L., b. Oct. 21, 1858; m. April 27, 1877, John F. Roberts of Lynn.

Children:

1. Clarence O. Roberts, b. Jan. 10, 1878.
2. Ruth M. Roberts, b. June 14, 1882.

iv. Carrie M., b. July 22, 1867; m. Dec. 24, 1884, ———— Van Cowan of Plymouth, Me.

Children:

1. Nellie L. Cowan, b. July 15, 1885.
2. Florence M. Cowan, b. Oct. 12, 1888.
3. Alice L. Cowan, b. May 27, 1891.
4. Viola B. Cowan, b. May 2, 1893.
5. Ethel M. Cowan, b. July 10, 1894.
6. Charles E. Cowan, b. Aug. 20, 1895.

211

OLIVER PAUL[6] (*Samuel,[5] Samuel,[4] Samuel,[3] Stephen,[2] James[1]*), born in Eliot, Me., Feb. 26, 1826; married

Nov. 18, 1851, at Tusceola, Mich., Augusta Melvina
Slafter, born in Norwich, Vt., July 11, 1826. He
left Eliot at the age of 13; lived in Michigan many
years; later made his home at Eugene, Oregon.
Children:

335. i.   Edgar Oliver,[7] b. Dec. 31, 1852.
336. ii. Frederick Wayland, b. Feb. 21, 1855.
337. iii. William Lincoln, b. July 18, 1860.
     iv. Mary Alice, b. June 11, 1868; d. unm. April 19,
        1890.
338. v. Frank Lovell, b. Jan. 7, 1871.

230

WILLIAM[6] (*Lemuel,*[5] *William,*[4] *Samuel,*[3] *Richard,*[2]
James[1]), born in Portland, Me., Jan. 9, 1817; married
at Thomaston, Me., in June, 1844, Lucinda, daughter
of Capt. Joseph and Sarah (Jones) Flint* of Damariscotta, Me., born Feb. 9, 1819, died May 2, 1882. He
was a sailmaker and master mariner. He died of
embolism, May 2, 1882.
Children:

350. i.   William Joseph,[7] b. April 14, 1845.
     ii. Sarah Elizabeth, b. March 31, 1848; m. July 31,
        1872, Capt. Frederick W. Stackpole, of Thomas-
        ton. Capt. Stackpole retired from the sea in
        1885, when he removed to Washington, Kan.,
        and entered into banking business.
     iii. Martha Ellen, b. June 25, 1851; m. Samuel Frank
        Robinson, of Thomaston, tailor, now of Brook-
        lyn, N. Y.
     iv. Abbie Frances, b. Oct. 31, 1853, m. Dec. 12, 1874,
        Wendell P. Rice, of Thomaston.
     v. Lucinda, b. Sept. 30, 1855; d. in Oct., 1894.
351. vi. Charles Edward, b. Dec. 20, 1857.
352. vii. Frank Herbert, b. Nov. 28, 1859.

* See Note, p. 279.

241

RICHARD BROOKS[6] (*Richard,*[5] *Richard,*[4] *Isaac,*[3] *Richard,*[2] *James*[1]), born in New Gloucester, Me., March 10, 1797; married Betsey ———. Resided some time at Pittsfield, Me.

Child:

355.　　　Richard Brooks,[7] b. in 1825.

242

CLEMENT FICKETT[6] (*Richard,*[5] *Richard,*[4] *Isaac,*[3] *Richard,*[2] *James*[1]), born in New Gloucester, Me., Aug. 13, 1799; married.

He removed to East Corinth, Me., about 1835, and after half a century of reputable life there passed away in 1881.

243

CHRISTOPHER COLUMBUS[6] (*Richard,*[5] *Richard,*[4] *Isaac,*[3] *Richard,*[2] *James*[1]), born in New Gloucester, Me., Jan. 20, 1803; married Lucy G.

He was graduated from Bowdoin Medical School in 1829; was in practice in New Gloucester in 1833; removed to Portland and became cashier of a bank; removed again to Netawaka, Kan., and resumed the practice of medicine. He died Aug. 12, 1885.

244

GEORGE WASHINGTON[6] (*Richard,*[5] *Richard,*[4] *Isaac,*[3] *Richard,*[2] *James*[1]), born in New Gloucester, Me., Nov. 7, 1805; married June 23, 1831, Sarah Demeritt, of Durham, Me., born May 1, 1807, died Oct. 10, 1858.

He worked on his father's farm through his youth, attending the town schools; and fitted himself for the work of teaching in the public schools. He taught first at the age of 17 in the town of Lisbon, Me. At

the age of 21 he began to teach at Orono, Me.,
where he continued for three years. After his marriage he resided in Levant, Me. He followed the work
of teaching as a profession. His life was not long.
He died in June, 1833.

Child:

Sarah Ellen,[7] b. March 4, 1832; m. Nov. 14,
1852, John Keaton Nelson, b. in Palermo, Me.,
Feb. 5, 1830, son of Daniel and Susan Nelson.
He was a millwright and farmer; removed in
1856 to Bridgewater, Aroostook county, Me.
Was in various town offices; d. April 26, 1896.

Children:

1. Elma Celestia Nelson, b. Oct. 21, 1853; m. Dec.
   7, 1872, Perley Haynes, of Amherst, Me.:
   rem. to Stockton, Cal.; is in U. S. mail service.

2. Ellen Augusta Nelson, b. June 13, 1855; m.
   July 14, 1877, James Archibald, attorney at
   law; res. Houlton, Me.

3. Fred P. Nelson, b. Oct. 12, 1857; m. (1) Oct.
   1, 1881, Ida Bean, who d. Jan. 14, 1889.
   He m. (2) Nov. 14, 1900, Bessie Agnes Peabody. Res. Houlton, Me.; dealer in Music
   and Musical Instruments. Sold business in
   1902 and removed to Washington, Pa. ; d.
   March 29, 1903.

4. Octavia Nelson, b. Dec. 1, 1859; m. Dec. 24,
   1878, James Duncan Ross. Res. Littleton,
   Me. He is a farmer and potato dealer.

5. Vesta Nelson, b. May 20, 1862; m. Sept. 24,
   1882, Jarvis H. Kitchen, of Houlton; a dealer
   in horses; he d. Dec. 13, 1900.

6. Frances Nelson, b. Dec. 20, 1864; m. Dec. 25,
   1886, Myron Eugene Hill; res. at the time of
   her death, Jan. 7, 1898, at Dorchester, Mass.

7. Forest Nelson, b. March 15, 1868; m. Sept. 5,
   1894, Bessie Clapp Dunning. Res. Bath, Me.
   He grad. Eastman Com. College, Poughkeep-

sie, N. Y.; is bookkeeper for the N. E. Ship-
building Co., Bath, Me.; also agent for North-
western Life Insurance Co.
8. Berton Jerome Nelson, b. June 11, 1870; m.
   March 6, 1901, Lizzie Maude Burns; res.
   Bridgewater, Me.; farmer and shipper of po-
   tatoes.

245

DANIEL LEWIS[6] (*Richard,[5] Richard,[4] Isaac,[3] Richard,[2] James[1]*), born in New Gloucester, Me., March
11, 1811; died in Auburn, Me., Oct. 30, 1901; married in 1858 Mary W. Merrill, of Freeport, Me. She
was sick a long time, and died in 1896. Their only
child, a daughter, died in infancy. Mr. Tobie was a
successful public school teacher in early manhood;
afterward learned the business of pump-making, which
he followed through his long life. He preserved his
vigor remarkably, being an active business man until
he had completed his eighty-ninth year. He laid the
first aqueduct in Auburn. He was a robust and pow-
erful man; a great lover of manly sports. Was a member of the Baptist church, and a kind, helpful, generous man; "a great temperance man"; kind to children
and considerate of all.

246

EDWARD PARSONS[6] (*Jonathan L.,[5] Richard,[4] Isaac,[3]
Richard,[2] James[1]*) born in New Gloucester, Me., Oct.
13, 1800; married first, Jan. 15, 1829, Caroline, daughter of Dean Frye, of Lewiston; she died in 1838. He
married second, Feb. 19, 1840, Jane E., daughter of
John Harmon, who outlived him.

He served an apprenticeship at carding wool and
dressing cloth, and went to Lewiston, Me., in 1823,
where he was engaged in that business which has been
so large a part of the city's activity and source of

EDWARD PARSONS TOBIE.

wealth in the years since. Except for a residence of ten years at Keith's Mills at Chesterville, Me., he spent his life in Lewiston. Disabled by an accident, receiving injuries which finally caused his death, he was chosen town clerk, filling the office thirty-five years, and then being chosen the first clerk of the city under its charter. He was a teacher in the Sunday School, and active in all the work of the Free Baptist church, of which he was a deacon; the first citizen in town to cast a vote in opposition to slavery, and a strong advocate of its abolition; helped on fugitive slaves escaping to Canada; stood up staunchly against the use of and traffic in strong drink, and was always on the side of conscience and faith.

Many were his friends, for his heart was tender toward all, especially the needy and weak; he was a lover of little children. Great sorrow was felt at his death; his memory is fragrant. He died Monday, March 29, 1875.

Children:

    i.   Sarah F.,' b. in Chesterville, Me., Nov. 16, 1829; became a remarkably successful teacher ; did thorough and uplifting work for her pupils ; occupied eminent positions in High schools, Academies and Institutes in a good many places ; taught five years at the Normal School in Westfield, and was at the time of her death in the High School of Springfield. Her influence over young people was unusually helpful. She died Oct. 13, 1877.

    ii.   Mary Frye; m. George W. Garcelon ; residence Riverside, Cal. He d. March 9, 1905.

365. iii.   Edward Parsons, Jr., b. in Lewiston, Me., March 19, 1838.

366. iv.   Leroy Harmon, b. Jan. 18, 1843.

    v.   A child who died in infancy.

20

248

ELBRIDGE[6] (*Jonathan L.,[5] Richard,[4] Isaac,[3] Richard,[2] James[1]*), Resided in Portland, Me. Carried on the business of tanning; was long a partner of J. S. Ricker. Stood high in the community for character, ability and business efficiency; died Feb. 14, 1884.

Child:

367.　　Charles M.[7], b. March 27, 1833.

249

JOSHUA A.[6] (*William,[5] Richard,[4] Isaac,[3] Richard,[2] James[1]*), born at Poland, Me., July 20, 1807; married.

He became a Methodist Episcopal minister, and did good service many years; when beyond the age of continuous pastorate he was a useful "local preacher." He died at Mechanic Falls, Me., Feb. 13, 1881, "leaving a wife but no children."

250

WILLIAM A.[6](*William,[5] Richard,[4] Isaac,[3] Richard,[2] James[1]*), born in Poland, Me., about 1811; married first, —— Waterhouse; married second, Jerusha Perkins; married third. Received a deed of land from his father in Poland, May 20, 1842. He was captain of Co. K, 5th Me. Vol. Inf., in the War of the Rebellion, commissioned in June, 1861, resigned in Sept., 1861.

He died at Mechanic Falls May 4, 1899, "aged 88 years."

Children:

370. i.　　Merritt[7]; removed to the West.
371. ii.　　Asa, removed to Lynn, Mass.
372. iii　　Frank; resided at Lisbon Falls, Me., in 1899.

iv. Ada F., b. in 1848; d. in Boston, single, æ. 45,
April 22, 1893.
373. v. Charles Henry, b. Aug. 8, 1849; grad. Bowdoin
Medical School, 1880. Practising physician at
Mechanic Falls, Me.
vi. Rose.

253

JONATHAN⁶ (*William*,⁵ *Richard*,⁴ *Isaac*,³ *Richard*²,
*James*¹), born in Poland, Me.; married Augusta——.
Children:
i. Llewellyn,⁷ b. 1870; m. in Boston, May 2, 1892,
Annie, dau. of Oscar and Bridget Perry, b. in
Boston in 1870.
ii. Carrie M., b. in 1875, m. April 18, 1891, Robert
L. Sanderson, son of Simeon and George Sander-
son, b. in 1870.

254

EZRA LEVI⁶ (*Ezra*,⁵ *Richard*,⁴ *Isaac*,³ *Richard*,²
*James*¹), born in New Gloucester, Me., July 5, 1826;
married Mary D. Nutting. He died Aug. 18, 1859,
and the widow married second, Charles Wilson.
Children:
i. Joseph,⁷ b. in May, 1853, d. Nov. 14, 1854.
ii. Nathan, b. in Dec. 1854, d. July 3, 1856.
iii. Jessie Fremont, b. Aug. 14, 1856; m. Stillman
Tenny; res. Raymond, Me.
iv. Mary, b. and d. in 1858.

265

IRA WADLEIGH⁶ (*Nathan*,⁵ *William*,⁴ *Isaac*,³ *Richard*,² *James*¹), born in Montville, Me.; married Emeline ⸺, born in Paris, Me. He became a physician; practised in Boston some years. "Was a man
of remarkable gifts and attainments in his profession."

[Boston Transcript.] He died in Boston, of enlargement of the liver, Oct. 29, 1867, aged 48–8–26.
Child:

Arthur Huntington,[7] b. in Boston, Feb. 22, 1860

[handwritten: Delia H. m J W. Mosher; Emma m F. Kidder]

SEVENTH GENERATION.

301

JOSIAH, 3d[7] (*Josiah,[6] Josiah,[5] William,[4] Samuel,[3] Stephen,[2] James[1]*), born at Kittery, Me., Dec. 25, 1822; married, Jan. 1, 1845, Elizabeth F. Mitchell.
Children:

400.   i.   Herbert C.,[8] b. 1853; carriage trimmer; m. in Boston, April 12, 1876, Flora D., dau. of Samuel D. and Nancy Weeks, b. in 1858.

     ii.   Fred; m. in Boston, April 2, 1891, Jennie, dau. of Albert and Sophronia Sellars, b. in Rockland, Me., in 1860.

    iii.   Albert E., b. 1866; stair builder; m. in Boston, Oct. 9, 1895, Ida M., dau. of John R. and Mary Swett, b. in Wolfboro, N. H., in 1870.

303

SAMUEL LEWIS[7] (*Josiah, Jr.,[6] Josiah,[5] William,[4] Samuel,[3] Stephen,[2] James[1]*), born at Kittery, Me., June 9, 1828; married, Dec. 25, 1855, Roxanna Parsons, daughter of John and Priscilla (Patch) Waldron; she died Dec. 1, 1900.

He was a seaman, and during the latter part of his life was pilot on the Piscataqua river to Portsmouth, N. H. He died May 15, 1901, at Kittery, where he had always lived.

Children:

406. i. Manning Phillips,⁶ b. Feb. 12, 1857.
    ii. Samuel Lewis, b. March 18, 1859. Resides at Kittery, Me.

319

MARTIN ·PARRY⁷ (*James S.,⁶ James,⁵ Samuel,⁴ Samuel,³ Stephen,² James¹*), born in Eliot, Me., Jan. 15, 1840; married, May 1, 1882, Abbie Elvena, daughter of Charles W. and Mary A. (Paul) Rogers, b. July 1, 1858.

He went to sea when a boy in the ship Rockingham — the last ship sunk by the Alabama. Was driven ashore in Bristol Channel, Eng., in the great hurricane of 1859. Served as an apprentice in the U. S. Navy Yard at Kittery, Me., during the building of the Kearsarge that sunk the Alabama. Afterward entered the employ of the American Fire Alarm Telegraph Co. as an electrician; worked in seventeen different cities. Was an inspector on the Automatic Telegraph Co.'s line from New York to Washington. Was one of the owners of the schooner Piscataqua, built in Kittery, and one of the projectors of the Eliot Hotel Company. Resides (1902) on the old homestead. Has done much to help on this genealogy.

Children:

420. i. Roger Parry,⁸ b. July 18, 1884.
    ii. Alice Hunter, b. Aug. 9, 1888.
421. iii. Walter Bartlett, b. Sept. 2, 1891.

320

JAMES W.⁷ (*William,⁶ James,⁵ Samuel,⁴ Samuel,³ Stephen,² James¹*), born May 4, 1830; married first, April 16, 1856, Hannah Martin. Resided at Milford (Mass.) some years. He married second, at Chelsea, Aug. 23, 1868, Lydia Catherine, daughter of John A.

and Mary Morrill of Chelsea, born in Limerick, Me.,
in 1832. Resides in Boston.
Children:
    i.   Clarence,⁸ b. April 16, d. June 19, 1858.
422. ii.   Rufus Tolman, b. July 12, 1859.
    iii.   Florence Martin, b. Aug. 23, 1873.

321

JOHN GOODWIN⁷ (*William,⁶ James,⁵ Samuel,⁴ Samuel,³ Stephen,² James¹*), born Jan. 29, 1834; married,
May 7, 1855, Emily A. Leighton. He removed to
Worcester, and resided there some years. Removed
to Portsmouth, N. H., where he has been a real estate
merchant and auctioneer.
Children:
423. i.   William Leighton,⁸ b. in Worcester, Nov. 4, 1860.
    ii.   A daughter, b. in Worcester; d. July 2, 1872.
424. iii.   John Goodwin, b. in Worcester, Nov. 10, 1873.

322

HENRY C.⁷ (*William,⁶ James,⁵ Samuel,⁴ Samuel,³
Stephen,² James¹*), born March 11, 1840; married,
June 4, 1865, Ellen A. Goodwin. He died March 19,
1901.
Children:
    i.   Harry H.,⁸ b. Dec. 6, 1869; d. Sept. 20, 1882.
    ii.   Rosa B., b. June 24, 1876.

323

FRANKLIN O.⁷ (*William,⁶ James,⁵ Samuel,⁴ Samuel,³ Stephen,² James¹*), born Feb. 10, 1845; married
Lucy Chamberlain. Lived in Boston some years,
later in Somerville. Machinist.
Child:
    Frederick Chamberlain,⁸ b. in Boston, Jan. 12,
    1878. Grad. Bowdoin Medical School 1891.
    Physician Eye and Ear Infirmary, Portland, Me.

330

NATHANIEL DIXON[7] (*Samuel,[6] Samuel,[5] Samuel,[4] Samuel,[3] Stephen,[2] James[1]*), born in Eliot, Me., Feb. 21, 1833; married first, in Medford, Oct. 1, 1853, Maria, daughter of Charles Dunn, born in New Yor'x in 1834; married second, Sarah E. Davis. He is a ship-carpenter. Removed in 1863 to California, worked some time at the U. S. Navy Yard at Vallejo; removed to Port Hadlock, Wash.

Children:

  i. Ida Anna,[8] b. in Boston, June 22, 1855; d. young.
  ii. Guy Mills, b. in California, April 20, 1871.

331

SAMUEL AUGUSTUS[7] (*Samuel,[6] Samuel,[5] Samuel,[4] Samuel,[3] Stephen,[2] James[1]*), born in Eliot, Me., Oct. 23, 1841; married first, Aug. 25, 1864, Annie R. Cole; married second, Jan. 28, 1885, Mary, daughter of Robert and Christie (McLain) Bowron, b. Sept. 18, 1860.

He is a carpenter and builder; has worked on ships and buildings, understanding all departments of the trade. Resides in Cambridge. He enlisted in Co. G, 27th Me. Vol. Inf., Sept. 30, 1862, and served till mustered out in July, 1863. Is a member of the Order of Pilgrim Fathers, the Odd Fellows and the Grand Army.

Children:

  i. Ida B.,[8] b. Sept. 3, 1865; m. in Cambridge, Jan. 12, 1888, Herbert E. Smith of Plymouth, Fla., b. in Cambridge in 1864, son of Samuel and Mary Smith.
431. ii. William Clinton, b. April 12, 1867.
  iii. Samuel Oscar, b. Sept. 29, 1870; d. March 6, 1898.

432. iv. Ralph Elwood, b. July 4, 1875; m. July, 1902,
Bessie Scott. Resides at Mattapan; clerk of Victoria Copper Mining Co., Boston.
  v. Gordon Eliot, b. Nov. 11, 1891.
  vi. Howard Blaine, b. Dec. 11, 1893.

332

WILLIAM WALLACE[7] (*Samuel,[6] Samuel,[5] Samuel,[4] Samuel,[3] Stephen,[2] James[1]*), born April 2, 1844; was published in Boston, Sept. 20, 1868, to Elizabeth R., daughter of George and Mary Kennedy, born in Portland, Me., in 1850; married in Boston, April 12, 1869, Annie M., daughter of Nathan and Susan Paul, born in Eliot, Me., in 1851. Carpenter and builder. Res. Cambridge.

Children:

433. i. Wallace Alexis,[8] b. Aug. 2, 1871.
434. ii. Nathan Paul, b. Jan. 25, 1873.

333

GEORGE[7] (*Alexander,[6] Samuel,[5] Samuel,[4] Samuel,[3] Stephen,[2] James,[1]*), born Aug. 8, 1838; married May 17, 1863, Constantia Tetherly, of Eliot, Me.

Children:

i. John R.,[8] b. April 12, 1865.
ii. Anna, b. March 24, 1867; married first, Dec. 10, 1884, Willis Tetherly, of Eliot; she married second, Nov. 9, 1899, Walter Langley, of Eliot.

Children:

1. Eva Tetherly, b. Dec. 28, 1888.
2. Charles E. Tetherly, b. Dec. 20, 1890.
3. Lester H. Tetherly, b. Feb. 9, 1893.
4. Morris E. Langley, b. June 9, 1890.

iii. Alice M., b. Oct. 10, 1872; d. Dec. 15, 1873.
441. iv. George A., b. July 2, 1874.
  v. Charles, b. Aug. 10, 1876; d. Dec. 15, 1890.

334

EDWIN[7] (*Alexander,[6] Samuel,[5] Samuel,[4] Samuel,[3] Stephen,[2] James[1]*), born June 10, 1840; married June 30, 1863, Olive Staples of Eliot, and resides there.
Children:

 i. Luella F.,[8] b. Feb. 2, 1867; m. Sept., 1885, Edgar S. Paul, of Eliot, Me.
  Children:
   1. Blanche Paul, b. June 21, 1887.
   2. Eugene S. Paul, b. June 10, 1890.
   3. Harry Paul, b. June 28, 1894.
442. ii. Arthur E., b. May 15, 1870.

335

EDGAR OLIVER[7] (*Oliver Paul,[6] Samuel,[5] Samuel,[4] Samuel,[3] Stephen,[2] James[1]*), born at Tusceola, Mich., Dec. 31, 1852; married at Halsey, Oregon, Dec. 7, 1892, Inez V. Cummings, born at Halsey, July 30, 1870.
Children:

 i. Frank E.,[8] b. at Olex, Ore., Oct. 19, 1893.
 ii. Myrtle Grace, b. Nov. 29, 1894.
 iii. Ralph Berry, b. Jan. 2, 1897.

336

FREDERICK WAYLAND[7] (*Oliver Paul,[6] Samuel,[5] Samuel,[4] Samuel,[3] Stephen,[2] James[1]*), born at Tusceola, Mich., Feb. 21, 1855; married there Dec. 18, 1883, Minnie Gertrude Fisher, born there Aug. 7, 1860.
Children:

 i. Alice Augusta,[8] b. at Olex, Ore., Feb. 10, 1885.
 ii. Carl F., b. at Olex, Nov. 1, 1893.
 iii. Etta Mary, b. at Arlington, Ore., June 21, 1896.
 iv. Vera Gertrude, b. at same place, Jan. 22, 1899.

312

337

WILLIAM LINCOLN[7] (*Oliver Paul,[6] Samuel,[5] Samuel,[4] Samuel,[3] Stephen,[2] James[1]*), born at Tusceola, Mich., July 18, 1860; married at Detroit, Mich., Feb. 21, 1895, Mamie M. Silvers, born at St. Johns, Mich., May 1, 1873.
Children:
  i.   Neita Ann,[8] b. at Vassar, Mich., Nov. 14, 1897.
  ii. Wilma Florence, b. at Olex, Mich., May 22, 1899.

338

FRANK LOVELL[7] (*Oliver Paul,[6] Samuel,[5] Samuel,[4] Samuel,[3] Stephen,[2] James[1]*), born at Tusceola, Mich., Jan. 7, 1871; married at Helena, Ark., Aug. 29, 1897, Retta M. Hall, born May 9, 1871.

350

WILLIAM JOSEPH[7] (*William,[6] Lemuel,[5] William,[4] Samuel,[3] Richard,[2] James[1]*), born at Thomaston, Me., April 14, 1845; married in Boston, Feb. 4, 1876, Lucy Amelia, daughter of William and Susan Amelia Henderson, born in Thomaston, Me., May 14, 1855. He became a sailmaker and master mariner; followed the sea 21 years; passed Cape Horn 35 times, besides making many voyages in other directions "off soundings." In 1885 he retired from the sea and removed to Washington, Kan., where he and his brother in law Capt. F. W. Stackpole have carried on a banking institution. They also have a bank at Greenleaf, Kan.
Children:
  i.   Alice Henderson,[8] b. in Medford, Mass., Jan. 20, 1878; d. at Rockford (Ill.) Female College, May 14, 1898.
  ii. William Henderson, b. in Oakland, Cal., May 12, 1879; grad. Kansas University, 1902; is a mining engineer.
  iii. Lucy Amelia, b. in Washington, Kan., Sept. 27, 1887; grad. High School, 1905.

Children of Samuel Frank and Ellen (Tobey) Robinson:
1. Frank Warren Robinson, b. April 9, 1877; 2. Harriet
Lucinda Robinson, b. May 28, 1880; 3. Helen Tobey Robinson, b. July 28, 1882; 4. Agnes Clara Robinson, b. Sept.
13, 1884; 5. Wendell Rice Robinson, b. Jan. 1, 1889.

351

CHARLES EDWARD[7] (*William*,[6] *Lemuel*,[5] *William*,[4]
Samuel,[3] *Richard*,[2] *James*[1]), born in Thomaston, Me.,
December 20, 1857; married at Cuba, Kan., Sept. 21,
1887, Helen, daughter of Sidney and Emily Case, born
in Youngstown, Ohio, Oct. 27, 1865.

He resides at Greenleaf, Kan., and is assistant cashier of the Greenleaf State Bank, of which his brother
in law, Frederick W. Stackpole, is president, and his
brother, William J. Tobey, is cashier.

Children:

  i.   Louise Case,[8] b. at Cuba, Kan., Nov. 14, 1889;
       d. at Crete, Neb., Sept. 11, 1890.
  ii. Sidney Case, b. at Cuba, Kan., Feb. 4, 1891.

352

FRANK HERBERT[7] (*William*,[6] *Lemuel*,[5] *William*,[4]
Samuel,[3] *Richard*,[2] *James*[1]), born in Thomaston, Me.,
Nov. 28, 1859; married in Nov., 1887, Lucy Amelia,
daughter of Col. Samuel H. Allen, at one time Warden
of the Maine State Prison at Thomaston, later Superintendent of the Soldiers' Home at Togus, Me.

Mr. Tobey died of appendicitis in Boston, Jan. 25,
1904.

355

RICHARD BROOKS[7] (*Richard Brooks*,[6] *Richard*,[5]
Richard,[4] *Isaac*,[3] *Richard*,[2] *James*[1]), born in Pittsfield,
Me., in 1825; married 1st ———; married 2d in West-
ford, Mass., March 28, 1878 (residing in Lowell, a
farmer), Eunice J. Hildreth (residing in Westford),
born in Durham, N. H. He resided at Charleston,
Me., and afterward removed to Perham, Me., where
he was living in 1900.

Child:

Brooks Roswell,⁸ b. in Charleston, Me., in 1867; m. at Medway, Mass., Dec. 28, 1898, Sarah Elizabeth, dau. of Fletcher Thompson, b. at Millville in 1873.

365

EDWARD PARSONS, JR.⁷ (*Edward Parsons,⁶ Jonathan,⁵ Richard,⁴ Isaac,³ Richard,² James¹*), born in Lewiston, Me., March 19, 1838. He married at Bradford, Penobscot county, Me., March 18, 1866, Addie (Adeline Aldrich), daughter of William H. and Sarah P. (Hart) Phipps of Bradford, Me., born there Sept. 28, 1843: she died at Pawtucket, Providence county, R. I., April 25, 1891.

He learned the printer's trade in the office of the Evening Journal of Lewiston; then worked some time in Andover, Mass.

He enlisted September 21, 1861, in Co. G, First Maine Cavalry; mustered in October 31, 1861, as private; saw active service; left at Falmouth, Virginia, sick, May 28, 1862, and sent to Fairfax Seminary Hospital, Alexandria, Virginia; in hospital on duty as clerk when able until November, 1862, when detailed as clerk at headquarters of Col. Allen, military governor, Frederick, Maryland; rejoined company January 11, 1863; promoted corporal February 13, 1863; wounded and taken prisoner at Brandy Station, June 9, 1863; taken to Richmond, Virginia, paroled and sent to Annapolis, June 13, 1863; exchanged and rejoined company October 26, 1863; re-enlisted January 1, 1864; promoted sergeant in April, 1864; slightly wounded in action at Deep Bottom, Virginia, August 16, 1864; detailed quartermaster sergeant at cavalry depot August 29, 1864; detailed orderly sergeant Second Division Cavalry Corps, November 9, 1864; rejoined regiment and promoted sergeant-major December 12, 1864; wounded slightly in action at Sailor's Creek, April 6, 1865, and in the charge at Farmville, Virginia, April 7, 1865, but did not leave the regiment; horse killed under him in the last-named engage-

EDWARD PARSONS TOBIE, JR.

ment; performed the duties of adjutant of the regiment during
the campaign of the spring of 1865, the last campaign of the
Army of the Potomac under General Sheridan, and was made
honorable mention of in the official report of that campaign;
commissioned second lieutenant of Co. E, First Maine Cavalry,
May 8, 1865; acting regimental adjutant until June 6, 1865;
detailed sub-superintendent Freedmen's Bureau in Buckingham
County, Virginia, July 15, 1865, but detail countermanded on
the muster-out of the regiment, August 1, 1865; historian of
the regiment; awarded a medal of honor under act of Congress
approved March 3, 1863, for distinguished gallantry in action,
March 22, 1898; admitted to Massachusetts Commandery, Military Order of the Loyal Legion of the United States, as an
original companion, January 2, 1895.

Returning to Lewiston after the war he became
foreman of the composing department of the Journal;
in 1868 he removed to Providence, R. I., and became
city editor of the Providence Journal. For 12 years
he reported the sessions of the General Assembly and
wrote the political news of the city and State. In
1887 he published a much praised history of the First
Maine Cavalry. He was elected editor of the Providence Telegram in 1880, but in 1881 resumed his connection with the Journal, and took charge of its interests in Pawtucket, to which he removed. He took
an active interest in city affairs, especially the public
schools; was a member of the school committee of
Pawtucket for six years; was a member and for one
year commander of Tower Post, No. 17, Department
of Rhode Island, G. A. R. He wrote several poems
of a patriotic character, and one on the 400th anniver-
sary of the Landing of Columbus.

He died Sunday, Jan. 24, 1900, of Bright's disease;
he had many friends, and was much lamented and
honored at his decease.

Children:

    i.   Edward Parsons[8] Tobie, Jr., born at North Provi-
        dence, R. I. (in that portion annexed to the city

of Providence, May 1, 1874), Sept. 14, 1870.
Enlisted May 5, 1898, in 1st Rhode Island U. S.
Vol. Inft.; mustered in as musician of Co. L,
May 16, 1898; promoted corporal July 5, 1898;
clerk at regimental headquarters from Feb. 15,
1899, until muster out of regiment, March 30,
1899. Married at Lincoln, Providence Co., R. I.,
June 18, 1902, Mabel Frances, daughter of William Francis and Nellie C. (Boland) Goodwin,
born at Rumford, East Providence, Providence
Co., R. I., Feb. 22, 1876. Journalist.

ii. Willis³ Tobie, born at Providence, R. I., March 21,
1874. Enlisted in Light Battery A, 1st Rhode
Island U. S. Vol. Artillery, and mustered in
June 25, 1898, as private; mustered out with
battery, October 25, 1898. Married at Nantucket, November 14, 1901, Mary Emma, daughter of Oliver Cromwell and Ellen (Morton) Hatch,
born at Nantucket, Feb. 15, 1871. Printer.

366

LEROY HARMON⁷ (*Edward Parsons,⁶ Jonathan L.,⁵
Richard,⁴ Isaac,³ Richard,² James¹*), born in Lewiston, Me., Jan 18, 1843; married Jan. 26, 1867, Belle
Pollard, daughter of Daniel and Abigail Soule (Porter) Hodges, born at Hallowell, Me., 13 Oct., 1843.
Learned the trade of machinist, and worked at it in
various places. On the breaking out of the Rebellion
he stood ready to help in its suppression, and enlisted
Oct. 4, 1861, in Company K of the 10th Me. Vol. Inf.,
and served till he was mustered out with the regiment,
May 7, 1863. Re-enlisted in Aug., 1864, in Co. G,
1st Me. Cavalry; was wounded in the battle of Din-
widdie C. H., March 31, 1865, and discharged for disability from wounds, July 27, 1865. Has held the
office of commander of Bosworth Post, No. 2, G.A.R.,
and member of the staff of the Grand Commander.
Has been fʿr many years in the Portland U. S. Cus-

tom House, where he is clerk and Acting Deputy Collector.
Children:
 i. Grace Eveleth,[8] b. Jan. 20, 1868; m. Oct. 14,
   1894, Thomas West Wilson Atwood, of Portland,
   b. in Barrington, N. S., a son of John and Lydia
   Ann (Wilson) Atwood.
 Children :
   1. Marjorie Tobie Atwood, b. Dec. 22, 1895.
   2. Edward Wilson Atwood, b. June 27, 1897.

455. ii. Walter Eaton, b. Dec. 12, 1869; Bowdoin College
   Medical School, M.D., 1899; a practising phy-
   sician in Portland and an instructor in the Medical
   School.
 iii. Le Roy Fessenden, b. July 26, 1873; is Assistant
   Passenger and Freight Agent of the Washington
   County Railway Co. at Calais, Me.

367

CHARLES M.[7] (Elbridge,[6] Jonathan L.,[5] Richard,[4]
Isaac,[3] Richard,[2] James[1]), born in Portland, Me.
He learned the trade of tanner, and followed the
business successfully; was president of the Casco
Tanning Company of Portland, Me., where he long
resided. Had a high reputation for sterling worth;
was a constant and valued member of the First Free
Baptist church. He died of apoplexy Feb. 2, 1896.
Child:
457. Charles F.,[8] b. March 22, 1860.

380

OTIS CROSS[7] (Joseph C.,[6] Nathan,[5] William,[4] Isaac,[3]
Richard,[2] James[1]), born in Montville, Me., March 23,
1832; married at Knox, Me., Feb. 3, 1856, Affinee
Adelaide, daughter of Harry Hatch and Eliza Dudley (Doty) Sherman, born March 24, 1838.

He died at Liberty, Me., March 13, 1880; the widow married second, at Great Falls, N. H., Feb. 14, 1882, Charles Morton Plummer.

Children:

   i.   Edgar Fremont,[8] b. Sept. 8, 1856; d. Sept. 24, 1860.
   ii.   Frank Oscar, b. July 1, 1858; d. Sept. 18, 1860.
   iii.   Frank Edgar, b. Sept. 24, 1863.
   iv.   Walter Leslie, b. March 1, 1868.
   v.   Lida Arley, b. Oct. 18, 1876; d. May 15, 1881.
   vi.   Fred Berton, b. June 12, d. Dec. 6, 1878.

[Doten-Dotey Genealogy.]

EIGHTH GENERATION.

406

MANNING PHILLIPS[8] (*Samuel Lewis,*[7] *Josiah, Jr.,*[6] *Josiah,*[5] *William,*[4] *Samuel,*[3] *Stephen,*[2] *Thomas*[1]), born in Kittery, Me., Feb. 12, 1857; graduated from New Hampton (N. H.) Institute in 1880; from Bates College in 1885, and from Cobb Divinity School in 1888. Began his ministry with the Free Will Baptist Church of Water Village, Ossipee, N. H., Aug. 5, 1885, and was ordained there Nov. 3, 1885, Prof. James A. Howe of Lewiston, Me., preaching the sermon. He has had other pastorates at Gilmanton Iron Works, N. H., Georgetown, Me., and Taunton, Mass., his present parish.

He married, July 8, 1890, Jane, daughter of Capt. Abner Collins of Kittery, Me.

Child:

       Grace C.,[9] b. June 6, 1893.

422

RUFUS TOLMAN[8] (*James W.,[7] William,[6] James,[5] Samuel,[4] Samuel,[3] Stephen,[2] James[1]*), born in Boston, July 12, 1859; m. Aug. 25, 1892, Mary A., daughter of William Alner and Abigail (Adams) Sherry, born in Boston, Sept. 4, 1859. He is a jeweler in Boston.
Child:
  James Alner,[9] b. July 15, 1894.

423

WILLIAM LEIGHTON[8] (*John G.,[7] William,[6] James,[5] Samuel,[4] Samuel,[3] Stephen,[2] James[1]*), born in Worcester, Nov. 4, 1860; married in Boston, Dec. 1, 1898, Margaret S., daughter of Henry D. and Agnes Campbell, born at Calais, Me., in 1862.

431

WILLIAM CLINTON[8] (*Samuel A.,[7] Samuel,[6] Samuel,[5] Samuel,[4] Samuel,[3] Stephen,[2] James[1]*), born in Eliot, Me., April 12, 1867; married at Cambridge, April 5, 1887, Della M., daughter of Elisha and Alice Payne of East Boston, born in 1869. He has been a commercial traveler; is now foreman of a Granolithic Co. at Lynbrook, Long Island.
Children:
  i.   Alice Della,[9] b. April 7, 1890.
  ii. Marion A., b. Sept. 14, 1894.
  iii. Carl Payne, b. April 27, 1902.

433

WALLACE ALEXIS[8] (*William W.,[7] Samuel,[6] Samuel,[5] Samuel,[4] Samuel,[3] Stephen,[2] James[1]*), born Aug. 2, 1871; married, Aug. 16, 1890, Mary E. Blennerhassett of Cambridge. Residence, Cambridge; in the employ of B. & M. R.R.

21

Children:
  i.   Mabel Pauline,* b. April 28, 1892.
  ii. Chester Wallace, b. Aug. 20, 1900.

434

NATHAN PAUL[8] (*William W.,[7] Samuel,[6] Samuel,[5] Samuel,[4] Samuel,[3] Stephen,[2] James[1]*), born in Eliot, Me., Jan. 25, 1873; married in Fall River, Nov. 10, 1902, Teresa, daughter of Luke and Rebecca (Graham) Driver, born in Fall River in 1882.

He is a druggist in Fall River. He and his wife were canoeing on Coles' River, at Touisset, near their summer home, Sept. 11, 1905, when the canoe capsized, and Mrs. Tobey was drowned in spite of his heroic efforts to save her; help came too late for her restoration; he was restored with difficulty.

Child:

Alton B.,* b. Sept. 15, 1904.

441

GEORGE A.[8] (*George,[7] Alexander,[6] Samuel,[5] Samuel,[4] Samuel,[2] Stephen,[3] James[1]*), born July 2, 1874; married, Sept. 10, 1894, Evelyn Foster of Portsmouth, N. H.

Children:
  i.   Gertrude,* b. Oct. 10, 1895.
  ii. Clara, b. July 2, 1897.

442

ARTHUR E.[8] (*Edwin,[7] Alexander,[6] Samuel,[5] Samuel,[4] Samuel,[3] Stephen,[2] James[1]*), born May 15, 1870; married, June 12, 1894, Mary, daughter of Henry and Jennie (Carter) Von Drethen, born in 1873.

Child:

Arthur Harold,* b. July 10, 1900.

455

WALTER EATON[8] (*Leroy Harmon,*[7] *Edward Parsons,*[6] *Jonathan L.,*[5] *Richard,*[4] *Isaac,*[3] *Richard,*[2] *James*[1]), born in Portland, Me., Dec. 12, 1869; married, Nov. 5, 1902, Mabel, daughter of George Howard and Mary Gardner (Folger) Cary, born in Pittsfield, Mass., Oct. 24, 1872.

He was graduated from the Medical School of Bowdoin College, M.D., in 1899; entered into practice in the city of Portland, Me., and has also been appointed an instructor in the Bowdoin Medical School.

Children:

    i.   Walter Cary,[9] b. Nov. 5, 1903.
    ii. Alice Cary, b. May 1, 1905.

TOBEYS IN PART FIRST.

324 TOBEY GENEALOGY.

George Angell, 214
George B., 147, 189, 191, 206, 229, 231
George Edwin, 235, 245
George Frederick, 191, 231
George Gibbs, 141, 197
George Gibbs Finch, 197, 236
George H., 209
George Loring, 216
George O., 206, 238, 239
George R., 142, 223
George W., 105, 156, 211, 240
Georgia Anna, 223
Gerard Burnside, 239
Gerard Curtis, 207
Gershom, 12, 20-3, 33-5, 51, 55-7, 93
Gertrude A., 245
Gilbert Russell, 146, 203
Grace, 82, 83, 90, 228, 234
Gustavus Bassett, 220
Guy Davis, 215

H. E., 210
Hannah, 18-23, 27, 28, 33, 40, 47, 58, 65, 71, 82, 83, 99, 101, 107, 114, 116, 119, 120, 126, 131, 149, 164, 165, 173, 182, 193, 199
Hannah B., 139
Hannah Brown, 182
Hannah Brown Sprague, 186
Hannah C., 168
Hannah E., 210
Hannah Elizabeth, 210
Hannah Etta, 211
Hannah L., 192
Hannah Nye, 129
Hannah Sears, 126
Hanson, 149, 209
Harlow, 125, 140, 171, 172
Harold, 214
Harold Grant, 215
Harriet, 92, 144, 159, 171, 200
Harriet Adeline Gibbs, 150
Harriet B., 193, 197, 241
Harriet Finch, 236
Harriet Foster, 145
Harriet Francis, 105
Harriet Jones, 180
Harriet I., 149
Harriet Newell, 162
Harriet Sophronia, 138
Harriet Submit, 197
Harrison Loring, 173, 226
Harry, 139, 210
Harry A., 213
Harry Wolcott, 220
Hathorne Parker, 223
Hattie F., 219
Hattie French, 237
Hattie M., 206
Hattie Swift, 175
Helen, 96, 97, 180
Helen Adell, 244
Helen Amelia, 173
Helen Aurelia, 239
Helen C., 224
Helen M., 189, 219, 226
Heman, Herman, 47, 71, 78, 83, 92, 113, 124, 130, 138, 164, 178, 193, 232
Henrietta, 147

Henrietta A., 215
Henry, 11, 96, 104, 124, 125, 136, 138, 145, 154, 159, 171, 192
Henry A., 137, 189, 223
Henry Archibald, 171, 243
Henry Augustus, 191, 231
Henry Davis, 164
Henry Edwards, 223
Henry Fales, 109, 161-162
Henry H., 189
Henry Jackson, 145
Henry M., 196
Henry Marshall, 139, 194
Henry Pratt, 244
Henry Richmond, 142, 196
Henry S., 193, 232
Henry Villars, 140
Hephsibah, 102, 148
Herbert A., 212, 241
Herman, see Heman.
Hettie, Hittie, see Mehitabel.
Hope Briggs, 148
Horace, 167
Horace M., 193, 231
Horace N., 193
Horace Pratt, 206
Horatio N., 215
Hylon, 140, 195

Ida A., 210
Ida Louisa, 230
Innocent, 93
Irene, 189, 196
Isaac, 53, 86, 87
Isaac Franklin, 128
Isaac S., 68, 69, 81, 86
Isaac Smith, 109
Isabella G., 128
Isadore, 235
Isaiah Nye, 99, 146

Jabez, 32
Jacob, 117
James, 11, 40, 41, 59, 61, 62, 96, 101, 103, 150
James Edwin, 159, 214
James K., 166, 222
James H., 130, 179
James Hall, 106, 159
James Osbert, 161, 215
James Phillip, 230
James Riley, 199
James Snow, 181
James William, 151
Jane, Jean, 24, 25, 39, 40, 77, 78, 107, 123, 125, 164, 169, 172, 192, 196, 209
Jane A., 146
Jane Anna, 174
Jane Eliza, 128
Jane Frances, 127
Jane Gould, 190
Jane Loring, 190
Jane M., 213
Jane West, 144
Janet Augusta, 165
Janet Elizabeth, 196
Jemimah, 27
Jennie B., 222
Jennie Lester, 214
Jennie May, 223
Jerusha, 34, 35, 140
Jesse, 56, 92, 141, 197, 220

Jesse Cook, 220, 242
Jesse Weston, 236
Jessie Howard, 213
Jessie Lathrop, 235
Joanna, 31, 32, 47, 71
Joanna Amelia, 205
Job Gibbs, 92, 141
Job Townsend, 69, 108, 109, 116
John, 19, 23-25, 38-40, 42, 48, 59, 60, 62, 64, 74, 79, 87, 93, 95, 97-99, 117, 120, 125, 130, 135, 143-6, 193, 200, 238
John Albert, 147, 206
John B., 189, 191
John Brayton, 230
John E., 138, 223
John Elbert, 171
John Foster, 139, 194
John Fry, 178, 226
John H., 203
John Henry, 145
John Himan, 117, 178
John L., 154
John Lewis, 211
John Reuben, 244
John S., 142, 196
John William Edmunds, 150
John Williams, 125
Jonathan, 20, 21, 23, 28-32, 45, 46, 48, 49, 67, 68, 79-81, 92, 93, 126, 138
Jonathan Bowen, 132, 182
Jonathan Burr, 82, 83, 131
Jonathan Ellis, 130
Jonathan Franklin, 127, 174
Jonathan Howes, 96, 97, 144, 201, 202
Jonathan Pratt, 138, 191
Joseph, 41, 55, 63, 78, 97, 102, 104, 106, 123, 149, 155, 159, 169, 209
Joseph Delano, 169
Joseph H., 155, 211
Joseph Terry, 129, 175
Joshua, 41, 47, 52, 70, 71, 87, 93, 109, 110, 116, 165
Joshua Briggs, 148, 206
Joshua Fessenden, 165, 219
Joshua Lincoln, 219
Josiah, 60-2, 93, 96, 101, 145, 148
Josiah Goddard, 123, 124, 170
Judith Ann, 161
Judith K., 206
Julia Frances, 192
Julia T., 145

Kate, 222
Katherine, see also Catherine, 194
Katherine Hart, 233
Katherine Libby, 238
Keziah, 68, 69, 76, 146

Laura, 139, 141, 203
Laura Ann Bartley, 127
Laura C., 222
Laura Hathaway, 181
Laura Pyne, 244
Laura Wallace, 246
Lauretta Eliza, 215

TOBEYS IN PART SECOND.

Katherine, 249, 255
Katie A., 297

Lemuel, 266, 273, 277, 282, 308
Leroy F., 317
Leroy H., 303, 316
Levi, 270, 290
Llewellyn, 305
Lizzie G., 298
Lois, 260
Louise Case, 313
Lucinda, 299
Lucretia, 290
Lucy, 266, 273, 277, 282, 308
Lucy A., 277, 296
Lucy Amelia, 312
Luella F., 311
Lydia, 257, 258, 275, 281
Lydia Catherine, 307
Lydia Cummings, 290
Lydia Parsons, 281

Mabel, 321
Mabel Frances, 316
Mabel Pauline, 320
Malinda, 292
Mamie M., 312
Manning Phillips, 307, 318
Marcia, 266
Margaret, 253, 259
Margaret S., 319
Maria, 309
Marion A., 319
Martha (Patty), 253, 256, 257, 260
Martha A. S., 266, 279
Martha Ellen, 299
Martha H., 296
Martha J., 296
Martha Jane, 293
Martin Parry, 293, 307
Mary, 252, 253, 257-260, 264, 265, 275, 282, 298, 305, 309, 320
Mary A., 282, 319
Mary Abigail, 295
Mary Alice, 299
Mary Ann, 280, 292
Mary D., 305

Mary E., 319
Mary Elizabeth, 291, 292
Mary Emma, 316
Mary Frye, 303
Mary Hammond, 294
Mary Jane, 293
Mary Paul, 277
Mary W., 302
Mercy, 266, 270
Merritt, 273, 291
Minnie Gertrude, 311
Miriam, 273, 291
Myrtle Grace, 311

Nancy, 289
Nathan, 271, 290, 291, 305
Nathan Paul, 310, 320
Nathaniel, 258, 264
Nathaniel D., 295, 309
Nathaniel H., 280
Neita Ann, 312

Olive, 275, 311
Olive Augusta, 278
Olive Jane, 296
Oliver Paul, 278, 296
Olivia M., 294
Otis Cross, 317

Page, 263, 272
Persis Temple, 269
Polly, see also Mary, 257, 258, 274, 294

Ralph B., 311
Ralph E., 310
Retta M., 312
Rhoda L., 290
Richard, 253, 256, 257, 261, 263, 266, 268-270, 280, 281
Richard Brooks, 280, 300, 313
Robert, 266
Roger Parry, 307
Rosa B., 308
Rose, 305
Rosilla Merrill, 288
Roxanna Parsons, 306
Rozan C., 294
Rufus Tolman, 308, 319
Ruth R., 280

Samuel, 254, 255, 257, 258, 260-2, 264, 265, 267, 274, 277, 279, 281, 294
Samuel Augustus, 296, 309
Samuel Brooks, 263, 271, 272
Samuel Lewis, 291, 306, 307
Samuel Oscar, 309
Sarah, Sally, 257, 258, 260, 264, 270, 274, 275, 277, 278, 265, 274, 275, 292, 296
Sarah Adelaide, 295
Sarah E., 282, 309
Sarah Elizabeth, 299, 313
Sarah Ellen, 301
Sarah K., 289
Sarah F., 303
Sidney Case, 313
Standish, 290
Stephen, 251-5, 258-260, 264, 265, 274, 275, 292, 296
Submit, 265, 266
Submit Cox, 279

Tabitha, 265, 266
Temperance, 292
Teresa, 320
Thankful Hobbs, 287
Thomas, 281, 292
Thomas Haskell, 270, 282

Vera, 311

Wallace A., 310, 319
Walter B., 307
Walter C., 321
Walter E., 317, 321
Walter L., 318
William, 251-3, 255, 257, 258, 261-5, 270, 271, 273-5, 277-9, 281, 290-3, 299
William A., 281, 304
William C., 309, 319
William H., 312
William J., 299, 312
William L., 308, 319
William W., 296, 310
Willis, 316
Wilma F., 312

GENERAL INDEX.

APPENDIX.

VARIOUS RECORDS OF TOBEYS.

UNASSIGNED OR RECEIVED LATE.

ALFRED A., "b. in Norridgewock, Me., in 1831, shoemaker, son of William [No. 228?] and Sarah (Holway) Tobey," m. at Middleborough July 29, 1859, "Eliza W., dau. of Sylvanus and Sally Hinckley, b. in M. in 1837." Res. Middleborough; m. (2) April 27, 1887, Esther F. Austin, widow, b. in Boston, dau. of James S. and Sarah F. (Taylor).
Children:
1. Clarence E., b. June 20, 1868, d. in Worcester Nov. 12, 1895; m.
2. Julia H., b. June 20, 1868.
3. Eliza B., b. May 12, 1871. [Mid. and Worc. rec.]

ASA S., born in Sandwich, died at Falmouth May 1, 1868, ae. 61; mariner, married. Eunice S., his widow, dau. of Charles and Bathsheba Weeks, d. Jan. 4, 1892.

CAROLINE AMELIA TOBEY, dau. of Apollos (No. 230) and Hannah (Crane) Tobey of Berkeley, b. Oct. 28, 1812; m. (published Nov. 25, 1842) Abel Babbitt Sanford, who d. in Philadelphia, Pa., July 4, 1887; she d. there March 18, 1888.
Children:
1. Helen Amelia Sanford, b. at Taunton July 13, 1845; m. Jan. 2, 1866, Thomas Devlin, who was b. in county Derry, Ireland, April 8, 1838. He is president of the Thomas Devlin Manufacturing Co. of Philadelphia, Pa., manufacturers of iron, steel and brass castings, builders' hardware, etc.
   Children:
   (1) William John Devlin, b. at Philadelphia, Pa., Dec. 25, 1886.
   (2) Thomas Francis Devlin, b. Jan. 20, 1869.
   (3) Walter Edward Emmett Devlin, b. Feb. 10, 1871.
   (4) Helen Regina Devlin, b. Aug. 5, 1873, d. Dec. 24, 1889.
   (5) Frederick Matthew Devlin, b. Nov. 16, 1875.
   (6) Harry Augustine Devlin, b. Dec. 2, 1877.
   (7) Albert Joseph Devlin, b. May 22, 1880.
   (8) Caroline Mary Devlin, b. March 28, 1882.
   (9) Charles Louis Devlin, b. Jan. 16, d. March 28, 1885.
   (10) Raymond Anthony Devlin, b. April 7, 1888.
   (11) Clarence Joseph Devlin, b. May 6, 1890.
2. Eliza Crane Sanford, b. Sept. 1, 1847, d. July 22, 1902.
3. Ella Hannah Sanford, b. June 27, 1849.
4. Francis Herbert Sanford, b. May 31, 1851, m. Emily Glocker; d. at Philadelphia Aug. 22, 1900.
   Children:
   (1) William Sanford.
   (2) Francis Sanford.
5. Emma Tobey Sanford, b. at Utica, N. Y., Aug. 1, 1853.
6. Mary Tobey Sanford, b. at Atlanta, Ill., July 18, 1856.

4   TOBEY GENEALOGY.

CAROLINE MARTIN, wife of Samuel, No. 222, who was b. Nov. 28, 1773, was b. Sept. 18, 1768 dau. of John (b. Nov. 1738, d. March 3, 1800) and Susanna (Millet) (b. Feb. 28, 1749, d. March 31, 1830) Martin.

DEBORAH, dau. of Zaccheus No. 199, m. James Sloane.
Children:
1. John Sloane.
2. James Sloane.
3. Alexander Sloane, all d. young.
4. Sarah Sloane, m. Andrew Derrickson; 4 children.
5. Mary Ann Sloane, m. Jonathan Woodcock; had children.
6. Harriet Matilda Sloane, m. Horatio N. Kent; 4 children.
7. Levi Sloane, d. young.
8. Christopher Gifford Sloane, b. Oct. 11, 1819, m. Clarissa Permelia Stone June, 1845; d. June 27, 1856 in Rush Co., Ind.
Children:
(1) Theodore Albert Sloane, b. Sept. 2, 1847; m. Ellen Roselle Hinsdale at Lamont, Mich. Feb. 2, 1875; located in Pueblo, Colo., and has resided there and at Colorado Springs. Children: Edwin Hinsdale Sloane, b. Oct. 24, 1875, d. March 7, 1880; Theodore Albert Sloane, b. Aug. 30, 1877, d. April 17, 1878; Edith Clara Sloane, b. Feb. 18, 1880; Helen Adeline Sloane, b. March 28, 1887; Norman Hinsdale Sloane, b. June 24, 1890.
(2) Harriet Fidelia Sloane, b. Oct. 27, 1849, d. Feb. 28, 1903.
(3) Lucy Ella Sloane, b. April 30, 1853.
9. Amelia Emma Sloane, m. John Gunning.
10. Deborah Tabor Sloane, m. John Lawrence; 5 children.
11. Elijah Sloane, m. (1) Zarilda Washburn; m. (2) Susanna Myers; 7 children.

ELISHA and Henrietta, their dau. Maria F., b. in Sandwich in 1837, m. at No. Bridgewater Oct. 14, 1856, John C. Hamblin, mariner, son of Benjamin and Betsey Hamblin, b. in 1828. Elisha and Henrietta's son, Albert W., 22, mariner, res. Sandwich, m. at Falmouth Jan. 22, 1873, Helen M., dau. of Josiah and Susan Burgess, b. in F. in 1852.

ELISHA, son of Joseph and Polly [see Joseph below] m. second, June 28, 1855, Mehitabel Draper, widow, dau. of Nathan Bourne.

FRANK, of Middleboro', his wife, Clara E., dau of Orin and Eliza Farnsworth, b. in Norridgewock, Me., Jan. 11, 1848, d. at Middleboro' Feb 7. 1892.

FREEMAN CROWELL[6] No. 322, (Thomas Howes,[5] John,[4] Eleazer,[3] John,[2] Thomas[1]), b. in Falmouth May 8, 1806; d. at Barnstable Nov. 26, 1863 m. Olive ——, b. in Maine, who d. at Chelsea May, 30, 1881, aged 73 yrs., 1 mo., 8 days.

GERSHOM TOBEY, of Sandwich, and Innocent, his wife, formerly widow of Joshua Ellis, sold her rights of dower in Ellis property March 17, 1797. (No. 102, p. 93.)

HENRY A., of New Bedford, made will April 11, proved Sept. 1, 1882. Wife L. Sophia principal heir; bequests to niece Mary Tobey, sister Harriet T. Doane and mother Mary; wife exec. Mary, the mother, made will 24 April, 1882, proved Oct. 5, 1883, giving to son's wife L. Sophia and dau. Mary, dau. Harriet T. Doane, bro. Isaac Bassett, niece Francis D. Herrick, nephew James Fuller.

HENRY AUGUSTUS, No. 750, d. April 22, 1903.

503. HENRY VILLERS⁸ (Ephraim,⁸ Elisha,⁴ Ephraim,³ Gershom,² Thomas¹), son of Ephraim and Zady, b. March 18, 1806, at Alford, Mass.; d. Oct. 27, 1854, in Kentucky; m. Dec. 21, 1837, Elizabeth F. Mitchell, who was b. Oct. 28, 1819, d. June 1, 1894.

He left Mass. as a young man, going first to Virginia, and soon afterwards to Kentucky, where he was employed as clerk in a dry-goods store. After marrying, he bought a farm, settled on it, and engaged in farming and stock raising. He was also engaged in the manufacture of salt several years previous to his death.

Children:
1. William Elzy,' b. Jan. 14, 1839, in Green County, Ky.; m. Feb. 23, 1869, Mary E. Jones, who was b. in Barren County, Ky., Nov. 29, 1848. He is engaged in farming in Metcalfe County.
Children born in Metcalfe County:
(1) Charles Edwin,⁸ b. Jan. 25, 1870; d. Oct. 25, 1870.
(2) Henry Sampson, b. Dec. 10, 1871; in mercantile business at Liletown, Ky.
(3) Anna Laura, b. Sept. 15, 1873; lives with her parents.
(4) Mary Ella, b. Dec. 13, 1875.
(5) James Albert, b. Nov. 7, 1879.
2. Mary Ellen b. Jan. 29, 1844, in Barren Co., Ky.; d. June 2, 1861.
3. Sarah Elizabeth, b. March 8, 1847, in Barren Co.; m. Feb. 24. 1868, Dr. William Henry Scott, who was b. Sept. 1, 1842, d. Sept. 1, 1874.
Children:
(1) Samuel Henry Scott, b. Dec. 22, 1868. Farmer.
(2) Eugene Robbins Scott, b. Sept. 22, 1870; d. Sept. 7, 1900.
(3) Florence Wood Scott, b. Oct. 24, 1872.
(4) John William Scott, b. Sept. 9, 1874. Farmer.
4. Henrietta Villers, b. April 10, 1854, in Barren Co., d. Aug. 29, 1892; m. Jan. 10, 1876, Joseph Thomas Lambirth, farmer. No children.

HIRAM, of Kittery, Me., born Dec. 28, 1807; married (published Oct. 9, 1831) Salome Phillips born Aug. 9, 1811.
Children:
1. John P., b. July 13, 1832; m. (pub. July 24, 1852), Elizabeth A. White.
2. Mary A., b. Nov. 7, 1833.
3. George W., b. Oct. 1, 1835, d. May 17, 1848.
4. Eunice E., b. Dec. 3, 1837.
5. Hiram, Jr., b. Nov. 30, 1839; m. March 24, 1864, Esther J. Sayward of Alfred, Me.
6. Elizabeth C., b. July 26, 1841, d. Aug. 29, 1844.
7. Miriam E., b. June 8, 1842.
8. Charles C., b. Nov. 30, 1844.
9. Henry F., b. Oct. 16, 1845.
10. Susan E. [Kittery records.]

ISAAC S., son of William (page 81) and Roxanna, died at Taunton Oct. 5, 1873, ae. 61.

6   TOBEY GENEALOGY.

REV. JACOB, m. Sarah Hayes, dau. of Hon. James and Pamelia W.
(Skelton) Adams, of Charlestown, b. Dec. 7, 1848. (She was a niece
of the wife of Rev. Alvan Tobey.)

JOEL WELLINGTON, " b. in Norridgewock, Me., carpenter," m. at New
Bedford Jan. 18, 1844, Elizabeth Esther, dau. of John and Esther
Fessenden, b. in Sandwich May 10, 1823, d. Jan. 12, 1892.
    Children :
1. Emma E., b. in Mid. April 13, 1849.
3. Mary L., b. in Carver Aug. 27, 1851.
3. Sarah E., d. in Mid. June 1, ae. 11. 2. 3.

JONATHAN, No. 261, d. June 26, 1843.

JONATHAN HOWES, No. 303, m. second, Nov. 18, 1852, widow Mary
B. Burgess, dau. of Thomas and Lucy B. Pope.

JANE, widow of Isiah Nye (No. 319), daughter of Asa and Annie
(Phinney), died at Falmouth Sept. 29, 1889, aged 77 yrs., 4 days.

JAMES SULLIVAN TOBEY, b. at Fairfield, Me., Aug. 12, 1808, Bowd.
Coll. M. D., 1832; physician at Athens, Me.; d. Oct. 22, 1891.

JOSEPH TOBEY, blacksmith, of New York, gave power of attorney
to his father Lemuel * Tobey, blacksmith, of Portland, Me., with
reference to inheritance from Maria Tobey, of Sandwich, widow of
Joshua Tobey, Oct. 16, 1826; and Lemuel receipted for $52.29 on this
account Dec. 30th.

JOSEPH TOBEY of Sandwich, m. at Wareham Dec. 6, 1804, Mary
Swift, of W.
    Children :
1. Franklin, b. June 8, 1807.
2. Elisha, b. July 25, 1809. [See Elisha, above.]
3. Lewis, Jr., b. Sept. 14, 1812. [Sand. rec.]
4. Mary, b. 1818, m. at Falmouth April 12, 1855, Matthew Baker,
    mariner. [Fal. rec.]

JOSIAH, No. 325, died at Falmouth Oct. 31, 1890.

I. LEMUEL¹ TOBEY, of Fairfield [Me.] and wife Joanna, dau. of Roland
Ellis, of Sandwich, sold land in S. June 13, 1792. [Barns. Co.
Deeds.]
I believe this to be No. 78, Lemuel⁴ (Eliakim,³ Samuel,² Thomas¹),
b. in Sandwich Oct. 30, 1755. — C. H. P.
    Children :
1. Ansel, b. April 18, 1780, d. Nov. 14, 1830.
2. Althea, b. July 17, 1782, d. May 3, 1784.
3. Lemuel, b. July 20, 1784, d. Feb. 8, 1821.
4. Alethea, b. July 25, 1787, d. April 21, 1808.
5. Elizabeth, b. June 18, 1789.
6. Joanna, b. April 29, 1792.
7. Abigail, b. June 30, 1794.

* This seems to be Lemuel, No. 189, and adds something to the article
on him.

APPENDIX. 7

Capt. Lemuel Tobey and Mrs. Betsey Phillips were married Dec. 18, 1814, by Moses Appleton, Justice of the Peace.

II. ANSEL and Mehitable his wife (she was b. March 10, 1787, d. Nov. 16, 1867).
  Children:
 (1) Thomas E., b. Oct. 23, 1802, d. April 25, 1804.
 (2) Henry S., b. Aug. 8, 1804.
 (3) Nancy, b. Sept. 11, 1806, d. July 7, 1829.
 (4) Martha, b. Jan. 23, 1809.
 (5) Caroline, b. Jan. 17, 1814, d. Jan. 30 1840.
 (6) George N., b. March 17, 1814, d. Dec. 25, 1847.
 (7) Julia Ann, b. Nov. 22, 1819.
 (8) Sophia, b. Nov. 11, 1822, d. Feb. 13, 1826.
 (9) Pe . . . , b. April 11, 1825.
 (10) Fr . . . , b. April 11, 1825.

III. HENRY S., m. (1) Sept. 2, 1830, Lydia S. Lawrence; m. (2) July 10, 1845, Mercy D. Lawrence; m. (3) Dec. 7, 1871, Ann M. Cannon.
  Children:
 (1) Cordelia Frances, b. June 21, 1831, d. Nov. 18, 1831.
 (2) Henry Washington, b. Sept. 16, 1832, d. Dec. 26, 1863.
 (3) Ellen Augusta, b. Jan. 17, 1835, d. Dec. 27, 1835.
 (4) Juliette, b. Nov. 29, 1836, d. Jan. 27, 1862.
 (5) Ellen Frances, b. March 14, 1839, d. July 13, 1840.
 (6) Churchill Gardner, b. Oct. 13, 1841, d. Aug. 26, 1894.
  Joseph Lawrence of Barnstable, Mass.
  Joseph Lawrence, b. Dec. 2, 1775, d. April 23, 1843.
  Mercy D. Blossom, b. March 24, 1775.
  Lydia S. Lawrence, b. March 3, 1804, d. Dec. 14, 1844.
  Sarah B. Lawrence, b. July 7, 1806.
  Hannah D. Lawrence, b. March 30, 1808.
  Mercy D. Lawrence, b. Oct. 2, 1810, d. May 4, 1871.
  Churchill B. Lawrence, b. Sept. 25, 1813, d. Aug. 11, 1835.
  Maria A. Lawrence, b. Aug. 2, 1814.
  Olive J. Lawrence, b. Feb. 18, 1819.

IV. CHURCHILL GARDNER, m. Susan L. Parlin, who was b. Nov. 22, 1846, and d. July 6, 1895.
  Children:
 (1) George Henry, b. April 30, 1869.
 (2) Charles Sumner, b. Sept. 15, 1871; res. Lewiston, Me.

V. GEORGE HENRY, m. in Charlestown Oct. 15, 1893, Emma, dau. of John and Lavinia Brenton, b. at Brookfield, N. S., June 3, 1872. He is a painter and decorator in Boston (Tobey & Co., 88 Warrenton St.); res. at Revere. By his courtesy we have been allowed to copy the foregoing records of five generations from the family Bible of his grandfather, Henry S. Tobey, Nov. 1, 1905.

LEONARD TOBEY, grad. Williams Coll., 1826; A. M.; tutor at Waterville Coll. 1827-8; hon. A. M. 1829; d. 1851, ae. 51.

LEWIS, b. Nov. 28, 1803, of Poughkeepsie, N. Y., d. April, 1878; m. Jan. 9, 1843, Deborah Tobey Adams, b. in Attleboro Feb. 15, 1811. Child, Deborah L., b. July 30, 1843; m. Sept. 18, 1867, S. Fred Davis. [Adams Genealogy.]

MARY, wife of Samuel, No. 75, was b. Nov. 6, 1749, and d. April, 1827.

MATTHEW TOBIE was published in Falmouth (before the incorporation of Portland) April 5, 1755, to Deliverance Trott. [Portland records.]

NATHANIEL B.[6] (Nathaniel,[5] No. 164, Stephen,[4] Samuel,[3] Jonathan,[2] Thomas[1]), "son of Nathaniel and Mary, b. at Ballston Springs, N. Y., married," d. at Shirley, Mass., June 19, 1871.

MARY N., daughter of Thomas Howes, No. 135, married at Sandwich Sept. 24, 1843, George Giddings, son of Joshua and Abigail Giddings.

NOAH, No. 70.
     Ballston, May the 20, 1804
     Noah Tobey his Book and bible
Sunday May the 20th day 1783, then my son Samuel was born
     then June the 10th day Heman was born 1785.
Noah Tobey died March 9, 1812; Elizabeth [his second wife] died Sept. 15, 1882. [Family Bible in possession of Mrs. Melinda M. (Tobey) Cook, of Lunda, O.]

PATIENCE N., dau. of John, No. 133, and Patience, unm., d. at Falmouth, Jan. 21, 1895.

PRATT LORENZO, No. 885, his child Pratt Lorenzo, Jr., was b. Nov. 17, 1902; the father d. Nov. 19, 1904.

REMEMBER NYE, daughter of John (No. 133) died at Falmouth Oct. 21, 1871, ae. 69 yrs., 7 mos., 25 days.

ROXANNA (wife of Russell, No. 318) dau. of Noah and Roxanna Hatch, d. of phthisis May 23, 1861, aged 60 yrs., 7 m. 24 days.

SALLY, daughter of Timothy (No. 80), born at Conway, died in Shelburne July 5, 1877, ae. 81, unmarried.

SAMUEL, No. 368, p. 160, continued
Children:
1. Hannah M., b. Sept. 17, 1825; m. Capt. William Johnson and sailed with him on many long voyages, visiting points along the coast of the U. S., West Indies and So. America; rem. to Worcester in 1872, where she still resides. Children: Mrs. Ernest R. Merrill, with whom she lives; Mrs. L. E. Dennis, of So. Norwalk, Conn., and William D. N. Johnson, of Lake View.
2. Horatio Nelson (No. 631, cont.) b. Feb. 29, 1828; m. Nov. 29, 1849, Sarah E. Foster, b. Nov. 21, 1831.
Children:
1. William Burton, b. Jan. 11, 1851; educated at town schools, Washington Academy at E. Machias and Bangor Com. Coll.; clerk in Portland, Me., several years, then paymaster and clerk at North Berwick (Me.) Woolen Mill, 1877 to 1881, when he was chosen agent and treasurer, which position he still holds. A director in the

No. Berwick Nat. Bank and other corporations. Was a delegate to the Chicago Republican Convention in 1886; in religion a liberal. He m. (1) in Oct. 1875, Ariana A. Small; she d. in 1887; he m. (2) Oct. 23, 1889, Julia H. M. Whittier, of Bangor, Me.
Children:
(1) Thad. B., b. Oct. 10, 1876; m. in Boston Jan. 18, 1897, Fannie E. Sweet.
(2) William Homer, b. Jan. 20, 1880.
(3) Dorothy Ingersoll, b. Nov. 19, 1890.
2. Henry Herbert, b. in Machiasport, Me. July 7, 1853, m. Ada Higgins, of Portland, Me. Accountant in Portland and New York City.
Children:
(1) Lester. (2) Florence.
3. Frank Nelson, b. and d. in 1854.
4. Lizzie Ella, b. Sept. 3, 1856; m. Capt. Wm. E. Dennison, of Portland, Me., long commander of steamer *City of Richmond* from Portland to Machiasport (now deceased). Res. Portland.
Children:
(1) William Dennison. (2) Adelaide Dennison.
5. Samuel Nelson, b. Dec. 6, 1858; m. Eva Cates. Was an accountant several years in New York City; returned to Machiasport, Me., and was instrumental in getting a large "Sardine" factory located there, and superintended the construction of the buildings. Has taken prominent part in town affairs, holding office continuously; also postmaster at present.
Child:
Madeline.
6. Eugene Cameron, b. Aug. 1, 1870; educated in town schools and Washington Academy; m. Mallie Curtis, of Portland, Me. Was clerk in New York city a few years; then in employ of Me. Central R. R. at Portland, promoted to be Asst. Paymaster. Enlisted in Naval Reserves in Spanish American War; Asst. Paymaster afterward in regular U. S. service; appointed Asst. Paymaster and served at Puget Sound and at the Philippines; transferred to Brooklyn Navy Yard and promoted to Paymaster. In 1904 appointed disbursing officer of the Isthmian Canal Commission and sent to the Isthmus, where he has also been Customs Collector and Postmaster General of the Zone, and later Chief of the Supply and Material Department. Child: Nelson Shaw.
7. Clarence Nelson, b. May 22, 1872, d. April 12, 1877.
8. Nettie Marion, b. May 11, 1874; m. Samuel Gilbert, of Portland, Me. Child: Elizabeth Marian Gilbert.
3. Benjamin Franklin, b. at Machiasport, Me., Jan. 1, 1830; m. Amanda C. Campbell, who d. in 1901. He was a carpenter and builder, res. at the old home town; d. in 1893.
Children:
(1) Howard. (2) Alden. (3) Mary.
4. James Prince Fuller, b. Dec. 11, 1832; d. Oct. 8, 1896; m. Louisa Phinney. He was a block and spar maker by trade. Served in the War of the Rebellion, First Lieut. of 31st Me. Vol. Inf.; was in Andersonville Rebel Prison 6 months.
Child:
Maurice M.
5. George Loring (No. 633, p. 216 *ante*).

SAMUEL,[6] No. 236, (Nathaniel,[4] Samuel,[8] Samuel,[2] Thomas[1]), b. July 12, 1790 (correcting imperfect statement on page 86); rem. to Caroline, Tompkins County, N. Y.; m. Sept. 4, 1813, Sophia Bunnsville, b. May 17, 1794. He d. Sept. 19, 1830.
Children:
1. Samuel Edwin,[6] b. Oct. 23, 1814; d. Jan. 16, 1815.
2. Alvan Burt, b. Dec. 25, 1815; m. and resided at Chicago, Ill.
3. William Chamberlain, b. Oct. 6, 1818; d. of consumption at Harrisburg, Pa. Aug. 2, 1854.
4. Mary Ann, b. Nov. 23, 1820.
5. Edwin, b. June 6, 1823; served in the U. S. Army in Mexico, and d. there of typhoid fever Feb., 1848.
6. Samuel, Jr., b. Sept. 10, 1825.
7. William Harrison, b. June 2, 1829.
8. Sophia, b. Oct. 11, 1830; d. Sept. 23, 1850, at Waukegan, Ill., of typhoid fever.

SAMUEL, Jr.[6] (above), m. at Providence, R. I., May 3, 1849, Susan Matilda, dau. of Sylvester and Susan (Hammond) Hunt, b. Sept. 21, 1829. Mr. Hunt was a resident of Ithaca, N. Y., later of Rehoboth and then of Chelsea, Mass. Mr. Tobey removed from Providence, R. I., to Rockport, Me., and engaged in West India comerce with the Talbots of that place. Was a very active worker in the Temperance reform, a teetotaler and helper in the Prohibitory movement; a man of deep Christian character. He d. of diabetes at Chelsea, at the house of his father-in-law, Nov. 27, 1854. Mrs. Tobey died of typhoid fever Aug. 6, 1878.
Child:
SAMUEL EDWIN,[7] b. in Providence, R. I. June 2, 1850; m. (1) at Charlestown, July 17, 1873, Catherine J., dau. of Nathaniel and Catherine Loomis, b. in Boston; m. (2) at Boston, March 19, 1895, Barbara, dau. of John and Helen (Russell) McLeod, b. in Glasgow, Scotland, Aug. 17, 1866. He was educated in the public schools of Chelsea and trained in his profession in the offices of some of the leading architects of Boston. Is an architect of wide range of operations, having designed and superintended the erection of many private dwellings and public buildings in various parts of the United States. Some of these are the Medfield Insane Asylum; the Pierce Building, Copley Square; the College of Pharmacy, Boston; the National Life Insurance building in Montpelier, Vt., and the Dime Savings and Trust Co.'s bank in Peoria, Ill.

SAMUEL DAVIES, M. D., Ann Arbor, Mich., 1860; was asst. surgeon, 8th Mich. Vol. Cavalry, 1862; res. at Oakland, Ia., in 1898.

SILAS W., of Boston, merchant, with his wife, Mary G. Tobey, sold in connection with other heirs their rights in lands which had belonged to Thomas Stetson, late of Harvard, 3 Feb., 1829. [Worcester Deeds.]

SOLOMON, of Dighton, bought of Ephraim Atwood and Ruth his wife of the same land in that part of Dighton called Taunton South purchase Dec. 9, 1772; bought other land 3 May, 1782.
He married in Providence Oct. 22, 1770, Martha Fuller.

SOLOMON, of Dighton, cooper, with wife Martha, sold house and land there Aug. 26, 1783; made another sale in 1784.

SARAH TOBEY, b. [Falmouth, Me.?] May 2, 1768; m. (1) July 15, 1791, Enoch Cox, of Falmouth Me.; m. (2) Feb. 14, 1807, Jonathan Sawyer, of same; d. Jan. 24, 1821. Children: 1. Joseph Cox, b. Sept. 1, 1792, d. March 28, 1843; 2. Lemuel Cox, b. and d. 1795; 3. Dorcas Cox, b. Oct. 1, 1796; 4. Frederick Sawyer, b. April 24, 1809, d. Dec. 21, 1858; 5. Lucy Ann C. Sawyer, b. Oct. 4, 1811, d. Jan. 8, 1849; 6. Lemuel C. Sawyer, b. March 7, 1813, d. Oct. 17, 1814. [Fred L. Eastman.]

TEMPERANCE, widow of James (No. 137) born in Sandwich, died at Falmouth Dec. 28, 1872, ae. 90 yrs., 2 mos., 10 days.

"WILLIAM Tobe and Elizabeth Robins Both of Yarmouth Design marriage. Entred January ye 9 1756 Thomas Toby town clerk."

WILLIAM, "son of William [No. 228?] and Sarah, b. in Waterville, Me., 1814," m. "second" at Charlestown Nov. 22, 1858, "Sarah E., dau. of John and Rebecca Gilling," b. in Boston (her "first" marriage.)

WILLIAM MERCHANT, No. 440, b. in Uxbridge, m. Nancy S., b. in Plympton; child, Frank A., d. at Watertown March 4, 1864, ae. 1 mo. 14 d.

MARRIAGES AT CONWAY.

Pheby, of Conway, and Samuel Allen of Ashfield, Dec. 6, 1792.
Lovina, of Conway, and Lemuel Howes of Ashfield, Jan. 1, 1809.
Anna, of Conway, and George Stocking of Ashfield, April 29, 1809.
Ardelia, of Conway, and Peter Look of Shelburne, Oct. 1, 1824.
Polly, and Rufus Chapin, Nov. 15, 1791.
William, of Peoria, Ill., 44 years old, and Jane B. Wing of Conway, April 1, 1863.
Joshua A., and Persis Jane Maynard of Conway, Jan. 17, 1850.

TOBY, of Rockbeare, county of Devon, England. From this ancient stock there came a branch to America in 1790; resided at Philadelphia, Pa. A grandson of the pioneer, Mr. Simeon Toby, born in New Orleans in July, 1828, wrote us a cordial letter in 1902; George Parmly Toby, of New York city, a son of Simeon, is one of our subscribers.

REVOLUTIONARY RECORDS

NOT ASSIGNED; FROM MASS. ARCHIVES.

ABSALOM. Private, on pay roll of Capt. Joseph Fox's (3d) co., Col. Henry Jackson's (16th) regt., for service from July 29 to Aug. 1, 1780; also, in a descriptive list of men raised to reinforce the Continental Army for the term of 6 months, agreeable to resolve of June 5, 1780; age, 16 years; res. Harwich; arrived at Springfield, July 19, 1790; 21st division marched to camp same day under the command of Capt. Clark.

AMMON. Private, on muster and pay roll of Capt. Joseph Griffith's co., Col. John Jacob's regt., from Aug. 3 to Sept. 12, 1778; served 1 month, 15 days; res. Yarmouth.

ANSON. Seaman, on Portledge bill of the officers and crew of the Sloop "Republic," Capt. John Foster Williams, from Aug. 7 to Nov. 18, 1776; served 3 months, 11 days; discharged at Boston; also, on muster and pay roll of the officers and crew of the Sloop "Republic," Capt. John F. Williams, from Aug. 7 to Oct. 1, 1776; served 1 month, 23 days; also, seaman, on descriptive list dated Dec. 11, 1776, of the officers and crew of the Sloop "Republic," commanded by John F. Williams; service from Aug. 7 to Nov. 18, 1776.

DANIEL. Private, on muster and pay roll of Capt. Tobias Lord's co., from May 31 to Aug. 31, 1776; served 3 months; stationed at Falmouth; on muster and pay roll of Capt. George White's co., Col. Ebenezer Francis' regt.; enlisted Dec. 13, 1776; served 3 months, 8 days; belonged to Falmouth; private, on muster roll of Capt. George White's co., Col. Benjamin Tupper's regt., dated at West Point, April 1, 1779; enlisted Dec. 13, 1776; served 2 years, 3 months, 18 days; also, private, on Continental Army pay accounts of Capt. White's co., Col. Tupper's regt., for service from Jan. 1, 1777, to Dec. 31, 1779; res. Falmouth; also, in a list of the men enlisted into the Continental Army out of the 1st Cumberland Co. regt., Col. Peter Noyes, made upon settlement authorized by resolve of April 29, 1778; belonged to Falmouth; enlisted for Falmouth; served in Capt. Skillen's co., Col. Francis' regt.; served 3 years; also, private, on an account rendered against the United States by the Commonwealth of Massachusetts for amounts paid officers and men of Col. Benjamin A. Tupper's regt. on account of depreciation of their wages for the first three years' service in the Continental Army from 1777 to 1780; also, private, on Continental Army pay accounts for 1780 of Capt. White's co., Col. Tupper's regt.; res. Falmouth; also, in a statement of continental balances in Col. Tupper's regt.; time engaged, 3 years; certified May 20, 1780.

JETHRO Tobey was in the grade of "boy" on muster and pay roll of the officers and crew of the brigantine Tyrannicide, commanded by Capt. Allen Hallett, Feb. 22 to April 30, 1779, and on the same vessel, commanded by John Cathcart, Esq., from May 12 to Sept. 6, 1779.

JETHRO, of Boston, deceased; Sarah Freeman, widow, of same place, admitted admx. Feb. 11, 1794.

APPENDIX. **13**

Job Tobey appears on an order on David Jeffries, pay master, payable to
Lt. Matthias Tobey, dated Boston, June 16, 1776, signed by said Tobey and
others belonging to Capt. Micah Hamlen's co., Col. Thomas Marshall's regt.,
for advance pay for one month, etc.; also, private on muster and pay roll of
Capt. George Claghorne's co., Col. Abial Mitchell's regt., from July 31 to Oct.
31, 1780; also, on a warrant to pay officers and men, borne on a roll dated
March 27, 1781, same company; also, private on muster and pay roll of Capt.
Henry Jenne's co., from March 14 to March 18, 1781.
Job Tobey and Mary Perry were published in Dartmouth Aug. 19, 1785. Job
Tobey of New Bedford with wife Mary sold land in N. B. March 19, 1788, to
Seth Jenne.

. JOSEPH, private, on muster and pay roll of Capt. Abel Dinsmore's co., Col.
Elisha Porter's regt from July 24, to Aug. 31, 1779; served 1 month, 13 days;
also, Joseph of Conway, among a list of men raised for the 6 months service and
returned by Brig. Gen. Patterson as having passed muster, in a return dated,
Camp Totoway, Oct. 25, 1780; age 21; arrived at Springfield July 16 1780; 18th
division marched to camp same day under Capt. Zebulon King; also, Joseph
Tobey, seaman, time of entry on list of Continental frigate Raleigh, at Portsmouth, N. H., July 29, 1776; wages $8; stature 5 ft. 8 in; complexion dark.

PETER Tobey appears in a list of soldiers belonging to "Fort Sulervan," Eli-
phalet Daniel, commander, Nov. 25, 1775, and in another list dated Dec. 2, 1775.
Simon Tobey appears in the same list. [N. H. Rev. Rolls.]; also, taken in the
sloop Charming Polly May 16, 1777; one of the prisoners committed to the Old
Mill Prison, Plymouth, Eng. [N. E. Reg.]; also, seaman, time of enlistment
July 29, 1776; stature 5 ft. 5½ in., on list of Continental frigate Raleigh, of
Portsmouth, N. H.; also, Peter Tobey appears in a list of officers and men
mustered in Barnstable county, to serve in Capt. Wordsworth's co., Col. Bradford's regt., by a return made May 31, 1777, by Joseph Otis, muster master;
residence, Falmouth; also, appears in a list of men enlisted into the Continental
army from Barnstable county, Col. Nathaniel Freeman's (1st) regt.; dated
June 10, 1777; residence Falmouth; served 3 years in Capt. Wadsworth's company, Col. Bradford's regt.; also, private on Continental army pay accounts,
Capt. Wadsworth's co., Col. Bradford's regt., for service from March 14, 1777,
to June 3, 1778; residence Sandwich; reported to have died June 3, 1778; also,
private, on an account against the United States by the Commonwealth of Massachusetts for amounts paid officers and men of Col. Bradford's regt. on account
of depreciation of their wages for the first 3 years service in Continental army,
1777 to 1780; exhibited by a committee Sept. 21, 1787.

SAMUEL, private, on muster and pay roll of Capt. John Lane's co., from June
19, to Nov. 1, and from Nov. 1, to Dec. 31, 1775; served 2 months and 5 days;
roll dated Cape Ann; res. Falmouth; also, in an order on David Jeffries paymaster, payable to lieut. Matthias Tobey, dated Boston, June 16, 1776; signed
by said Tobey and others belonging to Capt. Micah Hamlin's co., Col. Thomas
Marshall's regt. for advance pay for 1 month etc.; also, corporal, on muster and
pay roll of Capt. Micah Hamlin's co., Col. Thomas Marshall's regt. from June 6,
to Oct. 31, 1776; res. Yarmouth; also, seaman, upon a list of prisoners sent in
the Cartel Silver Eel from Halifax to Boston, Oct. 8, 1778 to be exchanged;
also, private, on pay abstract of Capt. Nathan Merrill's co., Col. Jonathan Mitchell's Det. for mileage; res. Windham; Det. raised in Cumberland co., for expedition against Penobscot; first drew rations at Falmouth; sworn to No.
Yarmouth, Nov. 3, 1779; also, private, on muster and pay roll of Capt. Abel
Babbit's co., Col. John Hathaway's regt. for service at Rhode Island on alarm
from Aug. 1, to Aug. 7, 1780; served 7 days; marched by order of Council of
July 22, 1780; also, Samuel, Jr., private, on muster and pay roll of Abiel Whit-
marsh's co., Col. Thomas Carpenter's regt. for service at Rhode Island on alarm,

from July 29, to July 31, 1780; served 3 days; marched to Tiverton by order of July 22, 1870.

Simon Tobey is mentioned in "A return of Capt. Robert Follett's Artillery men at Kittery Point, Me. Nov. 5, 1775"; also, in lists of soldiers belonging to "Fort Sulervan Eliphalet Daniel commander," Nov. 25, 1775, and Dec. 2, 1775.

Stephen, corporal on muster and pay roll of Capt. Joseph Palmer's co., Col. John Cushing's regt. for service at Rhode Island on alarm from Sept. 21 to Nov. 22, 1776; served 1 month 25 days; stationed at Newport, R. I.; also, in a list of men mustered in Suffolk county to serve on Capt. Norse's co., Col. Putnam's regt. by a return made by Nathaniel Barber, Boston, Aug. 31, 1777; also, on muster roll of Capt. Perez Cushing's co., Col. Craft's regt.; served 30 days; company reported as Boston militia and stationed at Hull from July 26, to Sept. 11, 1777; also, in a list of men mustered in Suffolk co., to serve in Capt. Norses' co., Col. Putnam's regt. by a return made by Nathaniel Barber, Boston, Aug. 31, 1777; also, private, on muster and pay roll of Capt. Manasseh Kempton's co., Col. Freeman's regt. for service at Rhode Island on alarm, from Sept. 27, to Oct. 29, 1777; served 1 month, 4 days; marched on a secret expedition; also, private on a return of Capt. (late) Gates' co., Col. Rufus Putnam's (4th) regt. for gratuity; dated Feb. 9, 1778; also dated April 22, 1779; also, private, on muster and pay roll of Capt. Simeon Fish's co., Col. Freeman's regt.; service on alarm, Sept. 1778, at Falmouth; also from Sept. 11, to Sept. 12, 1779; served 2 days; also, private, on Continental army pay accounts of Col. Putnam's regt. from Jan. 1, to Dec. 31, 1780; also, corporal, on muster and pay roll of Capt. Henry Jenne's co., Col. John Hathaway's regt.. from Aug. 2, to Aug. 8, 1780; served 6 days; service at Rhode Island on an alarm; also, in a list of men in Col. Putnam's 5th regt. showing balance of wages due by account certified Oct. 20, 1780; term of enlistment during war; also, private, on Continental pay accounts of Capt. Gardner's co., Col. Putnam's regt., for service from Jan. 1, 1777, to Dec. 31, 1779; credited to the town of Attleborough; also, Stephen appears upon a list of men who paid money to John Ellis, as a bounty or 3 years enlistment; dated at Lee, March 25, 1781.

Thomas, private on a muster return of Capt. Israel Davis' co., Col. Edward Wigglesworth's regt.; res. Bristol; enlisted for Salisbury; mustered by Major Ellsby; also, in a statement of Continental balances in Col. Smith's (late Wigglesworth's) regt.; served 3 years; also, private, on company return of Capt. Wyman's co., Col. Paterson's regt.; res. Falmouth; also, on a pay abstract Capt. Davis' co., Col. Edward Wigglesworth's regt. for service 4 months, 17 days from Feb. 14, 1777; reported as having been refused payment of wages due previous to July 1, 1777, by Jonathan Trumbull P. M. G., at Albany for the reason of not having joined regt. at Peekskill before said date; dated, Boston; also Thomas, sergeant, on a pay roll of Capt. Edward Sparrow's co., Col. Danforth Keyes' regt. for service 1 month from time of enlistment, Sept. 1, (1777); dated N. Kingston, Dec. 4, 1777; also, private, on Continental army pay accounts of Capt. Woodbridge's co., Col. Smith's regt. from Feb. 14, 1777 to Dec. 31, 1779; credited to town of Salisbury; also, private, on muster and pay roll of Capt. Edward Sparrow's co., Col. Danforth Keyes' regt. from Sept. 1, to Dec. 31, 1777; served 4 months; service at Rhode Island; also, private, on an account rendered against the United States by the Commonwealth of Massachusetts for amounts paid officers and men of Col. Calvin Smith's regt. on account of depreciation of their wages for the first 3 years' service in the Continental arms from 1777 to 1780; account exhibited by committee on claims in behalf of Massachusetts, Sept. 21, 1787; also, in a return of men enlisted into the Continental army from Capt. Benjamin Evan's co., dated Essex co., Feb. 13, 1778, belonged to Bristol; enlisted for Salisbury for 3 years; joined Capt. Davis' co., Col. Wigglesworth's regt.; *also*, sergeant, on muster and pay roll of Capt. Edward Sparrow's co. Col. Danforth Keyes' regt. from Dec. 1, 1777, to Jan. 2, 1778; dated at Providence; *also*, Thomas, private, on muster roll of Capt. Israel Davis' co., Col. Edward Wigglesworth's regt., May 1778; dated camp at Valley Forge, June 2, 1778; also from Oct. 1, to Nov. 1, 1778; *also*, seaman, on muster and pay roll of the officers and crew of the ship "Protector" commanded by John F. Williams, from March 1, to Aug. 17, 1780; *also*, private, on muster roll of Capt. Luke Hitchcock's co., Col. Joseph Vose's (1st) regt. from June 15, 1781 to Feb. 17, 1782; roll dated "Hutts"; *also*, Thomas; private, on muster roll of Capt. Hitchcock's co., Col. Joseph Vose's (1st) regt. for Sept. 1781; enlisted June 15, 1781 for 3 years; *also*, private, on Continental army pay accounts of Capt. Woodbridge's co., Col. Smith's regt. for service from Jan. 1, to Feb. 2, 1780; res. Boothbay; reported 3 years enlistment.

WILLIAM, private, on muster and pay roll of Capt. Joseph Noyes' co. from July 13, to Dec. 31, 1775; stationed at Falmouth; *also*, sergeant, on muster and pay roll of Capt. Elisha Nye's co., from Feb. 4, to Feb. 5, to Sept. 1, 1776; stationed at Elizabeth Islands; *also*, 2d lieutenant, on muster and pay roll of Capt. Elisha Nye's co., from Sept. 1, to Nov. 21, 1776; stationed at Elizabeth Islands; *also*, ensign, in Capt. Micah Hamlin's co., Col. Cary's regt.; dated 1776; *also*, private, on muster and pay roll of Capt. William Crocker's co., from March 1, to May 31, and from Aug. 31, to Nov. 23, 1776; stationed at Falmouth, Cumberland co.; *also*, on a petition dated Nov. 1776 asking for pay of 2d lieutenant since he had performed the duties of that office; rank, 1st sergeant, in Capt. Elisha Nye's co., in service at Island of "Naushon"; *also*, private, on muster and pay roll of Capt. Job Crocker's co., Col. Nathan Sparhawk's regt., from July 2, to Dec. 12, 1777; *also*, private, on a return of Capt. Ward Swift's co., for bounty allowed for service on secret expedition to Rhode Island Oct. 1777; res. Falmouth; *also*, private, on muster and pay roll of Capt. Manasseh Kempton's co., Col. Freeman's regt. for service at Rhode Island on alarm from Sept. 27, to Oct. 29, 1779; marched on a secret expedition; *also*, matross, on muster and pay roll from Jan. 1, to March 31, 1777; on a return of Capt. Abner Lowell's co.; stationed at Falmouth, Cumberland co.; said company reported Aug. 11, 1777, as mustered by Col. Noyes, agreeable to sea coast establishment; roll dated, Falmouth, July 31, 1777; *also*, private, on muster and pay roll of Capt. Joseph Palmer's co., from April 2, to Nov. 16 1779; raised by resolve of Feb. 23, and April 9, 1779; stationed at Falmouth; *also*, private on muster and pay roll of Capt. Simeon Fish's co., Col. Freeman's regt. Sept. 1778; service on alarm at Dartmouth and Falmouth; *also*, private, on muster and pay roll of Capt. Jacob Fuller's co., Col. John Jacob's regt. for service at Rhode Island from Aug. 10, 1778 to Jan. 1, 1779; res. Falmouth; *also*, private, on a pay roll of Capt. Joseph Palmer's co., Col. Freeman's regt. Company marched on alarm at Falmouth, Feb. 4, April 2 and May 16, 1779; roll sworn to in Barnstable co.; *also*, private on a pay abstract of Col. Simeon Fish's co., Col. Freeman's regt.; marched on alarm at Falmouth, Sept. 1779, by order of Brig. Otis; *also*, private on muster and pay roll of Capt. Henry Jenne's co., from March 14, to March 18, 1781; marched under resolve of Feb. 28, 1781.

TOBEYS IN APPENDIX.

Abigail, 6
Ada, 9
Albert W., 4
Alden, 9
Alfred A., 3
Althea, 6
Alvan, 6
Alvan B., 10
Amanda C., 9
Ann M., 7
Anna, 11
Ansel, 6, 7
Apollos, 3
Ardelia, 11
Ariana A., 9
Asa S., 3

Barbara, 10
Benjamin F., 9
Betsey, 7

Caroline, 7
Caroline Amelia, 3
Caroline M., 4
Catherine J., 10
Charles C., 6
Charles S., 7
Churchill Gardner, 7
Clara E., 4
Clarence E., 3
Clarence N., 9
Cordelia F., 7

Deborah, 4, 7
Deborah L., 8
Deliverance, 8
Dorothy I., 9

Edwin, 10
Elisha, 4, 6
Eliza B., 3
Eliza W., 3
Elizabeth, 6, 8, 11
Elizabeth A., 6
Elizabeth C., 6
Elizabeth E., 6
Elizabeth F., 6
Ellen A., 7
Ellen F., 7
Emma, 7
Emma E., 6
Ephraim, 6
Esther F., 3
Esther J., 6
Eugene C., 9
Eunice E., 6
Eunice S., 3
Eva, 9

Fannie E., 9
Florence, 9
Frank, 4
Frank A., 11
Frank N., 9
Franklin, 6
Freeman C., 4

George H., 7
George L., 9
George P., 11
George N., 7
George W., 6
Gershom, 4

Hannah, 3
Hannah M., 8
Harriet T., 6
Helen M., 4
Heman, 8
Henrietta, 4
Henrietta V., 6
Henry A., 4, 6
Henry F., 6
Henry H., 9
Henry S., 7
Henry V., 6
Henry W., 7
Hiram, 6
Horatio N., 8
Howard, 9

Innocent, 4
Isaac S., 6
Isaiah N., 6

Jacob, 6
James, 11
James P. F., 9
James S., 6
Jane, 6
Jane B., 11
Joanna, 6
Joel W., 6
John, 8
John P., 6
Jonathan, 6
Jonathan H., 6
Joseph, 4, 6
Joshua, 6
Joshua A., 11
Josiah, 6
Julia A., 7
Julia H., 3
Julia H. M., 9
Juliette, 7

L. Sophia, 4, 6
Lemuel, 6, 7
Leonard, 7
Lester, 9
Lewis, 6, 7
Lizzie E., 9
Louisa, 9
Lovina, 11
Lydia S., 7

Madeline, 9
Mallie, 9
Maria, 6
Maria F., 4
Martha, 7, 10
Mary, 4, 6, 6, 8, 9

Mary A., 6, 10
Mary B., 6
Mary E., 6
Mary G., 10
Mary L., 6
Mary N., 8
Matthew, 8
Maurice M., 9
Mehitabel, 4, 7
Melinda M., 8
Mercy D., 7
Miriam E., 6

Nancy, 7
Nancy S., 11
Nathaniel, 8
Nathaniel B., 8
Nelson S., 9
Nettie M., 9
Noah, 8

Olive, 4

Patience, 8
Patience N., 8
Persis J., 11
Pheby, 11
Polly, 4, 11
Pratt L., 8

Remember N., 8
Roxanna, 6, 8
Russell, 8

Sally, 8
Salome, 6
Samuel, 4, 6, 8, 10
Samuel D., 10
Samuel E., 10
Samuel N., 9
Sarah, 3, 6, 11
Sarah E., 6, 6, 8
Sarah H., 6
Silas W., 10
Simeon, 11
Solomon, 10
Sophia, 7, 10
Susan E., 6
Susan L., 7
Susan M., 10

Temperance, 11
Thad. B., 9
Thomas E., 7
Thomas H., 8
Timothy, 8

William, 3, 6, 11
William B., 8
William C., 10
William E., 6
William H., 9, 10
William M., 11

Zady, 6

ADDITIONS AND CORRECTIONS

TO THE

TOBEY GENEALOGY

1906

Imprimis. Since the issue of the Genealogy, Mr. Pope has discovered in "The Scrap Book" at Plymouth Court House, a signature of the founder of the Sandwich line, attached to the Inventory of the estate of Robert Bolock (Bullock) of Sandwich, 15 Sept. 1669.

ABRAHAM, No. 268; dau. Minerva m. George W. Brown, of Canaan, N. Y., d. May 6, 1878; dau. Jerusha, b. April 23, 1807, m. W. H. Edwards, of West Stockbridge; son Albert, b. Sept. 11, 1811, d. Sept. 24, 1841; son Franklin, b. April 17, 1818.

ABRAHAM, No. 507, b. Sept. 9, 1805.

ALBERT, No. 496, d. Oct. 16, 1875, æ. 74, 10, 15; Emily, his wife, d. Oct 16, 1871, æ. 66, 7, 10. [Gravestones at Sharon, Ct., where they had lived.] Their son was born at the adjoining town of Amenia, N. Y.

AUGUSTUS, No. 491, m. Huldah ———, who survived him and m. July 26, 1846, Nathaniel Tremain; she d. Oct. 18, 1849; child Amy m. April 18, 1832, Dr. Noah H. Warner, and res. at Buffalo, N. Y.

BARNABAS, No. 262, d. April 22, 1836, æ. 67. First wife, Lucinda, d. Dec. 1, 1807, æ. 41; second wife, Abigail (Hurd) Pray, d. Dec. 1841, æ. 67. Orville (of first wife) d. July 16, 1799, æ. 14 months; Ira d. June 22, 1804, æ. 22 months; Lucinda, d. July 17, 1815, æ. 9 yrs. 7 mos.

BENJAMIN, No. 267, m. Polly, dau. of Zechariah and Hannah (Pope) Fairchild, whose sister m. William Cullen Bryant. He removed to Bloomfield, N. Y.

BENNETT HYDE, No. 820, served in the Spanish American War as Major of the 14th N. Y. Vol. Inf.

BLISS, under Seth Fish, No. 577, change middle initial of No. 1 to T. and erase No. 6.

CHARLES, No. 870, b. in July, not Sept. His grandson Charles Alphonso Coffin was b. July 17, not 7.

CHARLES, No. 321, became a captain of a whaling ship; d. at Waquoit, April 7, 1876.

CORNELIA, No. ii in No. 465 (not Cornelius).

CURTIS, No. 807, had children: i. Amelia, b. June 4, 1875; d. 25, 1898; ii. Curtis, Jr., b. Feb. 19, 1873; iii. Theodosia K., b. June 18, 1883.

EDWARD, No. 777, did not remove to Cambridge, but d. in Pittsfield, May 31, 1878.

EDWIN, No. 776, was a tinner (not a tanner).

EGBERT PRINDLE, No. 502, d. May 16, 1854; his widow m. Merritt Bristol.

ELISHA, No. 97, m. Susanna, dau. of Jonathan and Abigail Pratt, b. Jan. 9, 1748-9, d. Feb. 4, 1821. Elisha d. Feb. 22, 1809. [Gr. st.]

EPHRAIM, No. 30, lived in Sandwich till about 1750, and his child Martha was b. in Lebanon, Ct., to which he had moved. It was after his death that the family removed to Sharon, Ct., and there his widow m. July 24, 1763, Miles Washburn; dau. Mehitabel m. April, 1764, Daniel Ticknor. Ephraim d. before Jan. 14, 1756, when administration on his estate was granted to his widow Reliance. She was also made guardian of the youngest children Ephraim and Martha. She presented her account Nov. 15, 1760, showing an estate of £86-2-5, out of which she had paid £42-3-11, leaving a balance of £43-18-6 to be divided. This, in accordance with her petition, was duly set off to the heirs by a commission; to the widow her thirds, to Elisha, the eldest son, a double portion of the remainder, and single shares to Jesse, George, Benjamin, Ephraim, Mehitabel and Martha.

EPHRAIM, No. 101, was b. in Lebanon (not Sharon), Ct.

FRANK GEORGE, No. 690, had his middle name perverted by reason of bad reading of written statement duly made.

FRANKLIN, No. 508, b. April 17, 1813; m. March 12, 1843, Elizabeth Pratt, of Catskill, N. Y.; he d. Aug. 25, 1885. Children: i. Ellen Elizabeth, m. William H. Halsey. ii. Amelia, b. Aug. 11, 1845; m. April 15, 1874, Lucius A. Vasey; d. June 12, 1879. iii. Frances Adeline, b. Jan. 22, 1849; m. Willis Baldwin, of Hunter, N. Y. iv. Sarah Minerva, b. May 29, 1851; m. Sept. 14, 1881, Lucius A. Vasey. v. Mary Eliza, b. March 18, 1853; d. Feb. 6, 1875.

FREDERICK, No. 506, d. at Canaan, N. Y., Aug. 13, 1835.

GEORGE, No. 99, m. Jan. 17, 1766. [A. T.]

GEORGE EDWIN, No. 895. Child ii. George Albert, b. Jan. 21, 1906.

GERSHOM, No. 31, removed to Fairfield, Me., where he was noted as "78 years old" in 1826, by Coffin in his "Journal." [A. T.]

GUSTAVUS BASSETT, No. 649, date of marriage was May 8 (not 7), 1856.

HEMAN, No. 264, m. —— Dorr, and lived in Canaan, N. Y.

JAMES OSBERT, No. 634, dau. Lelia (not Celia) Philena, b. Nov. 22, 1870.

JESSE, No. 98, his eldest daughter's name was Reliance Ada (not Rehameradah); she m. Rev. John Bristol; d. Dec. 9, 1849, æ. 86 yrs.

JESSE, No. 509. Children: i. Wales; ii. Dillon; iii. Jessie; iv. Clara; v. Franklin.

JONATHAN, No. 213, Mr. Tobey (not Sears) subject of second paragraph.

THE OLD TOBEY HOUSE, SANDWICH, MASS.

JONATHAN, No. 261, d. June 26, 1842 (not 1832). He m. (1) March 25, 1787, Anna Hatch. who d. Feb. 6, 1797, æ. 27; he m. (2) June 6, 1799, Ruth Wilcox, who d. Nov. 29, 1801. æ. 26; he m. (3) Mary or Polly Dyer; he m. (4) widow Anna (Hill) Dodge.

JOSEPH, No. 49, had children bapt. at Sandwich: Isaac, Feb. 14, 1768; Benjamin, Oct. 27, 1771. [A. T.]

JOSHUA BRIGGS, No. 575. We present his portrait herewith.

MARY ANN, dau. of Richard, No. 118 (James), d. since issue of book, Dec. 6, 1905.

POMEROY, No. 504, d. Aug. 4, 1834. Dau. Sophia m. Aaron Kellogg, of Sempronius, N. Y.

PRATT LORENZO, No. 885, d. Nov. 1904.

REGINALD SPRAGUE, No. 880, son Edward Sprague (not Edmund).

RUTH, dau. of Jonathan Howes, No. 303, whose marriage to Asa Shiverick is stated on page 201, had children :
1. Bessie Crowell Shiverick, b. July 25, 1858 ; d. April 24, 1904.
2. Lunette Shiverick, b. Jan. 25, 1860; m. Jan. 27, 1886, Walter Otis Luscombe. Children : (1) Helen Luscombe, b. Feb. 14, 1888; (2) Walter Otis Luscombe, b. June 17, 1893.
3. Asa Frank Shiverick, b. Sept. 26, 1861; m. April 23, 1891, Ruth Anna Hatch. Children : (1) Arthur Shiverick, b. April 22, 1892; (2) Francis Tobey Shiverick, b. Sept. 18, 1896.
4. Arthur Shiverick, b. Aug. 20, 1863; d. Feb. 4, 1906.
5. Seth Tobey Shiverick, b. July, 1866; d. in infancy.
6. Ruth Tobey Shiverick, b. Nov. 3, 1867; m. June 25, 1902, George Monroe Morley.

SAMUEL, No. 192. Statements " copied from a record at Holmes' Hole in 1855," give Samuel b. June 8, 1739, and d. Feb. 17, 1771; his first child Nathaniel, b. July 28, 1766, drowned Nov. 14, 1791.

SETH, No. 47, m. (1) April 19, 1750, Abigail Perry; m. (2) March 26, 1761, Mary Moxom. [Sandwich record.]

SIDNEY BERKELEY, No. 724 (not his brother Edward Silas), a member of the Penna. Soc. Sons of the Revolution.

SILAS, No. 94, children : Silas, bapt. at Sandwich, Aug. 4, 1766; Desire, bapt. Sept. 27, 1778.

STACKPOLE, under No. 230 (James ; Frederick Tobey Stackpole, son of Capt. Frederick W. and Sarah Elizabeth (Tobey) Stackpole, m. Jan. 22, 1903, at Tacoma, Wash., Harriet Lowe. Child : Joseph Frederick Stackpole, b. at Seattle, Wash., April 14, 1904.

THEODORE POMEROY, No. 781, child Clara Flint, b. June 16, 1870, m. (not Francis K. Matterson but only) F. L. Peck.

THOMAS HASKELL, No. 121 (James), second wife d. in August (not in April). On p. 286, Marion Lucy Titus, b. Nov. 20 (not 10), 1880, member of Phi Beta Kappa Society. On p. 287 change name of iii. to Elvira La Fayette Prentiss; on p. 288 middle name of 1 in vii to Twombly, and of (1) to Vivian, and front name of (1) in 3 is Perley.

TIMOTHY, No. 143, date of marriage Jan. 18, 1795. [A. T.]

WALTER DANFORTH, No. 808; second wife's father was P. S. Lincoln.

WILLIAM HAYWARD, No. 860, second child William Robert, b. Jan. 16, 1906.

These additions have been compiled and issued, and are sent to sub-scribers, through the generosity of Eugene H. Robbins, of Pittsfield, Mass. The picture of the old Tobey house has been furnished by Rev. Rufus B. Tobey, of Boston, and the portrait of Mr. J. B. Tobey by his son.

Printed in the USA
CPSIA information can be obtained
at www.ICGtesting.com
LVHW092122131023
761043LV00003B/108